The Making of Tocqueville's America

HISTORICAL STUDIES OF URBAN AMERICA

A Series Edited by Edward Gray, Stephen Mihm, and Mark Peterson

Also in the series:

PLANTERS, MERCHANTS, AND SLAVES: PLANTATION SOCIETIES IN BRITISH AMERICA, 1650–1820 *by Trevor Burnard*

RIOTOUS FLESH: WOMEN, PHYSIOLOGY AND THE SOLITARY VICE IN NINETEENTH-CENTURY AMERICA *by April R. Haynes*

HOLY NATION: THE TRANSATLANTIC QUAKER MINISTRY IN AN AGE OF REVOLUTION *by Sarah Crabtree*

A HERCULES IN THE CRADLE: WAR, MONEY, AND THE AMERICAN STATE, 1783–1867 *by Max M. Edling*

FRONTIER SEAPORT: DETROIT'S TRANSFORMATION INTO AN ATLANTIC ENTREPÔT *by Catherine Cangany*

BEYOND REDEMPTION: RACE, VIOLENCE, AND THE AMERICAN SOUTH AFTER THE CIVIL WAR *by Carole Emberton*

THE REPUBLIC AFLOAT: LAW, HONOR: AND CITIZENSHIP IN MARITIME AMERICA *by Matthew Taylor Raffety*

CONCEIVED IN DOUBT: RELIGION AND POLITICS IN THE NEW AMERICAN NATION *by Amanda Porterfield*

The Making of Tocqueville's America

Law and Association in the Early United States

KEVIN BUTTERFIELD

The University of Chicago Press
Chicago and London

Kevin Butterfield is assistant professor of classics and letters at the University of Oklahoma, where he is also senior associate director of the Institute for the American Constitutional Heritage.

The University of Chicago Press, Chicago 60637
The University of Chicago Press, Ltd., London

Printed in the United States of America

24 23 22 21 20 19 18 17 16 15   1 2 3 4 5

ISBN-13: 978-0-226-29708-8 (cloth)
ISBN-13: 978-0-226-29711-8 (e-book)
DOI: 10.7208/chicago/9780226297118.001.0001

{~?~CIP data to come}

♾ This paper meets the requirements of ANSI/NISO Z39.48-1992 (Permanence of Paper).

CONTENTS

ACKNOWLEDGMENTS

This is a book about belonging. It is an attempt to think seriously about the bonds that people create to bring themselves together. Especially if we want to understand the post-Revolutionary United States, I believe, we need to understand how and why the first generations of American citizens joined together in the ways that they did. Nearly every word of this book is devoted to telling that story, because I think it's an important one. The next few paragraphs are devoted to a much more recent story of belonging.

I have had the great fortune to be bound together with some truly amazing people as I thought about these themes for the last nine years. The project had its genesis at Washington University in St. Louis, where the Department of History and the American Culture Studies program were supportive in every way. I cannot imagine this project without the advice and the friendships of Michelle Repice, Daniel Scallet, and Jennie Sutton. Thanks, too, to Tom and Gen Coghill, for making me feel at home every Friday and Saturday night at the Iron Barley (the best restaurant in a great food city) and for the chance to stop thinking about American history and, instead, to play American music.

When I joined the faculty at the University of Oklahoma, I found another extraordinarily supportive group of people. There really are too many to name, so forgive me for naming only two. Kyle Harper, who brought me in as the first faculty member in a new program in constitutional studies, has been unfailingly encouraging. And Paul Gilje has been both a mentor and a friend. Institutionally, the university has helped immensely to facilitate this research, and I am grateful to the College of Arts and Sciences and to the Office of the Vice President for Research for all of their support.

I joined another welcoming group of people when I had the unbelievable good fortune to spend a year as the National Endowment for the

Humanities Research Fellow at the New-York Historical Society. I learned a lot about how to be a historian from my fellow fellows—Drew Lipman, Catherine McNeur, Dael Norwood, and Robin Vandome—and I will probably always see the reading room at the N-YHS as my favorite place to write a sentence (or a thousand). A huge amount of the archival research in the pages to follow could not have been done without the generous fellowships I received from the Colonial Williamsburg Foundation; the Gilder Lehrman Institute of American History; the Henry E. Huntington Library; the New England Regional Fellowship Consortium; the New York State Archives; the Robert H. Smith International Center for Jefferson Studies; and the Virginia Historical Society. Once a manuscript began to take shape, Tim Mennel and the American Beginnings series editors at the University of Chicago Press were everything I could have hoped for, and the comments and advice of people who read the entire manuscript—John Brooke and Johann Neem, in particular—have been invaluable.

This book would never have been written were it not for David Konig. I will never know another mentor like him. And my parents, Ken and Debbie Butterfield, and my sister, Kelly Nellums, have been supportive since long before I knew I wanted to be a historian. I owe them all so much. Tokyo, Lucky, Denny Matthews, and the Kansas City Royals kept me company through much of the writing, and I want to thank them though I'm skeptical any of them will ever read the book. And since the early days of this project, ever since my Huntington summer romance with a Shakespeare scholar from Canada, I have had a wonderful partner in life. Thanks, Sara Coodin, for everything.

INTRODUCTION

Americans are joiners, and they have been self-consciously aware of that fact for nearly two hundred years. Confronted with a problem, or simply seeking a way to socialize with other like-minded people, men and women in the United States have chosen, remarkably often, to create a formally organized club or association to meet the need. Sometimes their goals have been especially ambitious, such as ridding the nation of the evil of slavery or the pestilence of alcohol. Other times, their purposes have been the most ordinary, pedestrian things imaginable, such as a musical society formed by a handful of men in Wakefield, New Hampshire, in 1815 "for the purpose of practicing on their several and respective instruments." If it were not for the fact that the penchant for formal association has become so deeply fixed in our collective way of being, we would no doubt ask why they needed committees, a formally ratified constitution (one that they frequently took the time to amend), and bylaws in order to play their horns and violins. There is much that is extraordinary in these everyday experiences of membership and association. For countless observers since the early days of the nation's history, the very tendency of Americans to join together at all, so often and with such exuberance, was itself truly extraordinary. But perhaps the most remarkable thing of all was not so much the fact that people joined together, but the ways in which they did it: by choosing formalities over friendship, by emphasizing law, procedural fairness, and even constitutionalism as the best means to bind men and women together. This was not simply a nation of joiners. It was a nation in which people bound themselves together by law.[1]

In some ways, the sheer magnitude of Americans' eagerness to join together has kept even the keenest observers from noticing much else. A young Alexis de Tocqueville noticed it in his American travels in 1831, and he was among the first observers to draw attention to Americans' propensity to form voluntary associations and to join them with a fervor and a frequency unmatched anywhere in the world. He was by no means the last. The idea that Americans of the early nineteenth century were, in Tocqueville's words, "forever forming associations" has become something more than a commonplace. It has become a subfield of American historical studies, one that has grown immensely in the past two decades as people attempt to explain what works about American "civil society" or the American "public sphere"—and why it is so important. Really, as far back as the 1940s, describing America as a "nation of joiners" had already become one of the most frequently invoked explanations for why American democracy has thrived while others have suffered under more despotic forms of government. The fall of the Iron Curtain and more recent Western efforts to establish democracies around the globe has given cause anew to contemplate why some republics survive and others do not.[2]

But the phenomenon of America's flourishing civil society was not something apparent only to foreign observers or to those writing at the remove of a century or more. Many contemporary Americans were more than aware by the 1830s that something new was appearing among them. Francis Wayland designated voluntary associations "the peculiar glory of the present age" in 1838, though he did so dryly and without pleasure. Even outspoken advocates of cooperative organization such as Ohio lawyer Timothy Walker acknowledged concerns that "individual freedom of action shall be swallowed up" in what he called "the prevailing spirit of association." In truth, many Americans were anxious that the most ambitious voluntary associations being formed throughout the nation by the 1830s—groups formed to oppose slavery, to end the widespread use of alcohol, to evangelize to all the world, and so on—were dangerous "Instruments of Power," in the words of Boston minister Baron Stow. And the worry was not just that such groups would foist their will on everyone else. Rather, Stow believed, they posed a genuine threat to their own members! "Personal independence is crippled" in such groups, according to Stow, "and the inward man is subjected to a species of control not far removed from despotism." For Stow, and for many other antebellum Americans, these were problems worth worrying about.[3]

Those apprehensions were expressed in many different ways, none more memorable than the announcement in 1838 by a group of New Englanders that they had formed yet another voluntary society to solve some problem—in this case, the incessant ringing of bells in Boston. But this was satire, not civic activism. Truth be told, they could not have cared less about noise in the city. Rather, they wished to draw attention to what they saw as a ridiculous 1838 law forbidding the ringing of bells in the streets of the city. At the same time, it quickly became clear, they wanted to call notice to the astonishing ubiquity of collective activism, initiated for every purpose under the sun, in antebellum America. And so they drew up a constitution for the Anti-Bell-Ringing Society. "We hold this truth to be self-evident, that all good and sensible men are created equal," they declared in the preamble, "and therefore that we have the same right to unite and form an Anti-Bell-Ringing Society, as others of our fellow citizens have to unite together and form Anti-Slavery, Anti-Swearing, Anti-Smoking, Anti-Tea-and-Coffee-Drinking, Anti-Skating, Anti-Swimming, Anti-Rope-Skipping, Anti-Marble-Playing, Anti-Nine-Pin-Rolling, Anti-Kissing, Anti-Courting, and other Moral and Benevolent Societies already in existence."

It was extolled, and it was decried; it was embraced, and it was mocked. But the associational impulse on display in the early United States could not be ignored. Men and women established and joined voluntary associations of all kinds in astounding numbers in the first fifty or sixty or years of the American republic. Although some kinds of voluntary associations, such as fraternal clubs and charitable societies, had existed in colonial British America, their membership was not extensive and was limited to a handful of urban centers. After the Revolution, something new appeared: men and women at all levels of social standing, white and black, and in communities large and small, embraced voluntarism and self-created, relatively formal organizations as the very best of means to improve society and their own lives.

But how, precisely, could these groups hold together? How were they supposed to function effectively, and make a difference? In an age when the survival of even the new republic appeared to be tenuous, the associational impulse also presents us with thousands of separate efforts to muster effective cooperation from previously unaffiliated individuals. What did Americans not long removed from a republican Revolution believe could and should be used to make that happen, to create *unum* out of *pluribus*?

The second article of the constitution of the Anti-Bell-Ringing Society, though cloaked in satire, can point us to an answer at which most Americans had arrived over the course of the late eighteenth and early nineteenth centuries. There, in article 2, it was declared that the members of the Anti-Bell-Ringing Society were not permitted to violate any provisions of the law of the universe, the United States, the Commonwealth of Massachusetts, the city of Boston, or "the Constitutions, By-Laws, Resolves, Orders, Rules and Regulations of this Society or all other Societies, of whatever name or nature, already in existence or which may hereafter exist, here or elsewhere, adopted for the government of its or their members, 'or for any other purpose,' here or elsewhere, whether committed here or elsewhere." This idea of the nesting spheres of legality of the federal American republic, with each jurisdiction encompassed by more than a few others, was presented as both a reflection and a joke by the Anti-Bell-Ringing Society—one that an American in the 1830s might find funny precisely because of the kernel of truth around which it was formed.[4]

In the everyday experience of voluntary membership and in the crucible of the inevitable conflicts that would arise between member and group, Americans had concluded that what could bring them together was law. As people in post-Revolutionary America worked hard to build new institutions and to devise new forms of concerted action, there was a distinct, conscious move toward increasingly legalistic ways of thinking about social cooperation. They drew up constitutions and bylaws, elected officers, and abided by the decisions of the majority. There continued to be encomia about the natural sociability of man and the tender ties of affection, but in practice Americans began to embrace a wholly different model of associated action. The rules by which the joiners organized themselves evinced a trend toward greater precision and an increasing emphasis on legalistic formalities, and people began to speak up at the slightest indication that the agreed-upon procedural formalities were being ignored.

This is a crucial development for understanding the early American republic. Americans of the first post-Revolutionary generations were more than aware of the tensions between collective action and individual autonomy that arose when people attempted to join together to do much of anything, from the club to the nation. In important ways, hidden within the history of American civil society, of this great "nation of joiners," is the story of how the first generations of American citizens found in law and in an emphasis on procedural fairness a way to cohere.

But it was not an easy road. In some ways this tendency toward increasingly law-bound ways of acting was born of the quotidian experiences of membership. In other ways, it was born in conflict. Buried in the humor of Boston's first Anti-Bell-Ringing Society was a potentially troubling consequence of this legalistic understanding of voluntary membership: the growing numbers of voluntary associations in antebellum America, conjured up for purposes both important and trivial, were also creating new regimes of private authority for their many thousands, even millions, of members. That authority could be minuscule: take, for example, the many "cent societies" founded between 1800 and 1820, whose rules required that members (usually women) pay dues in the amount of exactly one cent per week. Or the authority could be profound, exacting, and even frightening: members of labor unions might regularly encounter the choice between abiding by the rules of a journeymen's society, such as rules to work only with fellow society members or for a certain wage, or watching their families starve when work suddenly became impossible to find.[5]

As the Anti-Bell-Ringers knew, though, the creation of rules—or laws, or bylaws, or articles, or regulations, or whatever they were called in a given club or society—was what gave existence to all of those voluntary societies whose existence they mocked. Such groups created standards of membership, admitted only those people who met those criteria, and continued as members only those who carried on abiding by the conditions of membership. Because no one was born a member, the most important part of what it meant to *be* a member was, simply put, to be bound by the rules. But the faux constitution of 1838 also brought into focus the idea that such rules were part of a much, much broader web of rules and relationships under which their members lived, from the laws of the "universe," nation, state, and city down through all the voluntary societies that could claim the allegiance of anyone.[6]

Only quite recently have scholars begun to explore the historical reality of something the Anti-Bell-Ringing Society observed in satire: voluntary associations were an integral part of the law-as-experienced by those nineteenth-century Americans who were a part of one, or of many. One historian has noted that, in the early American republic, a person's rights and duties were "the product of a very complicated and varied tally of the rules, regulations, and bylaws of the host of differentiated associations to which he belonged." This included the layers of federalism that Americans contemplate today—local, county, state, and federal governments—but also organizations that were, generally speaking, nongovernmental and entered voluntarily: clubs, churches, unions, corporations, and the like. There, too, individuals could find themselves required to pay dues or assessments, which they often called "taxes"; there, too, men and women drafted constitutions, amended them, acted in accordance with them, or found themselves fined, censured, or expelled.[7]

A better understanding of the importance of law in giving shape to early American civil society is long overdue. Part of the problem has been a matter of perspective. In creating formally organized, rule-bound, and wholly voluntary associations, Americans were forming what Philadelphia economist Samuel Blodget called "minor republics," and that way of thinking about associational activity has prompted historians and other students of associational activity to ask how Americans came to terms with the unanticipated prevalence of such entities *within* a republic, a body politic that the founding generation had hoped would never be broken into subunits of competing loyalties that might threaten the common good.[8] Scholars have more recently turned to a second question, one derived from the work of Jürgen Habermas, that asks what role these voluntary societies played in the formation of a public sphere between the state and its people, one integral to the success of the whole republican experiment. But, in both lines of inquiry, the central "unit of analysis" is the association, not the individuals who made them up.[9]

The next eight chapters will instead explore the phenomenon from the inside out, examining how Americans between the 1780s and the 1840s came to answer some fundamental questions about the nature of consent, voluntary obligation, and concerted action. What rights and duties should members have? Were there rights that people carried with them into any and all relationships? To what degree could individuals legally bind themselves to such private associations as fraternal clubs, business corporations, religious societies, and labor unions? And, once such a commitment had been made, was there any way both of enforcing it and of keeping it within its proper limits?

The answer to the last question provides a crucial insight for answering the others, and the answer was yes—in court. Americans were anxious, we will see, that their newly founded societies would work, and work well, to accomplish the myriad purposes they were being assembled to serve. When they formed these groups, they nearly always did so with clearly stated objectives, with transparent statements of the criteria and the conditions of membership, and with some document or other serving as a "constitution." And yet their legalistic framing of their own efforts to act collectively had another consequence: as more joiners in early national associations came to conceive of their participation as one of well-defined rights and obligations, legal institutions (chiefly, courts of law) occupied an increasingly important position in the monitoring of those internal relationships—precisely because those institutions were so frequently called upon to intervene by individuals aware of the importance of their own rights.

The result was a civil society that was shaped not solely or even primarily by the organizers and joiners themselves, but by the post-Revolutionary legal culture in which they lived and acted. For that legal culture shaped the everyday choices that they made, and in moments of serious internal conflicts between member and group it provided a vocabulary and a repertoire for how best to respond. And so this book offers an explanation for how individualism and the associational impulse could and did arise simultaneously, and it is an explanation that Tocqueville's emphasis on the spontaneity of the American associational impulse has long shielded from view. What allowed post-Revolutionary American civil society to become recognizably pluralistic was, ironically, the encompassment of all efforts at association within what rapidly became consistent patterns of behavior within the groups themselves and, just as important, a remarkably consistent jurisprudence—a body of law produced in moments of contestation—that helped to describe the rights and duties of membership in a way that limited, by law, the ways that a group could treat its members.

The twentieth-century political theorist L. T. Hobhouse once noted that "the function of Liberalism may be rather to protect the individual against the power of the association than to protect the right of association against the restriction of the law." An understanding of how and why that describes fairly well the tendency of the associational laws and practices of the early national United States, and of what became of the efforts to define the depth and breadth of voluntary commitments, reveals much about the conceptual and the practical aspects of a distinctively post-Revolutionary American political and social order. It rested on a liberalism that came to emphasize both procedural constraints on authority and formalized relationships among and between individuals. That is, liberalism, according to political theorist Nancy Rosenblum, "asks men and women to ignore all the other things they are in order to treat one another fairly in certain contexts and for certain purposes." By the second decade of the nineteenth century, this way of thinking about the member-to-group relationship had become predominant in ways that historians have yet to appreciate.[10]

Even as Americans were voluntarily joining a varied assortment of groups to meet needs large and small, and despite the multiplicity of ends to which they directed such collective endeavors, they shared practices, organizational forms, and technologies of association. Historians have done exceptional work describing the formation of an increasingly pluralist society in the early nineteenth century, with myriad interests and a wide variety of associational opportunities, but a vital component in the embrace of this pluralism has remained unexamined. In the early republic the view that all associations shared the same elemental unit—the rights-bearing individual—grew through contests large and small over the course of the nation's first several decades. And that way of thinking about voluntary affiliation served as a powerful stimulus to craft a legal means to temper associational authority and helped to ease the transition toward a recognizably plural society. By scrutinizing the law and the practices of voluntary association, we can discover the post-Revolutionary emergence of a set of beliefs that shaped

American attitudes toward the rule of law, toward constitutionalism, toward individualism and cooperation in ways that would resonate long after.

In the end, this study will offer a new account of one cultural development in the first fifty or sixty years of the American republic that has never really been explained. Why, exactly, did the United States witness the rise of the autonomous individual as an American cultural ideal just as new, more potent, and more effective forms of collective action—the corporation, the labor union, and the reform society—assumed a prominent place in the American social landscape? The more closely we look at moments of conflict between member and group, the more apparent the answer becomes: it was because of wide-ranging efforts, both internal and external, to extend to private groups a set of principles already present in the early republic, that (as Hendrik Hartog has observed in a different context) "when we are wronged there must be remedies, that patterns of illegitimate authority can be challenged, that public power must contain institutional mechanisms capable of undoing injustice." Only in that way could private associations and the autonomy of the individuals who made them up both, simultaneously, grow more robust and more secure. Limits could produce strength.

From within and from without, law-minded and law-bound ways of joining together would prevail in the post-Revolutionary era and nurture the growth of a diverse and vibrant civil society. That law-centered approach to association was preceded by an earlier, eighteenth-century emphasis on bonds of affection and sociability as providing the genesis and the lifeblood of the associational life of North America. And, by the fourth decade of the nineteenth century, as we will see in the final chapter, yet another way of thinking about voluntary affiliation would take center stage, as both the temperance and the antislavery movements found in the pledge—a deeply personal yet fully public profession of faith in a shared cause—a new variation on the meanings of voluntary affiliation that led some people to condemn them as absolutely threatening to deliberative democracy and to civic harmony in the republic.[11]

The first generations of American citizens chose to join together and act together in ways that still shape our society today. Though some aspects of their worldview began rapidly to disappear with the emergence of the radical reform movements of the antebellum era, in the post-Revolutionary contests about the meanings of membership we can witness men and women, consciously and deliberately, seeking to balance their need for effective, concerted action with their concerns for individual autonomy and personal rights. And the answers that they settled upon were essential to the creation of a civil society unlike any in the world.

PART ONE

The Concept of Membership in America, 1783–1815

Just as soon as the numbers of private, voluntary associations in the new American republic began to grow in the closing years of the eighteenth century, it became clear that they would prove disruptive. Thirteen republics had emerged from the Revolution, but each one had been established with hopes that it would speak and act with one voice on behalf of a shared, common good. As new forms of collective action came into being, it appeared that these new republics would soon be divided and split into various, particular interests. In time, and with experience, most people in the early republic would come to decide that this kind of fracture, these kinds of divisions, did not bode ill for the future of the United States. Initially, however, the associational diversity of post-Revolutionary America appeared to be utterly and completely divisive.

There was another way to see things, however. From the perspective of any man or woman who chose to join the ranks of a fraternal club, reform society, or any other kind of voluntary group, such associations were not divisive at all. They were unifying. Voluntary societies did not drive people apart. They brought them together.

The first generation of citizens of the new United States, between the conclusion of their successful War of Independence and the end of the War of 1812, was forced by daily experience and by the crucible of conflict to come to some shared understandings of the meanings and consequences of consent, coercion, and membership in the rapidly growing numbers of voluntary associations in the new nation. That last concept—membership—is one too easily taken for granted in a modern age of membership drives and annual membership renewal forms. But there was something new here, and it had to be defined. These newly created member-to-group relationships were unique. They were not like membership in a state, though the ways in which the two were different, particularly with the advent of written constitutions and explicitly consent-based governments, were not entirely clear. John Adams, in his draft preamble for the 1780 Massachusetts Constitution, for example, had noted that this "body politic" was "formed by a voluntary association of individuals." Like the new republican governments of the new American nation, however, these voluntary groups desired unanimity but nearly always found it fleeting. And so they seized upon the rule of law and procedural fairness as a means of creating fair but effective modes of private government.

Part 1 will explore how, in the everyday experiences of membership, there emerged a growing cultural consensus about what voluntary membership ought to look like and what it decidedly should not entail. In chapter 1, three important cultural developments will be examined. First, by looking at the travails of the embattled Society of the Cincinnati the chapter will examine the growing belief that effective voluntary association requires formalities and procedural regularity. No group can rely on mere affection or friendship. Second, I will begin a theme that will be continued in part 2: the increasingly sophisticated ways in which Americans embraced these kinds of formal practices within their own associations, by means of constitutions, bylaws, and resolute attention to procedure and predictability. Third, I will show just how pervasive these cultural practices were becoming by tracing the ways that they came to characterize practices in what was, for many American men and women, the most important of all associational connections: their own churches.

Chapter 2 will look at more explicitly political influences on the formation of a shared post-Revolutionary conception of voluntary membership. An important and revealing refrain emerged in the political debates of the 1790s and the first decade of the nineteenth century, when the first party debates between Federalists and Republicans took shape: the tension between collective political action and the ideally free and independent mind of the voting citizen. Many Americans, especially those who founded or joined one of the dozens of Democratic Republican societies that appeared throughout the nation during President George Washington's second term in office, believed that the creation of associations for political information and expression would make them better citizens—and keep the republic safe from harm. Their Federalist critics saw such groups as the wellspring of a terrifying political compulsion over the minds of men. One result was that the trends discussed in chapter 1, the emerging idea that members of nearly all kinds of voluntary associations ought to be knitted together by formalized and relatively attenuated bonds, found a powerful, post-Revolutionary impetus in the emergence of partisan conflict.

Chapter 3 will begin to show the ways that the Anglo-American legal culture of the early United States gave a particular shape and bent to the associational landscape that the first generations of American citizens were beginning to form among themselves. The cultural and political forces of the post-Revolutionary United States produced a jurisprudence that allowed civil rights claims to operate even within the ranks of private, voluntary associations, a jurisprudence founded on the idea that all groups comprised the same fundamental units—rights-bearing individuals. Some of these rights were defined in the articles of association (usually called "constitutions") of the group itself, but many were not. Some were creatures of the common law, which offered some useful terms, concepts, and remedies for those who sought to keep private, associational authority within positive bounds. And some of these rights were products of the American Revolution, of a republican belief in the idea that no governing authority, public or private, could pretend to certain kinds of authority over anyone, even one who had voluntarily chosen to be there.

Some of these struggles soon found their way into court. And the trials provide more than anecdote. It was in the arguments of counsel, the verdicts of juries, and the opinions of judges that conceptions of voluntary membership were tested and defined. There, the furthest limits of private governing authority were set. And, as it happened, all of the themes explored in part 1 were brought out into the open in a case decided by the Pennsylvania Supreme Court in 1810, after William Duane had a competing Philadelphia newspaper editor, John Binns, expelled from the St. Patrick Benevolent Society, which had been incorporated by the state of Pennsylvania, and from four other, unchartered associations. Binns took none of those expulsions lying down. He told the world of the tyrannies and injustices on display in each and every expulsion. He invoked ideas that resonated in the age in which he lived. He declared his certainty that it was not friendship that bound him to his fellow members, but rather rules and founding documents. He proclaimed his belief in the value of fair procedures and in constitutional limits on what majorities can legitimately do. He called out his worries about private governments as dangerous impediments to the independence of citizens. And, perhaps most important of all, he believed and he insisted that courts of law had an important role to play in solving the problems that faced him and countless others like him. By the time that the Supreme Court of Pennsylvania agreed with him, the foundations had been laid for the development of American civil society.

ONE

Friendship, Formalities, and Membership in Post-Revolutionary America

It did not take long at all. In 1783, in the immediate wake of the Treaty of Paris, the scent of gunpowder had yet to fade when a controversy of national reach gripped the American public. Officers of the Continental Army, who had just successfully waged war against what was still believed to be the world's greatest military power, formed the Society of the Cincinnati on the banks of the Hudson River on May 13, 1783. They named their association for the Roman general Lucius Quintus Cincinnatus who, rather than seeking power and glory, had returned to his farm after military triumph. The framers of the Cincinnati, led by General Henry Knox, whose brainchild it was, conceived of it as a "Society of Friends, to endure so long as they shall endure, or any of their eldest male posterity." By signing a copy of the parchment "Institution," or constitution, of the Cincinnati, more than a thousand Revolutionary War officers had joined within months of its formation.[1]

When the public first learned about its institution, critics of the Cincinnati—and they could be found from Massachusetts to South Carolina, even among American diplomats posted in Europe—began to engage in the first explicit discussions of the rights of citizens to form private societies and of the potential dangers that a closed institution of, by, and for the elite might pose for the infant American republic. It is not hard to imagine their concerns: American officers of the Revolution with at least three years' service (French officers, too, were invited) had chosen to form what could easily be seen as an association intended to create an aristocracy or even a knighthood. Members would gather together on regular, appointed occasions; they would wear an elaborate medal; membership would descend from them to their eldest sons, into perpetuity. It was utterly un-republican. John Adams called it "a deep design to overturn the whole Edifice of our Republican

Liberty." Its most vociferous critic, Judge Aedanus Burke of South Carolina, said that to permit the Cincinnati's existence "would give a fatal wound to civil liberty thro' the world."[2]

Two of the charges aimed at the Cincinnati have received a great deal of attention, at the time and over the past two centuries: The hereditary aspect of membership led some to believe that the club might result in the creation of an American peerage, even if the organizers had had no such intention. And, second, in a period when hardly any organization but Congress was truly national in scope, people could see the Cincinnati—with its federal structure, with national, state, and, in some places, district-level meetings—as something more than a club of former soldiers. It looked all too much like a self-created and parallel government. For many, it was an organization that simply reeked of political pretensions: as a legislative committee in Massachusetts reported, this "select Society" planned to "convene expressly for the purpose of deliberating upon, judging of, and adopting measures concerning matters, proper only for the cognizance of the legislative and their determination thereon, or of such other bodies as are known in the constitution." This was, in 1784, a dangerous *imperium in imperio*, an internal threat to republican government.[3]

But there was a third line of discussion. The reason that the founders and leading men of the Cincinnati gave for its very creation would generate a remarkable conversation that points the way toward how conceptions of voluntary membership would develop in the immediate aftermath of the American Revolution. The Cincinnati offered one reason that they believed the society ought to exist: to preserve friendships forged in war. The very existence of the Society of the Cincinnati exposes a desire by men in the late eighteenth century to come together in more-or-less organized forums for conversation and fellowship.[4]

This was an impulse in no way limited to the college man or to the soldier. A century earlier, in the late seventeenth century, English and Scottish thinkers began to develop a set of ideas that would shape Anglo-American views of social life for more than a century. Anthony Ashley Cooper, the third earl of Shaftesbury and a student of John Locke, was part of a group of influential writers who described an innate moral sense that was present in all human beings. This sympathy meant that all people were, by nature, sociable. That concept, especially as delineated in the works of Adam Smith, Dugald Stewart, and Francis Hutcheson, would echo in the political thought of the American Revolutionary generation and for decades to come. Even as they became anxious about the fate of "the social principle" by the mid-nineteenth century, orators and essayists continued to expound upon the "sacred tie of sympathy" that "binds man to his fellow man." In both the eighteenth and nineteenth centuries, such sensibility was seen as something that, although innate, must be nurtured and improved. And the stakes were high, as fostering sympathetic social bonds was thought to be crucial to holding a society together. The matter was not merely psychological, but intensely political.[5]

And organized groups were crucial. In a 1709 essay, "Sensus Communis," Shaftesbury emphasized the value of the club or conversation circle as an intimate community of shared interest and fellow feeling that gave men and women an opportunity to speak freely and to sharpen their wits. They could insulate themselves from the world outside "and grow better reasoners, by reasoning pleasantly, and at our ease," in these private societies of friends. Shared tastes would bring people together, often just a common interest "to furnish a rational amusement for the length of one Winter evening in a week," as one club in Annapolis described its goal in 1770. Beginning in the seventeenth century and in still greater numbers in the eighteenth, clubs of this sort spread throughout urban settings in England and British America. Before large numbers of outwardly oriented societies came into being—and they were notably called "projecting" societies by Daniel Defoe, meaning groups designed to offer something to those who were not members—private societies modeled on ideals of Shaftesburian sociability attracted educated men and women to fellowship throughout the English-speaking world. And the gentlemen's clubs, college fraternities, and coffeehouse gatherings of the colonial period, even if almost wholly founded on play and seeking little more than fellowship, served important discursive roles in the eighteenth century, as shown in the work of David Shields and others who since the late 1990s have applied the ideas of Jürgen Habermas to their studies of colonial and Revolutionary group life.[6]

But how much influence did such notions of belonging actually have in the years after the American Revolution, and into the nineteenth century, as Americans began to form and join increasingly diverse kinds of voluntary societies? How were their ideas about membership shaped by these older ideals of affectionate harmony? We know that the clubs and societies of Anglo-American civil society, generally seen to hold little political resonance before the Revolution, were transformed by the twin processes of winning independence and of building a nation in the decades that followed. During the Revolution, participants in the correspondence societies and other revolutionary groups met in private and forged strong relationships but acted directly to transform American politics in a way that had not, generally speaking, been the practice in British American associational life. In the Revolution's wake, many associations continued their direct engagement with the world around them, seeking social and political reform in ways undreamed of in colonial society. The question had to be asked of whether the nation as a whole could be held together through the sorts of sentimental bonds seen in these Shaftesburian clubs, though it seemed desperately unlikely.[7]

The furor over the Cincinnati helped some Americans arrive at some answers. In a way that mirrored the important distinction drawn by Revolutionary writers between society and government—one natural, the other artificial; one, as Thomas Paine said, "produced by our wants"; the other, "by our wickedness"—so too were critics of the Cincinnati profoundly skeptical of the Society's claim to be founded in "mutual friendships which have been formed under the pressure of common danger" in a time of war. If friendship was the goal, why then create a national, hereditary order, complete with auxiliary societies and constitutions?[8]

From the moment that the first eyebrow was raised concerning this veteran's organization, defenders of the Cincinnati insisted—and most scholars believe there is little reason to doubt them—that the organization was not a conservative, hierarchical reaction to the leveling tendencies of the Revolution, but a product of heartfelt desires to preserve the friendships forged in a long and destructive war. According to one Maryland member, the war produced friendships that "were strengthened by adversity, and finally cemented (as our establishment expresses it) by the blood of the parties." These were generally "of too endearing a nature to be for ever dissolved by the separation which necessarily followed the discharge of the army," and, because "no mode so unexceptionable as this could be devised to render them lasting," the Society of the Cincinnati was formed. In 1787, New York's Morgan Lewis would similarly call to mind how "a gallant band of patriots, who, for eight years, had lived together in the habits of the strictest friendship,—together borne the numerous hardships incident to the soldiers' life—together braved the various dangers of the field—together fought, bled, and conquered, saw themselves on the eve of separation, and could not bear the thought that it should be forever."[9]

Perhaps the Cincinnati was intended to be a "Society of Friends." But men such as Thomas Jefferson, who was not a member, and George Washington, who was, gave serious thought to the idea that the very act of organizing might threaten that goal. Nothing corrupted friendship, they believed, like formal association. Jefferson put his finger directly on the issue in a letter he wrote to George Washington in April 1784, and the perceived distinction between association and amity continued to shape attitudes toward

1. Society of the Cincinnati, membership certificate of Robert Pemberton, Dec. 10, 1785, Certificate File, PR 014, New-York Historical Society.

voluntary associations in the decades to come: Friendship was a feature of natural society; formalities and organized collective action were elements of political society. That distinction would become hardened in the crucible of the first postwar national controversy. The result was a growing certainty that natural bonds of affection were so sufficiently distinct from the artificial bonds of any formally organized society—from the club to the nation—that each should be governed by entirely different rules of conduct.[10]

When the controversy exploded, George Washington—who had had the presidency of the Society thrust upon him—felt obliged to seek the advice of others about how he ought to respond, including Jefferson, who was then serving in the Confederation Congress in Annapolis. In a letter he sent to Washington on April 16, 1784, fully expecting that the two men would have a chance to discuss the matter in person soon after, Jefferson laid out his case for why the retired commander-in-chief should do everything in his considerable persuasive power to destroy the Cincinnati.[11]

Jefferson hit the expected, anti-aristocratic note in his letter to Washington. The Society of the Cincinnati, in granting the progeny of its members "preeminence by birth," was "against the letter of some of our constitutions; against the spirit of them all." The Cincinnati, he argued, might well be a first step toward a subversion of all of the Revolution's accomplishments—accomplishments that Jefferson believed had the potential to alter forever the course of human history.[12]

Though he hated the idea of the Society of the Cincinnati, Jefferson perceived better than most critics that the organization had genuinely admirable origins. He never swayed from that view, even years later. But he saw those origins as resting in a natural sociability that was, in fact, ill served by the artificial creation of a badge-wearing, meeting-holding, bylaw-adopting association. He began by telling Washington what the older man surely already knew. Jefferson assured him that "it was natural for men who had accompanied each other through so many scenes of hardship, of difficulty & danger, who in a variety of instances must have been rendered mutually dear by those aids & good offices to which their situations had given occasion, it was natural I say for these to seize with fondness any proposition which promised to bring them together again at certain & regular periods." Jefferson insisted, twice, that any effort to preserve the emotional ties of friendship was a "natural" act.[13]

Jefferson then detailed for Washington how the very manner of organization that the Society of the Cincinnati had chosen would destroy friendships, not foster them. "I doubt," he wrote, "whether in it's execution it would be found to answer the wishes of those who framed it, & to foster those friendships it was intended to preserve." The members of the Cincinnati would attend "their annual assemblies no longer to encounter a common enemy, but to encounter one another in debate & sentiment." He, somewhat snidely, told Washington that, although the Cincinnati may have little to do at their gatherings, "something I suppose is to be done," and "however unimportant, it will suffice to produce difference of opinion, contradiction & irritation." And nothing—of all the passages in Jefferson's letter, it was this one that Washington would quote directly in his speech to the first meeting of the Cincinnati—"loosens the bands of private friendship more, than for friends to pit themselves agst each other in public debate." Organized as it was, the friendships forged in war would be put at risk by a voluntary association that had been formed chiefly to nourish them.[14]

This was not a position taken up for this one argument, but one deeply grounded in Jefferson's political philosophy. His point that a natural impulse to friendly intercourse would fall prey to the artificial structures being crafted by Knox and his co-organizers arose from his conviction that the natural sociability of man was something to be sheltered, not subjected to manmade pressures of organized disputation. Jefferson would later observe that "an association of men who will not quarrel is a thing which never yet existed, from the greatest confederacy of nations down to a town meeting or vestry." The instinctive draw of social interaction was something Jefferson took seriously from the time he commonplaced that idea's greatest proponent, Lord Kames, well before drafting the Declaration of Independence. This distinction between natural society and the artifice of government was shared widely by members of the Revolutionary generation. As James Wilson noted in his famous 1790 law lectures, "We have all the emotions, which are necessary in order that society may be formed and maintained," including, he noted, "attachment to our friends." And government's purpose was to protect and to shelter that sphere, not to replace it. Government was "instituted for the happiness of society."[15]

Jefferson's letter hit its mark. Washington visited him in Annapolis not long after, and as Jefferson recalled, "we had much convers[atio]n on the institution," until Washington "declared his determination to use his utmost endeavor to have it entirely abolished."[16] After leaving Jefferson, Washington traveled to Philadelphia and presided over the first general meeting of the Cincinnati, where he would make his opinion known at the first opportunity. The only point on which he quoted Jefferson, albeit without attribution, was on the Cincinnati as a burden to genuine affection and friendship. As Washington put it in his own words, formally organizing as a society "might be more productive of dissention than harmony." Proving the point as much by his behavior as by his words, Washington was apparently genuinely upset. He gave two long speeches, on back-to-back days, and an observer noted that he spoke "with much warmth and agitation"—hardly adjectives we associate with Washington. The debate over hereditary membership was terribly important, but the argument over the meaning of friendship lay at the core of it all. Everyone present knew that, as they put it in a letter to French officers, the whole point of the Cincinnati was "riveting more strongly those indissoluble ties" of friendship. Washington made the case that it might destroy them.[17]

The results of both debates—that is, both the national controversy over the very existence of the Society of the Cincinnati as well as the internal one among the members of the Cincinnati themselves—served to sharpen the distinction between friendship and formal association that had stood out to Jefferson. He may have been among the first to engage the issue, but others were coming to similar conclusions. Most notably, those who opposed Washington's attempts to change the Society of the Cincinnati emphasized formal, even contractual ideas in defense of their "Society of Friends." New

Hampshire's John Sullivan, a general in the Continental army and then his state's attorney general, pointedly told Washington—and all other members of the Cincinnati, via a circular letter sent to all thirteen branches—that "we became Members of the Cincinnati upon the original plan & cannot conceive ourselves bound by Articles to which we never subscribed." If a new system was contrived "we shall Individually claim a right to determine for ourselves whether we will become members or we will not." Such men stuck to their original plans long enough for the attention of their critics to drift to other worries, long enough for most observers to see how innocuous the Society of the Cincinnati was. But they did so for a reason that would only drive home the essentially political nature of the group itself: *this* was the society they had consented to join, and no one could turn it into something essentially different without their renewed consent.[18]

What is more, opponents of the Cincinnati formed and proposed counter-organizations that were clearly political entities. One anonymous plan called for a Revolution Society that was to be far more inclusive—including any and all elected officials and militia officers across thirteen states—but would make no effort to be a "Society of Friends." In the state of Rhode Island, men formed "anti-Cincinnati" associations, which were essentially political action committees, to prompt the legislature to prohibit the society. And, most famously of all, the tavern keeper William Manning proposed to form a national association of mechanics and farmers, a "Society of Laborers," to counter societies such as the Cincinnati, collectives of the privileged few. He wanted it to be "formed as nearly after the order of the Cincinnati" as possible, but he saw it first and foremost as a mode of political combination and mutual education: fellow feeling was to have no part of it.[19]

For Jefferson, the distinction between formal association and the informalities of true friendship were clear. The relationships of the domestic sphere were, to him, the essence of personal interconnection. The familiar letter, exchanged amicably and intimately between two equals, was far more dear to him than was any kind of fraternal association. He had been a member of the Flat Hat Club in college, for instance, but he gave no attention to it and later spoke of it dismissively: "I was a member, but it had no useful object, nor do I know whether it now exists." He was by no means opposed to private associations that served some public purpose—the American Philosophical Society, for instance—and he even drew up a model constitution for the Albemarle Agricultural Society, but he viewed it solely as a convenient clearinghouse of information for "practical and observing husbandmen" living in the county.[20]

In the end, it was clear that the Society of the Cincinnati was not a club of some two thousand friends. The contention of politics would drive the point home, as when Luke and Elijah Day joined Shays's Rebellion and were unceremoniously booted out of the Massachusetts Cincinnati, which rewrote their membership history by resolving that "they are not and never have been considered as members of this Society." More tellingly, about a week before Aaron Burr shot Alexander Hamilton to death in 1804, the two men had dinner together as fellow members at the annual gathering of the Cincinnati in New York on July 4th, 1804. Friends indeed.[21]

There was an increasingly obvious distinction to be made between the practical, purpose-driven association—where membership was a means to a well-defined end, with strictly delimited duties and expectations—and what Jefferson and many others saw as wrongheaded efforts to organize formally in order to preserve and promote amity. That distinction would become a common cultural touchstone in discussions and debates about the nature of voluntary association, in large part because it accorded so well with a potent set of Revolutionary-era beliefs about the chasm that separated natural society from the artifice of governing authority, be it private or public. There may well be no such thing as a voluntary association of friends. Friends could gather, to be sure. In order to form an effective association among more than a few individuals, though, friendship was not enough.

Voluntarism in Post-Revolutionary America

After the Revolution, men and women at all levels of social standing, and in communities large and small, embraced collective and relatively formal organization as the very best of means to improve society and their own lives. That fact has become a commonplace in the historical literature because such groups really did become utterly commonplace. Parades in New York in the 1780s and 1790s, for instance, reveal the many associations being organized in what one historian has called the "rush by New Yorkers to form societies that would embody every conceivable interest." These societies were not at all similar to the committees of the Revolutionary period, which claimed to speak for whole communities, but rather were formed by and for specific ethnic, cultural, or interest groups and, particularly in the early nineteenth century, for particular segments of the laboring population. Many sought formal incorporation, and chartered corporations reached Americans of all social levels: "the members of these corporations are increasing rapidly and daily," noted one judge in 1810. So too did the proportion of Americans formally belonging to churches roughly double between

1776 and 1850. Astute citizens of the early American republic simply could not help noticing what James Kent called the "most astonishing" spread of organized collective action, as the practice reached new places and new people with every passing year.[22]

A great deal of effort has gone to determine why so many groups of individuals chose to join together, voluntarily and formally, to accomplish some shared purposes in the several decades following the American Revolution. Alexis de Tocqueville's contribution to this ongoing conversation was that the phenomenon was a virtually inevitable by-product of the general equality (and thus general impotence) of each solitary citizen. Associations, then, "must take the place of the powerful private persons whom equality of conditions has eliminated." To achieve anything at all, organized cooperation was needed.[23]

A particularly persuasive school of thought has credited the rise of associational activity to the revival of American Protestantism known as the Second Great Awakening. The very concept of voluntarism, for those living in the early republic and for their historians, evoked the religious disestablishment and pluralism of the late eighteenth and early nineteenth centuries. The relationship of one form of voluntarism to another was neither direct nor simple, but scholars can make a compelling case for their connection. The theological optimism of the age, a sense of responsibility to do good and thus demonstrate saving grace (or, for some historians, to find a means to induce conformity, whether that meant efforts at the social control of the unregenerate or even efforts of the orthodox to contain revivalism), and the search for an "organizing process" of a religious awakening as expressed in local group—all have been named as direct causes of an unprecedented spread in private, formally organized associations.[24]

A third explanation centers on the increasing modernization of the early United States. William Ellery Channing saw the connection clearly in 1829, asserting that "the main cause" in the explosion of associational action was "the immense facility given to intercourse by modern improvements, by increased commerce and travelling, by the post-office, by the steam-boat, and especially by the press, by newspapers, periodicals, tracts, and other publications." Some historians have correlated the rise in American associational activity, particularly of the creation of charitable and reform organizations, with a series of gradual (and not so gradual) economic, social, and demographic transformations that saw the people of British North America, and then the United States, becoming more capitalistic, more tightly interconnected, and, in sum, increasingly modern. With such changes, though by no means wholly restricted to Britain or the United States, came a newfound humanitarian sensibility and a greater cognizance not only of the need but also of the capacity that people could come together to ease the suffering of others.[25]

Building on scholarship concerning British associations, a fourth but closely related school holds that the proliferation of voluntary associations is best understood as a consequence of the decline of community, a *Gemeinschaft*-to-*Gesellschaft* narrative. According to a scholar of British voluntary association, with "the fragmentation of the communal coherence, the diminution of the organized sociability, and the sundering of the powerful cultural identity of the older, medieval city," clubs, charitable organizations, and mutual aid societies can be seen as a response to "a growing sense of social isolation and social distance." With the requisite modifications, many historians working in a North American context have embraced that model, with new kinds of groups filling a void left by the (supposedly) once tight-knit communities of generations past.[26]

In the end, the most persuasive explanations cede primacy of place to the American Revolution itself. According to this view, one pioneered by Richard Brown and whose adherents grant that broader demographic and religious change played supporting roles, after the Revolution—and in large part because of it—"supra-local perspectives" that simply had not existed in British America combined with both a secular and a religious optimism to encourage collective action. Problems could be solved, they had come to believe, and cooperation was a means to find solutions. As men and women became accustomed to formal, voluntary participation in one organization or another, or as they read or heard about such groups in neighboring communities, a cumulative effect created the world Tocqueville observed in 1831, one in which it appeared that associations of "a thousand different types" were formed in "all the affairs of social life." In communities that had scarcely changed at all in some measurable socioeconomic or demographic way, men and women in the first few decades following a republican revolution were forming and joining associations with a frenzy that would have seemed absolutely alien to their colonial forebears.[27]

The first generation of American citizens did not emerge from the Revolution with a fully developed set of ideas about how to organize those groups internally, however. It was no simple matter to find a way to balance the nearly inevitable tensions between individual members and the larger group. And yet the drift toward new and more culturally resonant ideas regarding procedural fairness and rights that were carried into diverse social relationships was, in fact, presaged by developments that spanned the eighteenth century on both sides of the British Atlantic world, many originating within the associations themselves.

The idea of having at least a handful of rules was essential. As early as 1698, for example, Josiah Woodward could write in London about the usefulness of certain religious societies that were appearing within the Church of England. And he emphasized the "*Rules* and *Orders*" that they had drawn up among themselves and how, at each meeting, the young men "kept to their *Rules*." In British North America, too, well before the Revolution, New Englanders such as a teenage Paul Revere, who helped to draw up a covenant for a bell ringers' association for other boys his age, carried many of the ideas that characterized New England town government into the more tight-knit associations that they concocted. In Revere's bell-ringing society, organized about 1750, the boys instituted a system of majority rule, but they had a clear preference for unanimity, such as their rule that no member be admitted but by unanimous vote. They established a rotation of office (every three months, they would choose a new moderator), and they made a mutual commitment among themselves to ring the bells for two hours once every week. Such rules were not terribly unlike those drawn up by John Locke decades earlier in England, though the spirit of Locke's rules—aimed at fostering discussion and mutual improvement—were perhaps better captured in another famous early American's first venture at organized association: Benjamin Franklin's "Junto," which he formed in 1727. There too the men created a set of mutually agreed-upon rules (the exact time and regularity of meetings, requirements for essay contributions, and so on) to help to make their shared goals of personal development and rewarding social exchange a reality. At least a smattering of rules, even for those societies such as the famous Tuesday Club of Annapolis that were primarily about food, drink, and conversation, were considered standard. In their first meeting, in May 1745, the members passed four "Laws" that described meeting times, the admission of new members, and, of course, the requisite food and drink.[28]

The organizers and joiners of voluntary groups in England and in British America had begun to become aware of the utility of rules and procedural organization, long before the Revolution and before such groups as the Cincinnati came into being. The most recent study of Philadelphia's colonial-era voluntary associations finds that the societies there took their organization, their record keeping, and their founding documents seriously, as more effective ways of achieving their collective objectives. From the last decades of the eighteenth century onward, a similar trend has been witnessed in the Old World, according to an intensive study of Edinburgh and an extensive study of British societies.[29]

These were practical efforts to make the newly founded groups function, and they cumulatively helped to produce what recent historical scholarship has described as a "technology" of association. Quite simply, the spread of the knowledge of *how* to associate—through print, through emulation of a nearby town, and through the geographical mobility of the members and organizers themselves—encouraged the practice, and it did so in ways that underscored the importance of rules and formal structures as the lifeblood of collective action. It was a long process, one greatly amplified by the political and cultural effects of the American Revolution.[30]

As the imbroglio over the Cincinnati suggests, certain ways of thinking about membership were already becoming widely shared among Americans as the smoke of the Revolution cleared, emerging from within the everyday practices of associations in the early United States. The most important conceptual image or parallel for most American joiners in this period was constitutional self-government. At this very moment, of course, ideas about membership in the state—that is, citizenship—were also in flux, with a growing tendency to describe it purely in volitional terms still largely uncertain and passionately debated. And concern about how a republic's citizens must avoid any encumbrances that would limit their independence of thought and action had unavoidable and far-reaching consequences. It helped to enshrine an ideal of the self-sufficient yeoman farmer in the philosophies of men such as James Madison and Thomas Jefferson, for instance. And it produced a growing emphasis on education and the instilling of civic virtue among the nation's youth.[31]

By the very early nineteenth century, the self-created constitutions, bylaws, and day-to-day practices found within American voluntary societies put on display a set of attitudes toward private association that embraced voluntary affiliation as fully a political act—which is to say, in the post-Revolutionary idiom, as something strictly based on consent and limited to achieving the members' common interests, by predetermined means, while safeguarding each member's rights. Voluntary affiliation, as historian Marc Harris has suggested, was coming to be seen as part of "a meta-constitutional order within which citizens organized themselves for the purposes they deemed necessary." This did not come to be by accident: rather, the ordinary, everyday experiences of American joiners and organizers had begun to contribute to a pervasive culture of constitutional self-government, one that did not begin and end with the political creations of the Revolutionary era.

Particularly, the historical record reveals serious and repeated attention to how, exactly, to protect minorities—even minorities of only one person—from a majority that chose to violate their rights or neglect their interests. In their own clubs and societies, many American joiners were beginning to display a staunch commitment to the idea that the right thing to do was to establish firm limits to what a given voluntary society might do, even if a majority chose to do it. Written constitutions were crucial.[32]

One of the most telling examples can be found in the records of that quintessential eighteenth-century voluntary association, Freemasonry. That there was something "constitutional" in the conduct of Freemasonry should not be surprising, of course. As early as 1723, as historian Steven Bullock has observed, it took eighteen pages to print all of the Masonic rules and regulations. The very term *constitution* was introduced to much of the world via the exportation of Freemasonry from England: the first time it appeared in French, in 1710, was in a Masonic context, for instance. And James Anderson's *Constitutions of the Free-Masons*—the first Masonic book printed in America, when Franklin reprinted the book in Philadelphia in 1734—emphasized certain irrevocable features in what Freemasonry could and should look like. From a very early date with the formation of the first Grand Lodge in London in 1717, Masons were articulate, if not always consistent, about those kinds of constitutional matters. And that self-reflective attentiveness to constitutional forms of government found on display in Freemasonry would grow in the wake of the American Revolution.[33]

Though Freemasonry was always deemed by its participants to be unique and especially conducive to the enlightenment of humankind, Masons in the decades following the American Revolution certainly saw their association as part of a broader constellation of post-Revolutionary American collective endeavors. DeWitt Clinton, while serving as mayor of New York City, was elected as grand master of Freemasons in the state of New York in 1806. His address on the occasion of his installation that June, which was published later that year, went on at great length about the natural desire of men to join together, still a refrain around the turn of the nineteenth century. He noted for his fellow Masons that the "propensity to associate may be observed in every stage of society, from the rude hunter of the forest to the polished inhabitant of the city." But the United States in the present age was witnessing the phenomenon of association to a degree not before known. Though he was addressing Freemasons and reserved his highest praise for the advantages of the Craft, he noted, too, "voluntary societies springing up in a thousand shapes, for the improvement of our physical, mental or moral faculties" across the nation.[34]

Masonry was bigger than any of them. Though it was never really one, united organization, it was often seen as one by Masons and non-Masons alike. In the 1770s and 1780s, it first had to survive a division with the growing appeal of Ancient Freemasonry over the, ironically, older version known as Modern Freemasonry, but by 1792 the newer competitor had won the day in most states. And there was great growth for Masonry across the new nation, particularly in the 1790s. From approximately two hundred lodges in 1793, the number grew to five hundred by 1800 (or more than doubled to 11 grand lodges and 347 subordinate lodges by a more conservative count), and they spread far outside of the few urban centers into much smaller communities. Freemasonry was, in many ways, well suited to the culture of the new republic, and its willingness to include men from outside of the realms of the social elite and to embrace the participation of people from almost all ranks of society aided its astounding growth.[35]

Despite Clinton's view that Masonry was one association among countless others in the panorama of voluntary societies in post-Revolutionary America, the lodges made great efforts to separate themselves from the society in which they existed, even the post-Revolutionary American society in which Freemasonry thrived. They found three means to that end: secrecy, ritual, and law. The lodges acted publicly, of course, in processions, parades, and cornerstone-laying ceremonies throughout the post-Revolutionary era. But there was always a level of secrecy about what took place in the lodge, its door guarded by a man wielding a sword. Most men who joined had only a loose idea of what it would entail. Second, initiation rituals also helped to draw a line between those who belonged and those who did not, a distinction that would become still more profound in the early nineteenth century with a new focus on complex, lengthy rituals and the invention of entirely new levels of Masonic membership, in the York Rite and the Scottish Rite.

Just as important, it seems, were the ways that Freemasonry had cordoned itself as a constitutional regime, with well-articulated constitutions, bylaws, and judicial procedures to govern the interior proceedings of each lodge. Especially when combined with the terrors of the unknown set loose by Masons' proclivity for secrecy in all things, this legalism would provoke some skepticism and, ultimately, hostility toward the institution—hostility that would ultimately explode into the Anti-Masonic furor of the 1820s and 1830s. Worries about dark and immoral oaths and concerns about what passed behind the veil of secrecy were only worsened by the existence of a fully fledged code of laws, far removed and intentionally kept separate from the laws of the state.

One does not need to look very far into the minutes of any lodge or grand lodge to see a Masonic legalism in post-Revolutionary America that was both separate from and parallel to the broader legal culture of the new republic. The Virginia Grand Lodge, for instance, described a complicated appellate process in cases of expulsion, noting the right of the expelled man to file an appeal with a superior lodge in a 1799 resolution: "*Resolved*, That the power of suspension and expulsion, in such cases, always hath been, and now is, inherent in every Lodge within this jurisdiction: provided always, that the right of appeal to the Grand Lodge can in no wise be weakened or affected." Disputes within Masonry, such as one in Farmington, Connecticut, in 1795, nearly always showed a serious attentiveness to an interior rule of law. When Josiah Holt was accused of misconduct toward the wife of a fellow Mason by his compatriots in his local lodge, he wrote a formal response to "the Brethren of Frederick Lodge No. 26," noting that he had very much expected to have had a formal reading of the charges against him and an opportunity to respond:

> In such a case it is natural to expect that my accusers who are my brethren and who are under the strongest obligation to support the reputation of the Craft and guide by the plumb line of virtue a wandering brother—would have taken me by the cable of tow and led me to that body to whom I am amenable for my conduct and there exhibit such charges against me as would justify their proceedings and the Lodge in passing such Censure on me as my Crimes deserve—had this taken place I should have had opportunity to made [*sic*] my defense and related those circumstances that I presume would in some measure have extenuated my crimes and rendered less aggravated the Injury I have done the Lodge.

But this had not yet happened, and Holt was certain of his right to a fair hearing—"under these considerations I have the presumtion to arraign myself before you"—by letter to confess his wrongs in hopes of remaining a member in good standing but also to tell his own side of the story.[36]

Masonry's very constitutionalism and legalism, complete with appellate procedures internal to the Masonic hierarchy, was only to become more pronounced in the early nineteenth century. Historian Steven Bullock has examined Masonry's "growing institutional infrastructure" and a "language of legality" that came increasingly naturally to Masonic brothers in the early 1800s. Dorothy Lipson has argued that the system was somewhat akin to church discipline: Like a church, Masons punished in order to bring the errant back into the fold or, in cases of expulsion, to rid themselves of them, and like churches they "employed confessions, repentance, and forgiveness to bring about a reformation." It was a legalism that, as the case of Josiah Holt made evident, Masons themselves desired.[37]

Legal structures, fair hearings, and legalistic language were absolutely expected by all participants in this, the largest fraternal society of the early American republic, even though in most states it had no formal relationship to governmental institutions of legislative or judicial authority. There was simply no other way for participants to conceive of how to resolve internal disputes and to administrate themselves in a voluntary society of such size and scope. For instance, decisions were made quite early to give each lodge in New England exclusive rights to admit members over a geographical region, with Masonic laws prohibiting a lodge from admitting a man who lived closer to another lodge without first receiving the approval of that nearer body. Virginia, too, was still tweaking its internal appellate procedures occasionally in the 1790s and the first decade of the nineteenth century, setting up a district system between the local lodges and the state's grand lodge. Clark Brown went on at great length in telling his fellow Vermont Freemasons in 1814 about how they ought to try to solve each and every dispute among themselves by making use of the elaborate judicial system set up among Masonic lodges and grand lodges. "If any member should feel himself aggrieved by any subordinate tribunal," Brown said, "let him appeal for trial before a higher authority, the Grand Lodge, to which the Lodge, in which his case had before been tried, is in subordination by charter and jurisdiction." Throughout the 1810s and 1820s, Masons would continue to put ever greater emphasis on procedural details and guarantees of fairness in disciplinary cases, particularly those meriting expulsion.[38]

Membership in America's Churches

Though Freemasonry was the largest single voluntary organization in the early national United States, there were, of course, far more men and women who were members of churches. Ideas about church membership changed a great deal in the decades following the American Revolution, and the growing formalization of religious societies paralleled the developments in other, secular organizations. Going back as far as the first debates on religious tolerance, as scholars such as Holly Brewer have begun to make clear, discussions as to what constituted consent in terms of religious affiliation were crucial to how people understood other kinds of allegiance. This was particularly true in the era of disestablishment in the new United States, for it was there that the relationship between the state and the group life of civil society was first being worked out.[39]

As had been the case in the colonial era, schisms, growing religious pluralism, and a drift toward genuine religious diversity all resulted in church membership as a category becoming more, not less, meaningful. As each and every state ended their establishments after the Revolution, it became well understood that "no person can now become a member of a religious society, until, by his voluntary act, he has united with it." In 1833, Massachusetts, the one state that had maintained a formal church-state relationship into the 1820s, would finally amend its constitution and terminate its religious establishment. No longer would tax monies be used to support any church in the United States. From that point forward, no American religious institution could exist but by the voluntary affiliation and support of its adherents. It was not just a legal but a cultural shift. As every church came to comprise only those who had chosen to enter, membership came to mean something different than it had.[40]

In some ways, this is a story we know well. In 1837, in the introductory piece to the new *United States Magazine and Democratic Review*, John O'Sullivan wrote to describe his views on exactly what American republican government ought to look like: it should mirror the churches of America in its reliance on voluntarism, not compulsion.

> Its domestic action should be confined to the administration of justice, for the protection of the natural equal rights of the citizen, and the preservation of social order. In all other respects, the VOLUNTARY PRINCIPLE, the principle of FREEDOM, suggested to us by the analogy of the divine government of the Creator, and already recognised by us with perfect success in the great social interest of Religion, affords the true "golden rule" which is alone abundantly competent to work out the best possible general result of order and happiness from that chaos of characters, ideas, motives, and interests—human society.[41]

And O'Sullivan was not alone in seizing upon this concept, the "voluntary principle," to describe the antebellum American religious environment.

Robert Baird, one of the first historians of American religion, writing in 1844, entitled one chapter in his book *Religion in America* "The Voluntary Principle in America: Its Action and Influence." There, he argued for the peculiar self-reliance of Americans in supporting their own religious institutions, voluntarily, and found in that very voluntarism a way to explain the country's fervent religiosity. At about the same time, the author of a book on

American demographics said much the same: "When it is considered that all these institutions for the support of religion, the exercise of benevolence, and the diffusion of knowledge, are sustained purely and entirely upon the voluntary principle, it is impossible not to be struck with its superior efficacy, as compared with the fruits of any system of compulsory support, especially for religion, in any country whatever." By the 1840s, when people wrote to describe American religion, they invariably described it as a domain that existed only by individual, voluntary affiliation and support.[42]

Already by the time of the American Revolution, most Americans would have agreed with the basic proposition that being a church member was something one chose, not something one had thrust upon them. In the American colonies and the new United States in the eighteenth century and the early nineteenth century, ideas about voluntary affiliation and informed consent in churches were developed still further by the demographic and sociopolitical realities of American life. The growing numbers of churches and denominations, particularly of evangelical churches such as Baptists and Methodists, produced an environment in which Americans were actively solicited as potential converts. Without doubt, similar trends can be traced back at least as far as the revivals of the early to mid-eighteenth century, popularly known as the Great Awakening, but the post-Revolutionary era witnessed something new. The Reverend Henry Pattillo of North Carolina noted in 1788 that "a change of religious profession has become almost as common, and as little noted, as the variation of the weather." Where there had formerly been something akin to a "gentlemen's agreement" against proselytizing from within the ranks of another church, the early nineteenth century saw newly aggressive attitudes about missions, even attempts to seduce the adherents of one church to join another.[43]

Additionally, the religious pluralism of the eighteenth century led states north and south to develop legal regimes that allowed dissenters some room to practice their faith, in ways that made concrete this growing acceptance of the voluntary principle. Some states, such as New York, had at least fourteen kinds of religious bodies in the eighteenth century, and no church was ever established there. And even before those colonies that had an official state religion such as Massachusetts, Connecticut, or Virginia had ended their formal religious establishments, they had each spent a great deal of time discussing and arranging for a certificate system that allowed dissenters to opt out of support for the established church and to have taxes assessed for support of religion to instead be directed to their own church. All three of those states adopted such laws in the eighteenth century. In the post-Revolutionary era, such laws were increasingly common and increasingly lax: the Connecticut certificate law, passed in May 1791, was amended later in that same year to simplify the whole process in a way that underscored the new, post-Revolutionary impulse toward voluntarism: people could write their own certificates (rather than applying to a justice of the peace), with no need for any official to attest to its validity. Vermont passed a similar law in 1801. Though critics asserted that such laws made churches nothing more than "loose flimsy private corporations," the trend toward such policies—and, ultimately, toward fully voluntary religious societies—appears in hindsight to have been all but inevitable by the turn of the nineteenth century.[44]

It would only accelerate: as William Warren Sweet famously noted, the small town of Princeton, Illinois, in the 1850s had eleven different kinds of Presbyterians. African Americans formed a limited number of separate churches in the South before emancipation, but it happened far more commonly in the Northern urban centers in the early American republic. Members of black churches such as Richard Allen's African Methodist Church in Philadelphia numbered in the tens of thousands by the 1820s. Allen emphasized the importance of this racial separation by issuing a public statement in 1794 limiting membership to "descendants of the African race," highlighting how the continuing fragmentation of American religious denominations only amplified the importance of how the church defined its standards of membership. Westward expansion would push this development still further. Counties that had been virtually uninhabited by white settlers before the American Revolution would contain a third of the young nation's population by 1790. The mass population shift westward added to the popular impetus to organize and join churches as a way to form community out of chaotic new settlements.[45]

So too did state constitutional guarantees of religious liberty further this trend toward greater emphasis on personal, volitional commitment as the sine qua non of post-Revolutionary religion. The first inclination in many new states after 1776—Georgia, South Carolina, Maryland, Connecticut, Massachusetts, and New Hampshire—had been to create some form of multiple establishment, supporting Christian denominations generally if not entirely equally. Most outlawed blasphemy; many limited state office-holding to Christians or even to Protestants. But particularly after the 1784–1786 debates in Virginia over the issue of the separation of church and state, which involved a powerful combination of evangelicals and rationalists such as Thomas Jefferson and James Madison arguing for the individual rights of conscience as forbidding any governmental preference for one religion over another, the way was paved for a disestablishment across the new United States. Most states had explicit descriptions of an unalienable right of conscience in religious matters in their constitutions, and many admitted after 1790 copied much of Pennsylvania's constitutional clause on religious liberty, which emphasized an individualist reading of religious rights and a "natural and indefeasible right to worship Almighty God" only in the manner that one chose.[46]

Jefferson was not alone in believing that disestablishment as it was taking shape in America boded well for the future of Christianity. He saw that Pennsylvania and New York had "long subsisted without any establishment at all," and now "they flourish infinitely. Religion is well supported," and "their harmony is unparalleled, and can be ascribed to nothing but their unbounded tolerance." New England's decision to end church-state connections ultimately led even clergymen of the formerly established church to agree. Connecticut minister Lyman Beecher recounted what he called the "Downfall of the Standing Order" in a surprising way. "Originally all were obliged to support the standing order. Every body paid without kicking. . . . When, however, other denominations began to rise, and complained of their consciences, the laws were modified." He believed at first that the damage done to the church was "irreparable," but he would change his mind. In a famous passage, he noted in his autobiography that "for several days I suffered what no tongue can tell *for the best thing that ever happened to the State of Connecticut*. It cut the churches loose from dependence on state support. It threw them wholly on their own resources and on God." Soaring numbers of churches, ministers, and church members in the nineteenth century left most observers convinced that the state of religion in the United States was one of revival and growth: Jon Butler estimates that 10,000 new churches were built between 1780 and 1820, with probably another 40,000 in the next forty years. One in fifteen Americans was a communing church member in 1800; one in eight had joined a church in 1835. Six times that number (40 and 75 percent, respectively) had some connection with a church.[47]

What did all of this mean for the concept of church membership in the post-Revolutionary era? That was no simple question, to them or to us. "The subject of membership in the Church of God, and the rights, privileges and duties of members, are subjects which necessarily require God's explicit and particular Legislation.—They are subjects that cannot be left to human wisdom, or prudence," wrote Presbyterian minister John M'Farland in 1828. But divine instruction on the matter was sufficiently open to interpretation that Americans before and after the Revolution spent a great deal of time and energy dealing with questions about "the rights, privileges and duties of members."[48]

The diversity of religious beliefs and practices as well as of models of church government in the new United States, which would only grow as the eighteenth century gave way to the nineteenth, meant that no one conception of religious membership could possibly prevail among all American church members. But the trends and debates in the 1790s and the first four decades of the nineteenth century ultimately produced something approaching a consensus as to what, in a general sense, it ought to look like in a country where the voluntary principle had come to prevail.

One aspect of this new consensus was, as we have seen, already apparent to the very first historians of American religion: as denominations split apart and new ones formed; as most states ended formal church-state relationships; and as communities were being broken up and new ones formed with the westward expansion of the young United States, American Protestants sought a new vision to unite a fragmented Christianity. And they found it in the voluntary principle. From the perspective of men writing in the age of Ralph Waldo Emerson, this was an exaltation of individual freedom, which could produce a new harmony among American believers, a "unity through diversity." According to many scholars of American religion since the mid-nineteenth century—from Robert Baird to Perry Miller, and many others since—Americans found a unity in their descriptions of the nature of church affiliation: it was to be wholly voluntary, resting on the discernment of the faithful.[49]

The focus on voluntary affiliation, however, was only one of a number of ways in which church membership helped give shape to ideas of membership in all varieties of voluntary associations being formed in the early national United States. There was also a growing interest in *formalizing* the member-to-church relationship, better defining the boundaries between who was included and who was not. The result was a system of church-member relationships that came to be described, increasingly often, as something quite like a constitutional relationship, with the formative documents of the church setting the furthest limits of churchly authority in a way that members could appeal to in cases of internal disputes. Churches also began to take unprecedented steps to define themselves and the roles to be played by their members, and the consequence was a new emphasis on mutual consent, the idea that both the church and the member had to agree, formally and specifically, to a fairly well-defined relationship.

This meant that churches after the Revolution were insulating themselves from the world around them in new, or at least newly emphasized, ways. In part, this was achieved through language. For one thing, minority religious groups in the late eighteenth century (and not before) began to name themselves, choosing their own nomenclature to define themselves rather than letting others do it (as had, say, the Quakers). Further, churches' creeds and covenants evolved from general statements of commonly held beliefs to something more precise, a way of describing exactly why this group of believers differed from another. Such covenants, though "a relatively modest means of collective self-definition," became "an instrument of group identity" beginning around the mid-eighteenth century, according to historian Chris Beneke.[50] Many Baptist churches began in the late eighteenth century to add to their longstanding use of confessions, or formal creedal statements, a covenant that spelled out how members were to behave toward one another and drew a boundary between those who belonged and those who did not. Such perspectives were to be embraced by the individual converts, who then saw themselves as having joined something, voluntarily, that would provide structure for the remainder of their lives.[51]

Not only covenants but church manuals, lists of members, and a growing level of ecclesiological bureaucracy became far more common. One historian, studying Congregationalist churches, observed that "many churches had become bodies of strangers desperately needing some formal mechanism to identify one another," and similar patterns can be seen among New England Baptists. The Reverend Seth Sweetser of the First [Congregational] Church in Worcester, Massachusetts, captured the flux of nineteenth-century church membership when he observed that "only about one third of those whose names were given me on my coming here [fourteen years earlier] remain with us," and his church brethren formed "Standing Committees" to compile accurate membership rosters.[52]

The nineteenth-century historian Robert Baird also noted this trend, casting it as a rational response to the challenges of creating religious community in a society so constantly in motion, both geographically and in terms of its professions of faith. A well-defined membership was, for Baird, a point of "inexpressible importance" for those evangelical churches that had come to comprise a majority of churched Christians: "I do not suppose that there is a single evangelical church in the country that does not keep a record of its members; I mean of those whom it has received according to some regular form or other *as members*, and who, as such, are entitled to come to the Lord's Supper." In a mobile, even transient society lacking any religious establishment and containing a remarkable diversity of religious sects, churches turned to increasingly formal modes of determining—and then recording—who belonged and who did not. Even Elias Smith's

Christian Church, which eschewed formal covenants as being an unscriptural infringement on the religious liberty of the faithful, kept membership lists and formally expelled the wayward.[53]

Also, church leaders came up with increasingly formal procedures to facilitate the members of one church finding another church family when they moved, such as letters of dismission. We know that such letters became standardized in the years following the Revolution, usually with preambles including doctrinal statements that allowed a recipient church to judge the doctrinal background of the prospective member. In some cases, they were even printed certificates, with a blank for the name, such as one from an African American Baptist church on Fayette Street in New York City, which read: "This may Certify to all persons whom it may Concern that *William Baker* is a member of the Baptist Church at Peekskill in good standing we therefore Recommend him as such to any other Church of the same faith and order." Such documents had the appearance and the form of printed government documents, such as summonses from a court: they were typeset, with blanks for names and signatures. In the fluidity and rootlessness of the early American republic, churches made efforts to deal with the challenges that such geographic mobility posed. The result was a world in which members' ability to join a church in their new place of residence was facilitated by procedural formalities that helped to make the status of *member* something portable. Baptist churches in the South even required that members not move without requesting a letter of dismission. By the early nineteenth century, then, people joined churches that defined what they expected from and offered to their members with a new degree of specificity; members' names were recorded formally; and their modes of entry and exit were well defined, often in published manuals and guides.[54]

By the early nineteenth century it appears that the internal government of churches was conceived of as, essentially, a constitutional matter, and the everyday experience of drafting and abiding by constitutions in American churches led people to see them as genuine constraints on church authority, as charters of liberty. Presbyterian minister John M'Farland, for instance, certainly described matters in just that way: "So long as I am in the Presbyterian church," he wrote, "I shall hold to the Confession of Faith, because I have read it, and I hope in some measure understand its nature and use. I value it not only for the doctrine it contains, but because I consider it a charter securing me, as a member of the Presbyterian church, against all ecclesiastical tyranny." One of the first things that happened when a Presbyterian church received new members—and in this they paralleled Baptist and Congregationalist churches—was that a minister would "read them our confession of faith and church-covenant." That approach, when coupled with a church's "insistence on their own jurisdiction over disputes of all kinds between their members," according to Monica Najar, "allowed churches to offer a form of 'citizenship' to their members," including women and African Americans. Though decisions as to who belonged and who ought to have voting privileges did of course vary by denomination and, in the case of decentralized denominations such as the Baptists, even among individual churches, some churches declared "that ecclesiastical power resided in every member," and thus in the South "antebellum Baptist churches usually granted female members—and often granted slaves—voting privileges." And a view such as that expressed by Presbyterian John Rice, who in 1816 described the "Introduction" to the published Presbyterian constitution as "our *Declaration of Rights,*" was becoming more and more common in the early nineteenth century.[55]

Each of these efforts to better define who belonged, why they belonged, and what obligations each member had vis-à-vis the church body produced a world in which church members had laid out in front of them, with relative precision, the rights and duties of membership. Coupled with the increasingly frequent appeals to prospective members that instilled in them a new sense of choice and self-confidence, such descriptions of internal church affairs produced something that the leaders of many churches would not have purposefully intended: not simply a description, but an *emphasis* on the individual members' rights, duties, and expectations.

The experiences and contests of the early national years led many joiners and organizers to abandon affective bonds of association in favor of law-minded ones, which included emphases on self-made rules of behavior, in the form of constitutions and bylaws. This way of thinking about collective organization would manifest itself in groups of all kinds, made up of men and women, young and old, in the first decades of the nineteenth century, which will be explored in chapter 4. Unsteadily but cumulatively, patterns of conduct within these voluntary associations would help to produce an acceptance of public scrutiny and judicial superintendence of these private arrangements of civil society. And the ideal of the autonomous, unfettered citizen and the post-Revolutionary impulse toward political association would play an immensely important role.

TWO

Politics, Citizenship, and Association

"The moment a man is attached to a club, his mind is not free," said the Reverend David Osgood in a fiery 1794 speech denouncing some of the first politically active voluntary associations of the post-Revolutionary era. He was not alone in these sentiments. In the first two decades after the conclusion of the American War for Independence, there was a powerful commitment shared by many, across the political spectrum, to the principle that no male citizen's autonomy as a political actor should ever be constrained or limited. It made no difference whether he had of his own volition joined a private association that concerned itself with electoral politics. His mind and his vote were his own, and they must remain so.[1]

This was a generation perpetually watchful for potential threats to the successful establishment of republican governments. In the 1790s, especially, we can witness Americans debating and rethinking the nature and the potentially dangerous consequences of membership in a species of association that prompted anxiety in the post-Revolutionary era: the politically oriented fraternal society. There was a pervasive concern, one expressed repeatedly in the early years of the American republic, about the dangers of joining or participating in politically active groups as the Democratic-Republican societies and their successors, such as the Federalist Washington Benevolent Societies. Thus, it should be no surprise that early American political debate helped to define and delimit the appropriate boundaries of voluntary affiliation.

Part 1 of this book explores how, by experience and through contest, many in the early national United States would come to think seriously about what it was that could and should hold people together. Rather than bonds of affection, they saw association as a product of individual, voluntary decisions to bind oneself on known and definite terms. In contemplating the

Society of the Cincinnati and lodges of Freemasons, many Americans began to put a new emphasis on formalities and the individual volition to join over a roseate image of bosom friendship. In religious societies, the "voluntary principle," or the idea that all churches existed purely by the deliberate, informed commitments of their parishioners, furthered that same idea, and it was in churches that some of the first intimations were made that *all* member-to-group relationships ought to be well defined and governed by procedurally fair systems of internal order. Unsteadily, a new way of thinking about voluntary membership emerged: it would become increasingly formalized, increasingly law-minded.

This is no story of easy consensus, however. There was also a series of public debates and impassioned criticisms of certain kinds of private associations, such as those that appeared to claim too much authority over their constituent members, or those that appeared selfishly to endanger the pursuit of the common good. Unfamiliar episodes within familiar stories provide much of the evidence of how, between the time of the Revolution and the early nineteenth century, a young nation came to formulate new ways of thinking about what the member-to-group relationship ought to entail.

The political turmoil of the early republic was transformative in this regard. The powerful commitment to the autonomy of each and every male citizen had weighty repercussions for the future of American civil society, even as political self-organization grew more common and more consequential. And so, in a series of influential episodes, a post-Revolutionary uneasiness with unchecked private governing authority and with threats to personal political autonomy fused with a growing attachment to law-minded, legally bounded ways of acting collectively to produce something new and useful: a vibrant civil society that the first generation of American citizens believed could be a benefit, not a bane, to the republic.

The Specter of Political Compulsion

The American Revolution witnessed no shortage of voluntary associations convened for political ends. Committees of correspondence, the Associators, the Sons of Liberty—all were quintessentially voluntary societies, in that they were organized for a defined purpose and were created not by a superior power, but by the volitional commitment of the people making up its rank and file. For decades to come, the obvious parallel would be made: it was by means of voluntary association that the United States had come to be. According to Thomas Mitchell, in a speech to a pro-temperance audience in 1830s Kentucky, the signers of the Declaration of Independence were nothing less than "the most august voluntary association ever formed since the world began." In the immediate wake of the Revolution, however, that same parallel generally cut the other way. That is, with the Revolutionary associations a close, vivid memory, it was argued that the only legitimate use of such political associations was to resist tyranny and corruption. Lacking those things, in a properly organized republic, politically active or politically vocal organizations simply ought not to exist. "Nobody will deny the usefulness of popular Societies, in cases of revolutions," a 1794 writer noted in the *Gazette of the United States*: "By forming the people together into clubs, and giving to all those clubs, a central point of union, a bad government may be shaken down." Did such groups even have a reason for being in post-Revolutionary America? Was the voice of the people, once heard on election day, supposed to remain silent thereafter?[2]

The answer did not come easily, for it necessitated wholly new understandings of who or what "the people" were, precisely how their voices were to be heard, and—though the debates on this last point have been understudied—whether formally organized clubs and societies would infringe upon the rights and political independence of their own members, creating a danger not just to outsiders and political elites but to the citizens who had formed them in the first place. When disputes arose between members of politically involved fraternal clubs in the years immediately following the Revolution, ideas about consent and the rule of law that had been essential to the vocabulary of the Revolution and then to the subsequent political discussions about groups such as the Cincinnati gave shape to the argument.

One early dispute, in what was perhaps the only club in early national New York to conduct political discussions and debates between the Revolution and the formation of the Democratic-Republican societies in 1793, is revealing. In 1789, a nineteen-year-old John Peter Van Ness was dismissed for repeated, unexcused absences from the Uranian Society, a literary club of students and alumni of Columbia College and young law students and clerks in Manhattan. Though the records are silent, a historian of the Van Ness family has reasonably speculated that he had been expelled less for his absences than for "basically political motives." On being informed that he had been kicked out, the recent Columbia graduate, who had been the society's librarian, decided to hold onto the books. He would do so until he had a chance "to convince them of their error," a hearing "demanded as a right, not solicited as a favor," he told the readers of the *New York Daily Advertiser*, "but the motion was most pompously negatived." Some days later, around the time that five members of the Uranian Society were "seen lurking about the house," Van Ness's trunk containing the books was "forced open by persons unknown" and its contents seized, including a few books belonging to him. Van Ness began running advertisements implying the club's culpability, and members of the Uranian Society decided to make a formal announcement of his expulsion and their seizure of the society's property. Van Ness responded. If the Uranian Society would not give him a chance to speak in his own defense, he declared, he would present his case to the people of New York.[3]

And the Uranian Society would meet him there, also putting their case "before the tribunal of the public." Just weeks after the first session of the First Federal Congress came to a close in New York City, residents were treated to a debate about the rights and duties of individuals who had willingly attached themselves one to another and engaged themselves to abide by certain rules. Van Ness had been absent too many times, a writer for the society told the readers of the *Daily Advertiser*, and he was, according to a bylaw, dismissed. It was nothing personal: "A decision different from this could not have been passed, without directly contradicting the letter and spirit of the law, and shewing the most unjustifiable partiality." Several men had met the same fate, and "did they pelter the Society with their demands and with their threats? No; they acted like gentlemen, and had Mr. Van Ness followed their example, he would have given us no trouble, and have saved his own reputation."

Van Ness's public assault on the Uranian Society's conduct was threefold. They had, first, damaged his reputation without basis by publishing that he had been "expelled." No, he wrote. The bylaw merely notes that excessive absences mean that the member has "*withdrawn* his name from the Society." Can this be expulsion, he asked? "Because I chuse to *avoid* the society of any man or set of men, am I therefore expelled therefrom?" Second, and most ridiculously, Van Ness did what he could to paint his "adversaries" as a bunch of petty children, listing all seventeen of them by their diminutive names—Charly Haight, Jemmy Cochran, Dicky Hicks. The Uranian Society, for its part, would not comment on Van Ness's "puerile metamorphosis of names."

It was Van Ness's third critique that can help to reveal the unsteady emergence of a law-minded, even constitutional approach to voluntary membership, one well suited to a post-Revolutionary America. He had, of course, "engaged to subscribe and obey the laws" of the society. But, he asked, "was I obliged to submit blindly and implicitly to the society, when one of its *fundamental* laws, and consequently a condition of the contract between us was supposed violated, and I in vain sought an opportunity of redress?" Among other things, Van Ness here draws attention to the distinction between ordinary and fundamental laws, something many Americans encountered for the first time in their own private, associational experiences but which a politically involved young man like Van Ness in 1789 had certainly contemplated in regard to New York and federal politics. Most importantly, it is apparent that Van Ness was sure that, if he was to be bound by the rules of the association, so too must the association be bound to operate by those rules and procedures when it dealt with him. He felt confident that he knew how such clubs should operate (Van Ness also served as president of the College Society for Progress in Letters, for example), and drawing from his own experiences as well as more abstract principles of fair treatment he was sure that he had been misused.[4]

After this public airing of grievances, nothing more came of the dispute. The Uranian Society would survive into the mid-1790s, compiling an impressive roster of young men of diverse political persuasions, including a young DeWitt Clinton. They described themselves as "a Society of Gentlemen whose main object is the promotion of Literature." With an active membership that ranged from twenty to thirty young men, they met weekly, on Tuesday evenings, often at City Hall, and debated a topic that had been agreed upon the previous week. Prospective members were nominated one week and voted in the next. It was in most ways typical of early American fraternal and literary societies. In New York alone that same year, eight Masonic lodges met, as did four national societies (St. George's, St. Patrick's, St. Andrew's, and the German Society) as well as a smattering of other social and literary clubs. And in the decades to come, such associations would proliferate beyond belief. But Americans were still feeling their way toward a shared understanding of what the bonds between member and society ought to involve. Were members of such groups merely compatriots who had drawn up a *leges conviviales*, a set of rules by which to get along? Was there to be a check on any abuses of those rules? And were they to be held to higher, extra-associational standards? In other words, should the calls of a Van Ness that he had been the victim of unfair and unjust treatment be taken seriously?[5]

With the dismissal of John Peter Van Ness, a man who later in life would serve in Congress and as mayor of Washington, DC, the men of the Uranian Society were forced to describe, in greater precision than they might have liked, the interior workings of their club. Anxiety about reputation hangs all about the arguments on both sides of this little dispute, and when Van Ness responded to the society's attempts at "wounding my character" in the press, he took them to task for, quite simply, not treating him fairly. "It illy became a society," he wrote, "to dispense with those laws by which the general society of mankind is supported"—that is, the rules of fair play. They could have "suspended the ordinary business, and granted this request [for a hearing] to one who they say, had been 'so much esteemed.'" They should have treated a friend better. At other moments in what was surely for some an uncomfortably public dispute, Van Ness called the society to task for not abiding by its own rules and bylaws. The whole Uranian Society affair is marked by an uneasy coexistence of languages of affection and friendship alongside invocations of formalities, laws, and procedural fairness.

Throughout the 1780s, as fraternal societies such as the Cincinnati or John Van Ness's Uranian Society formed in the uncertain terrain of a nation just emerging from a successful struggle for independence, there was a tension between ideals of genuine friendship and the challenges of association, both in terms of internal organization and the group's role in the larger society. Some of those things that seemed necessary to preserving fraternity in a voluntary society, such as limiting membership to those who shared the bond of wartime service, could be seen as the very things that made a particular society appear threatening. And still other discussions about voluntary association in the republic reveal real concerns that clubs and societies needed to be properly organized and held to their terms of agreement, or else even the most well-meaning member might find himself a mark for the vigilance of private tyranny.

Beginning in the 1790s, when politically active groups and fraternal societies that had been formed with explicitly political aims began to appear across the nation, such anxieties resonated with and alongside one another. That decade witnessed two periods of intense debate about the role of voluntary, or "self-created," societies in the post-Revolutionary public sphere: the Democratic-Republican Societies that formed during Washington's second term; and the fears of the Illuminati that arose during the Adams administration. In both cases, popular perceptions of the groups in question hinged on what people knew—and thought they knew—about the nature of individual participation in them.

To be certain, there were a handful of politically attuned clubs and societies before the formation, in 1793 and 1794, of societies of men up and down the Atlantic seaboard who were opposed to the Federalist policies of George Washington and Alexander Hamilton. The Society for the Preservation of Liberty existed for a short time in Virginia in 1784, including such members as James Madison, Patrick Henry, James Monroe, and Edmund Randolph. A more active but more obscure Political Club met regularly for several years in late 1780s Danville, Kentucky. And the Society for Political Inquiries, founded by Benjamin Franklin in February 1787 in Philadelphia, included such luminaries as Benjamin Rush, Tench Coxe, and David Rittenhouse, but was more along the lines of a learned, philosophical society than a group that might, as a body, engage in politics. The latter two, we know for certain, had clear and certain rules of procedure, which were generally followed as a means to better and less contentious discussion. All sought to discuss the science and the practice of government and political economy. All included men of diverse political affiliations and hoped to encourage impartial inquiry into better government. And, in all three cases, the members appear to have simply lost interest.[6]

A confluence of factors produced a much different species of political club in the United States in the early to mid-1790s. According to their critics, they looked like the Jacobin clubs of Revolutionary France, though their more immediate influences were probably the American associations of the Revolutionary era (one of the first Democratic Societies almost named itself the Sons of Liberty) and British political societies, such as the London Corresponding Society, which received a fair amount of American media attention in 1792. The increasing radicalism of the French Revolution by 1793—Louis XVI had lost his head, and Europe was at war—deepened the schism between the generally Francophile opposition and Washington's administration, which appeared to side with Britain and which embraced Alexander Hamilton's controversial and British-style fiscal policies.[7]

Probably more than fifty societies were formed in the 1790s, almost all of them in 1793 and 1794, in the nation's largest cities and far outside them, such as in Kentucky and in the backcountry of South Carolina. Members saw themselves as serving the indispensable purpose of observing the government, mutually informing and improving one another, and disseminating true and helpful information to their fellow citizens. They insisted they did nothing illegal or inappropriate: they came together for good, republican purposes, "for deliberating, for thinking, for exercising the faculties of the mind," one writer noted. "What statute has deprived us of the right?" To a certain extent, they *had* initially modeled themselves after the Sons of Liberty, groups organized to resist the injustices of British colonial government in the Revolution, but their purposes were not to end tyranny but rather merely to prevent a turn in that direction, by sharing information and keeping an eye on governmental authorities.[8]

The Democratic-Republican societies set themselves up according to what were rapidly becoming "the standard procedures of associational life," according to Albrecht Koschnik in his description of the Democratic Society of Pennsylvania. They met in regularly scheduled, well-advertised meetings. Their officers were elected annually; prospective members were proposed and voted in, often swearing an oath and signing the club's constitution. Outside of the cities, meetings were held monthly in county courthouses, and in both urban and rural areas "the principles underlying their organization were the same." In at least one case, the Massachusetts Constitutional Society, members were required to hold in hand a copy of the society's "articles and regulations." Debate, resolutions, and the reading and discussion of correspondence from similar societies around the country constituted much of their regular agendas. Bylaws called for the open participation of all members, and members were required to do their part individually in defense of good government. Those in Portland, Maine, were asked to do more than most when the club resolved "that every member of this society arm themselves as speedily as possible with every implement of war." All of their materials teemed with references to the natural rights of man—to such an extent that some called for martial action in defense of those rights—and the Democratic-Republican societies apparently extended those rights to their own membership in a way that shaped their internal policies. They went out of their way to describe their members as fellow "citizens," each engaged in a common goal, and all were actively to participate. As Sean Wilentz has observed, the Democratic-Republican societies were "models of democratic decorum," and it appears that they acted in accord with genuinely held beliefs about what made for good, just collective action. And yet they faced intense criticism about their internal affairs—about how they would dupe the gullible, exclude or silence dissent, and, worst of all, might make automatons out of their members.[9]

Membership in the Democratic societies mattered. They were not free-for-alls, lacking admissions policies or rules of conduct. One New York club held so strongly to the policy that only members could participate that, when hundreds of people in Ulster County, New York, showed up to a July 4th gathering of the Republican Society there, the club insisted that only members be admitted; they were forced to hold two separate dinners so that the newly arrived Ulster men could be duly admitted. Plans for intervisitation among the clubs took shape early, as a means to "strengthen our intercourse" and facilitate concerted action across the states. Certificates were issued, such as one that survives from the Democratic or Republican Society of Baltimore, as "credentials" intended to allow a member of one club to be "receive[d] with fraternity" by other societies.[10]

And it was for good reason that the status of member was important to the Democratic societies. There was more than one instance in which opponents of these groups sought to treat them like town hall meetings and would try to show up in sufficient numbers to outvote the republican contingent. In Newark, New Jersey, friends of the Washington administration showed up and voted simply that the people should disband and make no attempt to organize the proposed Democratic society. Another similarly frustrating intervention was made by the "Friends of Good Order" in New York City. It became clear that for the political society to achieve its purposes—or, for that matter, to exist at all—it would have to be limited to the like-minded. Thus it was that they tended to admit as members only those who had the support of two or three current members, were voted in at a regular meeting, and who would both pay a small amount of dues and agree by signing the constitution to support certain, clearly stated republican principles.[11]

Still, for all the reality behind the idea that membership in the Democratic societies was a well-ordered thing, the conservative critics of the groups made them out to be much more regimented than they ever really were. They alleged, repeatedly, that these were tight-knit cabals operating behind veils of secrecy. A man writing under the name Faithful Watchman reported to the *New-York Evening Post* in early 1795 that he "went last night to citizen Hunter's hotel, where the Democratic Society meets, and shocking to relate! a number of men had met together, for what purpose I cannot positively say, but I fear something dangerous to the community was going forward, as the doors were shut, and I, not being a member, was prohibited entering the room." Eugene Link, in the most detailed study of the Democratic-Republican clubs, labeled the charge of pervasive secrecy as largely unfounded Federalist propaganda. Indeed, the usual practice was for open, public meetings, though with a distinction between spectator and member. The same issue of the *New-York Evening Post* that featured the worries of A Faithful Watchman, for instance, also included a public announcement by a Democratic society, the Patriotic Society of the County of Newcastle, State of Delaware, concerning their open-door policy, both in terms of membership and spectatorship: "Every citizen, without distinction, who will support the laws and constitutions of our country (for they are the basis of our institution, and the preservation of them on their true principles, the foundation of all our proceedings)," the Wilmington club announced, "is freely admitted a member. We hold our meetings in the face of day, with our doors thrown wide open, that all who chuse may hear our discussions; the only secret we possess, being that of making every thing public." The purposes of these societies made secrecy an unlikely choice, but the public allegations and responses produced a lingering aversion to the closed-door political association that would resonate into the early nineteenth century.[12]

From the perspective of their opponents, the Democratic societies were a danger to republican government, and the critiques echoed those made about the Society of the Cincinnati: the clubs were "self-created," that is, not created by the people through constitutional means and thus "unknown to the laws of the country." George Washington was only the most prominent person to so label the societies. Much of the recent historical work on the political turmoil surrounding the clubs has focused on one set of criticisms—that they had no legitimacy in their claims to speak for "the people" when there were other, constitutional entities that did so—to the near exclusion of the equally significant charge that the societies themselves turned their members into bad citizens. The first set of concerns was no doubt important. Though their aims were expressly democratic, observed Noah Webster in 1794, "every club therefore formed for political purposes, is an *aristocracy* established over their brethren," a minority voice in the republic that might impose its will on everyone else.[13]

On the other hand, the point that really struck home with one of Webster's more prominent readers, the Reverend David Osgood, who quoted Webster at length in an often-reprinted address he gave in Medford, Massachusetts, concerned the bonds of membership. He paid a great deal of attention to Webster's point that "the moment a man is attached to a club, his mind is not free." A man who had been "an *independent freeman*," Osgood summarized, "is converted into a mere walking machine." These voluntary societies posed a real threat to the republic by sapping the autonomy of their members. It appeared they might subvert the independence of thought required for the American experiment in free government to succeed. A Federalist assemblyman in New York, William Willcocks, told readers of the *Evening Post* that this was to be expected in any and all such organizations: "I do know that in all societies, even in legislatures, a few, (and sometimes a single man of art and intrigue) often have led unsuspecting, honest-meaning men, to become instruments of injustice, and designs they have detested, when it was too late." Willcocks believed that many had become members out of curiosity; others, "beguiled by the pleasing sound of liberty, and democracy, became members from the best of motives." In all cases, though, he believed they became either willing or unknowing actors in deeds they as citizens should abhor.[14]

When farmers in western Pennsylvania convened and even armed themselves in resistance to a federal excise tax on whiskey in 1794, members of the Democratic-Republican societies were widely blamed as instigators. Many in those groups chose to differentiate their societies from the patently subversive "Whiskey Rebels." They disavowed those rebellious farmers, emphasizing that what made their own groups different was that they operated within, and not against, the law. Even groups formed in opposition to the existing government should fall within the purview of the rule of law. The Democratic-Republican societies' efforts to reassure their critics that they had pure, civic motives meant that even associations that had positioned themselves as watchdogs of the government, then, had begun to insist that all groups must act within the law, pursuing lawful ends by lawful means. All groups were bounded by the same constraints in what they could and could not do in this republic of citizens. And the public discussions about the benefits and dangers of clubs also included serious consideration that even the *interior* spaces of these groups ought to fall within the purview of the people—that, there too, there was an expectation of individual autonomy and democratic, fair process.[15]

Take, for example, the second period of unrest over voluntary societies of the 1790s, the Illuminati scare, where there were tales of binding oaths and impenetrable veils of secrecy surrounding anarchistic and antireligious "Illuminated" Masonic lodges, which had allegedly spread from Bavaria across Europe, encouraged a Revolution in France, and moved into the Western Hemisphere. A much-read exposé by Englishman John Robison went on at length about initiations (where a drawn sword and threats of "unavoidable vengeance" for disobedience accompanied the ceremony for a new "Illuminatus Minor"), secrecy, and potent oaths of allegiance. Similarly, when William Cobbett, as Peter Porcupine, announced the *Detection of a Conspiracy Formed by the United Irishmen* the same year that Robison's book was first published in the United States, he revealed at length their "constitution," outlining for his readers their oaths, secrecy, and designs against the nation by detailing what commitments each member made to the cause.[16]

When Judge Alexander Addison pounded the drum against the Illuminati in 1801, he too called attention to how the members of the secret society "were absolutely under it's control; and it's dominion over their minds was above any other dominion of God or man." Every member must "obey *all* the commands of the society" or face "instant vengeance." Within and surrounding every diatribe against subversive, conspiratorial groups around the turn of the nineteenth century—a literature that has received its share of historians' attention, for the good reason that the pamphlets, sermons, and tell-all books were so often reprinted, so much discussed in the press, and so popular a subject of conversation throughout the nation—were discussions of the dangerous bonds of membership, discussions that could not help but shape popular perceptions of what membership *should* look like.[17]

Indeed, much has been made of the differences between the Democratic-Republican societies of the 1790s and the political societies formed after 1800. The latter, it is said, made no claims to speak for "the people" but rather "only represented and spoke for their members and allowed them to organize as partisans," as Koschnik has described the distinction. This was certainly true. But also important for public perceptions of the politically oriented fraternities of the nineteenth century were the intentional efforts of such societies to organize their private associational life in a manner that accorded with the ideals and the widely shared assumptions about personal autonomy found in the broader, post-Revolutionary political culture. The uneasiness of the 1790s had its effects on the law and practice of associations, as the people who joined and managed such associations were feeling their way, unsteadily and unevenly, toward new ways of conceptualizing the bonds of membership.[18]

Membership in Political Associations in the Early Nineteenth Century

On March 17, 1802, a Hibernian Provident Society was formed by Irish political exiles in New York, for the purpose of providing relief for suffering members by collecting fees each month from the current membership. Two political criteria were set forth in their initial printed constitution: all members must be Democratic Republicans, and they must be opposed to the "dominion of Great-Britain over Ireland." They put in place a higher-than-usual barrier for prospective members: each was to be approved by seven-eighths of the current membership in order to be admitted. The Hibernian Society would remain relatively secure from opposition until later in the decade, and the club was even chartered in April 1807 under Governor Morgan Lewis. That year, though, in the run-up to an extraordinarily contested election, the way the mutual-aid society appeared to govern itself became an issue: it was cast by outsiders as a potential threat to republican government in the State of New York. The society had been "wickedly converted into an electioneering engine," it was alleged, at a meeting at the Union Hotel in early April, where "a formal resolution was proposed and carried": that any member *"who should be convicted of voting for Mr. Andrew Morris* [candidate for state assembly], *should be expelled and forfeit all his claims on the Society."* A meeting of voters in the Fifth Ward quickly published a resolution in response, describing the affairs of the Hibernian Society as being driven by a very recent Irish immigrant, Thomas Addis Emmet, "before he has a right to vote in our elections." It was, they said, "a species of tyranny, hitherto unknown in America," and only a "stranger to the principles of our government" could have conceived of it.[19]

That was, of course, not entirely true. The experiences of the Democratic Societies in the 1790s had shown the importance, if also the public-relations risks, of limiting membership to those who shared a particular political vision. Tammany in New York, for instance, famously became a Republican stronghold by the first decade of the nineteenth century, largely because, in 1795, many of its Federalist members quit in protest of a resolution condemning George Washington's attack on the "self-created societies" of Democratic Republicans. Such groups, limited to people of a particular political point of view, spread across northern states and westward into Ohio in the years to come. The key aspect here was not that people of likeminded political hopes had come together, but the way in which they had done it. The Irishmen had "unite[d] themselves into a separate body" and had "presumed *collectively* to interfere with the ensuing election; that it has proscribed such of its members as shall dare to think and act for themselves." It was the impositions being made on the autonomy of the members that alarmed so many, especially, of course, those who saw in that unity a threat to their own chances at election.[20]

And the potential danger was terrifying. As Richard Harison, New York Federalist and the federal district attorney through the Washington and Adams administrations, observed concerning New York's Hibernians, "no mode more effectual or infamous could be devised, for directing, controlling, and overawing the constituted authorities, than by making their election depend upon the joint ballot of a numerous and influential society, enforcing the concurrence of all its members, under the penalty of expulsion, and the personal inconveniences attached to it." This would be "reprehensible" even among "native citizens" but was especially so among those who lacked "the warm glow of affection which nature has implanted towards our native soil." The "personal inconveniences" that Harison noted would attend expulsion were, in part, financial: according to their published constitution, each man had paid admission fees and an additional 12 ½ cents each month to support those among them who needed a hand, fully in the hopes that, if misfortune befell him, the society would come to his aid as well. When a resolution put the continued availability of the funds to any member at risk if he was found to have voted the wrong way—in this, an age before the ubiquity of the secret ballot—it should not surprise anyone that some commentators, especially Federalists such as Harison, were outraged.[21]

The fact that these were foreigners, cordoning themselves off from those around them and joining together to act politically with unity and purpose, was, of course, an important element in how outsiders viewed the Hibernian Provident Society and their aims in 1807. Nothing shows that point more clearly than the fact that the local Federalists, who had only recently begun calling themselves Federal Republicans, changed their name once again to run their candidates on the "American ticket." The recent influx of Irishmen into the state, deeply opposed to the Anglophile Federalists, exacerbated New York's already tumultuous political environment.

A meeting of Federalists in Albany that April, shortly after news of the Hibernian Society's resolution broke, declared that the idea of national societies forming in the cities of the republic was not the problem. If Welshmen, Irishmen, or any other national group opted to form and incorporate a society for their mutual aid, those aims "are salutary for purposes of relief and charity." Such groups had a long history in North America, even before the Revolution. But the risk was large that "such societies, when perverted from the purposes of their institution to the purposes of intrigue," when they became "political clubs and party cabals," would pose a more serious threat to the republic than any other group, for the simple reason that foreigners lacked the instincts and habits of resistance to tyrannical authority that groups of the native-born were supposed to have. The recently arrived were "little accustomed to our peculiar principles, habits and public discipline, and imperfectly acquainted with our constitution and laws." Organizers of voluntary groups for the foreign-born, then, could manipulate their membership, and their club could in turn be manipulated by a powerful faction in the state of New York, all because the men who composed it lacked the "principles," the "habits," and the knowledge of how such groups should and should not act vis-à-vis their members.[22]

Debates such as this one, splashed across the papers as an election approached, played a role in the subsequent development of American civil society. That is, by articulating exactly how one group could form a "phalanx" to capture one election, the critics of the Hibernian Provident Society and of similar groups helped to inscribe in the minds of many an expectation that fraternal societies could, if organized improperly, exercise illegitimate and abusive power over their members in a way that was unhealthy for the republic. That the association was made up of Irishmen, each of whom appeared to native-born Americans to lack the fortitude to preserve his personal autonomy in the face of associational pressures, made some kind of formal, external solution appear to be necessary, something to ensure that individual participants could enter into the post-Revolutionary public sphere as autonomous citizens and as good republicans. In the end, it is just not clear whether the critics of the Hibernians failed in their effort to limit the power of the group over its members by calling public attention to it: there is no record that the group lifted its rule, though there is also no evidence that any member was punished for its breach. The American Party ticket failed miserably at the polls, though there was little likelihood that members of the Hibernian society would have voted for Andrew Morris with or without the resolution. But the important point is that these sorts of popular debates about the tensions between membership and citizenship affected popular perceptions, associational practices, and the legal constructions of membership over the coming years.[23]

When Stephen Dempsey was expelled from the Hibernians just a couple of years later, for example, his story garnered attention in the New York press. Dempsey was a medical doctor and member of the Hibernian Provident Society when, in the wake of the spring election in New York in 1809, he publicly objected when it appeared that some resolutions approved by the society had been unilaterally altered by the club's leadership *after* their adoption by the club. According to an account of Dempsey's story in the *American Citizen,* he "publicly withdrew his membership, and assigned his reasons for so doing" when a "self-created committee" took charge and amended and greatly sharpened a series of resolutions drafted to rebut an address recently published by some political opponents, who also happened to be Irish. For Dempsey, this was evidence that the Hibernians now were no longer "dealing out charity" but rather "dealt out nothing but proscription and blood." Those men "who boast that they can govern the Hibernian Provident Society as they please, and who have an eye to their own personal aggrandizement," were not fazed by Dempsey's withdrawal: "No member as he was, the leaders proceeded in form *to expel him,* and he was accordingly expelled with more than usual solemnity!" Dempsey had other members certify his version of the story, and the account in the *American Citizen* made a powerful case that the "expelling Junto" had taken the Hibernian Provident Society far astray from its original purposes and that its self-appointed leaders sought "universal thraldom, not emancipation." They had made public Dempsey's expulsion and denominated him a liar. The editor of the *American Citizen* concluded, "Editors who publish the expulsion, as it is ludicrously termed, are respectfully requested to publish the above." He had withdrawn himself, and he wanted that fact known.[24]

Those public and partisan criticisms in the first decade of the nineteenth century of efforts by Irishmen's societies to control their rank-and-file membership helped to make public a series of apparent abuses of private governing power. And, as we will see in chapter 3, they provided an impetus to bring into the United States certain common law principles regarding corporate membership and associational authority. There is a tendency, however, to read these discussions, these debates about what membership ought to look like, as distinctly partisan in nature. In many works on contemporary visions of American associations, differing views about the value of such groups have been divvied up, a bit too neatly, along partisan lines. And, certainly, the oppositional nature of public discourse in the period meant that much of the discussion of associational authority and the ostensibly antagonistic relationship between club membership and public citizenship came from those writing in support of a rival political faction.

But this was more than a conservative reaction to the organization of the recently immigrated and the potentially radical. Similar critiques were made by Republicans about the formation of Washington Benevolent Societies by the Federalist faithful just before and during the War of 1812, and it is apparent that the charges tapped into what was becoming a set of widely held beliefs about legitimate association. There was an important difference in the sorts of allegations levied by Republicans against Federalist political fraternities, but it was a distinction that had more to do with chronology than with political philosophy. By the time that Federalists had begun creating organizations of the sort that Republicans had been forming since the 1790s, their opponents could tap into an emerging consensus—one that stretched across party lines—on how such political fraternities ought to be organized.

Going as far back as the Federalist/Antifederalist division in the late 1780s George Washington had stood firmly opposed to self-formed voluntary associations because they created opportunities for abuses of private power. When his nephew Bushrod Washington proposed to form a Federalist Patriotic Society, Washington noted that there were inherent risks in that kind of political club, even one in whose purposes he personally believed: "May not a few members of this society direct the measures of it to private views of their own?" These sorts of appraisals of the risks associated with voluntary affiliation into organized political societies, then, had less to do with the principles being espoused than with the forms the societies took, the powerlessness of their members, and the lack of accountability for oligarchic control. William Willcocks had voiced similar concerns in the furor over the Democratic societies.[25]

After the turn of the nineteenth century, Federalists wasted little time in beginning to organize fraternal societies that mimicked the clubs of their opponents. No less a figure than Alexander Hamilton proposed to his friend James Bayard a "Christian Constitutional Society" in 1802, a society that he described at length in a letter. It had two objects, Hamilton wrote: to support the Christian religion and to support the federal Constitution. Its "means" were the "diffusion of information" by pamphlets and newspapers and the creation of groups that reached out to the meaner sort, just as did any number of societies formed in American cities that, thus far, had been almost wholly Jeffersonian in persuasion.[26]

The plan was recognizably Republican in method. Hamilton wrote to Bayard that one goal should be "the promoting of institutions of a charitable & useful nature in the management of Foederalists." He went on: "The populous cities ought particularly to be attended to. Perhaps it will be well to institute in such places 1st Societies for the relief of Emigrants—2nd. Academies each with one professor for instructing the different Classes of Mechanics in the principles of Mechanics & Elements of Chemistry." Such clubs would have "an act of association" that "need only designate the 'name' 'objects' & contain an engagement to promote the objects by all lawful means, and particularly by the diffusion of Information. This act to be signed by every member." Hamilton appeared to be well versed in how these kinds of clubs looked from the perspective of their members and prospective members. His proposal began with the "objects" of the institution, moved on to describe its officers and federal structure, and closed with a description of the duties and benefits of membership. What he proposed was, in all ways, a perfectly ordinary political fraternity.[27]

Bayard was unimpressed, and Hamilton did not have time to turn his plan into a reality before he fell to a shot from Aaron Burr in 1804. In the meantime, Republicans continued to organize political societies. "*Combinations*" that "exactly resemble the French *jacobin* clubs," according to one Federalist writer in New Jersey in 1803, were "the settled Democratic plan" for electoral success. Federalists, excepting Hamilton's unfulfilled proposal, were late to that game.[28]

When Federalist party organizers, several years after Hamilton's first description of a similar kind of organization, did begin to follow in their opponents' footsteps, they made use of what had become the prevailing model of political organization. That is, the societies would be open to all who shared some basic beliefs, at a cost that would not be prohibitive; they would be organized locally and be designed to serve both political and nonpolitical purposes; and they would promote themselves by publishing copies of their constitutions and bylaws. A few Federalist societies were organized with names such as the Society of American Republicans, formed in Philadelphia in 1808, but most of them adopted the politically invaluable name of George Washington. In states throughout the Northeast, more than two hundred Washington Benevolent Societies were formed. The younger generation of Federalists was crucial to this turn: when the "Federal Young Men of the city and county of Philadelphia" organized the Washington Association, they announced their hopes "to assist their senior fellow citizens in promoting the interest of the Federal cause."[29]

In 1808, three New York men, including a twenty-two-year-old Guilian Verplanck, formed the first Washington Benevolent Society (aside from a nonpolitical club started in Alexandria a month after Washington's death). Probably mirroring the Tammany Society in New York, the New York Washington Benevolent Society held its meetings in secret, though unlike Tammany it did not pretend to be, first and foremost, a ritual-centered fraternity. Like other Republican societies, it opened itself to all comers who were able to pay relatively inexpensive dues (an initiation fee of one dollar, and half that each year thereafter) and who adhered to the right political beliefs. In some of the Washington Benevolent Societies, there was even a clause that poor men could join and have their dues waived: nearly one third of the members of the Boston society, for which records have survived, were exempted. The monies were intended for benevolent purposes among members who fell on hard times. As the New York society put it in their constitution, paraphrasing Edmund Burke, they were quite consciously following the lead of their opponents, for "when bad men combine, it is absolutely necessary that good men should unite." They held their first meeting on Washington's Birthday in 1809, hearing an address from Samuel Hopkins before having a dinner that spilled into five separate taverns. By the Independence Day celebration that year, some two thousand men marched in procession as Washington Benevolents. And each society was intended to oppose local Republican political organization. The new mode of Federalist association "followed Tammany to Rhode Island," in Dixon Ryan Fox's reading of the situation, and Washington Benevolent Societies were formed in large numbers in each northeastern state that had a reasonably strong Republican presence. In states such as Connecticut, which had only a very few Republicans at all, the Washington Benevolent Societies were much less common.[30]

With the Embargo, the drive to create an effective, organized opposition to the party of Jefferson had taken on a new energy. Between 1808 and 1812, the formation of 208 societies can be established. More certainly existed. Each took what was becoming a ubiquitous form for a political fraternity. When Rhode Islanders "associated to inform, advise and otherwise assist American Citizens" by forming a Washington Benevolent Society in 1810, they drafted a constitution and bylaws that, like all the Republican societies, spelled out in precise terms who could apply for membership, how they were to be admitted, what they needed to do maintain that status, and what benefits would obtain. The standards were open, generally asking only that members be citizens "of good moral characters and true friends of the constitution of the United States," as the Rhode Island organizers put it. The fees were kept low or, for the needy, dispensed with altogether.[31]

There were, however, two kinds of constraints on membership that did matter: as with virtually all fraternal societies, prospective members would be voted on by the current members. Four blacks balls would be enough to prevent admission in the Rhode Island society; for another Washington Benevolent Society in the state of New York, the number of black balls was set at five. In all kinds of social clubs, such practices had the inevitable—and, in this case, very much intended—result of producing a membership roster of people with generally shared political views.[32] Second, even once admitted, men (this was a male-only institution, though no rule stated that explicitly) had to take an oath to support the institution and could be expelled for immoral conduct or for failure to pay dues. Such constraints were thought to be the only way "to establish a plain, obvious, and comprehensive bond of union between the members, and to ensure a proper degree of sympathy, and a certain community of sentiment, upon great and acknowledged principles of morals and policy," wrote the organizers of the nation's largest Washington Benevolent Society, the one in Philadelphia, which had three thousand members in 1816. The members all had to agree on their basic purposes for coming together and had to swear to obey the rules and to support their shared beliefs: "as members of the Washington Benevolent Society we will, in all things comply with its regulations, support its principles, and enforce its views." The little books published for members—usually containing a membership certificate, the constitution of the society, the US Constitution, Washington's Farewell Address, and, often, an engraving and short biography of him—contained all the political beliefs that the members ought to share. They wanted to emphasize, to their own members and to the world around them, that the members had beliefs that were "not indulged in obedience to fashion, nor formed by sympathy or communication" with one another. Rather, "the reluctant, unbiased, and solitary deductions of each individual," formed separately, had allowed each citizen-member to discover and to recognize each other "as political brethren."[33]

One orator noted in an address on *The Bond of Friendship* to his fellow members in 1812, "We do associate for the express purpose of manifesting benevolence, of cultivating friendship." For all their emphasis on shared beliefs, however, it was apparent in their articles of agreement that it was the rules, not friendship or camaraderie, that held the men together once admitted. Take, for instance, the society in Philadelphia, which had elaborate provisions regarding expulsion that allowed members' expulsions "for refusing to comply with the provisions of the constitution and by-laws; for abandoning the principles which entitled him to become a member of the association; for disorderly or improper conduct in the presence of the Society." But the procedure to be followed was detailed and, in every way, protective against arbitrary dismissal. The clause in the constitution went on: "But no member shall be expelled, unless at a regular meeting of the Society; nor unless two-thirds of the members present shall vote for his expulsion; nor unless notice shall have been given at a preceding meeting, that a motion for the expulsion of a member would then be made; nor unless a written notice of the facts charged, shall have been furnished to the member, in like manner as is directed in the trial of an accused officer, in the tenth article of the constitution." David Hackett Fischer has argued that, in practice, the Washington Benevolent Societies were "little oligarchies tightly controlled by the young Federalists who had founded them," but they were oligarchies that operated by committees according to constitutional rules. From the perspective of the members of the societies themselves, the clubs were well regulated and bound constitutionally to act in ways that would not subject a member to arbitrary authority. The Democratic-Republican clubs of the 1790s had few such explicit rules regarding the power of expulsion. Much had been learned about how such societies *ought* to be formed.[34]

From the perspective of Jeffersonian outsiders to the Washington Benevolent Societies, however, these were at worst dark and frightening bodies and, at best, obnoxious ones. Yet their mode of organization was, to all appearances, perfectly legitimate: they followed what had already become a common mode of Republican organization, and, in some cases, the societies sought and received incorporation. And so the critics of the Washington Benevolent Societies did not focus upon ways in which, institutionally, the societies fell short of good, republican modes of operation. Rather, Jeffersonian critiques of the societies generally focused upon their being comprised of bad men. They alleged that the clubs had malicious, even treasonable, designs, which were sheltered behind a veil of secrecy. That is, though some of the allegations concerning the Washington Benevolent Societies mirrored those made against Republican organizations in the first decade of the nineteenth century, for the most part the language focused on the ways in which the Federalist societies did not even meet their own stated standards. The Washington Benevolent Societies were created to cherish constitutional government, and yet they threatened it. They claimed to admit all men who believed in the principles of Washington and in the Constitution of the United States, and yet they admitted only opponents of the current Republican regime.

Many of the charges of evil intentions came out of Vermont, and they were reprinted widely. Vermont was a battleground, where Federalist societies believed they had a chance successfully to combat the state's Republican Party. In the run-up to an 1812 election, one Republican paper advised its readers to protect lists of Republican candidates from being destroyed by the Washington Benevolents, "for it is fully ascertained, from their organized system of operation, that threats, flattery, corruption, and deceptions of every kind will be practised on the honest and unsuspecting of our citizens." For many of their critics, the Federalist societies had not only appeared to play dirty in legitimate politics but also had genuinely subversive intentions: The *Green Mountain Farmer* in Bennington, Vermont, urged the conquest of Canada during the War of 1812 in part because of "their incitements of secret treasonable societies among us." They comprised "Tories, monarchists, and aristocrats . . . without regard to character or reputation," noted another Vermont paper, though a New Hampshire writer saw their hopes as resting on the seduction of "the young and credulous." And there was widespread belief that the societies were tearing apart local communities: "Churches are separating, dissolving, and dismissing their pastors in various places amidst the ravages of disunion in consequence of the Washington Benevolent Societies." Meetings were called for "investigating and enquiring into the origins, progress, and designs of certain secret self-created societies in various sections of our country," and in some places committees were established for keeping a watchful eye on the Washington Benevolent Societies.[35]

Two key points that are easily missed in all of the charges made against the Washington Benevolent Society are these: the Federalists adopted a mode of organization that most Americans, regardless of party affiliation, could accept as legitimate in how it admitted and treated its members; and, second, the clubs were faulted for not adhering to their own stated purposes more than they were criticized for anything else. As Sylvester Pond put it in a much-reprinted exposé about the Federalist club in his hometown in Vermont, "The principles of the Washington Benevolent Society are NOT to disseminate the principles of Washington and Benevolence; but to proselyte and build up a *party*, so as to be able to change the present Administration of government." They claimed to be open to political debate, but "every principle that does not favour their peculiar notions about politics is kept out of sight." They claimed to be open to supporters of the Constitution, but "then why reject all republicans and receive every federalist, let his character be what it may?" As conceptions of legitimate membership in these sorts of societies became more generally accepted, there was a tendency to fault the Washington Benevolent Societies most often for not even adhering to these, their own professed standards regarding individual membership.[36]

What is especially revealing is that it appears from the very few extant, private records of individual Washington Benevolent Societies that allegations of internal tyranny and political control were unfounded. Members of the club in Northwood, New Hampshire, went out of their way explicitly to deny any authority over their members in terms of how they voted. One week in early 1813, "at a former meeting of this Society which owing to the severity of the weather was not generally attended—a Committee was appointed to nominate candidates for the State County District and Town offices to be filled in March." But when they reconvened, and "upon more mature deliberation," they decided that "it does not appear consistent with the principles of this Society to descend to the business of electioneering or to concern as a body therein." They resolved, in fact, "that as this Society has no power, so it has no wish to dictate to any member the manner in which he shall exercise his privileges as a citizen—but would leave him as it finds him, responsible only to his own conscience his country and his God." These were not assertions made publicly to appease outsiders; these were proceedings recorded in a private book of minutes, displaying a genuinely held belief about the limits of associational authority and the need to make efforts to preserve individual members' autonomy.[37]

If the Washington Benevolent Societies and the responses to them reveal anything, it is that by the 1810s Federalists and Republicans agreed far more than they disagreed about the legitimate bonds of membership, including commitments to procedural protections against arbitrary power as well as to the existence of legally guaranteed rights, as citizens, that set limits to the authority of the association. There was, in short, an emerging consensus about the dangers of associational constraints on the ideally independent voter. Societies formed by partisans on both sides appear to have shared practices and goals. And, more important still, similar critiques were made toward those groups formed by one's rivals. Although the Washington Benevolent Societies appeared to wish to turn back the clock, they were a part of something new, something recognizable as a post-1800 phenomenon in the way they described and delineated what was expected of their members. Even though they held "the times of Washington for our hope," as did the Rhode Island Washington Benevolents, and though Daniel Webster proclaimed how much "the mind delights to associate with the spirits that have gone before it," the Washington Benevolent Societies—no less than their critics—were looking forward. They exemplified a new attitude toward voluntary affiliation, one reflective of the post-Revolutionary moment. In the histories of these societies and their critics can be found all the worry and uneasiness that the first republican generations had toward unchecked private power and toward potential threats to personal autonomy.[38]

Political ambition and the perceived need to counter the worst tactics of the opposition meant that there were no easy answers in working out a conception of voluntary membership in political societies that satisfied everyone. And yet, by and large, one was found. Ideas about political autonomy, fused with beliefs about friendship and formal association, helped many come to the conclusion that the best sort of relationship between member and group was an attenuated one—one defined, delimited, and bound by law.

THREE

A Common Law of Membership

If Thomas Paine's America in 1776 was already a land where "THE LAW IS KING," as he shouted in capital letters in *Common Sense,* then historians and legal scholars have begun to show that "THE LAW" became somehow more important, more powerful, more culturally pervasive by the dawn of the nineteenth century. Comprehending law and its broader, existential purposes in the post-Revolutionary era as providing nothing less than "the rule of human conduct in the state of society," as Zephaniah Swift described matters not long after the American Revolution, is essential. What is more, a better understanding of how Americans described and envisaged the law says a great deal about early American culture writ large. Law—not merely or even primarily as institutionally embodied, but rather as a way of *thinking* about all kinds of interpersonal relationships, on the small and the large scale—became what Christopher Tomlins has called "*the* paradigmatic discourse explaining life in America."[1]

The first generations of American citizens increasingly thought in legalistic—or, to use John Philip Reid's softer term and quite useful term, "law-minded"—ways about nearly all of their efforts to function in groups, be it in the state, the church, or other small, self-created associations. And that tendency was apparent among American men and women, across racial lines, particularly in urban areas but also in smaller communities in New England, the Mid-Atlantic, and the South, to act within their *own* voluntary associations in ways that emphasized procedural fairness, legalistic formalities, and compliance with their own originating documents, which they usually called constitutions. Such attitudes would only become amplified with the rising worries about political autonomy that emerged in the 1790s. As a consequence, growing numbers of Americans would come to settle upon increasingly precise, detailed, and rule-based modes of organization in their own groups—in part as a means to a better and more effective cooperation among themselves, and in part in response to criticisms by outsiders, ones expressed in the political controversies that accompanied the emergence of the first party system in the last decade of the eighteenth century.

Law must be understood, then, as a language, as a way of describing and determining social relationships. But it was also as a means, practical and effective, of conflict resolution. Legal historians have begun to make clear something profoundly simple and profoundly important: in the early republic, law gave shape to collective life, on the small and the large scale. When that literature is brought into conversation with recent studies in the history of early American civil society, it points the way to a fuller understanding of what happened in the early United States and why so many Americans came to believe that law-minded and law-bound ways of acting collectively were the single-best way to resolve the tensions inherent between individual autonomy and collective action. The cultural and political pressures on the member-to-group relationships in the growing numbers of post-Revolutionary voluntary associations helped to propel a law-minded way of thinking about affiliation and membership in private groups, but it also helped to nourish the belief among the joiners and organizers of those groups that members had a right to expect legal protections and judicial interventions when things went wrong. Moments of contest led to litigation. The discontented would compel adjudication. And one of the effects was to underscore the idea that the internal workings of private associations must ultimately be open to public scrutiny, must fall within a larger framework of legal superintendence. Imperatives toward a legalistic way of thinking about voluntary membership came simultaneously from within and from without.[2]

Interestingly, legal control of voluntary associations was, from the very first, promulgated as a way of defending the proliferation of private societies, not discouraging it. One defender of the Society of the Cincinnati in 1784, for instance, wrote that there was no reason to worry about the club because the government could so quickly destroy it: "*The arm of civil authority surrounds it*—only to *will* its destruction would be instant annihilation." Such reassurances went a long way toward alleviating the public's wariness about the Cincinnati, evidence of an early belief in the idea of public superintendence of voluntary groups. And those beliefs were well suited to—and, as it happened, were inseparable from—the post-Revolutionary notion that no partial interests ought to be allowed to fragment the unity of the republic.[3]

The legal encompassment of the associational life of American civil society would soon become more intimate, detailed, and well established. Private, voluntary associations—particularly but not exclusively those that held charters of legal incorporation—might not face "instant annihilation" at the whim of governmental authorities, at least not in the wake of the 1819 decision of *Dartmouth College v. Woodward,* which protected corporate charters from arbitrary changes at the hands of the legislature. But individual members of such groups, should they have a grievance about their treatment at the hands of the association, could and often did seek out some kind of legal remedy. In the crucible of conflict between members of an association—often, it is clear, in moments of genuine frustration—a particular way of thinking about voluntary membership emerged, one that had truly national reach. Many disputes were resolved internally and quietly; but other times, they became issues of public discussion, with people near and far reading and discussing some alleged scandal of unfair or illegal treatment within a private group; and, more than most people realize, sometimes they found their way into courtrooms.

For any discontented member of any group, there have always been three ways to respond, as Albert Hirschman noted decades ago in his pathbreaking work *Exit, Voice, and Loyalty*. Setting aside the simplest of a person's three options (doing nothing), an unhappy individual had two choices: he or she could leave the group, either by quitting or simply opting out of active involvement until expelled (what Hirschman labeled "exit"); or raise a protest, either internally or by calling on outside authority ("voice"). The option of exit, with its parallels to political independence, religious schism, and westward movement, was "accorded an extraordinarily privileged position in the American tradition." But in the civil associational life of the early republic, to use Hirschman's terms, "voice" helped to produce increasingly sophisticated and law-bound ways of thinking about how to join together.[4]

In their everyday experiences and, especially, in moments of contest, joiners and organizers of American private associations gave meaning and practical shape to the concept of voluntary membership in ways that reflect the anxieties and priorities of the post-Revolutionary moment. Their generation sought ways to cohere—in churches, in clubs and corporations, as republican communities, as states, as a nation—without compromising liberty and without giving power any foothold from which it might grow unchecked. Despite the more-or-less unquestioned belief in the idea that the greatest threats to personal liberty could be found in the exercise of public power, the citizens of the early American republic quickly came to see that, in some instances, private authority might also array itself against the liberties and against the happiness of the very people that had created it.

Legal structures, practices, and remedies that had their origins long before the American Revolution provided some of the ammunition with which many of the conflicts between member and group would be fought. Historical artifacts such as the charter of incorporation and the writ of mandamus would be transformed by revolution and constitutional change in the decades to follow, but they would be of great usefulness for aggrieved members and troubled associations. All of the themes being explored here—a growing law-mindedness among American joiners and organizers; a wariness of associational threats to personal political autonomy; and the importance of legal forms and institutions in determining the internal workings of post-Revolutionary private associations—culminated in a remarkable showdown between two Irish newspaper editors in Philadelphia. What followed was absolutely essential to the emergence of something Americans have long taken for granted: their ability, their desire, and their willingness to join together.

The Law of Membership: Charters and Writs

Like so many other writers of his day, Francis Lieber—an intensely intelligent European visitor to the antebellum United States, who unlike Alexis de Tocqueville opted to move there permanently—was especially struck by the associational diversity he witnessed in the New World. Like Tocqueville, he was impressed by the federal political structures of the American nation, the governments nestled within governments, and he saw the associational impulse and the layers of government as being two aspects of the same phenomenon. In 1830, he would describe the United States as "a concatenation of various corporations, political, civil, religious, social and economical," with the nation serving as a "great corporation, comprehending all others."[5]

Lieber was not speaking metaphorically. Leaving aside governments and municipal corporations, the numbers of chartered corporations—and of their members—soared in the early national period. Huge numbers of Americans were joining, contributing to the capital of countless new business associations by subscribing for stock. New York, which issued five corporate charters in 1800, incorporated seventy-three companies in 1832, and slightly more than a thousand in the interim. By 1830, New England states had incorporated almost 1,900 businesses, and in 1832 the world's first treatise on the law of private corporations was published in America. The authors of that treatise, Joseph K. Angell and Samuel Ames, wrote, "If a native of Europe should be informed, even with tolerable accuracy, of the number of Banking Companies, Insurance Companies, Canal Companies, Turnpike Companies, Manufacturing Companies, &c,—and of the literary, religious, and charitable associations . . . fully invested with corporate privileges, he could not be made to believe that he was told the truth." And recent scholarship has confirmed that not only were these incorporated associations quite common, but participation in them was extraordinarily widespread, even among Americans of modest means.[6]

The eventual embrace in post-Revolutionary America of the chartered corporation as a form of collective action that was both effective and well suited to a republican government is an important part of the story being told here. We know that the protection of corporate charters from unilateral revision at the hands of governments, by classifying those documents as contracts protected constitutionally from arbitrary amendment, was a means of securing the pluralism of civil society from government. But the charter was not merely an instrument of private corporate autonomy. It was, at the same moment, an instrument of public authority and a means of public supervision. It facilitated the penetration of civil society by public norms and allowed legislators and jurists to set and enforce limits to the legitimate exercise of corporate authority over members. In the post-Revolutionary age, many Americans expressed comfort with the idea that political and legal institutions could and should superintend affairs within the bounds of voluntary associations, secular and religious. The existence of charters—and a particular understanding of what exactly a charter *was*—provided one important opening for that level of legal superintendence.[7]

There was virtually no form of joining together that did not become increasingly "chartered" in the decades immediately following the American Revolution. "Literary and moral societies, like other religious, benevolent, and fraternal societies," William Novak has noted, "were viewed by legislators and jurists as another component of the public civil society being actively constructed in early nineteenth-century America," and he has compiled a list from the state of Georgia that helps to prove the point: between 1790 and 1860, the state formally incorporated 528 academies, 314 churches, 85 fraternal lodges, 64 manufacturing companies, 40 charitable societies, 14 scientific societies, 12 mutual benefit groups, 10 libraries, and 6 temperance societies. Novak drew from sheer numbers an argument about "the direct role of the state in the creation and policing of early American associationalism," though he also noted that "the judicial opinions in which so much of the American law of association is determined remain to be examined, to say nothing of the bottom-up records of local legal contests."

Within those materials can be found countless stories that reveal a great deal about early American understandings of law, personal rights, and the emergence of a functioning civil society.[8]

There were several different ways that charters influenced how Americans experienced and conceived of membership in incorporated groups. One was conceptual. To understand where a corporation got its power and its existence, Americans in the post-Revolutionary years soon came to center on the "concession" theory, in which any and all powers of a corporation were derived from its charter as specific concessions from the state. There was some experiment with general incorporation acts in the early republic: New York's trailblazing statutes permitted churches to incorporate without special charter (1784), followed by libraries (1796), turnpike companies (1807), and manufacturing corporations (1811), and some other states, though not moving quite so quickly, passed similar laws. But the special charter, incorporating one corporation at a time by means of a detailed statute, was the rule. State governments and communities wanted to keep their creations within defined bounds. People who wanted to join the corporation, too, were often wary of the unknown in deciding whether to become involved, and they therefore had an interest in delimiting the means and the ends that a corporation might pursue. The concession theory not only met those purposes but provided a more or less tangible explanation for how to create *unum* from *pluribus*.[9]

Through the charter, the means of corporate conduct remained closely connected, conceptually and practically, to state power, which would have the effect of encouraging legal authorities to take an active hand in matters wholly internal to the corporation. The ends, or goals, of corporate existence, on the other hand, moved somewhat more quickly away from that close identification with the state. By 1832, the idea that American states should create only those institutions that were needed to serve the interest of the commonwealth had given way to a looser but still public-regarding standard. As Angell and Ames would describe it, American states incorporated "all associations, whose object tends to the public advantage" but that might also "be established for the advantage of those who are members of it." The public interest was not left out of the equation; in the first four decades of the nineteenth century, of the many corporate charters issued by the states of New York, Maine, Ohio, Pennsylvania, Maryland, and New Jersey, more than half were for public utilities such as turnpikes, canals, and bridges. But those who reflected on the subject could see a drift away from the conceptions of incorporated bodies as instruments of government or as state-endorsed monopolies. As Oscar and Mary Handlin described the trend in Massachusetts, "Democratic unwillingness to confine the corporation to a favored few had dispersed it among many holders and that in turn had separated it from the state." In the past few years, the work of Johann Neem has further fleshed out this transition from corporations as public trusts to private, charter-protected institutions by emphasizing the role of partisan conflict and the contested space of the public sphere in the eventual walling off of what would become known as "private corporations, aggregate," from arbitrary government alteration.[10]

Without doubt, however, that transition was gradual. In a practical sense, the portrait of the corporations' insulation from government supervision and discretion after 1819 ignores the conditional charters, their strict construction, and persistent state regulation that remained long after. Conceptually, too, the predominance of public-oriented incorporations and endless debate in the political sphere over corporate policies helped prolong the belief, even after the *Dartmouth* decision, that chartered corporations were institutions that existed to serve the public, even if their capital foundations were wholly private.[11]

Legislatively approved charters, then, did not only spell out the rights and powers of corporations. They were also a way of delineating the rights of corporate *members* vis-à-vis the corporation itself. Indeed, the charter stood at center stage in American views of the corporation even before its designation as a contract securing the corporation from government meddling. The principle was in large part a constitutional one. The Handlins showed long ago how the corporate form rose to prominence even before those attributes with which we associate it, such as limited liability and contractual freedom from state interference, were legal realities, largely because the corporation as an instrument of public service suited American republican conceptions of how states should govern. That view has become standard. Pauline Maier extended that observation to show how Americans could embrace chartered entities because they were so comfortable with constitutional ones. In other words, perceptions of how states should govern their citizens (through limited means, demanding minimal taxation) encouraged the liberal use of the chartering power, so that a company, and not the state, would, say, build a bridge or improve a road. Perceptions of how states were governed *by* their citizens (constitutionally, with specifically delegated powers) nurtured a particular view of the corporation as a fictional entity with limited powers and aided in Americans' embrace of that concept. The desire for more and more corporations, wrote one legal commentator in 1830, "naturally grows from the genius of our institutions; for our governments, political and municipal, are founded on corporate principles." After 1819, from the vantage point of the state the corporate charter was a contract, one that could not be amended without the consent of the corporators. But from the perspective of those who made up the corporation, the charter was something still more profound: it was a constitution, an agreement that, like a government's constitution, laid out the basic rules by which all subsequent decisions would be made.[12]

In some states, legislatures extended this policy, through their incorporation statues, to include even churches. There was no consistent policy toward the incorporation of churches in the early American republic: New York and Pennsylvania, on the one hand, moved quickly to allow the incorporation of churches by simple application (1784 and 1791, respectively); Virginia, Kentucky, and Missouri in 1820, on the other hand, prohibited any and all churches from being incorporated. Most states fell somewhere in the middle, incorporating churches by special legislative act until midcentury. One reason there was as much resistance as there was to incorporating churches was an unwillingness to meddle too closely with internal church affairs. James Madison, for example, endorsed some kinds of church incorporation statutes, but while president he famously vetoed the act of incorporation for the Alexandria Episcopalian Church in 1811, because the bill "enacts into and establishes into law sundry rules and proceedings relative purely to the organization and the polity of the church incorporated, and comprehending even the election and removal of the minister of the same."[13]

Madison's observation, however, would also have accurately described how other states actually did utilize acts of incorporation to delineate with some precision how churches operated internally: New York's 1784 statute, revised in 1801, described who could be a voting member (a male over eighteen years, attending worship for at least one year and having "contributed to the support of said church, congregation, or society according to the usages and customs thereof"); specified how elections were to be announced ("at least fifteen days before"); and even had slightly different rules for Episcopal churches, Dutch Reformed churches, and all "other religious societies." Such rules were not exactly intrusive, but they evince an interest by early American state governments in setting minimum standards of democratic practices in incorporated religious societies.[14]

Charters, then, had consequences for the experience of membership in the thousands of associations, of all kinds, that were formally incorporated in the early decades of the American republic. People could appeal to the charter as a declaration of what the corporation could and could not legitimately do. This applied to corporate deeds of all kinds, including those involving their own members. In 1810, in one of the most important cases in this emerging body of law, examined at length later in this chapter, Pennsylvania Chief Justice William Tilghman declared that the law would protect "the right of membership" in an incorporated society, because that right was "valuable, and not to be taken away without an authority fairly derived either from the charter, or the nature of corporate bodies."[15]

Tilghman penned those words in response to a formal request by the printer John Binns that a writ of mandamus be issued to compel the charter-bearing St. Patrick Benevolent Society to readmit him after he had been expelled for "vilifying" the reputation of fellow member and rival printer William Duane. Here was another way that the charter had an impact on how early citizens of the United States contemplated the meanings and the consequences of voluntary membership. Once accepting the idea that any corporation's powers were the creatures of a state-issued document, members knew precisely where to turn if they believed that an association had acted improperly—and they quickly learned just how and whom to ask. On several widely known and influential occasions, a court made use of the writ of mandamus to compel the readmission of an illegally expelled member, meaning that any and every member who believed he or she had been wrongfully ousted from the society of an incorporated organization had a ready remedy.

It is a writ most famous now for being the legal remedy that William Marbury requested, unsuccessfully, from the US Supreme Court to compel Secretary of State James Madison to deliver Marbury's commission as a justice of the peace in the District of Columbia after outgoing president John Adams had appointed him to the post. That moment generated the foundational case for modern judicial review. But the writ was even more consequential than it appears in the thousands upon thousands of pages devoted to the study of *Marbury v. Madison*. For this was a writ by which a court could order a subordinate legal authority, whether it be a government officer or a chartered corporation, to perform any task it was legally required to do. Indeed, Marbury was informed by the Supreme Court that he was rightfully entitled to a mandamus to secure his vested, legal right to office; Chief Justice John Marshall, however, also declared that the law that granted the Supreme Court the *power* to issue writs of mandamus was an unconstitutional act of Congress, one that had improperly expanded the original jurisdiction of the federal Supreme Court. But the logic behind Marbury's legal right to hold the office—and, thus, to a mandamus to order his admittance to the post—was remarkably influential for shaping American civil society.[16]

Though nothing in English legal history made this degree of active superintendence in the United States inevitable, mandamus did play an important role in English and Anglo-American law long before 1776. For English jurists, mandamus was seen as a prerogative writ, an order emanating directly from the authority of the king. The preeminent eighteenth-century scholar of the common law, William Blackstone, described it as "a command issuing in the king's name from the court of king's bench, and directed to any person, corporation, or inferior court of judicature, within the king's dominions; requiring them to do some *particular* thing." It was a flexible means of addressing a vast array of injustices: after a brief attempt to list some of the ways mandamus was used in English law, Blackstone simply summed up that it could be used "for an infinite number of other purposes, which it is impossible to recite minutely."[17]

It is exaggerating only slightly to note that the writ itself was born in the mind of the great early modern English jurist Sir Edward Coke, and the sheer breadth of its potential uses remains startling. Though there were two prior reported uses of a "writ of restitution" (to restore a freeman to his borough franchise), Coke created something new—and, theoretically, immensely powerful—in *James Bagge's Case*, reported in 1616. Bagge, or Bagg, had been ousted from the municipal corporation at Plymouth, England, for especially uncivil conduct, such as calling one of his fellow freemen "a cozening knave." Sitting at the court of King's Bench, the highest court of the common law, Coke determined that "there was not any just cause to remove him" and ordered a writ to "restore" Bagge to his freehold. The most extensive historical appraisal of the matter concluded that Coke's decision was "singularly unsupported by authority," with Coke referring "only to the general language of Magna Carta" to justify his ruling. And, for Coke, this writ was an expression of the power of King's Bench "not only to correct errors in judicial proceedings, but other errors and misdemeanors extra-judicial," such that absolutely "no wrong or injury, either public or private, can be done, but that it shall be (here) reformed or punished by the due course of law." Here was an assertion of superintending power that had virtually no apparent limits to it, for Coke rested it on the unquestionable powers of the king to do justice, a royal power he had delegated to his court of King's Bench.[18]

Though there was a great deal of unease with what historian Edith Henderson called the "unlawyerlike generality" of Coke's decision in *Bagge's Case*, it proved to be the seed of an important new remedy in English law. He had created a new means of dispensing justice that reached outside of the ordinary bounds of legal institutions. It had an especially far-reaching logic and also, in a practical, jurisdictional sense, served to extend the supervisory powers of King's Bench. Where many earlier writs were addressed to sheriffs or other agents of law enforcement (e.g., habeas corpus, bail) or to lower judicial officials (e.g., prohibition, error), what by the 1640s was being called the writ of mandamus was essentially an order made out to an official who stood, according to Henderson, "*outside* the normal law enforcement system." In extending the reach of King's Bench, Coke's mandamus came to be of great use in the decades following his death in 1634, even as King's Bench came to be known by another name (the Upper Bench) in the kingless, Commonwealth era. In a nation racked by civil war, and then in the partisan divisions in the decades following the Restoration, disputes within English municipal corporations became embarrassingly common. And with the rising number of politically charged corporate dismissals, English jurists had an opportunity to flesh out the writ of mandamus and thereby provide a means of addressing the problem.[19]

The scope of Coke's imaginative writ, then, provided what historian Paul Halliday has labeled "an effective instrument" that allowed the court of King's Bench to become "a powerful arbiter of corporation disputes." The result was stability. When internal mechanisms for resolution failed, repeatedly, English borough corporations faced schism and crippling internal struggles, but they found a way to survive. Conflict need not tear associations apart, because it could be channeled into legal modes of resolution. When King's Bench began to act as superintendent of corporate disputes and began to order the readmission of political minorities who had been expelled in ways or for reasons not legally justifiable, raging partisan conflict became transmuted into niggling disputes over procedure. Battles that might otherwise threaten to tear everything apart were fought in a safer place—in court.[20]

As petitions for writs of mandamus became more common, those involved in English borough corporations saw still more reason to play by the rules. Because of the remarkable tendency to clothe American associational efforts in the garb of chartered corporations, then, Halliday's insight into the English attempts to find a way to manage partisan disputes proves to be incredibly useful for understanding the origins and the nature of early American civil society. We know this because mandamus became the chief means by which a dispute between a member of an incorporated organization and the larger group might be resolved.[21]

To be sure, it was not an inexorable or simple development. It took the incisive jurisprudential mind of Lord Mansfield, in a series of 1760s cases, to make fully coherent the ideas and practices surrounding mandamus, including a rationale for when it should *not* apply. In 1762 in *Rex v. Barker*, still the leading case regarding mandamus and one frequently cited by early national American lawyers and judges as the quintessential summation of what mandamus was, Mansfield noted that the writ "ought to be used upon all Occasions where the Law has established no Specific Remedy, and where in Justice and good Government there *ought* to be one. . . . If there be a right, and *no other* Specific Remedy," the writ of mandamus "should not be denied." One important limiting factor, then, was agreed upon in the eighteenth century: mandamus applied only where there was no other remedy available to the aggrieved party. And, as the American treatise writers on the corporation noted, nearly all of the "modern decisions" on mandamus "seem indeed to be made in the spirit of Lord Mansfield's rule—that wherever there is a *right*, and no other specific remedy, *this* will not be refused."[22]

Between the mid-seventeenth and the late eighteenth centuries, mandamus took shape in Anglo-American law as a preeminent means of addressing failures and misdeeds of those holding a position of authority by means of a corporate charter. In colonial British America, according to the most thorough historian of the matter, the writ of mandamus, increasingly removed from its origins in the prerogative authority of the king, became something more akin to a civil action, one sought as a remedy for a wrong that resulted from a failure of a public duty. By the early nineteenth century, as treatise writers noted on both sides of the Atlantic during the early nineteenth century, writs of mandamus had been "particularly applied to the regulation of Corporations, for the purpose of compelling them to observe the ordinances of their constitution, and to respect the rights of those who are entitled to participate in their privileges."[23]

The consequences of this writ went far beyond the occasional restoration of an expelled member. The very procedures and written forms that had to be followed in each petition for mandamus produced genuinely self-conscious and reflective attitudes toward the relationship between member and group. When a person believed a wrong had been done and opted to seek judicial redress, a court would issue an alternative writ of mandamus, meaning that the alleged wrongdoer, the corporation, had an opportunity to make amends (e.g., admit an expelled person back into its ranks) *or* to state the reasons that no injustice had been done—that is, to show cause why a writ of mandamus should not be issued. If the corporation's return was deemed to be insufficient, for reasons large or remarkably small, then a peremptory mandamus would follow, to which as Blackstone wrote "no other return will be admitted, but a certificate of perfect obedience and due execution of the writ." By the very nature of the legal process that accompanied any request for mandamus, then, officers and members of corporations had every reason to abide by their own rules or, at the very least, to always be prepared to make the detailed case in court that they had done so.[24]

One thing should be clear: this was not simply a matter of enforcing contracts made between members and the groups they joined. In treatises and in judicial opinions, it was noted repeatedly that mandamus would not be extended to enforce private rights that were the result of a contract, for many reasons, most important the fact that a victim of a breach of contract had other, obvious legal remedies available. But writers agreed, most emphatically, that mandamus was available to protect private rights that suffered as a result of a failure of someone—anyone, even an officer of a chartered but ostensibly "private" corporation—to perform a public duty. About a century ago, Zechariah Chafee laid out several compelling reasons that the law regarding membership and voluntary associations had little resemblance to contract law, despite claims for several decades by his time to the contrary. His reasoning was sound, and it is clear that wholly non-contractual understandings of voluntary membership were accepted implicitly in the early republic.[25]

In short, American associational life was not so much a multitude of jurisdictions as it was a wide array of opportunities for individual voluntarism that all fell within a larger body of law. The story of an emerging American law of membership reveals a remarkable degree of penetration by certain common law norms, even within the private and internal actions of a corporation or other voluntary association. The still-towering study of early English law written more than a hundred years ago by Frederick Pollock and Frederic Maitland points out that, centuries before the emergence of mandamus, "the common law does not come to close quarters with municipal by-laws," something that the history of mandamus reveals is intertwined with the emergence of a jurisprudence governing voluntary association generally. "It [the common law] is rarely, if ever, called upon to uphold them," Pollock and Maitland discovered, and "it is rarely called upon to condemn them, for he must be both a bold and a rich citizen who will call in the king against the city." To put the matter simply, that limitation was just not the case in post-Revolutionary America. A solitary man of ordinary means might effectively bring—and on multiple occasions did effectively bring—a higher power to bear on a private controversy affecting his perceived rights and interests as a member. The bonds of voluntary membership were governed and shaped by superintending authority, and, more important, many Americans came to believe that they *ought* to be so superintended.[26]

The jurisprudential efforts to define and delimit the power of voluntary associations over their members helped to place the voluntary association of the early American republic on an unquestionably liberal foundation, as courts proved willing to bring the associational activities of Americans within the embrace of a larger regime of civil rights. The parallels to an earlier transformation in Anglo-American law are worth noting, for the insights of Daniel Hulsebosch in writing a history of "the shift from a predominantly jurisdictional to a substantive understanding of the common law," or, as he more succinctly put it, how "writs were becoming rights," are of great relevance to this study. Remedies arising in one situation were applied in others. And, in states north and south, a surprisingly consistent and culturally resonant system of law governing voluntary membership came into being in the early decades of the nineteenth century. Michael Walzer's observations about contemporary civil life ring true for the early American republic as well: "The state can never be what it appears to be in liberal theory, a mere framework for civil society. It is also the instrument of the struggle, used to give a particular shape to the common life." After the turn of the nineteenth century, a jurisprudence emerged that served to limit the bonds of membership and to ensure that even those who voluntarily bound themselves could, when circumstances compelled action, find protection in the law.[27]

A Common Law of Membership

A commitment to the idea that there should be firm limits on what a majority could legitimately do—even in private, wholly voluntary associations—was becoming well established in post-Revolutionary American culture by the end of the first decade of the nineteenth century. In describing what held these groups together, too, American joiners and organizers had begun to emphasize the formalities of association over the affective bonds of friendship. The idea that there should be real and significant limits on the extent to which a private society could manage the political expressions of its own members had also become more widely shared, especially over the course of the 1790s. One consequence of all of these developments was that, after the turn of the nineteenth century, American courts were soon called upon to adjudicate internal disputes. Though it was variously embraced and resisted by the joiners and organizers of American civil society, judicial superintendence was crucial to its early history. And all of this came together when John Binns and William Duane, two Irish-born printers with a friendship that began in the Old World and was revived in the rough-and-tumble of Pennsylvania politics, grew to hate one another.

John Binns migrated from Dublin to London to Northumberland, Pennsylvania, where he arrived in 1801 and renewed an acquaintance with William Duane, whom he had come to know in the radical movement in London in the 1790s. Indeed, they first met when the proudly democratic London Corresponding Society began organizing protests against the Pitt government, protests that would lead the British government to crack down on politically active voluntary societies in a way the United States never duplicated. Soon after his voyage to America, Binns began publishing the *Northumberland Republican Argus* and was deeply involved in Pennsylvania politics as a Republican at a time when, owing to the weakened Federalist Party, Republicanism in Pennsylvania was increasingly factious. In 1807, Binns came to Philadelphia to set up a newspaper there, one intended to aid William Duane's *Aurora* in its political efforts. Initially supportive, Duane invited Binns into the clubs at the core of the city's party organization, including the Tammany Society, at which Binns even gave the Long Talk in May 1807, private militia units such as the Republican Greens, and the St. Patrick Benevolent Society, a group seeking "the relief of distressed Irishmen emigrating to these United States." As recent work has shown, his membership in these clubs as an entry into local politics should come as no surprise.[28]

For reasons coming out of that year's elections and the always tenuous relationship between the urban radicals for whom Duane spoke and the rural democrats of Simon Snyder, for whom Binns printed the party line, they very soon had a falling out. Duane had Binns expelled from the Tammany Society (a club Duane, his son, and Michael Leib, according to a moderate Republican newspaper, ran with a tyranny "unexampled in the most despotic governments of the world"), from another political organization called the Society of Friends of the People, from two private militia corps, and from the St. Patrick Benevolent Society.[29]

The strife began in late August 1807, when Binns began running a series of letters signed "Veritas" in which he attacked Michael Leib's political practices, including an angry letter on September 2nd discussing Leib's tactics as president of the Society of Friends of the People: "Will you permit me sir, to ask, with what propriety did you as chairman of a public society, refuse to give the health of Simon Snyder when it was regularly drawn up and handed by one of the company? How did it happen that after reading it over, you put it in your pocket without taking any public notice of it?" Duane responded, and it did not take long for two men with nearly identical political views, who had struggled together for democracy on both sides of the Atlantic for more than a decade, to become bitter rivals. Two days later, Binns ran a piece entitled "Aurora vs. Democratic Press," though he tried to hold the high ground as long as he could, on September 25nd calling Duane "a man of talents, who has rendered important services to the democratic cause," a man who was simply far too attached to the conniving Leib.[30]

That same edition of Binns's *Democratic Press* began telling the saga of his expulsion from those clubs he had joined on first arriving in Philadelphia. The night before, at a meeting of the Society of Friends of the People, Duane had denounced Binns ("in substance the same as his denunciation of this paper, but particularly distinguished by vulgar epithets and indecent allusions," Binns wrote). When Binns and others had left the room after their committee had reported, "under the impression that no other business would then be submitted," Duane acted. "A motion was made that John Binns be expelled [from] the society, without a hearing; which motion was carried!!!" The next day, Binns published the report of John Jennings, who had remained in the room and recalled that he "sat just before Dr. *Leib*," who held the chair, "and loudly said *no*." Many others, too, "spoke against the injustice of condemning without hearing." But, Jennings recounted, "the minority saw it was folly to contend against *the train*[ed] *bands*, and they silently gave up the business to be done as best suited the instigators, in the belief that such proceeding would have a different effect upon the public mind, from what was intended." Binns made sure of it.[31]

In early October, a month before the St. Patrick Benevolent Society would vote to expel Binns, Duane's *Aurora* announced that Binns had been expelled from four organizations. Those dismissals were testimony that he "must be considered . . . a *public disturber*." Binns, in his own newspaper, responded point by point. As far as the militia companies went, Duane was factually wrong: Binns remained a member of one and never had been a member of the other. For the Society of Friends of the People, from which he was expelled "*without a hearing*," he asked the public, "Is such a proceeding as this, more a reproach to the society, to the cowardly prevaricator, who was the cause of it, or to me?" A letter was printed on October 9th, just a few days before the state election, signed "No Body," which observed that such an expulsion ran "contrary not only to the fundamental principles of democracy, but even contrary to the laws and statutes of monarchical and aristocratic governments. John Binns is the fourth person expelled in this anti-democratic manner, by the Friends of the People." Though "No Body" was not at all explicit about what he thought those "fundamental principles of democracy" were, his declaration that the procedural unfairness experienced by Binns was decidedly undemocratic is telling, and it is indicative of the broader push in the early nineteenth century to envelop nongovernmental institutions within a broader framework of personal rights and interpersonal duties. Indeed, the parallel was made explicit when the writer, probably Binns, asked, "What Laws would be enacted if the rulers of that Society, held the reins of government?" Any man's authority over other citizens, either in public office or in private club, was to be exercised fairly, justly, democratically.[32]

Binns made a similar but distinct critique of his expulsion from the Tammany Society. There, Binns noted, Duane's offense was not just against legitimate and fair procedure (although in Tammany, too, Binns had had no hearing before he was booted out) but, in a move especially dishonorable, Duane's tactic ran contrary to the society's own constitution and its prohibition that "the accusation and vote both take place at the same stated meeting" whenever a member was brought up for expulsion. Not having an opportunity to be heard only compounded the greater offense, their violation of "the provisions of the constitution, and the solemn manner in which the members have pledged *their most sacred honor* to support it." Binns, quite pointedly, used such arguments to turn the tables on Duane: "After such a proceeding as this, Wm. Duane has the unblushing effrontery to publish it *as a reproach* to me," Binns wrote. Indeed, the affair did not reflect well on Duane and, perhaps, played some role in his humiliating loss (besides being a party spokesman, Duane was also a candidate for state senate) and the narrow reelection of Leib in a safe district when Election Day came a few days later, on October 13th.[33]

Before that election, Binns had made the most of each expulsion as evidence of the despotism and oppression Pennsylvanians would face if Duane or Leib ever held elective office. Duane, too, had continued his assault, telling the world that Binns was a man "without any thing but arrogance, vanity, egotism, and impudence to sustain him." Their rivalry would continue past that election, even years later. In his famous 1809 "tyranny of printers" letter, Alexander Dallas went on to write that the only issue left in Philadelphia was "the question whether Binns or Duane shall be the dictator."[34]

In the St. Patrick Benevolent Society, however, there was no question. When Duane sought Binns's expulsion, he got it, with 70 votes out of 71. The charges brought against him in November 1807 were that he had broken a bylaw making "villifying any of its members" a "crime against the society," as Duane put it. Duane, as president, ensured this time that the proper procedures were followed, and with seven days' notice and a hearing, Binns was expelled. Five weeks after that expulsion, Binns, through his attorney Walter Franklin, approached the Supreme Court of Pennsylvania and told them the society had "deprived him of the rights of Membership in which this Deponent has a beneficial interest—and that this Deponent has not to the best of his knowledge and belief any adequate and specific mode of redress or Relief in the premises other than by Mandamus" to "restore him to his right of Membership." A few days later, Binns entered into evidence a pamphlet copy of the club's constitution, with the relevant passages underlined.[35]

Binns seized upon the fact that the society held a charter from the state as a way that he might legally hold them to the standards to which, it was clear, he believed all voluntary associations should adhere. The court listened, and William Duane as president was ordered on New Year's Eve 1807 to either readmit Binns or show cause for his expulsion. Duane chose the latter course (no one expected him to do otherwise), describing for the court how Binns had printed allegations about Duane's improper conduct toward the widow of a man who died in the Irish cause. Such accusations, "besides having no foundation or any shape in truth, had no relation to American politics," and for insulting the reputation of a fellow member Binns was charged with "violating his obligation to the said Society." He could not be restored to membership.[36]

Binns's argument in court began with the fact that the St. Patrick Benevolent Society was incorporated in 1804 under the 1791 general incorporation statute. The attorney for the commonwealth—a writ of mandamus had the state prosecuting the society in the name of John Binns—insisted that Binns's case began there: for a bylaw to be valid, it must "assist the charitable design," but this bylaw was "merely political." It did nothing for the "good government" of the group but rather "controls the external conduct of members to each other, and might by the same principle regulate their behavior to the rest of the world." Last, the state's attorney cited *Rex v. Richardson*, for the first time in an American courtroom, a precedent from Lord Mansfield that held that the power to expel was indeed an incidental power of all corporations, but that it was reviewable—specifically, by the writ of mandamus—and was valid only in certain, clearly defined situations. Four things stand out in Binns's effort to restore himself to membership: his emphasis on what he called "the right of membership," as something of value; close attention to the charter-derived powers of the society and, by extension, his rejection of personal, affective bonds as providing the glue that held them together; his fear that excessive associational authority could "regulate [members'] behavior to the rest of the world" and thus infringe on the personal independence requisite in any model of republican citizenship; and a turn to the common law for solution.[37]

When Duane's attorney spoke, he emphasized a Shaftesburian model of association, one that had been facing serious challenge at least since the 1780s debates over the Society of the Cincinnati. "This is the case of a private charitable institution" were the first words out of his mouth, and a society such as this depends "for its existence upon the admission of new members, and upon the contribution of such as voluntarily continue to be members." He put the point bluntly: "It lives by union and co-operation. Whatever destroys these, goes to the destruction of the corporation," and thus a bylaw prohibiting the vilification of fellow members—and he was sure to note that the rule "does not interfere with the intercourse between members and strangers"—is absolutely "needful" to prevent the society's demise. Duane's emphasis on society, on a union of sentiment, as giving vitality to the association, stands in contrast to the prosecution's argument resting on the act of assembly, the charter, and the common law. As the debates two decades earlier might suggest, Duane's view, which emphasized the association's need for affection and mutuality as evidence that a bylaw against besmirching a fellow member's reputation was perfectly legitimate, fell flat. Notions of affinity or sociability were of no use to the Pennsylvania Supreme Court as it sought to define the rights and obligations of association members.[38]

But why did Binns petition for reinstatement at all? As Judith Shklar has observed, pluralism is a safeguard against the injury of permanent exclusion, and Binns had no shortage of other groups he could and did join. He became a member of the Hibernian Society, an older and relatively conservative Philadelphia club for Irishmen, in 1809, and he joined and even helped organize other political associations. And it was not as if Duane had bested him in the newspaper wars: between the 1807 expulsion and the 1810 reinstatement, Binns's man won the governorship, and Binns was able to announce to his readers that, owing to greater printing demands, he would be taking up new quarters at what had formerly been Duane's offices. But all that was, for John Binns, quite beside the point. He saw an injustice—and an opportunity to attack a political opponent for being a despot though he held no office—and he acted. And where the other expulsions, from the unincorporated Society of Friends of the People and from the Tammany Society, merely symbolized his estrangement from a school of political thought (one he had already walked away from), the loss of membership in the St. Patrick society perhaps represented an attempt to separate Binns from Philadelphia's Irish community, a threat to his Irish identity. We cannot know Binns's precise motives, but we know that he found a ready audience in the Pennsylvania Supreme Court.[39]

Binns had insisted that anything the St. Patrick Benevolent Society did was legitimately reviewable by the commonwealth. As Mary Sarah Bilder has argued, compellingly, the doctrine of judicial review grew out of the English practice of voiding corporate bylaws "repugnant" to the laws of the land, which practice "subsequently became a transatlantic constitution binding American colonial law by a similar standard." "Over a century later," she writes, "this practice gained a new name: judicial review." But the significance of that area of jurisprudence extends still further. It created a means by which much of the associational activity that, for foreign-born observers such as Tocqueville and Lieber, was a defining feature of American society could be superintended by legal and political institutions whose authority rested on popular sovereignty.[40]

But there was more here than the concession theory of corporate existence, the idea that any and all powers are derived from the charter because the corporation is a creature of the state. Broader concerns about the nature of membership and of voluntary, informed affiliation became expressed in how Americans treated their incorporated as well as their unchartered organizations. The superintendence of private groups by those institutions legitimated by popular sovereignty was central, a point made expressly in *Commonwealth v. St. Patrick Benevolent Society*. In America's first corporate law treatise, published in 1832, Tilghman's opinion ordering that Binns be readmitted is described at length. The authors describe the case as having imported into the American common law the principle that it is "a tacit condition annexed to the franchise of a member, that he will not oppose or injure the interests of the corporate body." But the member's expulsion can be evaluated, on the merits, based on the court's judgment of "the nature of the corporation."[41]

Chief Justice Tilghman directly addressed the rival visions of association offered by the two printers. Tilghman emphasized "the benevolent purposes of this society, and many others which have been lately incorporated on similar principles," giving him, he said, "a mind strongly disposed to give a liberal construction" to the society's powers. Duane's attorney had emphasized the imperative of a union of sentiment in the society: "the instant that personal abuse and vilification of the members are permitted, that instant the society decays." Duane's affective—as opposed to legalistic or law-minded—understanding of the St. Patrick Benevolent Society was reaffirmed in the weeks leading up to the court's ruling. Duane's *Aurora* published the proceedings of the society on May 17, 1810, including the announcement, "The Members of the St. Patrick Benevolent Society have proven their virtue by expelling from their confidence the reputed betrayer of Quigley, and proven apostate of moral principle." The allegation that Binns had betrayed a fellow Irish nationalist in 1798, who was then hanged, was invoked in their expulsion of Binns, not only from the club, but from the confidence of its members. No court order, Duane appeared to be suggesting, could alter that.[42]

Tilghman, however, took such assertions that sentimental bonds were the basis for effective association to help craft a liberal and legalistic principle on which to organize civil society in the early United States, and it was immediately influential. He stated clearly that "the great and single point" in the case was whether Binns was the victim of a violation of the terms of the charter. The society was authorized by charter to pass only bylaws that were "necessary for the good government and support of the affairs of the corporation," and Binns was penalized for a violation of a bylaw that, in Tilghman's view, did not meet that test. Indeed, the bylaw would only hamper the ability of the club to function smoothly. "Taking cognizance of such offenses" as vilifying a fellow member will, he said, "have the pernicious effect of introducing private feuds into the bosom of the society, and interrupting the transaction of business." In a post-Revolutionary age that increasingly saw association as an effective means to improve the human condition, that was not to be allowed. Adherence to rules legitimately passed was a means to accomplish good ends. And this was not to be an isolated position, relevant only to Binns and Duane, but rather a decision on which American private governing power was to be founded. "I consider it as a point of very great importance, in which thousands of persons are, or very soon will be interested; for the members of these corporations are increasing rapidly and daily." To Tilghman, "the right of membership" was "valuable"—valuable to Binns and to countless others—and it was "not to be taken away without an authority fairly derived either from the charter, or the nature of corporate bodies." The rights were valuable to individuals; the preservation of those rights by legal enforcement was invaluable to a thriving civil society. The Pennsylvania judiciary as well as jurists around the country seized on this principle, as we will see in part 2. As Justice John Bannister Gibson would put it in 1822, the courts of the commonwealth would come to stand as a "superintending power" over all the "inferior associations" of American civic life.[43]

That development and the broader trend it reflects of how Americans were beginning to conceive of membership and authority in any private group, incorporated or not, can open new possibilities for understanding the American culture that Alexis de Tocqueville would observe by the early 1830s. It rested upon a liberal understanding of how and why people could join together, but it was a liberalism that explicitly rejected a sharp division between legal authority and a private realm of association. Rather, it was founded upon a new, post-Revolutionary commitment to the principle that civil rights and fair procedure should be brought to bear in increasingly diverse areas of social activity. Regimes of legal and political rights were created, embodied in charters and in a common law of membership, that ultimately defined the nature of American civil society, developed in practice more than in theory, in the organization of new societies and in moments of conflict between members and associations.

The court-ordered membership of John Binns in the Irish benevolent society reflected both broader post-Revolutionary notions of legitimate associational activity and the willingness of jurists to bring common law principles of members' rights and duties to bear in internal operations. And this was a liberal note sounded again and again in the jurisprudence regarding early national voluntary associations. That is, liberalism, according to political theorist Nancy Rosenblum, "asks men and women to ignore all the other things they are in order to treat one another fairly in certain contexts and for certain purposes." Here, John Binns, a rude club member unwanted by a vote of seventy to one, was declared by the court to be a man improperly stripped by "the uncertain will of a majority of the members" of "the right of membership." By emphasizing the legal origins of associational authority rather than a rival, affective vision of concerted action that saw the powers of voluntary associations as deriving from the mutual agreement and, indeed, camaraderie of its members, the Pennsylvania Supreme Court proved willing to bring the St. Patrick Benevolent Society within the embrace of a larger regime of civil rights.[44]

As people sought to understand how Americans could come together, privately and voluntarily, without danger to state or to citizen, rhetoric and concepts important to the Revolution would be applied in contexts and in ways far removed from their original meanings. The willingness of members of voluntary associations to call for a judicial intervention meant that constitutionally ordained legal authorities would take an increasingly active hand. And one result was that, as Laura Edwards has noted in describing legal reforms in the post-Revolutionary South, these "encomiums to freemen's rights legitimized the concentration of authority in the state." In many ways, however, the effect was not constraining, but liberating—both for Binns and for the future of American civil society. For what allowed the post-Revolutionary associational landscape to become recognizably pluralistic was the encompassment of all efforts at association within this new jurisprudence that made use of older, common law remedies. What emerged from these moments of contest was a body of law that helped to define and to defend the rights, the duties, and the very meanings of voluntary membership.[45]

PART TWO

Practices and Limits, 1800–1840

As privately formed, voluntarily joined organizations became more common in American cities and towns, conflicts and contests from within their ranks were inevitable. The increasing ubiquity of the voluntary association—the growing numbers of Masonic lodges, debating societies, moral reform organizations, and so on—is a great story in its own right. And that story has been told a few different ways. It was a reflection of an emerging, distinctively American character, as Arthur Schlesinger described it in the mid-twentieth century. It was something that, along with the growing print culture of the early republic, created and shaped an American public sphere that, as John Brooke has written, could operate as a "flywheel" between the people and their governments. The act of joining together, formally and voluntarily, created new kinds of connections between and among people, and the social consequences were tremendous.[1]

But joining together also created new occasions for people to split apart. Admitting men and women to membership allowed new opportunities to exclude and to expel. Those conflicts had to be resolved one way or another, and the ways that ordinary people who joined or organized these groups dealt with the tensions that surfaced are extraordinarily revealing. How judges and juries adjudicated the cases brought by one or more discontented members are no less illuminating, for distinct but related reasons. Over the first third of the nineteenth century, as the Revolutionary generation gave way to the first generations of citizens born in a young United States, the accepted meanings and consequences of voluntary membership were shaped by priorities and concerns unique to a people just emerging from a republican revolution.

Chapter 4 will examine the ordinary experiences of membership and association over the first three decades of the nineteenth century. This chapter will emphasize some of the ways that many American men and women came to agree on how best to join together. All of those anxieties and priorities about voluntary affiliation that culminated in the dispute between John Binns and William Duane—emphases on law over affection, anxieties about arbitrary power and totalizing commitments, and a belief that informed consent and procedural regularity ought to serve as limits on associational authority—were played out on a daily basis in hundreds upon hundreds of associations in the early nineteenth century. How joiners and organizers chose to structure their collective endeavors was, essentially, the everyday experience of constitutional self-government, albeit in private, voluntary associations. And each one of those organizational moments gave American men and women opportunities to confront directly the tensions between individual autonomy and collective action. As the Binns-Duane affair revealed, legal institutions and legal remedies would come to play an increasingly important role in Americans' growing world of voluntary associations, but those external forces mirrored the priorities and practices of ordinary men and women as they joined together and acted together.

This will be a study of the forms and practices of association as drawn up by the organizers and joiners themselves, male and female. Women of the early nineteenth century, for instance, were eager participants in American voluntarism, forming reading societies, prayer groups, maternal associations, charitable institutions, missionary and education societies, Sunday school organizations, and moral reform associations in numbers that impressed every observer. And almost from the very beginning, the women who organized and joined those associations described and defined the rights and duties of membership in ways that reveal an American society that had come to embrace rules, formal procedure, and well-defined benefits and obligations in virtually every collective enterprise. Using John Phillip Reid's concept of "law-mindedness" as a lens through which to scrutinize early national approaches to social organization, this chapter will look at broad trends in men's and women's voluntary associations, many of which had little or no pecuniary element—reading clubs, debating societies, and the like—to survey the cultural pervasiveness of a law-minded approach to membership in America.

One of the most important factors at play in the story being told here involves parallels across different kinds of associations, in law and in everyday practice. Chapter 5 will look at organizations that in a very real sense were almost entirely focused on money, exploring some of the ways that controversies over the meanings of membership in mutual fire insurance cooperatives and stock-issuing business corporations echoed challenges faced elsewhere in America's now-burgeoning civil society. Both in the constitutional governments of the new nation as well as within privately created, voluntarily joined associations, effective concerted action depended on finding a balance between some kind of effective, centralized authority and the powers and rights of individual members. In the decades immediately after the Revolution, legal authorities played a vital role in determining that balance.

When the century began, there was no certain consensus as to how one even *became* a member of a business corporation and still less about what limits there might be to what a corporation could subsequently ask of those members. These were debates that had important parallels with—and important consequences for—broader American notions of belonging. In 1832, the world's first legal treatise covering the laws and practices of the private corporation was published in Boston, the creation of two young Rhode Island lawyers who began their landmark work with the observation that "we have in our country an infinite number of corporations aggregate." While the English tended to join together "by mere articles of agreement," wrote Joseph Angell and Samuel Ames, their American counterparts had taken a different tack: "What is done here by the co-operation of several persons, is, in the greater number of instances, the result of a consolidation effected by an express act or charter of incorporation." The American law of corporations, while it may have derived from English origins, was something new under the sun.

Angell and Ames were sure, too, that these ideas of corporate membership were a product of a shared American worldview, not abstracted legal thought. In the opening pages, they quoted and wholeheartedly agreed with words that Justice Moulton Rogers of Pennsylvania had penned in 1827, where he stressed that the law of corporations had undergone drastic change and that "this change in the law has arisen from a change of circumstances, from that silent legislation by the people themselves, which is continually going on in a country such as ours, the more wholesome, because it is gradual, and wisely adapted to the peculiar situation, wants and habits of our citizens." As the republican polity came of age, laws in the United States that governed what Angell and Ames called "the co-operation of several persons" were changing with it. Tensions between individual members' rights and the will of the majority were common and were fraught with tension, for the challenge was to create *effective* associations that accorded with post-Revolutionary ideas of fairness, accountability, and rule by consent.[2]

Chapter 6 will begin to tell the story of how and why the associational world of the mid-nineteenth century was becoming something essentially different from what came before. When John Binns and William Duane feuded in 1807, they could not have anticipated that the aftermath of their feud would help to shape American civil society for decades to come. The civic life that Americans and foreign visitors such as Alexis de Tocqueville so often commented upon by the 1830s was, to be sure, the creation of countless men and women who organized and joined voluntary groups for all kinds of diverse purposes. But it was also a world that had been constructed according to peculiarly post-Revolutionary political ideals and practices and, more important still, was shaped and encompassed by law. This chapter will return to the immediate legacy of the Binns-Duane dispute and the full-blown emergence of the writ of mandamus as a means of judicial superintendence of conflicts between member and group. What was created in the post-Revolutionary moment would give way by the 1830s to new, more contractual ways of describing the relationship between individual and group. The mutual benefit societies that became so common in urban America in the first third of the nineteenth century became the key battlegrounds, for in those groups people were admitted and expelled by the votes of their fellow members, and they had a powerful financial incentive to challenge any decision that stripped them of access to the society coffers in times of distress. What emerged after 1810, then, was a jurisprudence that, much like the early development of the law governing stock-issuing corporations, directly addressed the tensions between majority rule and minority rights.

The history of mutual benefit societies in the American republic provides powerful examples of how the legal and popular conceptions of the rights and duties of membership continued to evolve in the period between 1810 and 1840. They did so, by and large, in a direction already established in the post-Revolutionary years, with a growing emphasis on legally guaranteed rights and legal superintendence of the internal workings of private associations of nineteenth-century American life. But something would happen by the end of the 1830s that helps us to see just how remarkable the earlier, post-Revolutionary era really was. Courts would begin to withdraw themselves from an active superintendence of the internal affairs of these associations, setting a precedent that would hold for the rest of the century: members should be careful about the fine print in their agreements to join, for the obligations they had taken on as members would be upheld and the private regimes of authority they had entered would be respected.

That development, intertwined as it was with the emergence of contract as the organizing idea by which Americans would come to understand so many kinds of relationships, was transformative. The distinction between bonds of affection and law-minded, formal association can help us, looking back, to understand what shaped the associational world of the post-Revolutionary United States. By 1840, Americans' understanding of what voluntary membership ought to look like had been transformed still further, and they would use the language of law to describe it. In a chapter that Alexis de Tocqueville opted not to include in his *Democracy in America*, one describing "the Manner in Which American Governments Act toward Associations," he made an intriguing observation: the people in any democracy must "find the secret of being self-sufficient" by "uniting together," by embracing the "spirit of association." Once that happens, Tocqueville speculated, the people will have learned how to pursue and achieve their own goals by associating together, and the government "must withdraw its hand as they better understand the art of doing so." Over the first third of the nineteenth century, the American people accomplished that remarkable feat, the active hand of the state had begun to pull away, and a nation of joiners had come into being.[3]

FOUR

Everyday Constitutionalism in a Nation of Joiners

When a small group of women met in the front room of one of their homes in Norwich, Connecticut, to establish the Ladies' Literary Society in 1800, they knew they were doing something both common and controversial. "The social principal [*sic*] in human nature is so powerful and so opperative that there has not been a period of the civillized world when particular societies have not existed," one member would declare a year later in the first annual address of the society. "Even female societies are not unprecedented," she noted, such as "the amiable and rightly respected widows society in New York" or the "female society also which was instituted at Newport for the Benevolent purpose of Prayer for the universal good of mankind." But the members of the new club were also aware that they had their critics. Why bother joining together to do something—in this case, reading—that can be done just as well alone? The women had a response: "We would answer that feeble and desultory are the efforts of one alone, compared to the effect of an united circle of congenial friends." But questions remained. They could, of course, benefit from one another's company. But why did they need to band together so formally? Why, exactly, did they need to draw up a constitution and adopt bylaws, just to read books together?[1]

Some thirty years later, a French traveler to the United States would pay close attention to the American proclivity for formal association, and he asked similar questions of American temperance organizations. Why, Alexis de Tocqueville asked, did they need to join together in the first place? "For the moment," he wrote, he "did not see why these very abstemious citizens could not content themselves with drinking water by their own firesides." How was formal association supposed to help them lead temperate lives? Why bother with the formalities when one sought something so simple?[2]

American men and women had answers to these questions, ones that we have already begun to explore. In the half century after the American Revolution, many would have come to the belief that, indeed, formal association—groups in which participation was well defined at the outset, structured by formal rules and, quite often, by some kind of self-ordained, supreme law to which all those rules must always be subordinate—was the best way to accomplish goals large and small. Those hoping to end the scourge of drunkenness wanted to transform a nation, and so they chose to create a way of acting together that could be both replicated elsewhere and joined with ease by anyone who wanted to further the cause. Similarly, the women of Norwich would make clear both in their actions and in their words that they valued rules and formalities. The tendency toward law-minded practices and formalized commitments was apparent even in groups that had little to no money involved, groups that had little reason to anticipate friction or confusion. What is more, countless groups were formed that primarily concerned a private choice, such as whether to drink alcohol, and they overwhelmingly embraced procedural regularity and constitutional forms of self-organization.

Despite the fact that they all knew one another well, having been praying together for a decade when they formed the reading club, the small group of Norwich women decided to organize formally, inscribing in a book of records that "we the undersigned do agree to form ourselves into a Society, by the name of the Ladies Literary Society for the special purpose of Enlightening our understandings, expanding our Ideas, and promoting useful knowledge among our Sex; to this end we propose we assemble ev'ry other Wednesday eve, or ev'ry Wednesday from the first of October, to the first of March from 7 Oclock till 9." Their first meeting, on January 29th, held at one of the founders' homes, began with a reading from the book of Proverbs and turned next to discuss a history of Christopher Columbus. The women made "suitable comments on the Heroic deed of Queen Isabella, in being his patroness, when in vane did he apply to Kings for assistance for Eighteen years." At that first meeting, they also "agreed to purchase a blank-book at the Expense of the Society, to minute their proceedings."

Six weeks later, on March 12, 1800, a committee of six women was appointed "to frame a set of rules to be laid before the society which they approving shall pass into laws binding on every member of the society." When the rules were reported on March 19th, copies were made for all the members to read closely for discussion at the next meeting. At the same meeting—not coincidentally, one can presume—one of the women's readings was the United States Constitution.[3]

Their rules were not everything to them, but sometimes it almost seemed that they were. Mary Tyler, delivering the second annual address, noted that the Ladies' Literary Society of Norwich was not simply a "united circle of congenial friends," friends though they surely were. They had formed a society that had, quite purposefully, chosen to create rules to give shape to their proceedings. "We shall do well," Tyler said, "if we pay a *strict* attention to the rules of our institution: they were formed by the most judicious of our society, and calculated for the good of the whole. We have an equal right to petition for an amendment of any of the articles (two or three excepted) when ever we see room but in departing from them while they are in forced—we are sure of creating uneasiness for our selves and others." Indeed, at the very next meeting, they, with no intentional irony, showed a real reverence for their constitutional rules by breaking one: in derogation of their unalterable requirement that each meeting begin with a Bible reading, the women began by reading their own constitution aloud, first, and only then moving on to read a passage from First Corinthians.[4]

Miss Lydia Harris, giving the third annual address in 1803, echoed Tyler's call for strictly constitutional proceedings: "A strict adherence to our constitution, I would strongly recommend, as a diviation from it may have a tendency to create uneasiness." And she recommended "to our secretary in *future*, more exactness, in recording every event, and transaction, that occurs in the society, as in the course of the past year, many things have been omitted, which may be of consequence at some future period." There was a deliberate effort, here, to use formal rules and constitutional methods to create something more permanent than a mere circle of friends. According to Harris, the society was no "transitory thing." It should "be durable as time, and productive of much good to future generations."

There was certainly nothing necessary about their embrace of procedural formalities. Detailed studies of such groups have shown how closely connected the members generally were. They usually shared religious backgrounds and social status; they were usually friends, often even family. In this post-Revolutionary period, however, what could begin as a society founded on shared friendships, social networks, and familial relationships would be cast, almost instantly, in constitutional, procedurally bound forms. The consequence was a new way of thinking about old relationships, even in voluntary societies founded by women who shared sincere sentimental bonds. This is not to say that participants in small, tightly knit female associations of this period cared less for one another after they had drawn up their organizational documents than they had before: it is only to say that they made conscious decisions that, in a formal sense, affection was to have little or nothing to do with their membership.

Everyday practices, shared assumptions, and the common features of voluntary associations as drawn up by ordinary American joiners and associational organizers all tended toward the same priorities: in short, rules, procedural regularity, and even a robust distinction between ordinary rules and constitutional ones came to shape the concept of voluntary membership for American men and women in the formative decades of the young nation's increasingly vibrant civil society. As important as it is to know *why* people formed and joined one or many of the panoply of voluntary associations present in the early American republic, it is also useful to shift the focus, instead, to *how* precisely they chose to do it.[5]

Rules and the Technology of Association

In 1803, Lyman Beecher helped to organize a society in Long Island "for the suppression of vice, and the promotion of virtue, and useful knowledge; to be known by the name of the Moral Society." He was a preacher in his late twenties, a man who would go on to become a transformative figure in his day and the father of others who would in turn transform their own, such as Henry Ward Beecher and Harriet Beecher Stowe. On the last day of summer that year, Beecher stood before a group of people who had several months before decided to form an organization "where every member is a soldier, every soldier a sentinel," against the growing tendencies toward intemperance, excess, violation of the Sabbath, and every form of vicious behavior.[6]

Beecher extolled the idea of a passionate and motivated band of people coming together "to mark existing vices, to strip them of their disguise, to point out their origin, their consequences, and to prescribe the remedy." And he would spend much of the rest of his life organizing, supporting, and promoting such groups. A Connecticut society he endorsed in 1812 had thirty branch societies in little more than a year. The models he had in mind appear to have been threefold: English attempts at just these kinds of moral reform societies; existing New England institutions such as the town and the church itself, in their idealized, tight-knit forms; and, when he began to contemplate larger associations that reached across multiple communities, other voluntary associations that had been formed elsewhere for completely different purposes. "Associations of this general nature for the promotion of the arts and sciences," he would note in 1812, "have exerted a powerful influence, with great success; and no reason it is presumed may be given, why the cause of morals, may not be equally benefitted by similar associations." Evoking a wide array of influences and precursors, Beecher remained constant on what was to him the key point: good people must form themselves into a "disciplined moral militia, prepared to act upon every emergency, and repel every encroachment upon the liberties and morals of the state," as he told the people of New Haven, Connecticut: "By their numbers they embolden the timid and intimidate the enemy; and in every conflict the responsibility being divided among many, is not feared."[7]

A key point was missing, though: how, exactly, should they do this? He wanted to entice volunteers to help him to create an actual, disciplined moral militia, but doing so would call for something more than a rousing metaphor. In an appendix to his 1803 sermon, Beecher offered answers, but he offered different answers for different circumstances, in a way that reveals the embryonic nature of his beliefs about the importance of formalities and rules. "It is an obvious reflection, and one which in the formation of the society in this place was early realized, that the constitution of a moral society, must be adapted to the local circumstances of the people proposing to unite," he noted after describing the constitution of the Long Island association formed in 1803, which had only four articles and was largely lacking in specifics. "In populous cities, where neighbours have less intercourse, and vice is more bold, it may be practicable to stipulate what, in given cases, will be done," Beecher observed. But in a place like this, "in a country town, connected by ties of blood and neighbourhood, too great particularity in the constitution, would, it was found, intimidate the virtuous, excite the opposition of the vicious, and defeat the proposed union." Among strangers, the best way to join together might be formal rules. Those "connected by ties of blood and neighbourhood" had no need of such things.[8]

In drawing that distinction, Beecher revealed that the first generations of American citizens were aware of something important: rules and specificity were a virtual necessity in order for strangers to act collectively. Only then could they know what role they would be expected to play, what burdens and benefits awaited them. Twenty years later, he would give a series of sermons on temperance and go on to help to found a truly national organization—the American Society for the Promotion of Temperance, or the American Temperance Society—which would by 1834 unite some 5,000 local associations and more than a million individuals. Detailed constitutions and bylaws at the local, state, and national level were necessary. But would those same kinds of rules be counterproductive among an already tightly knit group of people? In 1803, at least, Beecher thought so. Strangers, though, had little choice but to delineate in advance what a particular association was to do and how it intended to do it.[9]

Many of his contemporaries, however, were already beginning to act as if they believed that rules were as valuable for small groups of people who already knew one another as they would be for sprawling associations of strangers. And many others may never have had a sense that another way of associating even existed, because of the ways in which associational forms and practices were circulated in the early American republic—a point to which this chapter will return shortly. The women of Norwich are a fascinating and self-conscious example of early American joiners aware of the importance of rules, even among an intimate group of people who knew one another well. A similar attention to order was seen in other women's reading societies formed in the years to come, such as when the women of the Female Reading Class adopted a set of rules governing their club in Colchester, Connecticut, in 1816, including detailed rules describing how new members could be admitted. A decade later a group of fourteen young men in New Hampshire formed the Boscawen Juvenile Fraternity by drawing up and signing a meticulously arranged constitution despite the fact that most of them had likely known one another all of their lives. Indeed, five of the members shared one surname and three shared another. And Beecher himself would go on to use established, detailed associational practices throughout his long career as an organizer and a joiner of voluntary societies formed to do good in the world.[10]

Everyday practices within the growing numbers of voluntary groups—and what ordinary men and women thought, said, and wrote about those ordinary goings-on in the clubs and societies they joined—reveal a conscious choice to embrace rules and detailed procedure in the self-created associations of the early United States. Mary Tyler's speech on the importance and utility of abiding by the rules in the Ladies' Literary Society simply put into words something that the very acts of drawing up constitutions, bylaws, and rules and then following them, week in and week out, evidenced even more strongly: the world of American voluntarism, as it became "the prevailing spirit of the present age," was law-minded and rule-bound. And so many of the people who joined these groups would not have had it any other way.[11]

Women's associations are a useful reference point for exploring the depth and pervasiveness of this post-Revolutionary emphasis on rule-bound association. There is little doubt that women clothed their participation in a different rhetoric from men, emphasizing their role in certain benevolent enterprises as "the proper business of women" and a natural extension of "the feelings of mothers." But in the interior lives of their societies, the commonalities with men's societies—the detailed articulation of the rights and duties of individual membership, the voluntary and well-delimited nature of these purely voluntary relationships—are equally significant in our understanding of early American civil society. One consequence of this focus is to emphasize not women's separation from political society, but their close relationship with it, in the ways they organized their own societies by using languages of informed consent, law, and personal rights. It was in those ways that women secured a space of their own.[12]

There is good reason to think that women who organized and joined these associations thought that formal procedure and well-defined, constitutional modes of operation were the ideal ways to assuage or prevent conflict and to create unity of purpose. In reading groups such as the Ladies' Literary Society, the participant women made that point explicitly. In those early societies that were affiliated with churches, too, unity and consensus were paramount goals. When William Patten addressed a group of three hundred women in Rhode Island on "The Advantages of Association to Promote Useful Purposes," he noted that "the members in general of the Society, especially those who are active in conducting its affairs, will studiously cultivate unanimity. Society denotes union, as well as numbers—without which there is only the name." And women found that an optimal means to that end was to create the sorts of relationships among one another that, in Conrad Wright's terms, "were neither as flexible nor as comprehensive as family relationships," with annual elections, dues, and well-defined ways of participating as "recurring reminders that voluntary relationships were impermanent." The women who joined were there because they chose to be, with articles of organization and bylaws telling each from the outset what would be expected of her.[13]

Quite early there was a belief that consensus was achieved more easily in these constitutionally organized, voluntary groups, formed exclusively as they were of people of shared mind and of formal, constitutional equality. Maternal societies to support and provide spiritual edification for mothers, as Nancy Cott has noted, did not leave much evidence of their existence because they were small, were organized locally, and did not participate much at all in the print culture of the nineteenth century. But they too, from their earliest instances in the 1810s, were organized with detailed constitutions. One maternal association whose manuscript records have survived affiliated with the First Congregational Church in Concord, New Hampshire, had a constitution of nine articles (including article 6, which enjoined its members to pray daily) and regularly kept minutes of their meetings. The maternal associations were but one representative example of this embrace of formalities and detailed procedures. As scholars such as Bruce Dorsey have recently noted, "Formal organizations of women were nearly nonexistent before the 1790s." But what came next, women's historians have discovered, was consistent: as Anne Scott summed up her wide-ranging study of nineteenth-century women's charitable groups, for instance: "No matter where they were, who the members were, or what they called themselves, organizational forms were remarkably similar. Written constitutions were universal: every society established rules about meetings, the uses of money, and qualifications for potential receipts of charity." To these can be added other universals: women's societies almost invariably described how one became a member, their duties while a member, and (usually) what one had to do to withdraw.[14]

That social unity was a primary goal of this tendency toward formal and constitutional organization is somewhat underscored by one element of the constitutions of women's societies that was common only in women's associations: a prohibition on gossip or other malicious talk. The Ladies' Benevolent Society of Roxbury, Massachusetts, explicitly forbade speaking "directly or indirectly against the character of any." The Female Moral Reform Convention that met in New York in 1839 included an article in their constitution to the effect that "no member shall circulate reports derogatory to the reputation of another unless the interests of society require the exposure. Any member, who shall intentionally and deliberately violate either of the above articles, shall forfeit the right of membership, unless the Society has satisfactory evidence of her amendment." Here, one of two things was true: social pressures that might keep gossip in check were seen to be insufficient; or the women simply wanted to make a point publicly that they would not tolerate such actions within the society. Either way, they sought a constitutional solution.[15]

In some instances, women who were participating in a society appeared to be firmly committed to procedural regularity and detailed record-keeping, not because they believed it helped them accomplish any particular goal, but because they simply believed that that was how voluntary societies worked. Take the Ladies Sewing Society of St. James Church Ledyard in Connecticut, which drew up its constitution and began meeting to do things such as knit socks in 1838. The book of minutes for that club was meticulously kept—though a great number of the entries simply read "not one of the ladies attended," or "not one attended." Just as the organizers and joiners of fundraising societies might decide that their charitable societies "would become more extensive and permanent, were its benefactions collected in some way, more systematic and uniform," as a group of New Hampshire women decided in 1812, so too did those who joined many other kinds of voluntary groups come to see formal organization, constitutionalism, and detailed record keeping as important to the effectiveness of their endeavors. And, sometimes, it appears that they acted in procedurally detailed ways because it just seemed that that was how it was done.[16]

The early history of American agricultural societies, an associational realm dominated by men, is equally revealing of a growing attentiveness to detailed procedure and full transparency regarding associational obligations. The earliest agricultural societies, which were formed on both sides of the Atlantic in the eighteenth century, generally included only the better sort. Made up of men of social standing and eclectic intellectual pursuits, these associations were quite unlike the more democratic agricultural societies that were formed by the 1810s and 1820s, many of them based on Elkanah Watson's "Berkshire model," which emphasized agricultural fairs and competitions and which he never tired of promoting. Before that time, agricultural societies continued to be, essentially, learned societies with a horticultural focus, and there was no real need to experiment with new or distinct organizational practices.[17]

This did not mean, though, that post-Revolutionary Americans such as Thomas Jefferson were not contemplating the potential benefits that formal organizations aimed at agricultural inquiries might provide to the nation and its people. When a fellow member of the American Philosophical Society, Isaac Briggs, took "the liberty of addressing its President" on his idea of forming state-level agricultural societies that would then convene "annually at the City of Washington," Jefferson responded positively, if not overly enthusiastically. He liked the idea, but as he often did he confessed that he, personally, might not be able "to do much towards the promotion of such an establishment." He knew that "private contributions" alone would not do much good; nor would direct governmental action, which "would probably end in providing resources for a few idle favorites & in little further."[18]

But even if Jefferson's priorities in 1801 did not include the formation of agricultural societies, he could see how they would aid in the dissemination of knowledge and innovation, and he would revisit the idea a decade later. After a conversation with Wilson Cary Nicholas in early 1811, Jefferson "ruminated" on the "proposition for the establishment of an Agricultural Society" while traveling to his property at Poplar Forest. Tellingly, Jefferson's rumination took the form of a constitution. As soon as he arrived, he "committed to writing" a proposed constitution for an Albemarle County agricultural society, one that would formalize and thereby extend the "considerable benefits" that farmers received "from an intercommunication of their plans & processes in husbandry." It was a plan, essentially, to extend and improve the value of conversation, to share useful knowledge that would provide "greater means of subsistence & of happiness to our fellow citizens." Point by point, then, in a manuscript draft that Jefferson sent to Nicholas, he detailed his proposals for what this agricultural society would look like: how often they would meet (the first Mondays of January, April, July, and October); how members would be admitted (a majority vote); and how one would resign his membership ("those who, for two whole years, shall not have attended any stated meeting, shall, ipso facto, cease to be members"). There was a high degree of formality in Jefferson's proposal, not surprising from one who in the 1780s had been clear on the point that friendship and actual association were very different things.[19]

It was a detailed plan, but it was also one that Jefferson specifically declared ought to weigh very lightly on its own members. "That we may not deter from becoming members those practical & observing husbandmen whose knoledge is the most valuable"—and he believed that that knowledge was most likely to be found among "that portion of citizens with whom the observance of economy is necessary"—Jefferson's proposed constitution clearly specified that "all duties of every kind should be performed gratis." Ever the advocate of local innovation, though, Jefferson was "far from presuming to offer this organisation, and these principles of constitution as compleat and worthy the implicit adoption of other societies." Others should do as they think best, and all of the various local societies would make "parts of one great whole."[20]

An Albemarle Agricultural Society was formed six years later, with Jefferson named to a five-member committee to prepare rules and regulations. The committee's proposed rules for the society, after being considerably modified in debate among the broader membership, were adopted in October 1817, but they were not much similar to Jefferson's rules from 1811. They bore signs of many of the same concerns that had interested the former president, but the organizational framework was more detailed, including, as was becoming common in agricultural societies, the establishment of three classes of members: charter, ordinary, and honorary. For his part, Jefferson never attended a meeting of the society or wrote a paper for it, though he remained interested in its proceedings, forwarding letters to it throughout the last years of his life.[21]

The importance of finding an organizational means to address the tensions between individual members' interests and the success and stability of the larger association were apparent both in Jefferson's 1811 musings and in the constitutional plan actually adopted several years later. According to a report of the society in November 1817, there was good reason to believe that "the former attempts to establish Agricultural Societies in this State have failed, not from a deficiency of useful subjects to occupy their attention, or valuable information, for which they form the proper channel of communication for the public, but from the indefinite nature of the duties devolving upon their members." Jefferson had worried about this problem, too, though his solution was to stipulate constitutionally that no one be asked to do very much at all. The drafters of the report, which included Jefferson's son-in-law, Thomas Mann Randolph, instead planned to "guard against this course of failure by giving immediate employment, and stipulated duties to every member of the Society." In both cases, though, the priority was a clear, direct, and procedural stipulation that members would know exactly what they would be expected to do. They would know from their moment of joining the furthest extent of their obligations. The organizational solutions embraced by Americans in the early republic reveal a growing awareness that well-defined obligations—and full disclosure of those duties—was essential.[22]

Learning How to Join Together

As American men and women began to join together more often, more regularly, and for more diverse purposes, rules mattered. And this happened because, deliberately and self-consciously, Americans decided that they would. The motive forces that underlay this growing tendency toward procedural regularity were, of course, diverse, including such basic concerns as what would allow the organization to recruit new members, as the Albemarle Agricultural Society had concluded. That fact alone might explain the common emphasis on detailed descriptions of the rights and duties of members, but there was another crucial factor at work here: the organizers of post-Revolutionary organizations were not acting in a void, were not forced each time to come up anew with a list of officers, an order of proceedings, or even basic turns of phrase for their constitutions and bylaws. The technology of how to associate spread widely and effectively in the early decades of the nineteenth century, and patterns established quite early in the emergence of widespread voluntarism would have lasting influence and would be repeated and re-publicized in ways that shaped the practice and experience of associational membership.

The most resonant influences for American men and women as they contemplated forming or joining a voluntary organization were English and colonial precedents or groups organized elsewhere by their contemporaries, and these were often known only by their constitutions or rules, which were published (separately or in annual reports), printed in a newspaper, or shared by request. In that context, there were two natural consequences. First, there would be a remarkable number of similarities in the forms and practices of voluntary associations. Second, contemporaries would come to share the belief that to associate together was essentially to form, adopt, and obey rules.

British models were especially important both for women's groups and for the largest antebellum organizations, such as the American Bible Society. British evangelical women had already begun organizing charitable and benevolent societies in the late eighteenth century, and their experiences were important influences on women on the western shores of the Atlantic, often quite directly. For example, Isabella Graham, a Scottish immigrant, based her 1796 formation of a Society for the Relief of Poor Widows and Small Children in New York on a London model. Some years later, Quaker activism in Britain was also deliberately utilized as a model for female-led organizations in the United States. For instance, Benjamin Lundy in his *Genius of Universal Emancipation* reproduced the writing of British Quaker activist Elizabeth Heyrick and even reprinted a British sample constitution for the formation of female antislavery societies. This mock-up, which was drawn from "the Proceedings at the organization of Ladies' Anti-Slavery Societies in England" and which the paper called a "formula," included such details as how to create committees, hold meetings, and even fill-in-the-blank forms for important organizational matters.[23]

This influence, in some cases, also extended into more inward-looking associations, such as literary societies. This is especially apparent in women's groups, such as Charlestown's Social Circle in 1845, which looked as much like a typical benevolent society as it did a reading club when they elected as their lead officer a "first directress," a term most commonly used in fundraising and socially active societies. And "annual reports issued by the literary societies at Townsend, Charlestown, and New-Hampton seminaries," according to historian Mary Kelley, "read as if they were records of a voluntary association dedicated to benevolence." There were very formal goings-on in each of these literary societies, and it appeared that women who had learned how to form and run an association in charitable groups had carried that knowledge with them into other groups with quite different goals. One cannot help but be struck by the parallels across truly diverse forms of collective organization.[24]

The British influence on American associational practices had, of course, begun in the colonial era and was as much a product of the fact that some of the most prominent colonial joiners had had firsthand experience in British societies—Benjamin Franklin and the Tuesday Club's Alexander Hamilton, for example—as it was of printed bylaws and published accounts in newspapers and magazines. But it was in the formation of the first large-scale organizations comprising smaller, "auxiliary" societies that the British influence was felt most keenly in the new republic. And once imported into the young United States, the auxiliary system was tremendously common and influential. The initial forays in that direction were self-conscious emulations of British models, however, in which a large, national organization had a formal relationship with smaller organizations, many of which were formed before the national group took shape and only later affiliated. These relationships were spelled out in the official documents of both the local and the national societies.[25]

The American Bible Society, formed on the template of the British and Foreign Bible Society, is a clear example. William Jay, who wrote an influential pamphlet called *A Memoir on the Subject of a General Bible Society for the United States of America*, offered up a model constitution for the new society. It was, he said, "with a few immaterial alterations, required chiefly by local peculiarities," a "literal copy of that of the British and Foreign Bible Society," which meant the Americans could benefit from "the experience of the last 12 years." According the latest historian of the American Bible Society, Jay's *Memoir* "cited British practice to justify every aspect" of the constitution he presented.[26]

Scholars have begun to reveal some of the ways that voluntary association spread as a technology, through the medium of print, by correspondence among societies, and by personal experiences of people who participated in multiple associations or who traveled to new communities. Johann Neem's work on the spread of civil society in Massachusetts showed that the spread of the knowledge of *how* to associate—through printed forms and constitutions, through emulation of a nearby town, and through the geographical mobility of the members and organizers themselves—was essential to the forming of new groups. In the first third of the nineteenth century, methods of creating organized, more-or-less permanent societies that would persist even if the original members were replaced by new ones found their way from community to community. It was so common—and from a twenty-first-century perspective it might appear to be so obvious—a way of spurring the spread of a cause that it is easy to miss the transformative potential of the spread of this kind of knowledge. It meant that people near and far were being educated in the methods of association, methods that were attached conceptually and practically with philanthropic goals that post-Revolutionary American men and women were keen to embrace.[27]

Agricultural societies, formed in nearly every corner of the young United States in the early decades of the nineteenth century, provide a good example of this technological dissemination. Elkanah Watson circulated promotional materials for his model of agricultural societies, including such widely distributed publications as his *History of the Rise, Progress, and Existing State of the Berkshire Agricultural Society*, the title of which included, most importantly, *Practical Directions for Societies Forming in North-Carolina, on the Berkshire Model.* Addressed to North Carolina but printed in New York (and clearly aiming at a wider audience), Watson drafted "Directions for forming Agricultural Societies" that spelled out a "plan of a constitution," with the most important organizational principles spelled out in the preamble: "We, the subscribers, do hereby, associate ourselves as an Agricultural Society, in the county of ________ and we do severally promise to pay the Treasurer of said society, one dollar [upon joining and every July 4th] as long as we shall severally continue members of the same—and we do hereby adopt, and establish the following CONSTITUTION." The essentials of membership were detailed in the first few dozen words of their society's founding document.[28]

At the most basic levels, it is hard to find a voluntary organization in the early American republic—regardless of gender, race, class, or in many ways even its basic purposes—that looked much unlike every other group. The fundamentals of organization, entrance, and exit would, with very few exceptions, appear and reappear across the organizing documents and bylaws of countless groups, male and female.

More than is commonly known, men and women joined associations alongside one another. When women formed organizations of their own, they had templates and examples to follow, not merely from the experiences of their relatives or from published constitutions and bylaws, but from their own participation in associations that included both men and women. Also, the direct and hands-on influence of ministers in the formation of women's groups helped to create a common set of shared practices. Ministers—particularly in New England communities and in the larger urban centers farther south—actively encouraged their female parishioners to form societies to raise funds, usually by tiny, individual donations or by sewing, for the support of good Christian efforts such as charity, missions, or the spread of the word of God by tract or Bible. For example, the Reverend

William White argued in Philadelphia in 1814 that, even though there was a society for the distribution of Bibles that women could contribute to at any time, women there still ought to form their own, to combine their own efforts in support of a Scripture that stood as "the charter of the female sex against degradation and oppression." While the role of ministers in women's societies would decline over time (a sewing circle called the Worcester Female Association, for instance, had a minister open its meetings by prayer for about a decade after its organization in the 1820s, but female officers assumed that role by 1836) clerical leadership was essential to many women's associations in the early part of the nineteenth century.[29]

All told, there was little regional distinction in the methods and practices of organizing associations, according to historians of women's societies. Though Southern female associations began to form later than those in the Northern cities—for example, the first Southern female benevolent society was founded in Savannah in 1801, a home for orphan girls, the entire board of managers being female—historian Anne Scott has noted that "the records of southern women's benevolent societies are indistinguishable from other parts of the country, and it is clear that societies existed even in small communities." There is, she found, "no case to be made for southern exceptionalism from the voluntary association evidence." Mary Kelley disagrees only to a degree in her discussion of women's literary clubs, finding Southern women more likely than Northerners to continue "to display their learning and accomplishments in heterosocial gatherings of friends and family," but there was far more similarity than difference. And the same can be said for women's societies in the newly settled West: Cleveland and Cincinnati each saw the founding of several women's benevolent societies much like those found in the East in their first decades of settlement.[30]

Large-scale organizations that included auxiliaries were essential to carrying these influences far and wide. American men and women were fully conscious, often, that their participation was a part of a larger, incredibly ambitious, and quite organized social venture to transform their world. Often, a person could contribute by becoming a member of a large, national organization. More often, he or she could form or join a smaller group that was an integral part of the larger cause. In Philadelphia in 1814, women meeting with their minister at Sansom Street Baptist Church had "the impression . . . that the interests of the cause of Christ will be more effectually promoted by the formation of several Female Mission Societies in this city, than by one general Society, as that might become too unweildy [sic] for convenience," and they thus proceeded to "organize themselves into a Missionary Society." The auxiliary model was useful both as a means to spread the knowledge of how to associate and to give ordinary American men and women a sense simultaneously of being part of a larger cause and of running a local, tightly knit organization. In some cases, auxiliaries encompassed other auxiliaries! The Female Bible Society of Philadelphia was both a part of the national organization but also had eight subordinate groups in 1829, each of which included a one- or two-paragraph summary in the parent organization's annual report.[31]

Perhaps most crucial in the spread of the technology of association was the widespread use of model constitutions and rules in pamphlet form or in newspapers. For instance, the Branch Bible Society of Lebanon, Connecticut, had pasted into the first two pages of its minute book a smallish paper booklet entitled "Constitution for a Branch Bible Society." The widespread publication of constitutions, too, allowed people to emulate previously organized groups as they formed their own. This was common for men's, women's, and mixed associational efforts. The New Haven Mutual Aid Association, for instance, even included their point of reference in the preamble to their own constitution, noting that "we have formed ourselves into a society, (for the general plan of which we are indebted to a similar one now existing in Newark, N.J.) and we, the subscribers, do adopt the following Constitution and By-Laws for our government."[32]

To organize, it would seem, was to publish a constitution, making it almost unavoidable that new organizers and joiners had a fairly set notion of what an association ought to look like. The *Concord Observer*, for example, noted with regret in 1819 that it had not published as many accounts of the organization of new women's societies as were available to readers in other states and regions, where people had frequent descriptions of "the establishment of Female Societies for various charitable purposes" in "the Reports of other Societies, the monthly magazines, the weekly and even daily newspapers." The editor of the *Observer* apologized that that had not been the case in New Hampshire: "Their operations being more local" and women "naturally retiring from publick view, their numerous acts of benevolence have in a measure been private, or known to but a few." But the *Observer* sought to rectify this in a manner that says a great deal about how Americans were conceiving of voluntary association by 1819. The paper did not want to publish accounts of their charitable deeds, or the addresses and speeches given to and by them: the editors opted to do nothing more than "to collect copies of the Constitutions of Female Societies and Associations . . . for publication in the Observer." Agricultural societies, too, would often use periodicals to publicize their modes of organization, to "afford useful hints to those who are about forming similar Societies," as the *Genesee Farmer and Gardener's Journal* noted in 1837 when it published, in full, the bylaws of the Chautaque County Agricultural Society. That was the public face of American associationalism in the early nineteenth century—not promotional materials, mission statements, or even detailed accounts of the need for a particular charitable effort, but constitutions comprising articles and bylaws. It was, in a sense, a matter of marketing.[33]

When William Jay offered his advice for how to get the American Bible Society off the ground successfully, he pointed out to the readers of the pamphlet he anonymously published in 1816 that the national society might well get congressional approval for a franking privilege. The key benefit of that free postage, he believed, would be that it would "greatly facilitate another mode of obtaining patronage, and it would be, to make the constitution of the society, with the names of its members and officers as extensively known as possible." The constitution itself—though of course coupled with the impressive list of notable leaders and members—would be indispensable to making the society publicly visible and widely supported. "Not a Hamlet in the country," Jay wrote, "should be without the constitution of the society and suitable addresses explaining the nature and importance of the Institution." And, in many states, probably very few were.[34]

In sum, organizers of many of the voluntary associations beginning to populate the American social landscape very much wanted others to emulate their example. And because the mode of organization that the organizers seized upon was to draw up, approve, and abide by a set of written articles of agreement, most commonly called a constitution—and then to *publicize* these agreed-upon rules—these documents came to be seen as the starting point, the basis, the very foundation of collective action.

Inevitably, the rule-bound ways of joining together and the ways that this technology would spread became streamlined over time. When a group of women formed the Wapping Female Missionary Society in Connecticut in 1839, they penned six very short articles that declared the name, purposes, officers, and requirements of membership, all filling less than a page at the front of their book of minutes. It was an extraordinarily simple document, but it covered every essential; and it did so in a way that accomplished everything that they set out to do. By 1845, they had 53 female and 34 male members, collecting $34.38 to support foreign missionary efforts. It was not a grand endeavor to transform the world, but a small and contributory effort for a good cause. And the organizers knew how to accomplish their purposes effectively, efficiently, and with the benefit of decades of experience by men and women around the nation.[35]

It should be noted, too, that for some groups there were other incentives for publicizing the precise constitutional framework of a voluntary association. The insistence on publicity came less as a matter of marketing than as a way of countering concerns about impropriety and, especially, secrecy. Many people involved in voluntary groups had fervent hopes that they could, by publishing their foundational documents, prevent nonmembers from feeling wary or skeptical of what the group was up to. So, for instance, the New Hampshire Juvenile Fraternity published their entire constitution in the form of a broadside in their efforts "to avoid all unfavorable impressions, which commonly arise against the societies of youth, to explain the grounds on which we have been induced to introduce an institution of this kind, and to give the community an opportunity to judge of its merits." And so they chose to publish the constitution they had just adopted and "by which we have agreed to abide in all our transactions in the society."[36]

All of these factors helped to make the practices of association and the experience of membership take on the appearance, to people both within and outside a given club or society, of being essentially rule-bound, law-minded relationships. And that mindset about joining together had consequences. A common practice and emphasis on rules, laws, and constitutions would give shape to a great many of the social relationships formed by American men and women in the early republic. It was not their moral characters or their mutual affection but their own and self-made constitutions that would bind them together.

Everyday Constitutionalism in the Early American Republic

In 1787, men from twelve of the thirteen United States gathered in Philadelphia to draw up a constitution to reorganize the federal relationship among the states. That same year, two privately organized societies that had been formed in the colonial period—the Humane Society of Philadelphia, organized in 1770 to teach resuscitation techniques, and the Pennsylvania Society for Promoting the Abolition of Slavery, founded in 1775—also did something they had not done before. They too drew up constitutions. They had had rules before, without doubt. And there are examples of private, voluntary associations as early as the 1760s in British America drawing up what they called "constitutions." But the term "constitution" and the common forms that we associate with it (a preamble describing the purposes of organization, articles laying out precisely who held what power, exact description of the modes of amendment, which almost invariably called for a supermajority, and, most importantly, a clear distinction between it and "ordinary" rules or law) were an artifact of the post-Revolutionary era.[37]

Many voting American citizens—and many of those excluded from American political life—found in these privately organized, constitutionally formed societies opportunities to develop and practice skills of constitutional government. The practical, everyday experience of membership in these societies not only gave ordinary Americans opportunities to think and to act "constitutionally," but it did something more. Americans by these experiences came to believe that constitutions were not intended simply to allocate power, but to protect the rights of minorities, even minorities of one, against anything resembling arbitrary authority. And many people were beginning to see these constitutionally organized bodies as something that ought to be effectively encompassed and superintended by the legal and political institutions of their republican governments. But here it is important to address a newfound tendency that emerged in the everyday practices of countless voluntary associations, not merely to follow rules, but to distinguish between those rules and the fundamental laws that were inscribed in their founding documents. It was not only the drafters of state and federal constitutions in the post-Revolutionary era that were self-consciously drawing up rules for their rules.

The women of Norwich, Connecticut, were perfectly aware of this. Not only did they read together the federal Constitution as they prepared to draw up their own, but the constitution they crafted reveals, in 1800, a sophisticated understanding of what a constitution should do. On April 2nd, after some debate, the members of the Ladies' Literary Society had drafted their own constitution, which was "read and then passed almost unanimously." The constitution included descriptions of how, where, when, and by whom each meeting was to be conducted (it would rotate among members' homes, in the order that their names were inscribed on the constitution). And the articles reveal the women's familiarity with the idea of a constitution as serving the purpose, not just of describing the rules, but of constraining even a majority of the members from later changing them at will. They had drawn up a constitution that included four articles that, it was explicitly stated, could never be amended: each meeting would begin with a Bible reading; each week, members would make a "contribution" of four pence (more could be given voluntarily but could never be required); "any member dishonoring herself, or the society, shall be expeld, if the opinion of two thirds of the house concur"; and "no religious, or political disputes shall ever enter this Society." Any other article could be amended with the consent of two-thirds of the members. But, like Ulysses tied to the mast, the women set aside four issues and made sure they could never change their minds.[38]

Constitutions were virtually ubiquitous, in both men's and women's associations. For example, a minister's wife who proposed the formation of the Female Cent Society in Concord, New Hampshire, at about the same time also took the lead in the establishment of the Female Charitable Society in Concord. Elizabeth McFarland proposed the group "at a social gathering in the Christmas season of 1811," and what she did next was almost universal. She drew up a constitution. Then, with the help of two other women of the community she gathered the signed support of seventeen others in a matter of days, all of whom agreed "to form ourselves into a Society for charitable purposes—to choose such officers, and establish such rules and regulations, as may be necessary for effecting the design of such an institution." In countless other clubs, the founding members also met once and appointed a committee to draw up a constitution, which was then approved at their second meeting. The founders of the Providence Association of Mechanics and Manufacturers, for example, appointed a committee "to draft the form of a Constitution," which, when reported, was "read, and debated Paragraph by Paragraph, and amended" before it was unanimously agreed to.[39]

For many of the women who formed voluntary associations in the early American republic, it is likely that their constitution writing and their focus on rule-bound ways of collaborating was on some level an implied criticism of all those other, disorderly ways of gathering together. Mary Kelley's groundbreaking work on female participation in civil society is helpful in understanding why this was the case. Denied access to a public sphere of organized politics, women were free and were even encouraged to participate in civil society, and they chose to do so in remarkably rule-bound ways. Women in the first part of the nineteenth century, in addition to their participation in heterosocial salons and conversation circles, began forming literary societies where, according to Kelley, they "practiced the art of persuasive self-presentation, and instructed themselves in the values and vocabularies of civil society." One of those vocabularies, as the women of Norwich declared directly and repeatedly, was simply making use of constitutional articles and formal rules. Thus, while historians such as Rosemarie Zagarri have given some attention to the subject matter of the conversations of the Ladies' Literary Society for evidence of their engagement with early national politics, the way in which they organized themselves in order to have those discussions may be more telling and more significant than what they chose to talk about.[40]

Drafting private constitutions and abiding by detailed rules were acts that, in themselves, offered a political statement about post-Revolutionary society. Early national politics became increasingly institutionalized and formally organized, especially after 1800. Political fraternities, partisan volunteer militias, and other modes of civic expression were organized and orchestrated, in what was often a deliberate attempt to replace the Revolutionary-era mob and bring a new kind of order to the celebratory political culture of parades, processions, and patriotic gatherings of the 1790s. Women's societies, too, made a similar transformation at just about the same historical moment. How people chose to organize their societies—their constitutional manner of organization, their frequent and regular elections, and, most obviously, their expressed beliefs that it was vitally important, not merely to make rules, but to abide by them—were, in many cases, embraced as a means to an end (for example, to smooth over differences), but sometimes that choice was an end in itself.[41]

In both men and women's associations, founding members tended to take the task of drafting a constitution seriously, even if the members had joined many clubs before and clearly knew the ropes. In 1814, a committee was appointed at the first meeting of the Literary and Philosophical Society of New York, a gathering of some of the leading men in the nation's largest city, "to prepare a Constitution for the Association and report thereon to the next meeting." When the committee, the next week, "reported a *code of fundamental Rules* for the Society" the full membership "proceeded to consider the Constitution by paragraphs, which being amended in several respects was agreed to." And it was a serious, full, and complete document. A few months later, a committee that had been appointed to create a set of bylaws reported that "so full & judicious" are the constitutional rules "that there seems to be little room left for bye laws." The constitution covered "all matters which usually form the subject of bye laws with literary & philosophical societies in other places." Still—and this again speaks to the importance of rules in the private associations of the early United States—the committee proposed four bylaws, and the full membership added another five the very next week.[42]

Joiners were coming to learn that a formal declaration of allegiance to the constitution of a private society was important, for it was that document that bound all the members together. Typically, this took the form of a signature or, less often, of an oath. The significance of the act of formally acceding to the text of the constitution, though, was reiterated countless times in the early republic. In 1800 a group of men in Schenectady, New York, for example, founded a "Social Society" as a mutual benefit society, a form of voluntary association that is the focus of chapter 6. And no one who had been elected as a member of this society was entitled to anything at all—that is, he could receive no benefits should he fall on hard times—unless he had physically subscribed to the constitution. Such a requirement was commonplace long before the explosion in the numbers of voluntary groups in the post-Revolutionary era. The founding document, or the Institution, of the veterans' Society of the Cincinnati, for example, had included such a policy.[43]

The subscription requirement, though, would take on new meaning in an early national era in which the importance of founding documents would only grow. It became an element so universally accepted and expected in the joining of a voluntary association that there are numerous instances of people who assumed they had never become members of an association because they had never signed a constitution. In the wake of a corruption scandal, one Charles Walker wrote to the American Institute of the City of New York, an organization created to hold agricultural and mechanical fairs and to encourage invention, to clarify that he did not consider himself—or wish to be considered—a member of the association, despite having paid three dollars in dues. He had believed that that money would entitle him to "free admission to the exhibitions for one year," but he "did not intend thereby to become a permanent member, and signed no articles or constitutions." Lacking that step of actually subscribing to a constitution, even a man who had paid dues had every reason to believe he was not, in actuality, a member of the association.[44]

And the consequences of thinking constitutionally about voluntary affiliation were remarkable. The Social Society in Schenectady at the turn of the nineteenth century was not breaking new ground when it required a considered, supermajoritarian vote for any amendment, but the emphasis is striking in a post-Revolutionary age that had come to embrace the constitution as the essence of political, or civil, society. Members of the Social Society were resolved that there could be no amendment to the constitution without its having been read at "four stated meetings, before the question is taken," and then only "by consent of three-fourths of the members present; nor shall the vote be taken, until they are duly summoned to attend for that purpose." Such founding documents were not to be tampered with lightly.

If nothing else, the documents themselves were often treated as being tremendously important as symbols of unity. One society in New York, the Christian Benevolent Society, which included notable members such as Francis Wayland, not only planned to have five hundred copies of its constitution printed but also agreed that not one but "two copies of the Constitution should be framed and hung in some part of the Meeting House at the discretion of the Committee." Another group, the Young Men's Association for Mutual Improvement, which formed in Norwich some three decades after the Ladies' Literary Society had first convened in the same Connecticut town, revealed their respect for their founding document in a slightly different way. Their constitutional rules included something like a membership agreement, and two weeks after voting to print copies of the constitution and bylaws the men further resolved "that on the signing of the Constitution by any person or persons that the president read the obligation in solemn and impressive manner." Constitutions, then, and the regime of rule-bound collective action that they represented were not merely a public face of American associations. They also served a special role in the interior lives of these groups, at times having almost totemic value. From both outside the group and from within, the constitution was, as Judge Peter Oxenbridge Thacher would describe it in the context of a journeymen's bootmaking society, the thing that gave the association its very existence. It was, he said, "the soul of the club." Few Americans would have disagreed.[45]

The emphasis on constitutions as the promotional tool of American associations that was examined in the previous section, then, was something more than a savvy marketing tactic. It was related, too, to the attachment felt by members of these associations to their own founding texts. Judging by their words and their actions, many men and women who joined and organized voluntary associations of various kinds in the early years of the new American republic appear to have known that it was in the written constitutions, which defined the ins and outs of members' duties and rights, that they could and should put their trust. We see them, too, keeping detailed records, extolling the importance of rules, and taking steps to ensure that any new members followed those procedures and practices established by the old.[46]

The emerging American practices of association, in both men's and women's associations, was integrally related to the broader culture of legality that has been described in the preceding chapters: the idea that human relationships not only were governed by law, but they *ought* to be governed by law—or, where law as an instrument of state authority did not present itself, by legalistic ways of members' conceiving of their own organization. A constitution would be and should be abided by, operating as a sort of fundamental law from which all associational power derived.

That way of thinking about voluntarism and about private authority became nearly universal for reasons that go far beyond a mirror effect of the larger political order. The organizational forms that were agreed upon tended to suit potential joiners' preferences for associations that would not forever be making unpredictable demands on them. Individual obligations would ordinarily be well defined at the outset, would not be perpetual, and would take a form that joiners would recognize as having parallels with other forms of collective action. Therefore, a vocabulary for dealing with potential or actual conflicts was already at hand. All of these factors would combine to make America's associational world one of formalities and of written, detailed organizational practices that were to be always in accordance with the founding document, or constitution, of the society.

Much of this, then, helps to explain something that had so mystified Alexis de Tocqueville. He was confused about the Americans' strange urge to sign formal documents, create structured organizations, and take pledges before one another—all to do something as simple as not drink alcohol. He recorded his train of thought in book 2 of *Democracy in America*. He initially could not make sense of the strange practice of remarkably widespread formal organization for such a private choice as "drinking water by their own firesides" rather than something a bit stronger. But he came to conclude in his chapter "Of the Use That Americans Make of Association in Civil Life" that "these hundred thousand Americans, frightened by the progress of drunkenness around them, wanted to support sobriety by their patronage. They were acting in just the same way as some great territorial magnate who dresses very plainly to encourage a contempt of luxury among simple citizens." Initially, this European traveler who was enthralled but mystified by the ubiquity of formal associations in the United States, even for things concerning such a private choice as what to drink—things that, by all appearances, had no need for founding documents, bylaws, or regularly appointed meetings—fell back on an Old World explanation. People wanted to be *seen* organizing for this or that purpose, and so they did it in the most formal and public manner they could think of. He included that explanation in his finished analysis of *Democracy in America*.[47]

But Tocqueville also touched on some of the ways that many men and women in the United States had simply come to conclude that formal organization was a particularly useful way to accomplish something great or small or just to spend time together. And many more men and women, it would seem, followed patterns set by others. The sheer malleability and transportability of these methods of association, though, were even more important than Tocqueville recognized. The spread of the technology of association produced an associational world of shared practices. In this post-Revolutionary moment, membership tended to be impermanent: annual memberships, not perpetual ones, were the rule, something particularly apparent in the backlash against Freemasonry of the 1820s and 1830s that will be described in chapter 6. Moreover, most of these joiners and organizers were defining membership in ways that were respectful of the joiner: associations would define at the outset what was expected and what one would gain by joining ranks. People would join together, would write constitutions and bylaws, and generally speaking would abide by them in a manner that showed knowledge, sophistication, and even reverence for the idea of constitutional self-government.

It became a commonplace by the 1830s that, as a writer in the *New England Magazine* noted, "certainly, no age has been so remarkable for societies for the improvement of mankind as the present." Tocqueville, of course, would rightly note that people in the United States were not simply forming associations for the grand idea of the improvement of mankind. Rather, they were creating formal organizations for every conceivable purpose. And those who joined together in the young United States increasingly tended to do so in law-minded ways. Members of temperance organizations and antislavery societies would soon be binding themselves together in a way that diverged from the more attenuated commitments of most of the associational world of the early United States, as we will see in the concluding chapter, but the prevailing pattern was clear: an emphasis on constitutional self-government and on the importance, not merely of uniting their efforts, but of abiding by all of those rules by which they had chosen to do so.[48]

Across these same decades, between roughly 1800 and 1830, participation by ordinary Americans in private, profit-seeking corporations would become astonishingly widespread. And in ways that have nearly become lost in historical accounts of origins of corporate law and the theories of the firm, Americans would draw parallels between participation in private corporations and other forms of voluntary association. And that conceptual joining of the two had consequences, both for the future of corporate law and for post-Revolutionary American ideas about voluntarism writ large.

FIVE

When Shareholders Were Members: The Business Corporation as Voluntary Association

It began with Independence. Where there had been very few chartered business corporations in the colonial era, the number of charters of incorporation for profit-seeking enterprises skyrocketed after the Revolution, with some 317 issued by state legislatures between 1780 and 1801. And it did not stop there. Over the course of the following three decades, from approximately 1800 until 1830, people in the youthful American republic found themselves increasingly surrounded by private, profit-seeking business corporations, numbering in the thousands. Over those same decades, the modern law of corporations was pieced together, built on eighteenth-century common law roots but expanded and developed in utterly transformative ways.

Over those same decades, Americans understood the private business corporation in a way that they would not by midcentury. They saw these organizations, essentially, as one form of association that belonged in a larger family of collective, voluntary groups. The corporate form was embraced primarily as a way of bringing together, not dollars, but people. In the twenty-first century, one would be hard put to come up with any similarities at all between a major business corporation such as, say, IBM and a more quintessentially "voluntary" organization, like a gardening club or a Bible-study group. For an American observer in the early nineteenth century it was the parallels, not the differences, that would have first come to mind. And the perceived resemblance between the private business corporation and other forms of collective endeavor was fundamental to the historical evolution of both. Explaining how and why will require no small amount of immersion into the laws and practices of corporate membership—what we would now call shareholding—in the early nineteenth century.[1]

There is a lot to look at. The first three decades of the nineteenth century, to put the matter more bluntly than historians usually do, were without exception the most transformative years in the history of American corporate law. For today's economists and legal theorists, there are four features that serve to divide the corporation from other forms of business organization: perpetual succession; limited liability for investors; free transferability of shares; and centralized leadership. In 1800, only the first of these, barring statutory provision otherwise, was true of American business corporations. By 1832, when the first American treatise on corporate law was published, all four were the common standard. The legal history of the American corporation in this early national era is not one of continuity or even gradual change, but of rapid and profound innovation.[2]

And these transformations occurred over the same period that more and more Americans were embracing the voluntary association as a means to accomplish so many diverse ends. The laws and practices of corporate shareholding reflected that larger cultural context. Only in the 1830s did a profit-centered perspective effectively occlude those aspects of early national business corporations that made them more akin to than different from other kinds of membership associations. Before that time, however, some of the most important issues that are involved in any voluntary endeavor were confronted in the experience and the legal adjudications surrounding early American corporate development: first, what constituted an enforceable agreement to bear the shared burdens of the group, and what did not; and, second and more important still, what rights did a minority have to keep the majority from trampling on their interests, or from transforming their common enterprise into something fundamentally different. And just as the St. Patrick Benevolent Society had learned when it was forced by court order to readmit a man they had expelled by near-unanimous vote, the early American republic was a place where tensions between majority rule and minority rights would be taken seriously and would often be channeled into legal forums to find resolution.

Limiting the Duties of Corporate Membership

Between 1804 and 1807, as many in the United States were still talking about the purchase of millions of acres of western land for the republic, William Marshall was trying to hold on to a small plot in Boston. After Marshall repeatedly had failed to pay assessments for the costs of road improvements he allegedly owed to the Front Street Corporation, Jabez Ellis purchased the land at public auction and sued to eject him. In the legal dispute that followed, Marshall had a strong argument for why he owed the corporation exactly nothing: he had never been associated with the corporation in any way, and he had explicitly refused on multiple occasions to join this project for street repairs. But in an age when corporations were relatively rare and were invariably thought to be created to serve some public purpose, the best lawyers in Massachusetts divided on whether a man who clearly stood to benefit from the corporation's endeavors could be compelled to share its costs as a member, to be unwillingly added to the body corporate.[3]

The new chief justice, Theophilus Parsons, was forced to sit out, having argued on behalf of Ellis and the Front Street Corporation before his appointment. Justice Joseph Parker heard the arguments, including the Attorney General James Sullivan's laments over the "seriously alarming" increase in the numbers of corporations. "A spirit is growing in the country which will be productive of the most mischievous effects," he pleaded on behalf of Marshall, and "to an independent and enlightened judiciary can we alone look" to check that spirit. The attorney general's argument hit its mark, as Parker concluded that Marshall could not be "press[ed] into the service" of a corporation that had been created by "a private act, obtained at the solicitation of individuals, for their emolument or advantage." He had been offered membership and had refused—and there was nothing more to say. He could stay on his land.[4]

In many ways, the modern law of private corporations begins with *Ellis v. Marshall*. When Rhode Island lawyers Joseph Kinnicut Angell and Samuel Ames published the very first American corporate law treatise, in 1832, they cited *Ellis v. Marshall* only once, but they took its central points—that a private corporation's existence begins with an offer by the state and a willing acceptance by private individuals; and whereas public corporations could require membership, a private corporation could not—as facts that were both too obvious to be belabored and absolutely essential to understanding the nature of the corporation. What was uncertain in 1807 was made out to be the only rational way to think about corporate existence in 1832, a fact that owed much to the bright line between public, or municipal, corporations (which could claim involuntary jurisdiction over citizens) and private ones that was drawn by the Supreme Court in 1819 in *Dartmouth College v. Woodward*. Story's concurring opinion in *Dartmouth*—which also cited *Ellis*—was especially clear that the nature of the capital foundation of a corporation, not its intended purposes or its modes of action, determined whether it was public or private. Story applied the idea broadly, mentioning banks, insurance companies, canals, and turnpikes in his opinion. Angell and Ames embraced his view.[5]

Ellis v. Marshall did much more than aid in drawing a legal distinction between public and private, however. The matter immediately at hand had more to do with the authority of a corporation over an unwilling participant, a question of governing authority that resonated especially clearly in the immediate post-Revolutionary era, than it did with the broader political economy of corporate activity in the Commonwealth of Massachusetts. Indeed, it was indicative of a broader shift in how Americans conceptualized membership in private, corporate groups: only consent, expressed clearly and affirmatively, could make Marshall a member.

It may strike the modern ear as odd to refer to "members" of business corporations, a concept we usually denote with the words "shareholder" or "stockholder," or even "investor." But the term was heavily used, and was used interchangeably with the others, through much of the nineteenth century. Both the survival of the term *member* and the concomitant "rights and privileges" emphasized by corporate lawyers provide an opportunity to explore this transitional period in the evolution of the corporate form by taking the language and conceptual categories of the early nineteenth century seriously rather than shying away from them or, what is still more common, too hastily translating them into the lingo of modern theories of the firm.

Only a very few Americans, even those of some means, had ever owned a share of corporate stock before the last years of the eighteenth century. The number of colonial corporations was miniscule, partially owing to difficulties in using the joint-stock form in the aftermath of the South Sea Bubble of 1720 and still more to the simplicity of economic conditions in British America. Where there were eighteenth-century economic enterprises resembling modern corporations, in their freely transferable shares and in their concentration of power in an elected few, they were usually unchartered associations comprising mostly elite investors, often for the purpose of land speculation. In Middlesex County, outside Boston, corporate securities first appear in probate records in 1778 and became a much more common asset recorded there in the second and third decades of the nineteenth century. There were simply very few stock-issuing corporations before their numbers swelled in the post-Revolutionary years, even including unincorporated investment opportunities, and when someone sought to borrow capital or to join a business venture it usually took place in a face-to-face transaction.[6]

Over the next few decades in the United States, however, the numbers of private corporations exploded. And participating members in these corporations grew in number as well, reaching into lower strata of society to include Americans of no great means. Such people owned more shares in more corporations than has been recognized until recently; some thirty-eight thousand individuals purchased stock in Pennsylvania banks, turnpikes, and toll bridges between 1800 and 1821, for instance. When forty-two banks were chartered in that state in the year 1814, according to groundbreaking work by historian John Majewski, their stock was subscribed for by twenty thousand individuals, including many "carpenters, grocers, draymen, hatters, innkeepers, and tailors," who made up a full fifth of his sample of the investors of five Philadelphia banks. Angell and Ames noted that "there is scarcely an individual of respectable character in our community, who is not a member of, at least, one private company or society which is incorporated." The corporation was becoming a fixture in this associated American social order, and many Americans had a share.[7]

Tumultuous changes of the first third of the nineteenth century took the American corporation on a path sharply divergent from incorporated firms in England. Over the course of about five hundred pages, for instance, Joseph Angell and Samuel Ames in their 1832 treatise took occasion repeatedly to emphasize the fact that, even as English courts had begun to relax their constraints on corporate action (the Bubble Act had been repealed in 1825) and to modernize the corporate form, American courts and legislatures had far outpaced them. As an organizing theme, their focus on divergence was quite typical of American treatises in the post-Revolutionary era. For a treatise on corporations, it was inescapable. Theirs was the first major work on corporations to be written on either side of the Atlantic since Stewart Kyd's 1793 publication in London, which dealt primarily with municipal bodies. A distinction between public and private, in fact, was not a part of Kyd's work or, indeed, of the thinking of any British or American lawyer in 1793. And so much had changed in legal thinking regarding the corporation in the intervening decades, particularly in the United States.[8]

This was most noticeably true in the matters of corporate contracts, implied promises, and torts, but there was profound change, too, in conceptions of individual corporate membership. Looking at the questions of entrance, exit, participation, and authority, it becomes clear that, even as the corporate form was evolved in the early nineteenth century, many elements of what it was for an individual to be a part of a profit-seeking corporation did not stray too far from their eighteenth-century roots. But there were moves toward the better definition and delimitation of members' rights and responsibilities.

For profit-seeking institutions or, to use terms more commonly used in the early nineteenth century, "in monied institutions, such as banks, insurance, canal, and turnpike companies," it was the possession of a share of stock that signified membership: as a Pennsylvania court noted in 1836, "the mere owning of shares in the stock of the corporation, gives a right of voting; and a stockholder ceases to be a member by a transfer of stock." Those who held shares were the voting constituency of record. They held all authority not elsewhere ascribed in the charter. This possession need not be literal: even where the incorporating act declared that certificates shall issue to the stockholders, "still, for want of them, the stock holders would not lose their rights," determined the Supreme Court of Massachusetts in 1819. Certificates were, however, the usual practice. Unlike a bill of exchange or a promissory note, which was and is inseparable in a legal sense from the obligation represented, the stock certificate was and is only evidence of a person's title to shares in a company. Never an absolutely necessary element to establish corporate membership, it was rather only a convenient one.[9]

Legal challenges, and then legal change, resulted from the fact that the corporate share was rarely acquired by someone paying its full value, which meant that, very frequently, the corporation would come seeking more. The fully paid share—stock as it is commonly understood today—was a rarity in the early nineteenth century. A share representing, say, one hundred dollars' investment in a company was, in most cases, purchased with little at the outset, with the understanding that subsequent calls could be made up to the par value of the stock. In some instances, most consequentially in the Massachusetts turnpikes organized under the Turnpike Act of 1805, there was no stated value at all for the stock. Corporators simply subscribed for a certain number of shares, paid their assessments (which could amount to hundreds of dollars), and, they hoped, collected dividends proportionally.[10]

Although that method of financing corporations in the early republic led inevitably to legal challenges concerning delinquents, the method predominated through the early nineteenth century. Organizing a corporate business venture routinely followed the same course. When people sought to create a turnpike to connect Albany with Schenectady, New York, they met in November 1801 at the City Tavern in Albany and drew up articles of association, dividing the endeavor into two thousand shares, each worth fifty dollars. Those wishing to participate had a day to pay one dollar for each share subscribed, in order to defray initial organizing expenses. Once a charter of incorporation had been received from the legislature, they agreed, another four dollars would become due. As people subscribed, most commonly for about ten shares (some for as few as two, some as many as nineteen), elections were held and a committee selected to "to prepare a Bill to be presented to the Legislature at their next meeting for the purpose of

Incorporating the Turnpike Company," according to the company records. It was quickly passed. They soon prepared a circular seal for the corporation—"a stream of water with a bridge of three Arches across it, a road with Lombardy Poplar trees along the borders"—and the officers began the routine matters of turnpike construction (and the not-so-routine matter of purchasing ten thousand poplar trees). Over the next two years, the company assessed the members for five dollars, then six more, then another eight dollars in two installments. The year 1804 saw another fifteen dollars assessed, in three five-dollar installments, and the company secretary for the first time recorded discussions over what to do with delinquents. Not until 1805 (five more assessments, three dollars each) was the turnpike ready to open for business and toll collectors hired. In early 1806, a few weeks after another four dollars was assessed on each share, at last the first cash dividend was ready to distribute: 3 percent, or a dollar and half on each share, and additional dividends followed over the next seventeen years recorded in the company's ledger.[11]

Turnpike stock was especially widely held and yet famously unprofitable. Unlike English turnpikes, which were most commonly unincorporated trusts, those in the new United States were usually incorporated, although proprietorships did exist. It was quite often a desire for local economic development, especially efforts to ensure that one's town was not bypassed by a turnpike promoted by a rival community, that led people to purchase turnpike stock. Profits were not necessarily expected. And yet, rather than throw good money after bad, there were times when many individuals in the early nineteenth century would attempt to evade calls to pay, and thus legislators, in their general acts and charters, and judges and juries, when called upon by the companies to collect debts, had to come to terms with the exact nature of the turnpike shareholders' liabilities.[12]

The first time in reported case law that a court was asked to step in and compel a man to pay his assessments, it was money owed to the Union Turnpike in New York in 1803. People were uncertain how to treat the obligations owed by Thomas Jenkins upon his "promise to pay to the president, directors, and company of the Union Turnpike Road the sum of $25 for every share of stock in the said company, set opposite to our respective names, in such manner and proportion, and at such time and place, as shall be determined by the said president, directors, and company." Jenkins had not made the initial ten-dollar payment, and he had not responded to subsequent calls for five dollars. The Supreme Court of New York held Jenkins liable to pay, but the state's highest court, the Court for the Correction of

Errors, found differently. Two opinions were written, and each based a decision in favor of Jenkins on different grounds. Importantly, Senator Ezra L'Hommedieu held that the statute creating the turnpike had allowed the corporation only one remedy if Jenkins did not make his ten-dollar down payment: "The plaintiff, by this, forfeited his right to be a stockholder." The corporation could not compel Jenkins to pay anything at all, but they could sell off his shares. Feeling their way toward a principle that could be applied consistently (this was, L'Hommedieu observed, the first case of its kind), the judges could rest their decision against the Union Turnpike both on the incompleteness of Jenkins's subscription and on the fairness of the outcome, for just as the turnpike could not claim money from Jenkins, he could have made no claim on them: "In case the stock had rose, the company would have been under no obligation to have considered him as a stockholder."[13]

The reversed Supreme Court in New York, however, found two opportunities in the next decade to assert its stronger stand on the liability of subscribers to corporate stock for subsequent assessment, and these decisions would not be overturned. Corporate organizers had found a way to ensure that subscribers to stock could be held legally accountable for not paying their share. And they found it by ignoring corporate membership and its attendant rights and duties and, instead, insisting each member sign a separate contract to pay assessments. The crucial point in both cases—and, as Angell and Ames observed in 1832, in virtually all subsequent case law on stock subscription—was an explicit contractual commitment on the part of the stockholder, in a shape either analogous to or exactly in the form of a promissory note. In other words, both corporate organizers and the courts found that the best solution to the problem was to sever the concept of corporate membership from financial liability: those who joined would sign separate, express agreements that they would pay assessments. The courts of New York looked to those specific acts of personal obligation, finding there a way to authorize corporations' pursuit of delinquents in actions of assumpsit, or debt. In *Goshen and Minisink Turnpike Company v. Hurtin* in 1812, and in *Dutchess Manu-Factory Company v. Davis* five years later, the Supreme Court decided in favor of the corporation, "on the principle that the maker of a promissory note is liable." In the Empire State, there was an increasing emphasis that individual liability for corporate assessments was to be founded only on precise and express consent. And Massachusetts had done the same. When Aaron Willard signed an agreement to pay all assessments made by the Worcester Turnpike Corporation, and when Elijah Pope did so with the Taunton and South Boston Turnpike, Massachusetts courts decided that their personal promises to pay assessments gave each corporation another remedy, aside from the one provided by statute (the sale of delinquents' shares), should Willard or Pope fail to pay up.[14]

That point, though some states took a slightly looser view, became fixed in the American law of business corporations in 1809 when the Andover and Medford Turnpike brought an action against Abraham Gould, who had signed no such paper and who had only agreed, with many others, "to take in said road the number of shares set against our names, and be proprietors therein." Theophilus Parsons, while noting that assessment was not a corporate power at common law, had no problem with inferring the company's power to tax its members from an act that had not expressly given it. There was for Parsons no other way to read a statute that authorized the turnpikes (the Andover and Medford was formed under the general Turnpike Act of 1805) to sell the shares of delinquents. What he and the court would not countenance was inferring any other remedy than that spelled out by law; they could not pursue the money in a debt case and could instead only sell Gould's shares. The practical reasonableness of their position was apparent to them: although people approached to join a turnpike company "may not be able to judge of the probable expenses or profits," they are more likely to "join the association" as long as "they know, that if the assessments become grievous, they may abandon the enterprise by suffering their shares to be sold." As readers of the first American corporate law treatise would see, it was there established that "the members of a corporation are not liable to be proceeded against personally in a suit by the company for a legal assessment, unless there has been *a promise* on their part to pay it."[15]

While a United States senator, John Quincy Adams subscribed for ten shares in the New Bedford and Bridgewater Turnpike Corporation in Massachusetts, a company divided into five hundred shares. When assessments for his part of the company's $50,000 in expenses were made, his one-fiftieth portion came to $1,000. His refusal to pay, and the fact that the highest court in Massachusetts would not compel him to do so, reveals the relatively brief but consequential evolution by which membership in the stock-issuing business corporation moved toward limited and well-defined obligations. Adams's lawyer could insist, citing the *Andover* case, that the subscription paper he and others had signed "was not intended to give a remedy by action, but simply to make each subscriber a member of the corporation, subject to the legal duties belonging to him in that character." Those duties did include paying money to the company, in a sense, for if a shareholder failed to pay up, the corporation could terminate every one of that person's connections with the corporation. But the company could not compel payment, could not pursue the members' assets in court, because membership in the corporation was not enough to make a person financially liable. In order for an action to lie to collect, a second step was necessary, in which the member explicitly promised to pay assessments.[16]

It is certainly true, though some scholars have elided the point, that Massachusetts was less willing to allow actions to enforce assessments than were other states, such as Maryland, Connecticut, and Kentucky, where courts would not say that a statutory provision allowing the sale of a delinquent's shares necessarily prevented the corporation from also taking the shareholder to court to compel payment. Virginia took a direct route to resolve any confusion and passed a statute describing the steps a turnpike company must follow against a delinquent shareholder: the stock would be sold at auction, and if the sale price fell short of the amount the corporation was seeking, a motion would lie against the original shareholder to make up the difference. But a crucial point is that, in spite of the nuances of jurisdictional difference across the states of the early American republic, jurists and legal commentators perceived and promoted what they saw as a prevailing trend in the developing American law of corporations. As Angell and Ames described it, a person's liability "is, indeed, to be measured by the extent of his express engagement."[17]

One other development in the early United States underscores the point: the self-imposed obligations to pay lawful assessments were, with very rare exceptions, not applied to anyone who subsequently acquired the same shares. A person who held stock as a transferee had acquired the ordinary rights and obligations of membership in a private business corporation, as those rights and duties were understood, but that did *not* include a promise to pay assessments that was enforceable by legal action, even if such a promise had been made by the original stockholder. Thus it was that William Sansom, who owned twenty shares in the Delaware and Schuylkill Canal, was held liable for assessments on those five shares that he had purchased at the company's founding, having made an explicit promise to pay assessments up to two hundred dollars on each. Those fifteen shares he had acquired from others, the Pennsylvania Supreme Court decided, "stand on a different ground." Because there was only one remedy described in the statute, their forfeiture and sale, there was no express commitment on which to base a legal action for recovery. This was not the "Solomonic decision" that historian Andrew Schocket has described, in which the court "split the difference." It was a holding fully consistent with the nature of personal obligation and corporate commitments in post-Revolutionary America. For

Sansom in 1803, it was indeed the "express promise" that made all the difference. There had come to be an unwillingness to infer much of anything about personal obligations to private associations. The outcome of William Marshall's encounter with the Front Street Corporation, and the successful resistance of many others to claims against their property to support corporations that they had indeed become a part of, reveal a growing certainty that express consent—precise, direct, and personal—was required to create the sorts of interpersonal bonds that made association effective.[18]

Consider, too, what is probably the most famous development in early American corporate law: the birth of limited liability. In a much-studied divergence of American common law from its English heritage, American courts in the late 1810s began to decide that, in the absence of explicit charter or statutory provisions to the contrary, stockholders were not liable for corporate debts beyond their original investment. That is, in cases in which a shareholder had paid the full value of the shares they owned, they could not be pursued by the creditors of a bankrupt corporation for debts it had accumulated. It was a marked divergence from what had been a centuries-old common law standard for corporate bodies, one that has been explained in terms of economic imperatives (encouraging investment and lowering monitoring costs; accommodating the free transferability of shares) and as a more or less deliberate attempt to democratize the American marketplace by keeping entry into business markets open to all.[19]

Set next to developments in the law and the practice of corporate membership as a species of post-Revolutionary association, limited liability takes on a new hue. Clearly, even contemporaries were acutely aware that limiting shareholders' liability was productive: as Angell and Ames noted, "by such means persons are induced to hazard a certain amount of property for the purposes of trade and public improvement, who would abstain from doing so, were not their liability thus limited." But before courts had even made the turn toward a full articulation that, under the common law, corporate stockholders' liability was limited to their initial investment, people had begun to assume it. Early national conceptions of voluntary membership allowed little room for any other view. In the 1819 Massachusetts case generally cited as the turning point, *Spear v. Grant*, the judge noted that "public opinion" about individual responsibility clearly presupposed that corporate members were not liable. Although the fact that the court cited public opinion in a legal decision shocked the court reporter, the content of that public perception should come as no surprise. The broader practice of formal, voluntary association in the early American republic had by 1819 led people to assume that the obligations of voluntary membership, including participation in a profit-seeking corporation, would and should always be bounded and strictly delimited.[20]

Minority Rights and Majority Rule in the Early American Corporation

Ensuring that corporations could never impose membership on the unwilling was an important step, one taken in the first decade of the nineteenth century. Limiting that member's corporate responsibilities to those things he or she had explicitly taken on was another, and this too was fairly well established by the end of the second decade. A third challenge that confronted those who wished to create lasting and effective corporate institutions was confronted repeatedly, but never solved, over those same years: the question of minority rights in an incorporated association governed by majority rule. It is possible that a majority-ruled corporation can operate perfectly legitimately, acting democratically and acting within the bounds of its charter, and still trample on the interests of a minority in its ranks. By majority vote, they could transform the corporation into something fundamentally new, something different from what the individual members had consented to join in the first place. Could they still make legally enforceable demands of their members? What exactly would happen when a corporate majority sought and received an amendment to their charter by the legislature, one that took the corporation in an entirely new direction against the wishes of some members, or even against the wishes of one member? These were challenges that were faced in all kinds of collective endeavors in the early republic but that, judging from the number of legal contests, were felt especially keenly in two kinds of corporations: the mutual fire insurance cooperative and the turnpike corporation.

In an unincorporated association, no change was theoretically permissible without unreserved and unanimous consent—that is, unless the group did what nearly every group would do in the early republic, which was to make a special agreement at the outset defining a mode of amendment, or how exactly a majority may bind the minority. "But such a power must be clearly shown and established," as the complainant in one such case successfully argued before New York's chancellor, James Kent, in 1820, "for it is in derogation of the legal and natural rights of the minority." The authority of courts of equity to prevent by injunction, upon the application of a minority no matter how small, an unincorporated joint-stock company or partnership from using their funds to pursue a business outside the scope of their articles of agreement was well settled in the early nineteenth century. This was true both in legal and equitable terms as well as in how the broader culture understood collective agreements. As the influential social theorist Francis Wayland noted in the 1830s, once people join together, specifying both their objects and the means to be employed in pursuit of them, nothing can "properly be changed in any essential particular, without unanimous consent," making such an association, "from the nature of the case, essentially unalterable." As James Willard Hurst has noted, the extension of such a principle to corporate law, requiring unanimous consent to amend the charter, would have hindered the sort of "flexible continuity" that was essential in the increasingly unpredictable marketplace of the nineteenth-century United States.[21]

And yet there was also a clear and perceptible danger that allowing a private corporation to make *fundamental* changes in its purposes, its organization, or even its modes of operation might leave a minority shareholder legally bound to participate in something to which he or she had never assented. It was, in a sense, a reprise of the *Ellis v. Marshall* principle, in which William Marshall's refusal to consent to membership in the Front Street Corporation was held to have freed him from liability for corporate assessments. He could not be compelled to join. An express and direct agreement to become a member had become the starting point for American conceptions of belonging in increasingly varied kinds of group life in the post-Revolutionary decades. What remained to be seen in the years to follow, then, were the ways that such assent would be restrictive on the association. If it was, if a corporation could not make substantive changes in its goals or the means it would use to achieve them without facing legal challenge from members and, especially, without losing any legal claim to their pledged support, then profit-seeking organizations would face a formidable obstacle every time circumstances in the marketplace changed. There was a tension, then, between flexible continuity and the nature of personal obligation.

This was confronted, repeatedly, in a mutual fire insurance company in Virginia that exists still today. It was an organization that may have had more historically important members than any group outside of Congress. Men such as Thomas Jefferson, James Madison, John Marshall, St. George Tucker, Bushrod Washington—all were participants in the Mutual Assurance Society, a Virginia association formed and incorporated in 1794 to allow people statewide to share the costs of losses by fire. These men, and thousands of other men and women who joined and insured their property, confronted the inevitable tensions between individual autonomy and collective action. Throughout its early existence, Virginia's mutual fire insurance company had faced challenges as it sought to unite "two opposite & conflicting Sentiments, Benevolence & Self interest," as one of its leading officers, Samuel Greenhow, once described matters to Jefferson. And his organization often found self-interest the stronger inclination among its members. Legal institutions were an important arena in these moments of conflict, a fact true across the nation as mutual insurance associations sprang up in the years following the American Revolution. From a single colonial predecessor, the Philadelphia Contributionship, these cooperative societies, organizations "congenial with the warmest feelings of benevolence and the most enlightened maxims of civil society," had appeared in states north and south by 1800. To many, they served as perfect exemplars of the promise of the Revolutionary age, associations aiming not at profit but at mutual support, combining cooperation with self-improvement and security. As George Hay noted after a devastating fire in Norfolk, where many members of the Mutual Assurance Society of Virginia had insured their homes and businesses, such losses "would have been ruinous to the individuals who were the immediate sufferers, but being now divided among many, they are scarcely felt."[22]

Fire insurance of any kind was a relatively recent development, its earliest beginnings a consequence of the Great Fire of 1666 in London. There were a few attempts in colonial British America to establish some sort of insurance association, such as the Friendly Society in Charleston, South Carolina, begun in 1735. It closed only a few years later, when a fire destroyed two-thirds of the city and exhausted the group's funds. An immensely more successful venture, one that still offers insurance today, was founded in 1752 as the Philadelphia Contributionship for the Insurance of Houses from Loss by Fire. Incorporated in 1768, this organization was the first successful effort at a mutual insurance company in North America. It was modeled after a London association known as the Amicable Contributionship (or the Hand-in-Hand, owing to the design of its emblem and fire-mark), founded in 1696. Benjamin Franklin proposed the idea in 1750 to the thirty volunteer firefighters of the Union Fire Company, and they pooled their money in equal shares (half to be jointly invested) to provide compensation to any participant who lost his property to fire. The men soon shared their idea with other fire companies, drew up a deed of settlement (a constitution), and some thirty years later, having issued about two thousand policies in Philadelphia and undergone formal incorporation in 1768, remained the only fire insurance company in what had become the United States.[23]

Mutual fire insurance shared many features with more established sorts of indemnity such as marine insurance, especially its use of policies in which the property to be insured was intimately described and the terms of coverage were closely spelled out. The difference was in the internal organization of the association. The Contributionship announced in the first article of its deed of settlement that all persons insuring in the society "shall be taken and deemed as members of the same." Those policy holders were and are the entire company. The capital on which it was founded was not held by stockholders or partners but consisted solely of the premiums and fees paid by the insured. Those members elected officers to direct the affairs of the association, met annually to determine matters of particular importance, and were liable, often up to a previously determined limit, for further assessment in case of substantial losses. Thus, all members held an interest in determining who or what was to be insured.[24]

In the years between the Revolution and the turn of the century, mutual insurance cooperatives were formed in Massachusetts, New York, Maryland, Pennsylvania, Connecticut, Rhode Island, and Virginia. The most ambitious of these, the Mutual Assurance Society against Fire on Buildings of the State of Virginia, was brought into existence in 1794, the same year that witnessed the founding of the nation's first joint-stock fire insurance company. Unlike the other mutuals, this company endeavored to offer insurance, not to a single city, but to the entire commonwealth of Virginia. Also unlike all of the others, it was in its internal organization not a direct derivative of the Philadelphia Contributionship. It was instead based on a unique plan proposed by Prussian immigrant William Ast and modified by some of the leading lawyers of Virginia. From the start, however, participants in this effort at mutual insurance found themselves confronted with unanticipated burdens and a scheme of organization that one judge later insisted had "not been carried into effect, with an ability proportioned to the benevolence of the design."[25]

William Frederick Ast was in his late twenties when he began work to establish a mutual insurance association in his adopted state of Virginia, his ambition untempered by age. He unsuccessfully petitioned Congress that same year to establish mutual insurance companies "in every State in the Union, under the authority of the Government of the United States," proposing that "an additional tie or attachment would thereby be created from every individual whose property may be insured, to the Government." He was never shy about declaring the brilliance of his plan, and he sought from the legislature of Virginia "for his trouble in suggesting forming & publishing the said Plan and that he should be allowed annually out of the funds of the Society one Cent for each hundred Dollars that may be insured," which he received when the plan was adopted on December 22, 1794.[26]

Ast and those with whom he worked to establish the Virginia association remained hopeful through the first several years of the company that more and more citizens would join "one of the best institutions existing, the only object of which is to succour the unfortunate," thereby making the risks and potential costs miniscule for each individual member. In an 1802 publication that listed all the members of the Mutual Assurance Society and the amounts of their insured property—a list that, impressively enough, began with men such as Jefferson, Madison, and Marshall—Ast noted that if only "the people would all insure, there is no question but one premium would insure the houses situated in the country forever: therefore every one ought to lend an assisting hand to make it general."[27]

Virginia's General Assembly took great pains to ensure that the Mutual Assurance Society would be on a solid footing before it began collecting premiums, the initial payments that served as the consideration for the insurance contract and that, in these early mutuals, initially constituted the entirety of the capital stock. They required subscriptions for three million dollars' worth of property before the company could begin operation. Amazingly, this took only a year, and on December 17, 1795, a number of men gathered at the Capitol to formally organize the Mutual Assurance Society. At their request, an explanatory act was passed by the legislature a few days later to allow voting by proxy at the general meetings and to define a quorum as comprising delegates representing either a majority of individual subscribers or a majority of property subscribed. That made it possible for about twenty men, two representing only themselves but others representing dozens (two proxies, Thomas Newton of Norfolk and Ludwell Lee of Alexandria, cast more than 40 percent of the 450 votes), to approve a constitution, elect officers, and set Ast's experiment in motion.[28]

William Foushee, mayor of Richmond and already president of the James River Company, was elected to the presidency, and Ast served as principal agent. There were some elaborate provisions to serve as internal checks on potential abuse, including the purchase of a lockbox to hold the funds and stocks of the company that required four keys to open, each to be held by a different officer, as well as requirements that policies and payments be signed and countersigned by various officers. The internal bureaucracy, however, was largely irrelevant to the crises that the Mutual Assurance Society would face in the first decade of the nineteenth century. Those challenges would, instead, center on precisely how the enforceable rights and duties of members were defined and whether those rights and duties could be reworked entirely if a majority of the members so chose.[29]

The central duty each member had, of course, was payment of assessments when losses by fire caused a shortfall and a fellow member awaited compensation. Ideally, a mutual company would have the premiums set high enough to handle the costs of any losses, and funds could be invested and even periodically disbursed back to members as a dividend. But the Mutual Assurance Society instead found itself constantly running short in the wake of catastrophic losses, and the company placed a lien on the insured property as security for each member's required payments. Concerns that the Mutual Assurance Society might have been granted too much power over its own members were made especially acute when the Mutual Assurance Society sought and received authorization from the General Assembly to collect its monies by motion, a proceeding requiring only ten days' notice, rather than the usual form of a suit. As Henry St. George Tucker lectured his students in the 1830s, these sorts of "summary proceedings" have from time to time been "authorised by our laws in certain cases, deemed by the legislature particularly entitled to speedy redress," such as a client's claim against an attorney for money collected. But Thomas Jefferson, for one, instantly saw the potential problems of combining the power to proceed by motion with a lien on the full value of the property insured. When the vice president had gathered with several of his neighbors at Monticello to appraise his property, a step required to join the Mutual Assurance Society, he learned of this new statute. "We all declared off from that moment," he wrote to Ast. "We considered our houses as in ten times greater danger from such an establishment than from fire."[30]

In part, it was Jefferson's belief that the law should never work to the prejudice of the independent yeoman farmer that lay at the root of his worry. "To make a farmer's house liable to be sold at short hand when his resources come in but once a year," he wrote, "is to lay it under much greater danger than that of fire." Jefferson was also hesitant, throughout his life, to afford voluntary associations of any kind much real authority. It is not surprising, then, that Jefferson was initially uncomfortable with the powers that the mutual insurance association held over those who joined. It also appears that Jefferson may have been the first person to notice that the Mutual Assurance Society lacked any provision for unhappy members simply to withdraw, an omission rectified at the next general meeting.[31]

Ast responded to Jefferson's worries in a letter several months later. He noted the salutary changes that had been passed allowing members to depart, but he defended the summary proceeding. "To succour the unfortunate ought, I think go before any other payment upon this ground the fathers of the Land have granted a Summary process—as each has in general only a small Sum to pay, which is proportioned to his Riches, they can easily raise it: if they are willing—the Law is only for the hard hearted the tender heart will always come forward of his own accord in so laudable a Cause." He also made sure to correct Jefferson's beliefs on the low risks of fire in the countryside, referring to the lack of water and firefighting equipment and reminding him of "a certain Class of people who undergo often a severe discipline" on Virginia's plantations and occasionally "do a great deal of Mischief." Jefferson soon joined and insured Monticello.[32]

In the first years of the nineteenth century, the Mutual Assurance Society of Virginia would frustrate so many of its own members that it almost ceased to exist. As Henry St. George Tucker noted in 1831, William Ast's plan for the Mutual Assurance Society, "though he may have had the aid of some professional gentleman to throw it into the form of a law," had always remained "clumsy" and "drawn without system, and expressed, in many instances, in terms wholly inappropriate." Unsurprisingly, Tucker added, "it has been a fruitful source of litigation." The internal records and the reported and unreported case law regarding the Mutual Assurance Society show in detail how the administrators of the mutual were forced to make frequent changes in the organization of the institution. Most were small, though not inconsequential: as one member noted, "the alterations in the Constitution and Laws are so frequent, that it requires Vigilance to know when you are insured and when not."[33]

Ten years after its formation, the Mutual Assurance Society faced its greatest crisis when it adopted a plan put forward by Edmund Randolph that substantially (and, to some, very unequally) adjusted the demands it would make of some of its members at the expense of others. Such redefinitions of the burdens of membership would never have been necessary but for the horrific fires in Norfolk and Fredericksburg in 1799 and again in Norfolk in 1804. The heat of those conflagrations found its way into Virginia's courtrooms as an immature jurisprudence of fire insurance crossed paths with a developing law of membership. In 1805, a majority of the members of the Mutual Assurance Society approved Randolph's plan, a change so drastic that some denied they could possibly be held fast to commitments they had made to what, they believed, had once been a much different institution.[34]

When fire swept across the east side of Norfolk on February 23, 1804, a section of the city that had been consumed not five years before, the losses were estimated to approach $100,000. Many in the Mutual Assurance

Society believed that, as in 1799, a new assessment would have to be levied against the members. The members (or their proxies) were convened in Richmond in July to discuss whether a "quota" ought to be called for, and Littleton Waller Tazewell led the opposition, moving successfully that the losses should be paid by selling off tens of thousands of dollars invested in bank stocks. More important was the decision to appoint a committee, headed by Edmund Randolph, the former attorney general of the United States who had retired to private practice, to reexamine the whole nature of the institution and to explore ways to make more equitable the risks run by members outside of urban centers such as Norfolk. Including the recent losses in the February fire, members in cities had received ten times as much in insurance payments while paying, on average, only one-eighth more into the coffers than rural insurers. The inequities were apparent, and men such as Tazewell—whose Williamsburg holdings were classed in 1802 as "country" property—were tired of paying for city losses. Either the city members would begin to pay their share of the costs, it was becoming apparent in the fall of 1804, or the Mutual Assurance Society might just split in two, or falter entirely.[35]

In August and September, the newspaper editor Thomas Ritchie ran a three-part series in his influential *Richmond Enquirer*, examining both the philosophy and the recent, practical history of Virginia's mutual insurance company. Unlike a stock insurance company, in which an insurer makes annual payments to maintain indemnity, Ritchie noted, a mutual company was, by design, imprecise as to the demands it would make of its insuring members. If no losses occurred, the total assessment would be zero; if losses were exceptionally high in a given year, so too would be the sums assessed. Ritchie stressed, too, a second key difference between the mutual and the stock insurance company: in stock companies such as London's powerful Phoenix Insurance Company, the insurer had nothing whatever to do with the affairs of the company (other than his annual payments). In a mutual, however, an insuring member may monitor the use of his money "through all the mazes of its employment and disbursement." With the other members, "he gives his vote, and exerts his influence in the government of its concerns." As in any democratic body, a person had control over the course of the institution "as far as his zeal, or capacities may give him an ascendant power over the other members of the institution."[36]

Upon that foundation—in essence, an explanation of how both ballots and persuasion factored in to republican government—Ritchie built his case for a division of the funds of the town members from those of the country insurers, "though they may be conducted in the same office." He already knew of the policy proposals Randolph's committee would make at the next general meeting, to be held in January 1805. The third part of Ritchie's series, which included six tables and made public the ninefold disparity between town and country payouts, hinted that a measure separating the funds between urban and rural members would "most probably be adopted" and made a strong case for the justice of that division. But the issue was extraordinarily controversial. According to Francis Corbin, one Fredericksburg printer took the underhanded tactic of not printing notice of the resolution authorizing Randolph to investigate division because, Corbin alleged, he and others in "the *Towns* do not relish the idea of a separation."[37]

Randolph's proposal to divide the Mutual Assurance Society into two funds was approved by the members and given effect by a legislative act amending the constitution of the society, in January 1805. Nothing but such a drastic step, Randolph had declared, "can do away the objection, 'That, when a house takes fire in a town, a hundred or more houses may be destroyed, but when a house takes fire in the country, only one is consumed.' " Simply charging town members proportionally more was not a viable option (they could not realistically be expected to pay *nine times* more), but, even if separation was the most palatable remedy available, the officers of the society expected dissent. In the first issue of the *Enquirer* following the legislature's amendment of the charter, the founder and principal agent, William Ast, wrote a letter to inform members that, first, the change made it likely that the country members may never be assessed again and, second, that town members would still do better to be a part of this society than to insure anywhere else. "Where will they do better?" he wrote. "The annual premiums abroad are very expensive, and the security of a few individuals precarious."[38]

Indeed, the precariousness of the mutually insuring few was precisely the point. Many in the towns felt they were being left to shift for themselves, especially when, within a few weeks of the division, the town members—and only the town members—were assessed for an amount equal to half of the original premium (on the reasonable premise that neither fund should be allowed to fall below 1 percent of the value of the insured property). Opposition to the division and levy in Richmond, wrote the president of the society, Alexander McRae, was marked by "great zeal and assiduity," though he hoped that the dissidents could be persuaded. Others, such as Chief Justice John Marshall's brother, Charles, made special requests to ensure that their homes were not classed as urban property. In the short term, however, the dissent was kept relatively contained. Randolph's committee had proposed a loosening of the exit requirements, reducing the requisite notice from three months to six weeks, which was adopted, and some members, including the chief justice himself, simply left. At the annual meetings of 1806 and 1807, there was no great turnover in office, no business of interest. But James Currie, a medical doctor working in Richmond since long before the Revolution, resisted the attempt of the Mutual Assurance Society to collect a quota from him, questioning not only the justice of the society's recent decisions but its very authority to make them.[39]

Currie's was a bold and significant legal challenge, one that centered on the rights of individual members to resist the demands of the majority in democratically structured and formally chartered bodies. And he promptly lost. He was determined by the Petersburg district court to owe the society a substantial sum approaching three hundred dollars. This was a mere prelude, though, to the main event, which began after Currie's death in 1807. His administrators carried the matter to the newly organized Supreme Court of Appeals, claiming that the substantial changes made in 1805 were so far beyond the scope of the original charter, under which Currie had joined, that they could not be binding on the original members. No quota called for under the new town-country organization of the society could be collected from those who had joined before the divide. Further, even if the general meeting of the corporation, largely comprising proxies, had voted to put additional burdens on the town members, "those men were delegated to give effect to the charter as it was," and "a power to support is not a power to destroy." Currie had joined with certain expectations, including one that the insurance—the burdens and the benefits—were to be mutual and predictable, not periodically and unevenly reapportioned.[40]

The legal arguments for each side were lengthy, articulate, and very public. Not only the final opinions of justices Spencer Roane and William Fleming but the lawyers' positions were printed in full as soon as the ruling from Virginia's high court came down. The lawyers for the Mutual Assurance Society asserted that Currie was doubly bound to pay, both by the will of the majority of the association and by the sovereign decision of the legislature to amend the institutional arrangement. They knew that a decision against the society might cripple it, for more than half of the insured property lay in towns and was assessed for a quota in 1805. By 1809, moreover, an entirely new system of annual fees had been adopted—calling for one-seventh of a premium from country members and one-fifth from town members—and was potentially threatened.[41]

Virginia's high court upheld the lower court's decision and ruled against Currie, but scholars to this day have focused on exactly half of the court's rationale—and, as it happens, the less significant half. Attention to the emerging attitudes and legal principles regarding voluntary membership helps to show that this case has wrongly been seen through the prism of a case that came a decade later, *Dartmouth College v. Woodward*. Justice Spencer Roane did opine that one legislature cannot bind subsequent assemblies and that necessarily a corporate charter could be repealed or altered, a "doctrine" supposedly overturned in 1819 in *Dartmouth College*.[42]

Both Roane and William Fleming, who concurred, devoted the bulk of their opinions to something else entirely. Because the association itself had requested the change, the whole issue of legislative supremacy was obiter dicta, something Fleming made clear when he asserted that "as to the right of the assembly to alter the charter, I will just observe that it was, in effect, done by the society itself." The crux of the dispute was the authority of a majority to bind Currie, a dissenting minority (of one) who claimed that his duties had been defined in one way under the original charter and could not be fundamentally changed and continue to be legally enforceable. Indeed, Roane even took the position that the court could no doubt intervene to protect members such as Currie in certain, more extreme cases, but that it need not here. "It is enough for our purpose that the act of 1805, if it has produced any injustice at all to any class of subscribers, has fallen short of that crying grade of injustice, which alone can disarm the act of its operation," he wrote. "The society itself, at least, considered this, on the contrary, as a measure essential to the equalization of the risks; and, in this respect, I see no cause to differ from them in opinion."[43]

Crucial to Roane's opinion was the fact that, as he put it, any members who disagreed with the opinion of the majority are "protected from oppression, by the liberty guaranteed them, of withdrawing from the institution altogether." Though the Mutual Assurance Society had begun operation without any prescribed mode of withdrawal for its members, a provision for exit was established in 1800, six years after the society was formed, allowing for egress at the end of each calendar year with proper notice. Four years later, an amendment to the charter, legislatively approved, allowed for withdrawal upon six weeks' notice. Five years after that, in 1809, the society allowed immediate withdrawal upon receipt of written notice. The letter (following a form) of one exiting member in 1821 evokes the thrust of this trend, in which Abijah Janney did "hereby require you to issue to me such a discharge as to the said assurance as I am by the Rules and Regulations of the Society aforesaid, entitled to demand and receive." Though, as Michael Walzer has suggested, the idea that any aggrieved person can just leave is a legal philosophy that can be used to excuse a whole host of internal corporate evils, the right of withdrawal was a key way in which Currie's liberty was imagined throughout the legal battle over his rights as a member.[44]

Correlative to Currie's rights were his corporate duties, including the obligation to abide by the will of the majority (within limits, Roane was sure to note) or to get out of the way. John Marshall had made the central point many years earlier, as counsel in the British debt case *Ware v. Hylton*, that associational burdens should be no less binding because voluntarily assumed. "Banks, Canal Companies, and numerous associations of a similar description, are formed on the principle of voluntary subscription," Marshall told the Supreme Court in 1796. "The nation is desirous that such institutions should exist; individuals are invited to subscribe on the terms of the law; and, when they have subscribed, they are entitled to all the benefits, and are subject to all the inconveniences of the association." That idea, that law gained its force owing to the consent of the governed but must no less continue to govern, was as widely held and influential a premise of the American Revolutionaries as any had been. Those views were coupled in the judges' opinions in *Currie's Administrators* with an explicit defense of majoritarian democracy. In short, the challenges of the Mutual Assurance Society's first fifteen years had compelled Virginians to question how far they should extend their core principles of just government—notions of consent, representation, and the rule of law—into the internal workings of voluntary associations.[45]

How the Mutual Assurance Society visually portrayed itself over these years is telling. Between the 1790s and the crisis of division in 1805, the members and officers of the society itself were coming to see it as more a political entity and less a hopeful, utopian endeavor. In the engravings atop the earliest insurance policies, issued in 1796, stood the figure of Justice, her scales balanced, alongside two buildings, one burning and one fronted with scaffolding as it was being rebuilt (a two-part story also common to English policies). To her left was a line of men ready to provide offerings on an altar labeled "Relief." At her feet were the words of the Golden Rule.

When new printed forms were made necessary by the 1805 amendments, a new engraving was commissioned, and those words were replaced with a large stone tablet inscribed with a motto less religious and more political, "In Union There Is Safety." Firefighting was now a part of the story told (indicative of improving technologies and greater efforts to put out, and not simply contain, fires). Justice had lost her blindfold, her scales rested on the ground, and the central icon was now the fasces; one was cradled in her arms, two more appeared with the eagle above the scene. At her elbow

2. Mutual Assurance Society of Virginia, engraving on insurance policy (1799), Myers Burrage Graham Papers (I), 98 M99, Box 1, Folder 7, Special Collections Research Center, Earl Gregg Swem Library, College of William and Mary.

stood the Commonwealth of Virginia's emblematic figure, Liberty, with her foot pressed down on the defeated tyrant. In its words, its imagery, and its practices, the Mutual Assurance Society was becoming a thoroughly political entity. The charitable fervor was gone.[46]

By 1809, it was apparent that members in neither half of the divided association were terribly happy with the state of affairs. Even if, as William Ast informed a country member in 1807, such "great slams" as the fire of Norfolk could no longer affect the country branch, "it has since the division, sustained a good many losses, and as the delinquents do not pay up, as fast as they ought to do, the funds actually on hand are low." Just such a slam hit the town members' funds later that year, when Fredericksburg was ravaged, and "swept away the money & public stocks on hand." When the decision was made in February 1809 to assess members of both branches annually, and the charter was legislatively amended accordingly, it was because vast sums were owed to the society, which itself owed money to stricken members.

Even leaving the legal challenges of James Currie and his administrators aside, there were reasons in 1809 to worry that the Mutual Assurance Society might soon meet its end. "The present State of the Institution furnishes no very strong inducement to the house owners of Virginia to become members," Ast's replacement as principal agent, Samuel Greenhow, informed Jefferson. In an open letter to the *Enquirer* shortly before the *Currie's Administrators* decision came down, Greenhow publicly admitted that "the society has not been so punctual, as might be wished." In fact, he told Jefferson, the country branch of the society was owed $44,000 by nonpaying members and thus could not readily pay $12,000 in members' claims.[47]

3. Mutual Assurance Society of Virginia, engraving on insurance policy (1815), Virginia Cities Collection—Williamsburg, 39.4 V82ci, medium oversize, Series 32, sub-series 1, Box 12, Item 3, Special Collections Research Center, Earl Gregg Swem Library, College of William and Mary.

In Loudoun County, many people who had joined the Mutual Assurance Society were beginning to stage protests. Charles Fenton Mercer was a young and aspiring politician when he was nominated by "a very large and respectable meeting" of Loudoun County members of the Mutual Assurance Society to bring their grievances to the attention of Samuel Greenhow. He was to report back to "a more general meeting of the society" in Leesburg in two weeks, where they would decide whether to continue their support of the Mutual Assurance Society or should instead attempt "dissolving it, if the latter can be effected by judicial or legislative decision." Even if the insurance company could not be dissolved, there was a "*certainty* that, unless satisfactory information be furnished, the whole of those members will avail themselves of the mode, authorized by law, of withdrawing, individually, from the society." Within the four pages Mercer wrote to Greenhow were several of the most notable features of American associational activity in the early national period: the ad hoc but formalized nature of many associations, in this case one arising to address concerns about a larger corporation's abuses; the ever-present shadow of legal control, which as Mercer noted could come either legislatively or judicially; and the threat of exit to give force to internal dissent.[48]

Other moves to destroy the Mutual Assurance Society were also underway. Stephen C. Roszel, a delegate from Loudoun to the General Assembly, moved unsuccessfully to abolish the institution. And frustrations would not disappear after 1809. James Ewell Heath, an eighteen-year-old agent for the society in Prince William County in northern Virginia, wrote to Greenhow in 1810 to give those in Richmond some sense of the "angry brow of popular discontent" he faced every day and to request that he be replaced. With a new schedule of annual fees now in place but with the method of collecting no more refined, Heath rightly predicted that, before one quota was brought in, "those of 1810 and 1811 will perhaps be due—the consequence of which will be the irritation of the members & their ultimate disgust towards a Society which they will conceive a more complicated system of oppressive taxation and a more refined engine of legislative tyranny than was ever introduced in the country." Heath told his superiors he had no interest in exerting "any measure of coercion."[49]

He recounted for Greenhow an encounter with one Maryan Cave, a widow insuring her home on Main Street in Dumfries, who "gave vent to a torrent of opprobrious epithets, which she very bountifully bestowed upon the Society and its Officers." She was one of many who could not reconcile the practices of the Mutual Assurance Society "to their ideas of justice or expediency." Cave "spoke largely of the priviledges which she was entitled to, in a free country and of the violation of those priviledges in the inordinate demands of society." She refused to pay anything. Heath did not want Greenhow to think that he gave too much credence to "the unmeaning lingo of a woman," but her challenge that the Mutual Assurance Society's demands on its membership had no place in a free and republican polity stayed with him, and was echoed many times by members in these crisis years of the company. And it should be no surprise that there was little prospect of persuading people to join. Agent William Dawson described a typical exchange in 1811: "Is your House Insured Sir (no is the answer it is such a wreched Society, that those already in it would soon leave you if the[y] could git back there money &c)."[50]

John Marshall was another member who made known his dissent to the course the Mutual Assurance Society had taken in the first decade of the nineteenth century. Though his connection to the association went back to its formative moment (he served on a committee to examine the original plan of organization and to petition the legislature for a charter), Marshall terminated his membership some time before 1809, his motive "openly given at the time" to Greenhow. He noted specifically the legislative tinkering with the organization of the society and considered "the interference of the legislature in the management of our private affairs, whether those affairs are committed to a company or remain under individual direction, as equally dangerous & unwise." It was true that he may at times find himself circumstantially "compelled to subject my property to these interferences, & when compelled I shall submit; but I will not voluntarily expose myself to the exercise of a power which I think so improperly usurped." But Marshall had his finger on the key question: who protected those people who *had* voluntarily exposed themselves to the authority of an association such as the Mutual Assurance Society in the event that a majority of its members, with legislative approval, effectively reinvented the society?[51]

The *Currie's Administrators* decision had ultimately confirmed the authority of the majority in the Mutual Assurance Society to bind the whole, even if it meant holding individuals to commitments they had not foreseen, although Roane had suggested that his court would act to prevent patent injustices. The Supreme Court of the United States was first given an opportunity in 1810 to declare whether and how it would intervene, in a case that, in effect, asked the same questions posed by James Currie. And Marshall's Court took precisely the same position as Virginia's high court had the previous year. John Korn and Jacob Wisemiller, merchants in Alexandria and members of the Mutual Assurance Society, were bound by the decisions of the majority when the society adjusted the liabilities of town members.

Indeed, each member "is bound to consider it as his own individual act," as "every member, in fact, stands in the peculiar situation of being party of both sides, insurer and insured." Justice William Johnson, who had been Jefferson's first appointee and who wrote for the Court every time a mutual insurance case came before it, presented a rationale—"the majority of a corporate body must have power to bind its individuals," though that power is "restricted by the nature and object of its institution"—that established courts as a final arbiter while steadfastly supporting the power of the group to seek its own welfare. Johnson perceived that Korn and Wisemiller had "an obligation to conform to the laws of their own making, as members of the body politic," especially as they had signed insurance policies promising to abide by the regulations "which are already established, or may hereafter be established." When the merchants sought to avoid another levy against them three years later, the Court was forced to repeat itself: "in the capacity of an individual of the body corporate the Defendants are bound by the by-laws of the society as far as is consistent with the nature of its institution." Indeed, these two Supreme Court decisions confirm that *Currie's Administrators* has long been misunderstood, and the crux of the issue was not legislative authority to tinker with a charter but, instead, to what extent a member of such a corporate body was bound by majority rule.[52]

What checks remained, then, on the Mutual Assurance Society and its powers over its constituency? There remained, always, the courts, which Roane had insisted would intervene to prevent injustices, even if it had not exercised that option in Currie's case, and which Johnson positioned as a final arbiter of whether amended bylaws fell within the principles and purposes of the institution. He was clear that a majority could bind a minority to fulfill any new responsibilities only if the changes were in accord with "the nature and object" of the institution. The experiences of members of the Mutual Assurance Society reveal an institution that was designed to place the welfare of the whole as a priority but that had to be adjusted, amended, and adjudicated as individual interests came face to face with associational priorities. And at nearly every step, some judicial verification became necessary, an outcome produced not so much by design as by the popular belief in the new republic that legal institutions stood to preserve those rights held by individuals in what Maryan Cave called a "free country."[53]

Another check on corporate authority over its membership was their nature as public creations formed under a republican government, which meant that "their powers and privileges must therefore depend wholly on the act of Assembly," as St. George Tucker had noted. Not only were incorporated bodies very strictly limited in their powers to those delineated by the legislature (except for a very few general powers supposed to be implicit in all charters), but legislative props to corporate authority, such as facilitating the Mutual Assurance Society's collections by leaving it to sheriffs, could be and were withheld. That decision greatly weakened the institution, according to its officers and agents, and by 1819 the country branch was in "a very deranged state," according to John Marshall, largely because delinquent payments could not be collected and owing to what an investigating committee called "the extreme uncertainty of the real value of the houses insured" on isolated rural plots. The country office was shuttered three years later.[54]

Even without utilizing an arm of the state to delimit the private governing power of such institutions as a mutual insurance society, members and nonmembers preempted and responded to internal abuses. When a John Marshall or a Maryan Cave expressed their thoughts on the nature of the association and the ways in which it was veering off course, they made use of varied and diverse languages of rights, legal and political. Marshall described a private, personal sphere of authority into which outside "interferences" should venture only on occasional, necessary invitation. Cave stressed protections that participants in all collective endeavors, ranging from the state to the private corporation, could claim within a republican polity, her "free country." The liberal principle that individuals carried rights into any and all social relationships found increasingly insistent expression as the Mutual Assurance Society, adapting and evolving, engaged in increasingly complicated efforts to achieve the simple idea upon which it was founded.

In the end, idealized hopes of effecting a general insurance on pure, equitable principles had produced a Mutual Assurance Society that could succeed only by compulsion, by division, and, ultimately, when the country branch was lopped off, by exclusion. From the moment Thomas Jefferson first heard of it, he thought "the general idea of a mutual insurance against fire as a valuable one," but he was wary of vesting too much power in William Ast's proposed creation, such as authority to collect on short notice or to seize property ahead of the demands of other creditors. "It would be a good work to give it such modifications as might lend to it's general establishment," he told Ast, but the challenges were many. Over the course of a single decade, the Mutual Assurance Society had gone through a series of political challenges, from within and from without, until the hopeful optimism of mutual indemnity had little resemblance to reality.[55]

Each step of the way, however, the challenges of association, the inherent tensions between individual autonomy and collective action, were channeled into legal and political means of resolution. This was a period of emerging ideas, not settled ones. When Charles Clay, apparently a victim of a duplicitous insurance agent, wrote to William Ast in 1805 to complain that he was "as strangely compelled into a business as a voluntary agent as ever a freeman was in a free country," he was invoking concepts of great rhetorical power but of still uncertain meaning. The case of *Currie's Administrators*—no less than the internecine struggles and drastic modifications of the Mutual Assurance Society that produced it—provides an opportunity to witness jurists and active citizens in early national Virginia working through those ideas, thinking seriously about the rights and the duties of voluntary participants in any collective endeavor. There were parallels to other struggles large and small, ones arising in groups of people ranging in size from the smallest club to the sprawling nation, and it appears that these were parallels as apparent to the participants as they are to us. As we have already seen in the case of the dispute between John Binns and William Duane, in which "the right of membership" was declared to be of real and legally protected value, there existed a vocabulary and a means to address these kinds of disputes, a vocabulary rooted in the common law but suffused with the ideas and the rhetoric of a republican revolution. Ultimately, another kind of revolution—one based more in economic shifts than in political ones—would largely sever the world of the business corporation from this domain of rights-oriented legal protections of voluntary membership.[56]

Business Corporations, Voluntary Associations, and How Profit Divided the Two

The challenges of building turnpikes produced conflicts over individual members' responsibilities quite similar to those that plagued Virginia's mutual fire insurance endeavor. In corporations not founded on the mutual principle, however, American courts beginning in 1811 quickly settled into a practice of protecting individual members' rights by denying shareholders' liability to pay into the company coffers if the corporation was substantially modified. So established did this line of jurisprudence become, which one New Hampshire justice described as being a study of "the nature of the liabilities of members to their own corporation," that Nathan Dane in his influential 1823 digest denounced *Currie's Administrators* as fully wrong—and not because it had been superseded by *Dartmouth*. His concern was with the nature of the member-to-society relationship. As Dane saw it, "no vote of a majority, nor any corporate vote or legislative act, or these altogether, can vary the terms, and rights, and burdens" of individuals in what he called "property corporations." Such things cannot be done "without the consent of each and every such independent party," he opined, and "no such consent appears in Currie's case." Legal developments in the fourteen years since the 1809 *Currie's Administrators* case and the publication of Dane's digest influenced his reading of the case, developments that had begun to tighten and refine the definitions of the rights and duties of voluntary members in business corporations. About a decade after that, in the early 1830s, an entirely new principle would come to prevail, one that allowed certain kinds of corporate change by recasting the nature of corporate membership to center on the profit motive, and nothing else.[57]

Recent developments in the study of corporate governance are helpful here, particularly work on what had been a little-recognized attribute of the corporate form that was critical in its rise to preeminence in the modern market economy. Called both "entity shielding" and the "locking in" of capital, it is in effect the mirror image of shareholder limited liability. Just as the latter insulates shareholders from business debts, the former terms emphasize the ways in which the corporation has, historically, been legally protected from the demands of its stockholders, who otherwise might try to reclaim the capital they had invested, and even from the demands of the stockholders' personal creditors. A lasting and effective business institution came into being when corporate members made commitments, enforceable at law, that each would contribute what he or she promised *and* that the capital would stay with the corporation and could neither be withdrawn by fickle owners nor be pursued by their creditors.[58]

That, however, goes only part of the way toward the legal assurance of people's commitments to one another necessary to create lasting business institutions. History reveals an attendant concern, a second guarantee that was needed. Prospective corporate members also needed to be sure that that money—locked into the firm as it was—would be directed to the ends for which it was intended when they purchased a share and joined the endeavor. Put another way, potential shareholders must be assured that no one of them would be entirely at the mercy of the majority. To be clear, most corporations of this era were not massive, sprawling endeavors: of the 812 corporations created in New York State between 1790 and 1825, the average company had 74 members—the largest had 560 shareholders; the smallest, just three. One of the ways that early corporate organizers attempted to protect minority stakeholders in a corporation was to establish limitations on the practice of granting one vote per share held (rarely, they did this by giving each stockholder one vote, regardless of the number of shares owned, and much more commonly by establishing graduated voting rules). Of those 812 New York corporations, 48 percent had one-vote-per-share policies and roughly the same number (45 percent) had some kind of graduated system, granting large shareholders something less than one vote per share.[59]

But the logic of majority rule—and the obvious need for flexible continuity—remained powerful. The same kinds of challenges that faced Virginia's Mutual Assurance Society would appear, in superficially different forms, in many other corporations across the new United States. A proposed route of a turnpike, spelled out by charter, might later be found to be unworkable. A cap on the amount of property that a corporation might legally hold might need to be altered dramatically. It happened countless times that someone joined a corporation in the manner most common in the early nineteenth century, subscribing for a certain number of shares with a small down payment and promising, expressly and voluntarily, to pay in the remaining dollar value of the share when the company called for it. But what would happen if the corporation, making use of the proper decision-making mechanisms, decided that it needed to change in some significant way between the time of the promise and the time of the call?

Beginning just two years after the *Currie's Adminstrators* case, which had been decided in 1809 in favor of the majority's power to modify the demands that the corporation made of its rank-and-file membership, contests regarding members of turnpike corporations began, consistently, to angle the other way. If the corporation was deemed to have changed in any significant way, the member was released from any subsequent obligation to pay, and the shares would be sold. Why this was the case is, in itself, important and reflective of a republican frame of mind about private associational commitments that needs explanation. Why the issue would become more complicated after 1830, leading ultimately to a rule that prevails today permitting certain kinds of corporate change, is a second and no less significant question. And it helps us to understand why it is that the first generations of American citizens could contemplate the profit-seeking business corporation as being essentially akin to other forms of voluntary affiliation—and why, by the mid-nineteenth century, that affinity was no longer apparent.

The issue was first tested in 1811. Thomas Locke had subscribed for one share in the Middlesex Turnpike in 1805, agreeing to pay all legal assessments. The directors, with the approval of a majority vote of the stockholders in a regular meeting, sought a legislative amendment to the charter, and the legislature agreed in 1806, altering the route of the turnpike. The new route no longer passed near Locke's property, and he was not happy. He refused to consider himself still bound to pay assessments, arguing through his attorney that "the plaintiffs have no right to transfer his subscription for the promotion of one road to that of another, without his personal assent." Assessments piled up to the amount of $240 before Locke's case came to the Supreme Judicial Court of Massachusetts, who found, in the record, proof of two things: "of an engagement to pay assessments for making a turnpike in a certain specified direction; and of the making a turnpike in a different direction." This freed him of any obligation. Locke, according to the court's opinion, "may truly say, *Non hoec in foedera veni*. [To this I never agreed.] He was not bound by the application of the directors to the legislature for the alteration of the course of the road, nor by the consent of the corporation thereto." The court determined, "Much fraud might be put in practice under a contrary decision."[60]

The principle became even clearer when Samuel Swan successfully resisted a call from the same company for $1,440, or $240 on each of his six shares in the Middlesex Turnpike. Like Locke, he claimed "he was exonerated from his subscription, so far as it concerned his personal responsibility, on the ground that the turnpike had been located differently from the plan under which he subscribed, as established by the act of incorporation." The road as originally plotted was to pass near his property in Medford, but the charter amendment had stopped those plans. The turnpike's lawyer had a pretty compelling case to make that Swan had effectively given consent to the change in the route of the turnpike, however: not only had he served as a director, a treasurer, and a clerk for the company, but he had even signed the petition to the legislature to alter the charter and change the proposed course of the road. Doing so, they argued, "operated as a waiver of any right to rescind his contract, and was an assent to all the doings of the corporation." If anything could show the express consent of a shareholder to a corporate change, the Middlesex Turnpike's attorney claimed, would it not be his acting, as a corporate officer, to make that very amendment?[61]

The court could not disagree more, deciding that Swan owed nothing. In doing so, it drew a still brighter line between the duties of corporate membership and the express promissory commitment to pay assessments. The fact that Swan signed on to the corporate petition for amendment meant nothing, according to Justice Samuel Sewall. In two ways, Sewall wrote, Swan's alleged actions in support of the route change did not make him liable to support it financially: first, "the defendant may have been controlled by the will of the majority"; and, even if that were not the case, "if he concurred in the votes and proceedings of the corporation, it was as a corporator, not carrying with his concurrence any renewal of his supposed collateral promise." Here was the pivotal distinction. Although a corporate member was without doubt "subject to the by-laws, rules, votes, and undertakings, of the corporation, so far as these are within the scope of the original design," that was a matter entirely separate from the express promise that Swan had made—like the one made by so many other members of private corporations across the new United States—that he would pay all legal assessments in order to fund a corporation's enterprise. In that promise, according to Sewall, Swan "is not a corporator, but an individual contracting with the corporation; and he undertakes in that extraordinary manner, referring himself to what the legislature had done, not to any probable subsequent grant." The court refused to compel Swan to hand over more than a thousand dollars to a corporation seeking to do something substantially different from what it had initially set out to do.

Importantly, these were not cases hinging on whether, in passing these charter amendments, the state legislatures were in violation of a constitutional prohibition of the impairment of contracts. Each case, as a New Hampshire justice noted at the outset of an 1817 opinion, was rather "a dispute between a private corporation and one of its members," and thus "a recurrence to the nature of the liabilities of members to their own corporation will we apprehend divest the case of many of its difficulties." That case, in which Union Locks and Canals brought an action of assumpsit against Joseph Towne for seventeen unpaid assessments, was ultimately decided on a single point: did the charter amendments—changing the amount of property the company could own from six acres to one hundred, allowing them to charge tolls for an unlimited duration, and redefining the extent of the locks and canals to include new stretches of the Merrimack River—exonerate Towne from any liability to pay? Without doubt, the court held, for every shareholder "expects and indeed stipulates with the other owners, as a corporate body, to pay them his proportion of the expense," but only "in the promotion of the particular objects of the corporation." In that sense, Towne's decision to participate is "in the nature of a special contract, the terms of which contract are limited by the specific provisions, rights and liabilities detailed in the act of incorporation." Alter those unilaterally, and the deal is off.[62]

To skip to the end: There was a hint in *Union Locks* toward a consistently applicable principle by which to evaluate corporate evolution and the rights of individual stockholders, one that would, for the most part, come to prevail in the middle third of the century. That principle, what legal scholar Edwin Merrick Dodd called the incidental-change doctrine, allowed alterations to corporate charters even where unanimous consent would appear to be necessary (that is, where there is no particular mode of amendment described in the charter) "provided the alteration can be characterized by some such criticism-disarming adjective as auxiliary, incidental, or non-fundamental," as Dodd put it in the early twentieth century. As Dodd observed in his seminal article on dissenting stockholders and charter amendments, it is a rule that "grants to the majority in the interests of fairness and of progress a power which there is no evidence that the minority intended to confer on them." That is, while it may be *reasonable* to allow small and non-fundamental changes to corporate charters, it is done on the principle that there was an implied agreement among stockholders to allow minor, incidental changes without unanimous consent. (Of course, nothing the shareholders actually did carried such an implication; it was, wrote Dodd, "an agreement implied in law," not in fact.) And the historical origins of the concept are crucial to understanding the conceptual divergence between profit-seeking corporations and other, more traditionally "associational" forms of voluntary affiliation.[63]

In September 1830, a Pennsylvania man was freed from any financial obligation to the Indiana and Ebensburg Turnpike, by decision of the state's Supreme Court, because the legislature had split the corporation into two separate turnpike companies. One of the two sought to recover money owed by Armour Phillips based on his subscription to the original corporation. In this case, the first of its kind in reported case law regarding charter amendments and the rights of dissenting stockholders since the *Dartmouth* opinion of 1819, the issue of constitutional prohibitions against the impairment of corporate charters-as-contracts, was central. "It is impossible to avoid a conclusion," wrote Chief Justice John Bannister Gibson, "that the supplementary act is, as regards original stockholders who have not consented to be arranged to either of the new incorporations, in direct collision with the tenth section of the first article of the Constitution of the United States." Despite the turn toward constitutional law, however, the crux of the issue remained unchanged. It was the nature of Phillips's agreement at the moment of joining that mattered. And creating two corporations out of one was doubtless a new arrangement entirely: "The defendant has not thought fit to become a party, and his subscription cannot be demanded." Phillips was under no obligation to support the "new" corporation.[64]

With every emphasis on the magnitude of the changes being made affecting the obligations of Phillips or Towne, however, the hints were becoming more obvious that *less* significant changes could be made without unanimous consent. Nine months later, a divided Pennsylvania Supreme Court made the final turn in that direction. And their rationale indicates how the business corporation was coming to be understood, in an important way, as something wholly different from the other voluntary associations of the American social landscape. The prospect of profit was, for the first time, seen to be the only thing holding the members together.[65]

William Irvin subscribed for stock in the Susquehanna and Waterford Turnpike just before it was chartered in 1819. He was particularly pleased by the fact that the turnpike would run right by his property, even crossing the Susquehanna River "at or near the mouth of Anderson's creek," very near the Irvin estate. His son, who represented him at the time of the stock subscription, was assured by the turnpike commissioners of that fact, showing him an 1815 statute that described the route in detail. But, as had happened to Thomas Locke and Samuel Swan in Massachusetts, a new law was passed in 1820 that moved the turnpike away from Irvin's property. The act changed the location of the bridge to "the mouth of Sugar-camp run," about two miles farther downriver. With the requisite adjustments to the route, the road now passed on the other side of the river from Irvin's property. He refused to pay. Interestingly, Irvin lost before a jury, but he probably came with confidence to the Middle District of the Pennsylvania Supreme Court, as the relevant precedents appeared to be stacked in his favor, including not only Locke's and Swan's cases from two decades earlier but also the very same court's decision, not a year old, in *Indiana and Ebensburg Turnpike v. Phillips*. Two justices, indeed, did agree with Irvin's defense, but three, including Chief Justice Gibson in an elaborate opinion, did not.

There were for Gibson two issues that Irvin just did not seem to understand about the consideration for his corporate obligations. First, the consideration for investments such as Irvin's was, for Gibson, not solely private gain, but also the public good. Here Gibson was echoing a long history of emphasizing the public purposes of corporations, particularly in Pennsylvania: his predecessor, William Tilghman, noted in 1822 in describing the Hibernia Turnpike, for instance, that "there never has been, or certainly never ought to have been, a corporation created with a view solely to the private interest of the corporators." Gibson's language was largely the same.[66]

Second, and crucial to our understanding of the changing conceptions of corporate membership by the end of the first third of the century, Gibson described the "fallacy" in Irvin's argument: it lay in his "confounding the motive for entering into the contract with the consideration of it." Absolutely "nothing but the benefit to be received *as a corporator* is held out to the subscriber by the corporation or the state." Irvin had, as members do, engaged himself to certain burdens with the expectation of certain benefits, but he misunderstood what was included in the exchange. In the *Middlesex Turnpike* cases of Massachusetts, Gibson observed, promissory notes were substituted for the legislative charter's having "had prescribed neither contract nor conditions," and in those notes parties were "at liberty to establish any terms of responsibility which they might think proper to adopt." But it was different here, for the details of obligation were spelled out in the original charter. And it was, to Gibson, entirely clear that the liabilities of Irvin to pay the company on demand had "arisen from a promise in consideration of benefits to be drawn *from the profits of the corporation*, and not from a location of the road peculiarly beneficial to him as a landholder." He cannot complain of "a decrease of corporate interest, nor of a change of corporate object or identity; of nothing, in short, but a loss of advantages expected to be realized from the location of the bridge." His rights and duties as a corporate member were unchanged, even if he felt entirely betrayed, because the change was not deemed by the court to be essential or fundamental and because—in theory, anyway—the dividend checks would keep coming.[67]

Essentially, from this time forward Americans would not confuse the profit-seeking business corporation with other forms of collective, voluntary organization. Subsequent court decisions only underscored what Gibson had observed. In 1841, in *Gray v. Monongahela Navigation*, Gibson himself was able to elaborate on the distinction between fundamental and nonfundamental charter amendments. Members' obligations were unaffected by the ways in which a corporation may evolve, he declared, "provided it do not extend to a change of the structure of the association." As Chief Justice Samuel Nelson of the New York Supreme Court observed in an 1843 railroad case, Gibson's thinking was consistent: in *Gray* and in the *Irvin* case, the "general principle" of *Indiana and Ebensburg Turnpike v. Phillips* was maintained, "that the alteration by the Legislature may be so extensive and radical as to work a dissolution of the contract; but an effort is made so to modify and regulate the application of the principle as to admit of improvements in the charter, useful to the public and beneficial to the Company, without this consequence." Nelson also noted the crucial, consistent element in the case law regarding corporations' altering the terms of agreement: "corporations can exercise no power over the corporators, beyond those conferred by the charter to which they have subscribed, except on the condition of their agreement or consent." That proposition lay at the foundation of American conceptions of corporate membership, and yet courts had also come to embrace a new position: all those corporate agreements would be interpreted with the understanding that members of profit-seeking corporations had joined in order to profit themselves—and for no other reason that could serve as a constraint on what a majority could legitimately do.[68]

For Americans of the early nineteenth century, the "locking in" of capital to a business enterprise, stressed by today's scholarship as a vital step toward the success of the modern corporation, was necessarily accompanied by protections for the individual corporate member. The member's promise that allowed capital to be locked away was met by a guarantee that his or her corporate commitments would be absolved if the corporation became something essentially different. Over the course of a single generation, those ideas would begin to fade from view as the rise of the modern corporation, with its increasingly centralized management and growing emphasis on profit maximization, led both ordinary Americans and those with legal training to agree that a corporation could evolve so long as its members continued to have, unimpaired, the same claim on corporate profits.

Before that turn, however, the parallels between profit-seeking corporations and other forms of voluntary organization had powerful influences on the evolution of both. In the first third of the nineteenth century, those who formed and joined associations of all kinds believed that there were some basic principles that could and should pervade all of these efforts at concerted action. In 1819, for instance, a North Carolina contractor by the name of Delacy was stricken off the list of corporate members at a general meeting of the Neuse River Navigation Company for failure to pay assessments. Insisting that he had reached an agreement with the directors to do a particular job for the company in exchange for $1,000 *and* the amount he remained indebted for his shares of stock, he petitioned for a writ of mandamus to compel the company to restore him "to his franchise of a corporator from which he had been wrongfully removed." Most important, Delacy argued, was the fact that he had not been given a chance to state his case. The justices of the Supreme Court of North Carolina all agreed that Delacy had been deprived of "the undoubted right of every man to receive notice of any proceeding against him," and they ordered the company "to restore the applicant to the rights of a corporator." There were, the court determined, certain rights of which no person should be deprived. There was no charter provision on which the court based its decision that "no man shall be condemned or prejudiced in his rights, without an opportunity of being heard." Rather, the right to be heard was deemed to be one of those principles that always merited legal protection in the member-to-group relationship. In the first three decades of the nineteenth century, a period of unprecedented and still unparalleled evolution in the law of corporations, post-Revolutionary ideas about the nature of voluntary participation and assumptions about the rights and duties of membership in any kind of social organization played a vital part in American corporate development.[69]

The challenges posed by questions of minority rights within institutions directed by majority rule can be found in the histories of virtually every type of American associational activity in the post-Revolutionary and antebellum eras. The profit-seeking corporation, however, was entangled in a unique set of concerns. Over the course of the early nineteenth century the underlying assumption regarding why people joined those corporations—a presumed rationale that gave shape to legal interventions in the many disputes that arose between shareholders and corporations—came to be seen as solely pecuniary. But it did not begin that way. Rather, the history of American corporate law was intertwined with the experiences and the ideas of voluntary membership across the wide spectrum of the civic associational life of the early United States. Just as they had so often experienced in their own tireless efforts to create a Union that would cohere but not become a tyrannical force in their lives, the first generations of American citizens struggled to create new ways to cooperate effectively without creating new forms of power that could act without regard to the least among them.

SIX

Determining the Rights of Members

In 1807, John Binns, William Duane, and all of the other members of an Irishmen's benevolent society were swept up in a deeply personal contest between Binns and his former friend and rival printer Duane. But there was another party to the struggle. The highest court in Pennsylvania declared, for the first time in an American court, that what it called Binns's "right of membership" merited protection by the legal authorities of the commonwealth. His arbitrary dismissal on grounds that the court could not and did not approve of was reversed with the issuance of a writ of mandamus in 1810, ordering his readmission. Essentially, the Supreme Court of Pennsylvania held that membership in a fraternal society was to be treated as a legal relationship—with attendant guarantees, rights, and legal remedies—as opposed to an affectionate one. It mattered not at all how much Duane and a vast majority of the other members had grown to despise John Binns.

Similar quarrels would follow, in which members of incorporated but privately formed organizations would follow up on the influential precedent of *Commonwealth v. St. Patrick Benevolent Society*. And parallel disputes arising out of incorporated, profit-seeking organizations were finding their way into courtrooms over the same period, many of which centered on questions of majority rule and the rights of individual members. All of these cases would be reported widely and repeatedly, in the nascent but quickly growing legal literature of the early national United States. The consequences were profound, for it meant that ideas about voluntary membership that were already being put into practice in the civic associational life of the early republic—that, in short, everyone could join with the reasonable expectation that the internal affairs of those societies would be procedurally fair, law-minded, and constitutionally ordered—would be effectively protected by the legal apparatus of the early American state.

In the several years immediately following the Binns-Duane quarrel, Pennsylvania courts decided a series of cases arising out of membership disputes in associations formed exclusively for mutual financial aid. And these were developments that had national implications. When James Kent discussed "the various causes that have been adjudged sufficient or insufficient for the removal or disfranchisement of a member of a corporation" in his *Commentaries on American Law*, for instance, he cited only Stewart Kyd's eighteenth-century English treatise on corporate law and three Pennsylvania cases arising out of disputes in mutual aid groups that will be discussed in detail below. Thus, in the same brief span of time that saw a great deal of innovation in another kind of association tied together chiefly by pecuniary ties—the profit-seeking business corporation—American jurists also elaborated upon the legal meanings and consequences of membership in mutual benefit societies. Much like the cases involving business corporations, in which men such as James Currie and William Marshall turned to judges and juries when they believed they had been misused by a legally chartered organization, disputes that might at first glance appear to have centered on narrow points of law prove to have been grounded firmly in post-Revolutionary ideas about majority rule, personal rights, and the perceived dangers of arbitrary authority. The result was a solid and widely embraced legal foundation upon which an associational world would be built, one that Americans and foreign observers alike would marvel over by the time Alexis de Tocqueville visited the country in 1831.[1]

The Law of Mutual Aid

Mutual benefit societies were one of the oldest forms of voluntary association, but their numbers soared in the early American republic. Known as "friendly societies" in Great Britain, they had one purpose: to collect funds that would then be available to individual members in case of injury or illness, and to their families in case of death. Surrounding that core goal, of course, there was a lot that went on in these kinds of associations, most of which occurred at the regularly appointed gatherings of the group, usually monthly, that helped to foster a sense of fraternity and to provide accountability and transparency. These mutual benefit organizations were by no means unique to the United States: they existed in the Old World and in colonial British America in no small numbers. Indeed, they were not even unique to the modern era; something quite similar to an ordinary nineteenth-century mutual aid society is known to have existed in the Roman Empire, in Lavinium in AD 136, complete with monthly dues and initiation fees. But precisely because so many kinds of associational action were wholly new to the post-Revolutionary era, there is a great deal to be learned from those varieties of concerted action that existed long before and yet, also, began to adapt to a new world and its new social, legal, and political climates.[2]

For the most part, mutual benefit clubs were societies that, like the business corporation and the mutual fire insurance society, never claimed to be an institutional embodiment of brotherly love or close ties of affection. Procedural regularity and rigid enforcement of previously agreed-upon rules were expected. The societies were formed as a way for individuals of no great means to deal with unforeseen hardships, to prepare for the costs associated with their own death and burial, and to provide for their families. It was clearly to the advantage of those who organized these groups to choose their fellows carefully and to take those steps necessary to maintain a certain level of collegiality and financial stability. And thus, unlike other varieties of concerted action in the early American republic, the internal workings of mutual benefit societies did not become increasingly formalized and procedurally precise in the early nineteenth century, for both in Great Britain and in the early United States these societies were already, by the mid-eighteenth century, astonishingly detailed and specific in their descriptions of the rights and duties of membership.[3]

One reason for this was that precedents drawn from British societies provided a model for many American organizations, whose institutional forms were copied again and again. Though British organizations were detailed from a very early date, the 1793 Act for the Encouragement and Relief of Friendly Societies, passed by Parliament as a way to regularize their proceedings, prompted still greater formality of organization and set the pattern for the involvement of the state until 1834. The government in Britain became involved in order both to supervise against any kind of organized subversion (the passage of the act in the midst of the French Revolution was, of course, not coincidental, and it followed a 1792 act on seditious meetings) and to spur the formation of such societies and thus relieve demands on public support for the poor. One consequence was a direct superintendence over the internal workings of all groups that registered, meaning all such groups looked much the same. What many regarded as the most successful of the British groups, the Castle Eden Friendly Society, whose rules were published in 1798, was a particularly influential precedent in the United States, and the published rules of American societies looked much like those of their

British counterparts. What is more, nearly all of these groups shared the same problems and responded in noticeably similar ways. Indeed, the basic plan of organization would scarcely evolve at all in the coming decades even as it began to compete with other kinds of disability and life insurance in the nineteenth century, because the mutual benefit society was well adapted to the increased geographical mobility and changing occupational structures of the urban environment in both Britain and in the United States.[4]

Changing conceptions of membership over the first third of the nineteenth century would shape how Americans participated in groups that offered mutual aid to their members. In a brief span of time, participants in mutual benefit societies had learned that they could claim and receive legal protection for their rights as members by appealing to what can be called an American common law of membership. That development should also be understood in the context of the rise in the 1820s of the first third-party, single-issue movement in American history, the Anti-Masonic movement, which we will explore in the second section of this chapter. By the late 1830s, as we will see in the final section, the expectations of those who joined and the workings of mutual aid societies themselves tended to fall within an increasingly narrow spectrum of associational practices. At that point, courts became willing to withdraw themselves from a direct superintendence in favor of a standard that would prevail through the remainder of the century: what happened in the ordinary course of proceedings in such groups would not be second-guessed by the legal institutions of the state. It was a vital step toward the embrace of a pluralism that many would come to see as quintessentially American, but it was a product of decades of contest and change in the perceptions and legal definitions of voluntary membership.

Though they were an old idea, mutual aid societies boomed in the post-Revolutionary era, appearing in urban centers throughout the 1790s and the first decade of the next century. Philadelphia was a leader. By the 1810s, about a hundred such groups existed there, averaging sixty to a hundred members, many with similar initiation fees and monthly dues of about 37 cents each month, entitling a member or his family to support in case of sickness or death. And there was little to differentiate associations formed by whites from those organized by African Americans, aside from the fact that the first black men's societies were affiliated with churches: the Friendly Society of St. Thomas's African Church, one of about fourteen black mutual aid societies formed in Philadelphia by 1812, is indistinguishable in form from organizations created by and for whites. When James Mease described the social environment in 1811 Philadelphia, he spent several pages describing the city's mutual benefit societies, both in the aggregate and individually. Many were formed for distinct ethnic groups, others for specific occupational groups, and still others had more open membership policies. And yet, he wrote, "the objects, principles, and in general, the rules of these societies are the same." They served the same ends ("to prevent the degrading reflection arising from the circumstance of being relieved, while sick, by private or public charity") by the same means (fines for absences and other forbidden conduct, for instance). To Mease, the general practices of such groups were well established, well crafted, and perfectly appropriate for the workingmen of the city. "Such societies cannot be too strongly recommended," he wrote. "All classes of workmen, and others who depend upon their daily labour for their support; and who in case of their death would leave their families in distress, should be persuaded to form or join benevolent societies."[5]

Many had been incorporated under Pennsylvania's 1791 general incorporation act for religious, literary, and charitable societies, the same act under which the St. Patrick Benevolent Society had been organized. But for all their numbers in the late eighteenth and early nineteenth centuries, it was in the years immediately following the 1810 decision in *Commonwealth v. St. Patrick Benevolent Society* that the first cases involving members of such groups found their way into Pennsylvania courts. Indeed, the first such case came within a matter of months of Binns's successful petition for mandamus and had recognizable echoes, suggesting that the precedent regarding membership was immediately influential. By the end of the decade, mutual benefit societies were legally obligated to give their members notice and opportunities to mount a defense whenever their continued membership was up for decision by their fellow members. Decisions regarding members were, on multiple occasions, essentially retried in court, and associations' judgments were reevaluated on the merits. The Pennsylvania judiciary imposed, from without, their notions of justice and fair treatment into voluntary societies long seen to be the epitome of self-help and private mutuality.

In the same month that the decision in *St. Patrick Benevolent Society* came down, in March 1810, Joseph Vanderslice became a member of the American Beneficial Society, a group of about a hundred men. Before the end of the year, however, Vanderslice had been expelled, and he sought a writ of mandamus to compel readmission to the mutual benefit society. He gave sworn testimony that he had been "duly elected and admitted a member of the 'American Beneficial Society' and has paid into the hands of the Secretary thereof the sum required from every person becoming a member thereof." Notably, he gave the court a copy of the constitution and rules of

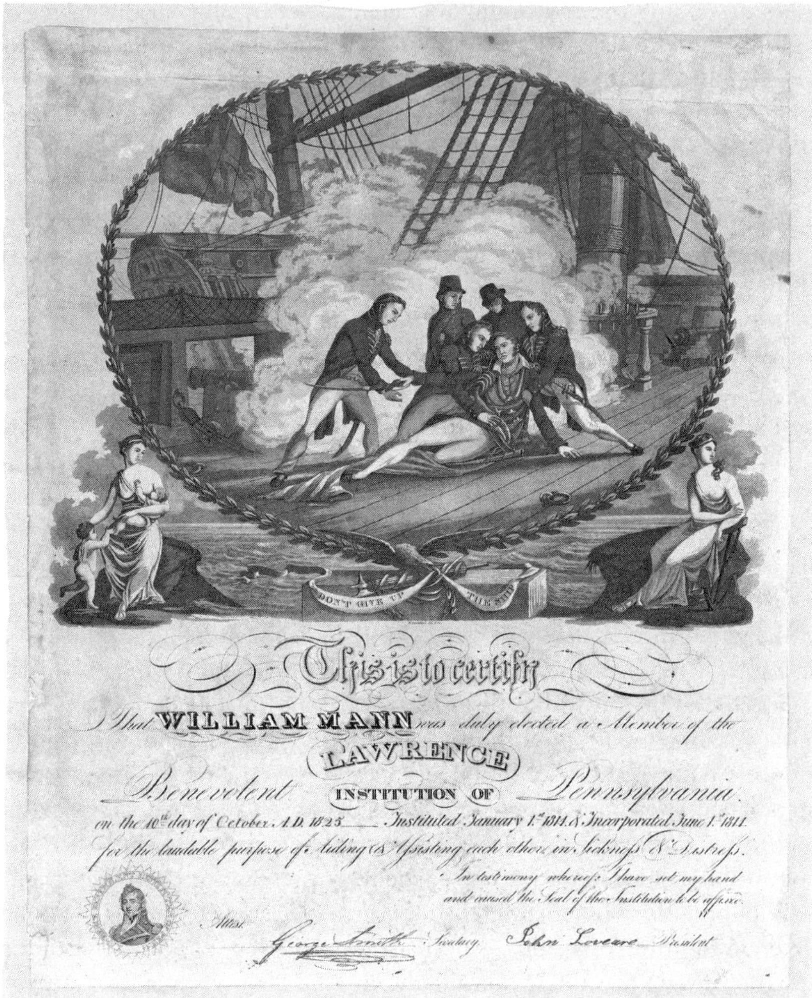

4. Lawrence Benevolent Institution of Philadelphia, membership certificate of William Mann, Oct. 10, 1825, Certificate File, PR 014, New-York Historical Society.

the society and swore that he had "not in any particular committed a breach thereof." The court, as was expected in such cases, asked the president of the American Beneficial Society to give cause for his expulsion. It followed, in most every detail, the course of events in *Commonwealth v. St. Patrick Benevolent Society*, with Vanderslice even including the same turn of phrase as had John Binns: the society had expelled him and "deprived him of the right of membership in which this Deponent has a beneficial interest." The Supreme Court of Pennsylvania, faced with Vanderslice's claim that he "has not to the best of his knowledge and belief any adequate or sufficient mode of relief in the premises other than by a mandamus to be issued by the Supreme Court of the State of Pennsylvania to restore him to his right of membership," was willing to listen.[6]

The American Beneficial Society had appointed a three-person committee to investigate charges levied against Vanderslice that he had suffered from infirmities at the time of his joining the society that, had they been disclosed, would have precluded his admission. The committee's report was conclusive that he had deceived them, and the society voted unanimously to expel him. The officers of the society were told by the Supreme Court to recount the proceedings that led to Vanderslice's expulsion, which they did. "Joseph H. Vanderslice was, previous to his iniciation, in the presence of the society asked the usual questions as has been established from the commencement of the Institution of which the following is the most connected with the present case," they reported. "Are you perfectly free from any bodily complaints or infirmities whatsoever. To which he answered, yes." But the committee claimed it could "prove that he was afflicted with a rupture sometime previous to the iniciation, by the person who put on him the truss to prevent any further injury." In their return to the court, the officers also made sure to spell out what they believed to be the legal basis of their authority to expel Vanderslice, and it was found in their own constitution: "The society conceive from the 5th article of the acts of incorporation 9th and latter claws of the 10th articles of the constitution together with the phisicians report to have been justifyable in having expelled the said J H. Vanderslice." Unfortunately, no further record exists. But it is clear that Vanderslice acted with confidence that he could find relief in court. So too did the officers of the society act with certainty that they were in the right and could prove it. They even concluded their return to the court by asking for assurance that "the court will permit them to have a further trial if the situation of the case requires it." But we cannot know what came next for Vanderslice and the American Beneficial Society.[7]

In the next few years, more cases of precisely this sort would find their way into Pennsylvania courtrooms. And they centered on the fairness of the proceedings against the expelled member. Records survive of three 1813 cases in which members of these kinds of mutual benefit societies had been expelled and sought to challenge the validity of their expulsion before the Supreme Court of Pennsylvania. Charles Hepburn was one. He had been expelled from the Independent Beneficial Society, an association "for the express purpose of raising a fund sufficient to relieve each other in certain exigencies," after having been a member for more than a year. He had joined not long after its incorporation in 1811 and in May 1813, "being incapable, by indisposition, of attending to his usual business, applied for the pecuniary assistance of the society." They denied his claim, believing that he "had feigned himself sick for the purpose of deriving benefit from the Society." They were probably right. According to the return the officers of the society filed to the Supreme Court, Hepburn had not been around when a visiting committee came to check on him. Later, when a doctor examined Hepburn, in accordance with the clause of the constitution calling for a physical examination in cases of doubt, Dr. Isaac Catherall reported that "from the state of his tongue and pulse together with the general appearance of his countenance he believed him not to be so much indisposed as to prevent him from attending to some parts of his business." Catherall went on to say that "he had forborne to be more explicit in his certificate from a reluctance to injure the character" of Hepburn, but "if he should say what he really thought it would be that the said Charles Hepburn was a lazy skulking fellow." He was expelled at a regular meeting of the society on August 10th, in accordance with the second article of the society's constitution, which permitted the removal of members who feigned illness and sought to collect benefits.[8]

According to Hepburn, however, he was expelled "whilst absent" from an August meeting "and without having any previous notice, or knowledge whatever that a motion would at said meeting, be made and acted upon for his expulsion and exclusion." He therefore believed "that his expulsion was illegal and unjust," and he petitioned the court "to grant to him a rule upon the Society to be directed to the proper officers thereof to appear at such time and place as your honours shall direct and shew cause why a mandamus shall not issue to restore your petitioner to all the rights and privileges of a member of said Society." Unfortunately, no outcome is recorded, but it is important to note the basis upon which Hepburn based his claim. He believed that not having been told that a vote would come for his expulsion was, in itself, enough to make his removal void and illegal.[9]

Even without surviving records of a judicial disposition of the petition, then, there is something to be learned. A week after the society filed their formal return to the Supreme Court, they followed it up with an additional attestation that Hepburn's complaint of a lack of notice was of no importance. First, according to the account given by society officer Libbeus Whitney, there was no need to give the man notice of his potential expulsion at the next meeting for the simple reason that no clause in the constitution, no "existing and established practice of the society," required them to. Second, he asserted, they gave Hepburn notice anyway, informing him that his case would be decided at the August 10th meeting. And though Hepburn "did willingly absent himself" he "did request a member of the said society," a Cornelius Campbell, "to appear for him and in his behalf." Indeed, when the society was ready to "postpone the consideration of the case" Campbell made a request on behalf of Hepburn for "a prompt and immediate decision upon his case." They even included Campbell's deposition about his conversations with Hepburn. Campbell described the moment when he informed Hepburn of his expulsion: "Hepburn said no more on the subject and made no complaints of want of notice or otherwise." It appears that all the participants here knew to center upon the question of notice. And that point is key for understanding the extent to which broader, extra-associational standards of fairness—and not simply fine-pointed details of procedure derived from charters or bylaws—were shaping the conduct of the associations of early national Pennsylvania.[10]

The act of seeking redress in court for questions regarding membership in private societies was quickly becoming common. Three men expelled from the German American True Loving Brotherhood, for instance—a society of which very little else is known aside from its receipt of a charter in 1801 under the general incorporation act of 1791—each filed nearly identical petitions and depositions to the Supreme Court in seeking a writ of mandamus to compel his readmission. Two were expelled on the same day, in December 1813, noting that each "did well and faithfully discharge all his duties as a member of the said Corporation, and did in all respects conform to the Constitution, rules, articles, and by-laws of the said corporation" before being "unjustly, illegally, and without sufficient cause expelled from the said Corporation." Another man, a Philadelphia baker named John Stief, was expelled some time later, on August 12, 1815, and his petition was substantially the same. He described how he had fulfilled his duties as a member, had been expelled anyway, and had no other "adequate and specific redress in the premises other than a mandamus to be issued by the supreme court of Pennsylvania to restore him to his right of membership." As they became more common, these efforts by aggrieved members to win what essentially amounted to judicial review for associational decisions would generate a body of reported case law that jurists nationally would cite, discuss, and endorse.[11]

Something else was becoming almost routine: the complaining member won. Time after time, courts would order a compulsory readmission. William M. Stewart was one exception that, in the eyes of a Pennsylvania chief justice writing some forty years after Stewart's case, proved the rule.

In 1813, William Stewart found himself estranged and expelled from the Philanthropic Society in Pennsylvania. Stewart had told them of an illness and, according to the rules of the institution, had presented a physician's bill for forty dollars, which he claimed to have paid, and he asked for compensation. It was obvious to his fellow members (and, indeed, is still obvious on the surviving scrap of paper in the Pennsylvania State Archives) that the doctor's bill had originally been for four dollars. Stewart had added a zero, and his request was denied. The society then expelled him, invoking the thirteenth article of the society's constitution, which permitted the expulsion of those "concerned in scandalous or improper proceedings which might injure the reputation of the society."[12]

Without shame, Stewart went to court. He called for a writ of mandamus to compel the society to restore him to "the standing and rights of a member of the Philanthropic Society." By the time Stewart had joined the society in 1808, admission fees had probably already been raised to five dollars, with quarterly dues of a dollar required to remain a member in good standing. Thus, even leaving aside his reputation, Stewart certainly believed that he had a sufficient investment in the Philanthropic Society to seek a remedy for what he believed to be a wrongful expulsion. According to Stewart, he was not shown to be guilty "of any of the offences" described in the constitution as meriting expulsion, but rather the charges were "altogether foreign to the interests and no relation to the legal objects of the society said incorporation." He asserted that the question posed by article 13—whether his conduct had, indeed, injured the reputation of the society—had not been formally decided or noted in the minutes of his expulsion proceedings. As it stood, the society had expelled him for reasons that fell outside the bounds of its authority.[13]

Stewart's argument failed. "If this was not forgery, it was very like it," wrote Chief Justice William Tilghman when the case was decided in 1813, three years after Tilghman had written his opinion in favor of Binns's successful petition against the St. Patrick Benevolent Society. "Did it tend to injure the reputation of the Society? No man can doubt it. A society that would not be injured by such a proceeding as this, on the part of one of its members, must be a society without reputation." He denied mandamus to compel Stewart's readmission. The case, though, left its mark on the emerging common law of membership. The court did not equivocate on its power and its willingness to look into the central questions of the case and into how Stewart's alleged fraud was treated by the society. It even took into evidence a copy of the minutes of the Philanthropic Society from all of the meetings in which Stewart's case was discussed. And two of the most influential treatises of the nineteenth century, James Kent's *Commentaries* and Joseph Angell and Samuel Ames's *Treatise on the Law of Private Corporations,* would refer to it as important in helping to establish the legal requirements of a member's expulsion.[14]

What is most remarkable about the case is how anomalous the outcome, the court's ultimate approval of the expulsion of a member of a private society, actually was. Writing in 1864, another chief justice of the Pennsylvania Supreme Court, George Washington Woodward, attempted to chronicle the long history of cases in English and American law regarding expulsions and the contested rights of membership. For him, Stewart's case provided something "very rare in the authorities, an instance of expulsion that was sustained." In reported appellate cases, courts rarely hesitated to compel the readmission of a member they believed had been wronged. Indeed, every other case cited by Kent on this point—and most every other American case involving a private corporation cited by Angell and Ames—ended with a court order to readmit the expelled person, many centering on the question of the apparent fairness of the proceedings against the expelled man.[15]

One of the most important of these cases in the decade following *Commonwealth v. St. Patrick Benevolent Society* was a mandamus hearing about an expulsion from the Pennsylvania Beneficial Institution—again, a voluntary society like dozens of others in its basic operations and mutual-benefit arrangements, this one incorporated on June 3, 1812. John Hansell was expelled for failure to pay dues, which, according to the officers of the society, "ipso facto forfeits the right of membership." It was, the officers said, "neither customary nor necessary to take a vote upon the subject as the delinquency carries with itself necessarily the exclusion of a member." But in a unanimous opinion of the Pennsylvania Supreme Court, Tilghman determined that the society's own articles of association called for something else: the fourteenth article, section 2, read that "should any member neglect to pay his arrearages for three months, he shall be expelled." For Tilghman, this meant that "there must be some act of the society, then, declaring the expulsion, and this cannot be without a vote of expulsion"—but, he went on—"after notice to the member supposed to be in default." The member may well have had an explanation, Tilghman reasoned, and justice required that it be heard. Simply put, according to the chief justice, "no man should be expelled in his absence without notice."[16]

Important for the outcome, it appears, was the fact that Hansell did indeed have "an excuse to offer," according to Tilghman: "the society was indebted to him, for his services as secretary, in a larger sum than the amount of the arrears of his monthly contribution." Had he had an opportunity to make this point clear to his fellow members, Tilghman thought, they may well have decided differently. "Be that as it may," wrote Tilghman, "he ought to have had the opportunity." Tilghman followed this up with a summation that made his argument sound more grounded in Pennsylvania law than it really was: "The terms of the charter have not been complied with." But coming as it did after an exposition of the apparent unfairness of Hansell's expulsion, the chief justice appeared to be contemplating matters of substantive justice even as he issued mandamus by invoking the society's charter.

Note especially Tilghman's additional and direct comment that "no man should be expelled in his absence without notice." The English common law governing municipal corporations did, indeed, help to lay the foundation for Tilghman's opinion. On the back of the return filed by the officers of the Pennsylvania Beneficial Institution, someone (probably Tilghman) wrote the citation of an English precedent relevant to the proceedings: *Rex v. May*, a case decided by Lord Mansfield that reinforced a longstanding rule that no man is to be deprived of an opportunity to be heard in his own defense in any matter affecting his interest in a municipal corporation. Notice should always be given before a decision was made affecting the rights of any part of the corporation, even a solitary member. Here, Tilghman was deliberately extending that principle to protect the rights of individual members of the vastly growing assortment of voluntary societies of the commonwealth.[17]

Pennsylvania jurists were willing to extend to societies that were voluntarily joined and were chartered by means of a 1791 statute for incorporating "religious, literary, and charitable societies," then, a common law standard that before 1810 had been used only for governmental or quasi-governmental bodies, such as municipalities. Just as would be decided a few years later in a case involving a profit-seeking business corporation in North Carolina, these private societies, when deciding a case involving one of their own members, were and ought to be treated as courts of justice. And they should be held to the standards and expectations that governed the conduct of any judicial tribunal. One of those—the right to be heard in one's own defense—was fundamental, and no member was to be deprived of it under any circumstances.[18]

The idea that membership was and ought to be a relationship defined by law—and, when push came to shove, secured by courts of law—developed into a robust and full legal reality over the course of second decade of the nineteenth century. Writers and compilers of American legal digests and treatises in the 1820s (such as James Kent) and the 1830s and 1840s (such as Angell and Ames, David Hoffman, and others) would cite and describe *Commonwealth v. St. Patrick Benevolent Society*, often alongside the Pennsylvania mutual benefit society cases that followed, as establishing the idea that expulsion from incorporated voluntary associations was something that could be legitimately challenged by mandamus. Participants in these associations were not there at the pleasure of their fellow members. The rights of membership, which included such things as the right to notice and to fair hearings regardless of whether such principles were spelled out in the articles of agreement, were protected by law.[19]

The "Anti-Masonick Excitement" and the Law of Membership

In 1826, one participant in a voluntary association was kidnapped and murdered by his fellow members. William Morgan had joined a fraternity voluntarily, taking a series of oaths that he would never reveal the secrets he would then learn behind the club's closed doors. And he paid the ultimate price when he dared to disobey the organization's rules and made plans to divulge those secrets to non-members. When local authorities began to look for his murderers, they found conspiracies of silence. Some twenty grand juries and a series of trials and legislative investigations all made little headway in investigating the matter, and no one was ever brought to justice.

This was the story told repeatedly for about a decade after the 1826 disappearance of William Morgan. The voluntary association in question was Freemasonry, undoubtedly the most prominent fraternal club in the Western world. After settling in Batavia, New York, Morgan began preparations to publish an exposé of Masonic rituals, passwords, and oaths that he intended to call *Illustrations of Masonry, by One of the Fraternity*. For reasons that remain unclear, the Virginian, despite being a Mason, had not been admitted into the local lodge, and it seems Morgan's motives for publishing the secrets were a combination of spite and potential profit. His plans became known in the late summer of 1826, and someone took action. He disappeared—some accounts had him shouting "Murder! Murder!" as he was forced into a coach barreling toward the Canada border—and his apparent kidnapping generated a political firestorm of unprecedented scope and animus. No singular vocabulary captured the motivations of many of the men and women who would proudly call themselves "Anti-Masons" in the late 1820s and the 1830s. It was often based in orthodox religion, with critics seeing the ritual of Masonry as a pseudo-religious threat to Christianity, deluding men away from true faith. And Freemasonry was also described as a subversive threat to republican government, creating an *imperium in imperio* of the sort that American citizens since the founding of the Society of the Cincinnati in 1783 had always been especially wary. There was even an element of political opportunism, as some men with bright political futures, such as Thaddeus Stevens and William Seward, seized an opportunity to take part in a social movement that carried with it opportunities to unseat and unsettle local and statewide political establishments. Not least, Anti-Masonry was also shaped by intense anxieties about modernization and the accompanying threats to the household economy and ideal of personal independence in the early republic, issues of great resonance in upstate New York where Morgan disappeared and throughout the Northeast where Anti-Masonry as a political movement would have its greatest success.[20]

But there was more to what became known as the Anti-Masonic excitement. Popular and legal understandings of voluntary membership—what it tended to look like by the mid-1820s, and more general ideas of what it ought to look like—informed and shaped the roughly decade-long movement that affected, in ways large and small, the politics of every state north of the Mason-Dixon line. (In the South, any political movement arrayed against the party of Andrew Jackson, an unrepentant Mason who held all the right positions on the issues of slavery and Indian removal, would make little headway.) According to many of its critics, Freemasonry demanded that its members take powerful, bloody oaths, and the lodges created an insulated, Masonic jurisprudence that could accuse, try, and punish one of its own members for their breach in ways unacceptable in 1820s America. Frederick Whittlesey could denounce Freemasonry as dangerous and murderous "in exercising jurisdiction over the lives of its members for crimes not known to the laws." A committee of upstate New York citizens focused in on the fact that Freemasonry was "an Institution in one instance at least stained with the blood of one of its members by a crime which has in an unequivocal manner received the sanction of the Order." In an era in which Americans of diverse walks of life were forming ever-greater numbers of voluntary organizations for one purpose or another and during which, as we have just seen, there was genuine and repeated attentiveness to the idea that these groups ought never trample the rights of their own members, Morgan's disappearance was a signal moment. It brought Freemasonry under scrutiny on the question of whether it had, in fact, established and enforced a law of membership impermissible in the young American republic, one at odds with and dangerously shielded from the popular will and from broader standards of justice.[21]

William Morgan's *Illustrations of Masonry*, published posthumously (or, at least, post-disappearance), included an unsigned introduction by his publisher, David C. Miller, who had also faced an episode of Masonic persecution when his offices were ransacked as he prepared Morgan's book. Notably, he began with the commonplace observation that humanity's development was, essentially, progress from a lawless state, when man was "weak, powerless, and defenceless," to a lawful one. "For his comfort and well being, as a member of society," Miller wrote, "rules and regulations are necessary." But the legal forms that men develop may well be outgrown. "In the various stages of his progress, these systematic improvements undergo various changes, according to circumstances and situations," he wrote, and "what is proper and necessary in one grade of society, is wholly useless, and may be alarming in another." Morgan's disappearance had proven the laws and practices of Freemasonry, as useful as they may have been in "olden times," "should come out before the open light of day, and be subjected to the rigid test of candid investigation." Miller's point was a revealing and an important one: the rules of Masonry ought to be subjected to scrutiny by the larger, republican community's standards of justice and right.[22]

For the Anti-Masons, the external superintendence of associational rules and practices was a salutary and needful thing. That belief, so important to understanding the emergence of post-Revolutionary American civil society, extended far outside of the courtroom, then, and played an important role in the first grassroots, third-party movement in American history. This was, as Anti-Masonic leaders such as Solomon Southwick were quick to point out, not exactly new. After arriving late to the 1828 Le Roy convention, a key moment in the transformation of the movement into a full-blown political endeavor, Southwick called to mind "with what jealousy the people of these United States had watched the introduction of societies and combinations anti-republican in their tendencies," and he "instanced the decline of the Cincinnatti society [sic], composed of many of the veterans of the Revolution, and the opposition to that article of our federal constitution which authorizes secret sessions of congress." But that "jealousy," or watchfulness, was more fully developed in the 1820s and 1830s assaults on the Masonic institution than it had ever been during the earlier episodes.[23]

Just in terms of its scope and *potential* influence in the early national United States, Masonry was not an organization like any other, something the Morgan affair had shown without doubt. It was no small thing to take on the fraternity that counted men such as George Washington and Andrew Jackson among its brotherhood. And Masonry was far bigger than any of the other fraternal societies against which Americans might choose to compare it. The number of Masons in the United States in the early 1820s has been estimated, probably conservatively, at 80,000, or about 5 percent of the adult white male population of the day. So too were its oaths more worrisome, the layers of secrecy more intriguing, than anything else in America. People began to fear the abstract, potential power of Freemasonry, the privileges it gave to its own. Even men who remained as distant from the Anti-Masonic movement as they could for as long as they could, such as John C. Spencer in New York (he had even served as counsel for the defense in the first Morgan abduction trial in January 1827), had by 1830 decided that the rule of law and, thus, the security of the republican experiment was threatened by the power of Freemasonry. Oaths, secrecy, and other Masonic obstructions that stood in the way of investigations into wrongdoing of any kind ought to be combated in every way. Massachusetts and Rhode Island passed laws prohibiting the administration of extra-judicial oaths in this period, directly aimed to limiting the ability of Masons to ask members and potential members to swear any kind of allegiance to the Craft. There were fears, as was argued in Connecticut, that the oaths asked of members "an unqualified surrender of natural and civil rights," something that no organization ought to be able to do to anyone, member or no. And Masonry had a power and a prominence that made potential threats appear to be, not abstract, but imminently looming.[24]

Without losing sight of the other factors in the genesis of the Anti-Masonic movement, it is also useful to explore how the changing associational landscape and the accompanying popular and legal conceptions of the meanings and consequences of voluntary membership affected how Americans viewed Freemasonry. For one thing, there were ever greater numbers of groups that provided fraternity to their members and vowed to support one another if times grew tough. For another, the vastly increasing numbers of mutual aid societies that appeared to be hybrids, of sorts, between mutual insurance companies and more recognizably fraternal societies spurred change in how all kinds of fraternity and voluntary affiliation were perceived. As a mutual benefit society, Masonry would lag behind the prevailing understandings of how the member-to-society relationship ought to be defined. Members who fell on hard times could *hope* for the support of their fellow Freemasons, but they could not expect it. They could not claim it as a right of membership. Masonic lodges in the nineteenth century, it was believed, were doing less and less in terms of philanthropic endeavors for the general, non-Masonic public. Any charitable support they did offer was to go to their own members. But still this mutual support remained discretionary. In a world of increasing anonymity and growing numbers of young men experiencing life as newly arrived strangers in towns and cities across the young nation, Masonry offered a great deal: contacts for personal advancement, a place of warmth and affection among brothers, and, ideally, a helping hand in times of distress. But what it would not offer—and what growing numbers of mutual benefit societies went out of their way to offer—was a guarantee.[25]

By the 1820s, after the spread of societies organized around the principle of guaranteed benefits for indigent or ill members, many had begun to expect that Masonry too would operate in this more definite mode of mutual insurance and support. Facing hard times, Jesse Bradley, a Mason in Connecticut, wrote to the King Hiram Lodge No. 12 that if "poverty and misfortune can claim a donation," he ought to be entitled to "ask of you some small charity." But when George Bradley took up his pen the next year after his father received no response, his tone was different: having been "a member of your chapter & having paid his money," it was "Just and Reasonable that he could (sins he has become Poor and penalis) have something Either in money or clothing." As historian Dorothy Lipson recounts this moment, George Bradley regarded his father's dues as "an insurance premium."[26]

That mode of thinking about Masonic membership would resonate among critics of the institution. The experience of membership in organizations founded as joint-stock or mutual insurance companies had effects on how many Americans conceived of Masonry. One man who was active with his pen in denouncing Freemasonry, Henry Dana Ward, pointed out in 1828 that the chief kind of support a Masonic lodge offered to its members—help in times of distress—was better performed by a proper mutual aid company. For one thing, in those clubs and fire insurance firms, Ward wrote in his *Anti-Masonic Review*, a person joined for a set period (not for life) and paid into the coffers. For another, that citizen then had a legal claim for support from the society in case of disaster. He would come, then, "as a freeman should come, demanding his right under guaranty of the laws of the country," not as an oath-bound member hoping for the charity of his fellow Masons.[27]

So, too, were many people in 1820s America troubled by the extent to which Masonry attempted to separate itself from the society in which it existed, even the post-Revolutionary American society in which it thrived. In many states, Masons were slow to form any sort of formal relationship with state governments. Most Masonic grand lodges operated without a charter from the state into the 1810s, precisely because they did not want to place themselves in a subservient role to an elected government. Virginia's Grand Lodge decided in 1803, unanimously, that "it is highly *inexpedient* and *dangerous* to apply to the legislature, for any act of incorporation of the Grand Lodge of Virginia, or of any officers or members thereof, either for general purposes." Kentucky Masons, too, reported to their Virginia brethren in 1804 that they had chosen to operate as an unchartered club. The inconveniences of merely having a group of Masons hold their property in trust, without a charter, was nothing compared to the risks associated with incorporation, they decided: "At present, *as a Society*, we acknowledge no superior.—If we should make an Application to the Legislature, it would be acknowledging ourselves under the law; and the legislature would become our *Legal Creators*. Whenever, therefore, that body should think proper, they would have a right (*acknowledged by us in the application to them*) to enquire into *all* our Workings."[28]

In New England, almost all clubs and societies formed for the purposes of mutual support were incorporated, and the Freemasons would eventually begin to seek charters in the 1810s and 1820s. When Masons received a charter, such as the Massachusetts Grand Lodge in 1817, the decision undoubtedly shaped how the organization functioned. One Massachusetts grand master, looking back a decade later at that incorporation, noted its effects: "an amended code of by-laws being required in consequence of that act, the Grand Master, then presiding, was induced to examine fully all the transactions of the Grand Lodge, view them in every possible relation, and adopt a system for the management of its various interests, which should be just to all, while it should require a faithful discharge of duty in all. This system has since been steadily and uniformly followed." And the charter would one day open the Masons up to a lengthy investigation, such as happened in the early 1830s, for failure to adhere to their terms. They surrendered their corporate charter in January 1834. This was a common occurrence: Connecticut's Grand Lodge received a charter in 1821, and some ten years later, in the height of the Anti-Masonic movement, that fact was seized upon by critics of Masonry as entitling the legislature to "enter into an inquiry relative to the nature and tendency of the Institution, particularly the nature of its oaths, obligations, and penalties."[29]

Where Masons consciously opted out of a plan of legal incorporation, outsiders saw it as deeply troubling. According to Richard Rush, addressing an Anti-Masonic State Convention in Pennsylvania in 1832, the Masons had deliberately opted not to seek incorporation in the commonwealth, leaving its opponents with no other option than to go to the people directly to bring the state's grand lodge to account: "If the Lodge existed by act of incorporation from any legislative power the facts proved upon its members on the Morgan trials would long since have led to a forfeiture of its privileges under a writ of *Quo Warranto*. But it stands upon no such footing, and society cannot have the benefit of this legal corrective." The grand lodge, he said, "is self created. It rides in a sphere of its own. . . . It is above the Judiciary."[30]

With or without a charter, a repeated cry of the Anti-Masonic crusaders was not that Masonry was conducted without law, but that it operated within its own legality. Masons could make claims of their fellows, but they need not expect fair treatment, since their claims did not fall "under guaranty of the laws of the country." There was no shortage of laws to which Masonic lodges, grand lodges, and individual members were required to adhere, but these laws, unlike the rules of other mutual benefit societies, were kept at a remove—by oaths, vows of secrecy, and the like—from a larger regime of civil rights that members carried into each private association.

It was with thoughts about the potential existence of a shadow government, complete with its own shadow legal system, that many who had never paid the fraternity much mind would turn against Masonry in the wake of the alleged murder of Morgan in September 1826. Masons were seen to have shielded themselves from the rule of law and from the power of the people through their elected governments. They were not lawless, by any means, but rather had erected their own legal system that Anti-Masonic critics saw as being completely unacceptable in a republican nation. The extremes to which critics of Masonry would go to prove this point bordered on the ridiculous. The Vermont Anti-Masonic Convention in 1831, for example, made one of its very first orders of business the creation of a committee to examine the degree to which Masons lived by their own legal code, and they quoted everything they could get their hands on to show the depth of this Masonic legality, even a line in a song: "Our *laws* all other laws excel." From this, the committee drew the conclusion that "here we are not only told, that masons have laws, but it is more than intimated that other laws cannot counteract them, and that the summum bonum of those laws are in the secrets of the art." The conclusion, then, was no joke. And these critics of an insulated Masonic legality saw only too clearly that "masonic oaths constitute a part of masonic law; and if a part of masonic law they can constitute only the very essence of the law from the very nature of their binding compact, without which the Institution would suddenly rush into its native chaos." Laws were what allowed societies of men to exist. Laws were what gave form to Freemasonry. In this case, however, the laws that Freemasons had agreed upon, among themselves, were a threat to the rule of law in the republic. It would be best, then, to destroy those laws and, thereby, to destroy Masonry.[31]

Masonic legalism cut both ways for Masons who hoped for their institution to coexist peacefully and benevolently with the world around them.

They, like so many other organizations, turned to procedure and well-articulated internal regulations to help their lodges function. Indeed, even their critics knew that it took laws and internal rules to create any well-functioning association. And Freemasons really did seek nothing less than real fraternal discipline; they were attempting to build better men. All mutual benefit societies asked members to participate in fraternal functions, not merely to sign up as insurance beneficiaries. Bringing men together as equals was important as a way to foster participation, encourage reciprocity, and allow such groups to be perceived as a joint affair among equals. And Masons certainly believed that those mutual benefit societies based more on financial contribution than on fraternal ties could never improve their members the way that Masonry could.[32]

As Dorothy Lipson has observed, however, they were then "vulnerable to the charges that they overlapped the jurisdiction of the civil courts, competed with the discipline of the churches, or invaded individual rights." In important ways, notions of what membership ought to look like were a factor in this decline. Lebbeus Armstrong, a minister and former Mason who became an outspoken critic of the Craft, saw that "men may live in a free country, be bound by righteous laws to observe truth and justice, be entitled to all the natural rights of citizenship" and yet find themselves "bound with chains of masonic despotism . . . to fulfil masonic obligations, and to escape the desert of masonic vengeance." To allow this, Armstrong told his readers, was to allow a "total dereliction of the rights of man." The murder of William Morgan—and, still more, the concealment of that murder—"shows the lodge to be too strong for the Law," according to Anti-Masonic politician Richard Rush. And this was not a problem simply faced by others: if it happened that William Morgan ("your free fellow citizen," as the first national Anti-Masonic convention made sure to call him) faced the tyranny of his fellow Freemasons, such a thing could happen to any man who found himself deceived or seduced into joining a lodge.[33]

When inquiry after inquiry, trial after trial, failed to find and hold anyone accountable for the disappearance of Morgan, it appeared to prove that the rule of law was threatened by Freemasonry. "The masonic oath was soon found to be a shackle upon the officers and ministers of the law," announced the Le Roy convention in 1828: "The lips of witnesses were sealed by a mysterious and invisible influence, or opened only in the utterance of falsehoods." Every informed observer by this time knew that even fully voluntary associations required rules and regulations to function effectively, but if those internal rules were unaccountable to—or, worse, were a threat to—the voice of the people and the rule of law, then it was simply too profound a danger to let be.[34]

So, too, did it appear to many Anti-Masons that Freemasonry was a threat to the *political* independence of American citizens. Here, Anti-Masons rehearsed many of the same criticisms leveled against the political organizations of the 1790s and 1800s. One former Freemason in Pennsylvania, named John Stem, was interviewed by Thaddeus Stevens's investigative committee in the Pennsylvania House of Representatives in 1836. He was asked whether he had "heard the subject of politics mentioned, and any injunction for masons to vote for each other?" His answer shows how widely shared this idea that no private association ought to dictate to its members how to vote had become. When informed that he needed to give his political support "in favour of a brother mason who was up for office," Stem spoke with "another member of the lodge, who was high in masonry," to tell him that he could not in good conscience support a man for office simply because he was a fellow Mason. The other member of the lodge informed Stem that "he did not know how I would get out of it, as it was my duty to vote for a brother mason, when requested." Stem held fast to his personal conviction that no Masonic lodge could dictate his vote, even though he showed no concerns that, as a loyal Democrat, he was indeed bound to support the party's favored candidates for office. As Stem recalled the exchange for the Stevens committee, "I told him if the applicant was regularly nominated by the democratic party, then only would I feel myself bound to vote for him." It was, for Stem, something essentially different to have committed oneself voluntarily to support the nominees of a political party, which by the 1820s were becoming generally accepted as a genuine expression of, not an infringement of, a citizen's political voice.[35]

The Anti-Masonic literature reveals to extent to which many Americans had come to embrace a particular conception of how the relationship between individual member and voluntary society ought to be well defined, limited, and effectively constrained by the laws of the community. Critics of Masonry adored associations that asked little of likeminded individuals and were governed by articles of agreement that, unlike Masonic laws and regulations, were fully a part of a larger, all-encompassing rule of law. Though they could not abide a Masonic regime of law, shielded from the will of the people by secrecy, oaths, and even violence, Anti-Masons were "joiners" through and through, organizing and forming membership organizations in order to make their voice heard. They formed clubs, drew up constitutions and bylaws with abandon, organized conventions, and named honorary members. But they did all these things in a manner that adhered to prevailing trends in associational practices in the 1820s and 1830s, eschewing oaths, secrecy, and lifelong commitments in favor of plans based on low membership dues and shared commitment to a single cause. The Young Men's Anti-Masonic Association in Boston, for instance, admitted men with payment of dues of fifty cents, made it clear in their constitution that meetings would be open to any and all spectators, and spelled out every one of their relevant beliefs in a lengthy, published preamble.[36]

The remarkable success of Odd Fellowship that occurred simultaneously with the decline of Masonry is also noteworthy. Odd Fellowship shared many features with Freemasonry, yet it swelled in numbers in the 1820s and 1830s even as Masonry was dwindling in some places to near non-existence. Begun in England in the late eighteenth century, Odd Fellows lodges were a part of the first confederated mutual benefit society, with local lodges all a part of a national network of Odd Fellows clubs. The first American lodge appeared in Baltimore in 1819, a gathering of working-class immigrants affiliated with the Manchester Unity in England. During the 1830s, in part fueled by exiles from Freemasonry, the Odd Fellows grew in numbers and in social standing, beginning to comprise lawyers, doctors, merchants, prosperous tradesmen, and other members of an American middle class, all part of a deliberate effort to bring a new, refined tone to Odd Fellowship led by the only native-born American to join in the first decade, Augustus Mathiot. In many ways, the Odd Fellows resembled Freemasonry, and they were in some ways becoming more, not less, alike. Odd Fellows made no attempt to dispense with secrecy and ritual, and they made deliberate attempts to create a governing system, even establishing a Grand Lodge of the United States, in 1825, before there were many members to speak of, giving the still-immature organization a federal structure.[37]

What the Odd Fellows did not have, from the perspective of many outsiders, was the same potential as Masonic institutions to infringe upon the rights of members and nonmembers. For one, and most obviously, they did not have the same breadth and potential power as did Freemasonry. For another, the Odd Fellows, early in their history, made a decision that made them more akin to the local mutual benefit society than to Freemasonry, despite all the Odd Fellows' interest in secrecy, ritual, and initiatory rites: they replaced charity, or passing the hat to help fellow members, "with a system of fixed weekly assessments" (probably instituted in Baltimore as early as 1825) and made a point to teach lodge treasurers "double-entry bookkeeping and money management."[38]

Odd Fellows were not guiltless from the perspective of many crusading Anti-Masons, to be sure. Thaddeus Stevens's investigative committee in Pennsylvania in 1836 appeared to be as anxious about Odd Fellowship as it was about Masonry, even appending "An Exposure of Odd Fellowship, by a Past Grand" to its final report. And published exposés often included descriptions of rituals from all kinds of secretive organizations, such as Masonry, Phi Beta Kappa, Odd Fellowship, and others. But one way to read the *success* of Odd Fellowship amid the decline of Freemasonry is to emphasize its closer adherence to prevailing norms of voluntary membership in 1820s and 1830s America. Masonry evoked the responses that it did for reasons that were peculiar to its size and scope, but those responses were shaped by changing notions of how the group life of civil society ought to be superintended by the legal and political institutions of the state. Decades of experience and evolution in the practice and the law of individual, voluntary affiliation provided a vocabulary and a frame of reference for the Anti-Masonic movement.[39]

By the time the Anti-Masonic crusade had essentially run its course, by the late 1830s, Freemasonry was a shell of its former self. New York's five hundred lodges in 1825 were dwindled to 75 a decade later, and the number of Masons nationwide was probably more than halved to 40,000 by 1835. But the conversation throughout much of the nation that began with disappearance of William Morgan also had a number of repercussions for American conceptions of voluntary membership. The central question that it asked—how private regimes of law were fitted into the larger political and legal order—had recognizable parallels with smaller-scale disputes such as those decided by Pennsylvania courts in the preceding decade.[40]

Defenders of Masonry were by no means silent, however. In fact, one important aspect of the Masonic response to the Anti-Masonic fervor of the 1820s and 1830s is revealing of a drift toward something new in popular and legal conceptions of membership: a new understanding of individual affiliation that came to center on the notion of contract. Sui juris individuals in the United States should be able to enter those groups that they wished, and be governed by those groups in the ways that they wished, unlimited by the state. Charles Moore, grand secretary of the Massachusetts Masonic Grand Lodge, provided a good expression of this view in an 1836 address to fellow Masons of a New Hampshire lodge. He argued that one truth firmly established over the course of the recent Anti-Masonic crisis was that the state ought not to limit the ability of each individual to enter into agreements with his fellow men, "to regulate, or interfere with the conventional obligations of private individuals, or associations," as long as "those obligations do not militate against their allegiance and duties as good and faithful citizens." Government "has not the power either to prohibit or to dictate the terms in which an individual may pledge himself to his fellow, whether that pledge assume the solemnity of an oath, or the ordinary form of a promise. In either case, it is a matter of conscience, the full and free enjoyment of which is secured to every citizen of this Republic, by the Constitution under which he lives." Moore, an impassioned defender of Freemasonry in Massachusetts throughout the period of the Anti-Masonic excitement, had founded a journal, the Boston *Masonic Mirror*, to advocate for Masonry on a monthly and then a weekly basis beginning in 1828. Eight years later, his energy and devotion to Freemasonry had not flagged, and he remained fully committed to the idea that a man ought to be able to join, voluntarily, a Masonic lodge and to swear his fealty to the values of reason, self-improvement, and cosmopolitanism that Masonry so effectively embodied.[41]

To allow these sorts of private commitments to be made and to be enforced by the groups themselves was a good and salutary thing, men such as Moore would begin to argue in the 1830s, precisely at the same time that men in labor unions were assuming a conspicuous role in the American associational landscape, making substantially the same arguments. As long as those associational commitments did not go *too* far, intruding on the ability of members to function as citizens in the republic, or leaving them vulnerable to unchecked private power, people ought to be allowed to join together in whatever manner they chose.

The End of Direct Legal Superintendence of the Rights of Members

It was with widespread agreement about what membership ought to look like that courts began to bring to an end their direct superintendence of the internal affairs of American voluntary societies. In its place, they would begin to insist that each man who considered joining a voluntary society must fully acquaint himself with the rights and duties of membership, and if he entered into that group he should consider himself bound by those previously agreed-upon rules and fully answerable to the society should he violate them. Disputes arising out of mutual benefit societies in Pennsylvania are powerful evidence of this turn, when courts in the late 1830s pointedly refused to intervene to restore expelled individuals to membership if there was no evidence that the group's decision-making *process* was improper, that it deviated from the group's own constitution or bylaws. When the Pennsylvania Supreme Court denied Isaac Vandyke in his attempt to challenge his expulsion from the Black and White Smiths' Society in Philadelphia in 1837, it helped to establish what became the prevailing jurisprudential standard: courts ought not to intervene in cases of expulsion from private societies if the proper procedures were followed by the proper associational authority. No attempt should be made to weigh the merits, to determine the justice or injustice, of that decision.

The Journeyman Black and White Smiths' Beneficial Society of the City and County of Philadelphia had been incorporated in 1829, under the same general incorporation statute that had facilitated the incorporation of mutual benefit societies since the Washington administration. Isaac Vandyke had been a member for "several years" before he was expelled on November 1, 1834. He had begun receiving sick benefits earlier that year, until the committee of stewards charged with supervising such matters determined "that his sickness was caused by intoxication and other outrageous conduct of his own," and they suspended his benefits and brought charges for his expulsion by the whole society. Vandyke had been given notice that his case would be decided at a coming meeting, and though he did not appear at the hearing "his guilt was voted by twenty-five to four, and his expulsion pronounced by twenty-three to six." He went to the alderman, then to the court of common pleas, filing an action on the case for the sick benefits due him, arguing that he had been illegally expelled.[42]

In perfect accordance with post-Revolutionary legal standards governing American voluntary groups, Vandyke won at the trial level. Lower courts do not commonly innovate, and thus he was declared to be entitled to twenty dollars in wrongfully withheld benefits. The court had closely read and entered into evidence the relevant bylaws, especially article 10, section 1, which read: "No member shall be entitled to receive any benefits from the society, whose complaints or disease has been the effect of debauchery, intoxication, wilful fighting, or any outrageous conduct of his own, which it shall be the duty of the stewards at all times particularly to investigate; and on proof thereof, such member or members shall not receive any benefits: and the stewards shall report thereof to the society at the next stated meeting; when, on sufficient proof thereof, such member or members shall be expelled." Most crucially, according to the appellate records the judge's charge to the jury had asked them to determine the *truth* of the charges against Vandyke, as had long been the rule. The jury was to determine, on the merits, whether the decision to expel had been properly made. When the society appealed the decision against them to the Pennsylvania Supreme Court, they objected to five aspects of the lower court's charge to the jury, all relating in one way or another to truth of the allegations against Vandyke.

The Black and White Smiths' Society objected to the charge "that if the defendant was expelled from the society for an alleged cause which was not founded in truth, he was entitled to recover benefits, alleged to have become due even after the date of such expulsion, in this form of action." They objected to the court's decision to admit any evidence proving or disproving Vandyke's intemperance. And they objected especially to the idea that the power to decide this case, granted to the association by its constitution, bylaws, and charter, was to be held null if a court decided that the society had reached the wrong conclusion. Thus, they strenuously objected to the court's charge "that although the society, under the constitution and by-laws, had a right, at the meeting of the 6th of September 1834, to receive the charge of the stewards against the defendant, and by a vote founded on that charge, to direct that the defendant should not receive further benefits; yet, if in this action that charge be proved to have been untrue, the defendant may recover." In sum, they argued that, be they ultimately right or wrong, the decision was theirs to make.

With a powerfully worded opinion written by Chief Justice John Bannister Gibson, the state supreme court overturned the lower court's decision. In an often-quoted passage at the close of his opinion, Gibson succinctly described the new approach that courts would take in such matters: "he was convicted and expelled by the requisite majority. Into the regularity of these proceedings, it is not permitted us to look. The sentence of the society, acting in a judicial capacity and with undoubted jurisdiction of the subject-matter, is not to be questioned collaterally, while it remains unreversed by superior authority." He went on to expand the implications of the court's decision, in order to encompass all the earlier cases in which mandamus had been the remedy sought: "If the plaintiff has been expelled irregularly, he has a remedy by mandamus to restore him, *but neither by mandamus nor action, can the merits of his expulsion be re-examined.*" Vandyke had opted to join this society, which operated according to "the charter to which the plaintiff expressly assented at his initiation; and he is consequently bound by everything done in accordance with it." The proper assembly of men had heard his case, according to the proper, charter-prescribed mode, and they had reached a conclusion that Gibson's court would not then question. Mandamus, Gibson made clear, was now to be limited to only those cases in which there was an "open disregard of the prescribed forms of procedure," regardless of whether that process had led to a just outcome.[43]

In 1844, a petition for a writ of mandamus came to the Pennsylvania Supreme Court that reinforced the turn that Gibson had described seven years earlier. John Bryan had been a member in good standing of the Pike Beneficial Society, but he had been expelled for violating the tenth article of the club's constitution, which held that "should any member, while deriving the benefit allowed by the society, be engaged at his usual business or occupation, or any other employment (except giving the necessary directions to those employed by him), he shall, on being convicted thereof, be expelled." According to the lower court's recounting of the fact of the case, on June 28, 1841, members of the society witnessed Bryan with a paintbrush in hand, doing some work, in clear violation of the club's rules. The society, in accordance with the eleventh article of their constitution, notified Bryan that he was to be brought up for expulsion at the next meeting. The requisite two-thirds of the Pike Beneficial Society then voted to expel Bryan. He took them to court.

The judge at the court of common pleas gave Bryan a sympathetic ear. Noting especially the fact that Bryan had not, in fact, done much work at all—"the only act of which it is alleged he has been guilty, is that of painting a latch to his own gate, or, to use the language of some of the witnesses, the 'handle' to the gate, a piece of wood used for its fastening, about ten inches long and three inches wide"—Judge Parsons informed the jury that they did not need to limit themselves in this case. "The plaintiff denies that he did paint it himself; but the evidence seems to be tolerably clear that he did. The cause mainly turns upon a question of law to be decided by the court. Hence we instruct you, that even if the jury believe that Bryan did do the painting to the gate, as testified to by the witnesses, he has not so far violated the laws of that association as to warrant his expulsion." Parsons told them that Bryan "simply took a porringer of paint, and with a brush painted the latch or fastening to his gate, that had got soiled; can it with propriety be said that he had been labouring for himself for gain, following his own business for profit, or doing any act which brings him within the provision of that article?" And so he instructed them "that, under the whole evidence in the cause, the law of that society has not been violated, in this instance, by the plaintiff, and that your verdict ought to be in his favour."[44]

The Supreme Court of Pennsylvania, however, decided to use this case to put to rest any further attempts to have courts reexamine cases of expulsion on the merits. In a succinct, one-paragraph opinion, Justice Thomas Sergeant writing for the court, insisted that "this case cannot be distinguished from that of White and Black Smith's Society v. Vandyke" [*sic*].

Because "the charter to the defendants below provides for the offence, directs the mode of proceeding, and authorizes the society, on conviction of the member, to expel him," the society had every right to determine Bryan's case for themselves. Seeing as "there is no allegation of the irregularity of the proceeding," the determination and the sentence of the Pike Beneficial Society "is conclusive on the merits, and cannot be inquired into collaterally either by *mandamus* or action, or in any other mode. It is like an award made by a tribunal of the party's own choosing; for he became a member under and subject to the articles and conditions of the charter, and, of course, to the provisions on this subject as well as others. The society acted judicially, and its sentence is conclusive, like that of any other judicial tribunal." His court would intervene if the previously-agreed-upon rules for resolving disputes in cases such as expulsion were not followed, but only in those cases. If the right procedures were followed, a man such as Bryan had no recourse at law: "The courts entertain a jurisdiction to preserve these tribunals in the line of order, and to correct abuses; but they do not inquire into the merits of what has passed *in rem judicatam* in a regular course of proceedings."[45]

At about the same moment that the Anti-Masonic crusade had run its course, then, courts began to withdraw themselves from direct superintendence of the internal workings of mutual benefit societies, setting the standards for judicial intervention in private associations for the remainder of the nineteenth century. Indeed, this turn has helped to obscure the earlier, post-Revolutionary tendency of courts to involve themselves and even to intervene in the internal workings of early American membership societies such as mutual benefit clubs. A still more powerful obscuring influence, described in chapter 8, was the rise a new form of pledge-oriented society that aimed at profound personal and social transformation, marked particularly by the rise of the temperance and antislavery societies of the 1830s. By the late 1800s, associational disputes were consistently resolved or ignored by jurists on the premise that the matter was a purely contractual one, embodied in an agreement that in itself contained the terms for (usually internal) modes of resolving the conflict. A modern conception of contracting as private lawmaking would come to prevail, one in which the parties, free and capable, created a legal regime to govern future conduct. Strictly contractual understandings of association would then face substantial criticism by those emphasizing an organic, corporate reality to collective action in the early twentieth century, and equitable relief took central place.

From the 1830s on, it was an accepted truth that members of such societies had all agreed upon the ways in which any decisions made regarding their rights and duties as members would be determined, and so they ought to consider themselves bound by the outcome. At least some of the fraternal mutual aid groups of the late nineteenth century fought tooth and nail against that development, this turn toward a contractual understanding of the whole collective endeavor, hoping to shield the mutual insurance of their own membership associations from the regulation of the law, as the recent work of Jonathan Levy has shown. They failed. For the antebellum era, however, this was a shift in the direction of greater associational autonomy. The outcome of decisions made within these contractual regimes—those decisions, at least, that were made by the proper authorities in the proper manner—would not be reexamined on the merits.[46]

It was Carol Weisbrod's *Boundaries of Utopia* that first brought out just how revealing it is that so very many nineteenth-century utopian communities were based upon membership agreements that were expressed and interpreted as contracts. From the perspective of the communitarians no less than those outside the society, that approach to membership did not deny but rather essentially rested upon judicial authority, even if courts quite often declared that they chose not to intervene in a particular dispute. Communal societies like the Shakers were not isolated and removed from the law; the Maine Supreme Court noted in 1825 that, if the Shaker community leaders "should be found to abuse their power, they are answerable both civilly and criminally for their misconduct." Nonetheless, courts would declare repeatedly that people ought to be able to submit, by signature, to the lawfully exercised authority of the communal group, even if it meant giving up all of their worldly possessions, in part because "the very formation and subscription of this covenant is an exercise of the inalienable right of liberty of conscience," as the same court would declare a year later.[47]

Weisbrod's conclusion that groups such as the Shakers were ultimately acceptable in nineteenth-century America so long as those outside of them were confident that every Shaker had entered voluntarily—and, importantly, could leave any time he or she wanted to—remains persuasive. State authority and broadly applicable legal principles served to mark the furthest limits of associational authority, but often in a way that reinforced the authority of utopian communities over their own, those who chose to stay. As the Shakers themselves noted repeatedly in the 1820s and 1830s, their members were duty bound to obey so long as they remained members: they were "required by the rules of the Society to do this, or withdraw." Obedience was "a matter of free choice." The legal regimes of the early United States, though not without much contestation and occasional legislative interventions, ultimately supported the Shakers' efforts to create a community of "subordination and obedience" that nonetheless rested on the voluntary assent to what they called, interchangeably, their "Covenant or Constitution."[48]

Utopian communities made use of membership contracts to create wholly new societies. And yet anything that appeared to take away the possibility of judicial superintendence would be and would remain impermissible. If individuals "had voluntarily joined communities under peculiarly rigorous contracts," Weisbrod observed, they had done so "in the exercise of rights available under the legal system, and that legal system remained available to scrutinize the contracts." And such an increasingly contractual understanding of individual membership would, by midcentury, come to pervade much of American voluntarism.[49]

By the 1840s, a widely agreed-upon element in that understanding was that individuals ought to be trusted to come to their own articles of agreement *and* that they ought always to know what those rules included. A handful of societies—particularly fire companies in the late eighteenth century and into the nineteenth—had included in their bylaws a requirement that members ought always to have their copy of the constitution at hand, sometimes under penalty of a small fine. And the fact that so many private constitutions and associational bylaws were printed in small, even pocket-sized pamphlets suggests that they were intended to be carried to meetings for ready reference. In 1842, the Pennsylvania Supreme Court seized upon that idea in a decision against a member of a Franklin Beneficial Society in a dispute that "is undoubtedly calculated to excite sympathy, and to enlist feelings in favour of the plaintiff." Although that plaintiff, a man who was denied benefits because he was unable, physically, to apply for them, "was so injured as to be deprived of the power of applying, there seems no sufficient reason why he might not have had it done for him by another, according to the forms prescribed in the pamphlet containing the constitution and laws, a copy of which every member as he has a deep interest in its contents, ought, in common prudence, to have always in his possession." By the 1840s, courts had grown willing to accept what might be seen as unfair or even cruel outcomes, under the pretense that the members of these societies had known—or, at least, ought to have known—the nature of their agreements and to have acted accordingly.[50]

It was a legal and a cultural shift that would help to shape American society well into the twentieth century. And the fact that the American law of membership would by the 1830s come to include a newfound focus on the individual member as being entitled and empowered to enter into agreements as he saw fit—even to join a group that might thereafter compel its members to do something that might seem to be a burden to him and a danger to the community, such as an agreement to work only for a certain, minimum wage—would come to its fullest expression in the most controversial of post-Revolutionary American societies: the labor union.

PART THREE

Consequences: Civil Society in Antebellum America

In 1764, long before separation from Great Britain was even contemplated, let alone desired, one of the great defenders of the rights of British America shared his thoughts about the place of smaller, voluntarily associations in a society of laws. James Otis did it by following the hierarchy of power and authority downward, from Almighty God, to the King-in-Parliament, and below. "It seems easy to conceive subordinate powers in gradation," he wrote in 1763, "till we descend to the legislative of a town council, or even a private social club. These have each 'a one whole legislative' subordinate, which, when it don't counteract the laws of any of its superiors, is to be indulged." And what should happen if, indeed, the lower and lesser authority should transgress its boundaries of authority? Otis had an answer: "The superior does not destroy the subordinate, but will negative its acts, as it may in all cases when disapproved." He believed that "this right of negative is essential, and may be inforced," though it was limited by "the essential rights of the subjects." Writing from British North America, with an obvious purpose of, as his title declared, asserting and proving the rights of the British colonies, Otis described a world not far different from the one that antebellum Americans would come to know.[1]

By the end of the first decade of the nineteenth century, American joiners found that their private associations were effectively encompassed within a broader jurisprudence governing voluntary membership, in which courts could be called upon by members and former members who believed they had been misused by the groups they had joined. But this was less an unwelcome intrusion than it was an extension and, perhaps, a fulfillment of the priorities and practices of the joiners and organizers themselves. Men and women embraced law-minded ways of joining together, and courts of law were willing to enforce the bonds and the boundaries of legitimate association. The concept of voluntary membership—how it ought to originate, the rights and duties that it produced—was something that was worked out by experience and contest, particularly through the institutions and the language of law.

Procedural fairness was key, both to the members themselves and from the perspectives of judges and juries that, through the 1830s, continued to play a key role in shaping American civil society by enforcing the idea that people carried rights into these relationships, rights that merited legal superintendence. Among these were the right to be a part of only those groups with which a person wished to be affiliated; rights to due process in private but incorporated groups, including the right to have an opportunity to speak in one's own defense in any hearing that might affect what was often called "the right of membership"; and the right to be protected from all claims of private, associational authority that were not founded on clear and informed consent.

It was from that vantage that, by the middle of the nineteenth century, even organized labor was beginning to be seen as falling within the boundaries of acceptability. Between the late eighteenth century and the seminal year of 1842, when for the first time a court ruled that labor unions had a legitimate place in the American social landscape, post-Revolutionary Americans' experiences with voluntary membership in organizations of the most ordinary kind—fraternal clubs, reform societies, profit-seeking businesses, and the like—gave them a vocabulary and an intellectual framework by which they would come to understand the labor union. As we will see in chapter 7, many people came to accept labor unions as a legitimate and acceptable presence in their communities for reasons that were more conceptual than legal, more ideational than economic. And these people, most notably Massachusetts Chief Justice Lemuel Shaw, would draw from ideas that arose out of the interesting career of the concept of voluntary membership in the post-Revolutionary United States.

The first generations of American citizens learned a great deal about how to join together in ways voluntary, effective, and safe for both the republic and the individual citizen. Something new did appear in the 1830s, however, when temperance and antislavery societies that were organized around a pledge—a public confession of faith in the cause and an internalized commitment to both personal and societal transformation—brought a novel and powerful kind of voluntary membership to the United States. And thus the post-Revolutionary emphasis on procedure and law-minded practices in American civil society sowed the seeds of its own historical obscurity, for the associational diversity that it nurtured had produced new ways of thinking about the meanings of voluntary membership, new ways of joining together. The pluralism of antebellum American civil society had opened the door to something new and radically transformative.

SEVEN

Labor Unions and an American Law of Membership

The very first man to take the stand in the very first conspiracy trial against a labor union in the United States was asked: "Did you join the society of you [*sic*] own free will, or were you compelled to join it?" The very next man was asked, "Did you join it voluntarily, or was you compelled?" In summing up the position of the prosecution, Jared Ingersoll condemned the union with the argument "that to force a man to become a member of any society whatever, is inconsistent with the imprescriptable rights of man." One of the essential elements of what it meant to be a member, it was clear, was informed and uncoerced consent. And some Americans of the early nineteenth century believed that there were degrees of compulsion among workingmen to join labor unions that made such groups stand out as something different, dangerous, and unacceptable.[1]

Organized labor was—and is—a species of collective action that evoked both fear and hope, that simultaneously elicited impassioned support and full-blown opposition, in ways that very few groups can. And, indeed, other citizens in the early United States saw the organization of workingmen quite differently. Caesar Rodney, a lawyer for the shoemakers in the first conspiracy trial, told the court that if his clients were to be deemed guilty of a crime for refusing to work alongside nonmembers, then the Whig and the Cliosophic societies of Princeton University might be next in court: "Would the members of either of those bodies," he asked, "be considered amenable in a court of criminal justice, for uniting in an act of expulsion or refusing to associate with the member when expelled?" The parallel he drew was, for the court, unpersuasive, but a generation later that kind of conceptual pairing of organized labor with other, more acceptable forms of voluntary association would transform labor law in the United States. Before 1842, however, ideas about what constituted compulsion and what constituted consent were central to an important conceptual line that was so often drawn between labor organizations and other forms of voluntarism.[2]

People in the early American republic frequently asked to what extent men (and, in some cases, women) really were free to choose their membership in laborers' organizations. And they wondered, too, how the answer to that question ought to change the way such groups were superintended by the legislative and judicial institutions of the state. The literature on the early American labor movement is immense and varied. But historians and legal scholars have tended to discuss early labor organizations and the legal and political debates regarding such associations without reference to contemporary discussions and beliefs regarding the meanings and consequences of voluntary membership. By examining the varieties of labor organizations that were formed in the late eighteenth and early nineteenth centuries as well as the labor trials for criminal conspiracy—from the first such case, in Philadelphia in 1806, through the seminal decision of Lemuel Shaw in Massachusetts in 1842—we can derive a better sense of how Americans in the early republic came to define what constituted compulsion, what constituted consent, and how the answers to both helped to draw a line among associations, between the innocuous and the unacceptable.

The common law and an emerging jurisprudence regarding voluntary membership appeared to many to offer the best means to guarantee that each American citizen had access to the same rights and remedies, regardless of whether he worked in a particular trade or had joined a particular society. When Shaw decided in 1842 that a journeymen's society did not, necessarily, commit a crime when it made concerted efforts to compel people to pay or work only for certain wages, he did so by deliberately evoking the examples of other kinds of associations—a temperance society, a joint-stock bakery—and asking, how are these things different? By 1842, as Americans were coming to agree on what membership in all of these kinds of associations ought to look like, Shaw could give an answer that his predecessors had not been able to give: they were not different at all.

General Societies and Masters' Trade Associations in Post-Revolutionary America

William Manning was an uneducated but remarkably aware political observer from Billerica, Massachusetts, when he drafted a series of radical commentaries on the new American republican order in the 1790s. One of the ideas that Manning hoped to bring before the reading public was that self-organization was a ubiquitous and even inevitable consequence of the fact that there were distinct interests in society. And formal association ought to be encouraged among the as-yet poorly organized multitudes of the uneducated and nonelite. He referred specifically to bar associations and societies of ministers, even to the Society of the Cincinnati organized by Revolutionary War veterans, but he did not declare that such groups were dangerous or at all regrettable. "I would not be understood to be against the associations of any orders of men, for to hinder them would hinder their improvements in their professions, and hinder them from being serviceable to the Many"—that is, to those who were neither professionals nor well-to-do. "There need only be one society more established," a society of the Many, what Michael Merrill and Sean Wilentz describe as "a national membership organization, with state, county, town, and neighborhood chapters." It would be called the Labouring Society, and he offered a constitution for its organization. He was only one of a very many people in the early American republic that looked around, saw all of the organizations that appeared to strengthen the positions of the elite—the merchants, doctors, ministers, and lawyers—and drew the conclusion that, perhaps, the lower orders of society ought to organize, too.[3]

Men who worked with their hands never did form a society that had national reach in the early American republic. Locally, however, there were growing numbers of mechanics' societies from the 1780s onward, usually organized according to trade and city but also including larger "general" societies that admitted men from any mechanical trade. Three kinds of labor organizations became increasingly active in American society in the late eighteenth and, still more, the early to mid-nineteenth centuries: general societies that had open membership policies (though they often included only the well-to-do); tradesmen's societies that tended to be formed by masters but often sought to include all practitioners of a particular craft; and societies organized solely for journeymen. It was the journeymen who faced nearly all of the formal charges of conspiracy levied against such associations. The changing experiences and conceptions of voluntary association—that is, the search for a shared understanding of the concept of voluntary membership—would inform and shape every one of those trials.

The general societies of the early national period began to be formed in the 1780s. The General Society of Mechanics and Tradesmen was founded in New York in 1785 (it would be incorporated in 1792), the same year that the Mechanics and Manufacturers of Boston sent a circular letter to mechanics in various cities in the new United States, hoping to form like organizations throughout the nation. They had a variety of goals in mind, but most significant was their hope to push forward a protectionist political agenda. Some years later, in 1789, while officially still removed from the new federal union by Rhode Island's tardy ratification of the Constitution, the Providence Association of Mechanics and Manufacturers formed. They happily informed the Boston mechanics that, although they were responding four years late, they were ready to join "with you as a 'Band of Brothers,' in a general Association . . . that we might thereby become one of the links in the chain, with our highly esteemed Brethren, the Mechanics and Manufacturers, of our Sister States." They were pleased to be able to describe their new charter of incorporation, and they sent their own letters out to the cities of the union, such as Philadelphia, hoping to further the spread of these new general societies of mechanics and manufacturers. The Providence group would number two hundred in the 1790s; the New York society had six or seven hundred members in the decade following.[4]

General societies in the 1790s had wide-ranging purposes but made fervent efforts to create a real sense of unity, something they had not bothered with before. In Baltimore in 1785, for instance, an Association of Tradesmen and Manufacturers formed, by and large, to pursue the passage of protective tariffs. Once its goal was achieved, the Association disappeared. But in 1792, a Baltimore Mechanical Society was formed to include the city's "mechanics and manufacturers," and it had for its stated purposes a much broader agenda. They met in January 1793 to draw up and ratify a constitution, one that included not only political activism in behalf of favorable trade policies but also the establishment of a benefit fund for its members. The General Society in New York also came to include aspects that made it something much more than a politically oriented association. According to historian Howard Rock, they instituted "Masonic-like secrecy and mystery, fostering a sense of exclusivity" and thereby enhanced "the prestige and esteem of the honored mechanic membership," and their iconography and language spoke with great power about the ties that bound the members together. Their use of formal ritual, in fact, was a forerunner to the sorts of fraternal elements that became ubiquitous in the later nineteenth century among labor unions and cooperative self-insurance associations, which found that handshakes and passwords could help to forge a level of solidarity necessary to their thriving.[5]

The general mechanics' societies of the early national era embraced associational practices, ranging from mutual support to formal ritual, that were derived from other kinds of groups but also evoked a preindustrial, guild-like past. They engaged in (noncoercive) membership drives, such as when the Providence Association appointed a committee "to wait on such the Mechanics and Manufacturers of this Town as have not yet joined the

5. General Society of Mechanics and Tradesmen of the City of New York, blank membership certificate, Certificate File, PR 014, New-York Historical Society.

Association." They followed virtually identical organizational practices as did the mariners who were also setting up voluntary associations in the same seaport cities, and their constitutions became increasingly detailed. The New York General Society, for one, set up formal policies dictating the exact procedures to be followed in cases of proposed expulsion, with full articulation of the rights of the accused. A sampling of the constitutions and charters of the general societies reveals a fairly consistent approach toward the definitions of membership, including both the manner in which men were to be admitted and the expectations regarding their behavior as members. These general mechanics' societies, one could say, were manifestations of a particular way of looking at the world, one centered on the idea that people of a chosen livelihood ought to look after one another. As Thomas Mercein of the General Society told an audience in 1820, "There seems to be a moral propriety in each class superintending the immediate concerns of the members of its distinct profession and pursuit, as well as of their Widows and their Orphans." And the manner in which they did so became increasingly organized, increasingly attentive to procedural regularity.[6]

Masters' craft societies, or those groups that were limited to masters in a specific trade, such as hatters or shoemakers, were also changing in similar ways. Such societies date to the colonial era, of course, such as the Carpenters' Company of Philadelphia, formed in 1724 "to obtain instruction in the science of Architecture, to assist such of its members, or the Widows and Children of members, as should by accident be in need of support," and, most important of all, the adoption of a table of prices. Not incorporated until 1790, at a time when other masters' societies, such as the Stone Cutters' Company, were also being formed in Philadelphia, the Carpenters' Company was one of the most exclusive associations in the city. These masters' societies became far more common after the Revolution, and they evolved quite quickly. Especially after 1800, the bulk of these groups were formed with mutual assistance as a primary purpose: in addition to anniversary celebrations and appearances as a group in local festivities and parades, they offered sick and death benefits to their members, widows, and children. Their creation of well-defined mutual assistance funds, their constitutional organization with its strict delineation of the rights and duties of membership, their professed purposes of education and internal mediation—all evinced a trend toward mutual support and improvement founded upon well-tested associational practices.[7]

Although these masters' craft societies and the general societies of mechanics increasingly resembled countless other voluntary groups of the period, they continued to evoke fear, and the reason was simple: the potential that they could organize to regulate their trades in a way that harmed the community. When the Boston mechanics formed a general society in 1785, they gained eighty-five members within their first three weeks and were able to announce to the world that Paul Revere would serve as their first president. And yet when they petitioned for incorporation in 1795 and again in 1796, they were denied. Only in 1806, with a name change (from the Associated Mechanics and Manufacturers of the Commonwealth of Massachusetts to the Massachusetts Charitable Mechanic Association) that emphasized benevolent over commercial goals, would it pass muster in the General Court and receive a charter.[8]

Associations of mechanics in Virginia, too, faced similar suspicions. Before 1819, according to legal scholar Bruce Campbell, "only two charters related to economic affairs contained general reservations [by the legislature] of power to alter, amend, or repeal the act of incorporation": a marine insurance group in Norfolk, for uncertain reasons, and the Mechanical Benevolent Society of the Borough of Norfolk for reasons far less mysterious. The Mechanical Benevolent Society was forbidden explicitly in their charter from passing any bylaw that regulated "trade, or the wages of labor," or that restricted the "number of apprentices to any trade or craft," but the reserve clause appears to have been intended as an additional level of security. Explicit denials of powers to regulate trade were common: the Albany Mechanics were chartered with a blanket denial that they could do anything other than collect and disperse benevolent funds. In the early republic, there was certainly worry that, in the words of one Massachusetts writer in 1806 (Christopher Tomlins has identified him as Peter Oxenbridge Thacher), "we frequently find brethren of the same craft constituting communities, enacting by-laws, and sanctioning them by the severe penalties of ignominy and ruin to the disobedient." Such groups, simply put, "should be repressed."[9]

In the post-Revolutionary era, the economic pressures of a rapidly evolving market economy would drive the interests of the employing masters and those of wage-earning journeymen further and further apart in the cities of the new United States. Ultimately it led many journeymen's societies to become trade unions in the late eighteenth and early nineteenth centuries, actively and collectively bargaining for better wages and conditions of employment. They would face fierce opposition. And the law of criminal conspiracy would be used to attempt to press them into submission.

Journeymen's Societies and Criminal Conspiracy

Seymour Martin Lipset once observed that the American labor union had needs that most organizations simply did not have. It made special demands of what might fairly be called its rank and file because it was, essentially, a "combat organization." Because of that, because it was a group "whose usefulness to its members lies in its collective strength in relation to management," he wrote, "the trade union has demanded more control over its individual members than do most types of associations." Throughout the post-Revolutionary period, there had already been long and well-argued disputes about what demands different kinds of private, nongovernmental organizations could justifiably make of their own members and about how effective association and individual autonomy could ever be reasonably balanced, one against the other. The history of organized labor must be understood in the context of those controversies.[10]

Journeymen of the early nineteenth century began more fervently to organize. As Howard Rock has written, they saw the beginnings of industrialization and wage-labor capitalism and "understood that self-control and self-reliance were necessary if they were to prove effective against the considerable capital resources of the masters and merchants." And they came to believe that they must unite in order to withstand the forces that appeared to be combining against them. In Boston, New York, Baltimore, and Philadelphia, the first journeymen's societies began to form between the end of the Revolution and early years of the nineteenth century, as class tensions somewhat akin to what the Old World was witnessing had begun to intrude. Work was being rearranged, and an emerging and, it appeared, permanent dependence on wages looked as if it would fully replace the prospect that skilled and diligent tradesmen would, over time, become masters of their own shops. The growing amount of wage work was largely a product of migration into the cities (both from abroad and from the countryside) and of commercial investment into large-scale industrial enterprises that were intended to include more wage-earning workers. Those workers had apparently dim prospects of ever becoming masters themselves. And as these journeymen witnessed the advent of an increasingly exploitative market system that posed threats, not only to their well-being, but also to the ideals of community and mutuality exemplified by the traditional workplace, they responded.[11]

A world of independence and virtue was disappearing, and many journeymen beginning in the last decade of the eighteenth century found that joining together was perhaps their only option. The deterioration in relations between journeymen and master craftsmen that began in the 1790s and grew worse in the early nineteenth century caused journeymen to form their own trade associations and even to "turn out," or strike, in struggles against their employers, who were also forming associations among themselves. In 1790, journeymen carpenters in Philadelphia created an association and in 1791 struck for better wages, declaring to the people of the city: "*Self preservation* has induced us to enter into *indissoluble union with each other*." These trends were largely confined to what have been called the "conflict trades," industries such as shoemaking, cabinetmaking, tailoring, carpentry, masonry, and printing. Perhaps the first instance of rival associations being formed by masters and journeymen came in 1790, when master cordwainers, or shoemakers, formed a society in Philadelphia. The best evidence suggests that the journeymen of their trade responded in kind, though it was to be a short-lived association. In 1794, however—the same year that a journeymen's society of cordwainers was also formed in Baltimore—the journeymen cordwainers of Philadelphia formed something more permanent, an association that survived up through the conspiracy trial of 1806.[12]

Within those trades, journeymen's societies quite quickly began to move beyond their benefit and price-setting roles to become collective-bargaining organizations, and many journeymen in the conflict trades banded together for fraternal and benevolent ends but especially to attempt to shore up their positions vis-à-vis their employers, against whom they were beginning to define themselves. The journeymen printers in New York, for example, amended their constitution in 1817 to note that "the interests of journeymen are separate and in some respects opposite to those of employers," and thus "when any member . . . shall become an employing printer he shall be considered without the limits of this society." Places of work were changing and becoming, in many cases, sites of large-scale production that depended on a permanent population of skilled or semiskilled wage labor: one of the masters who was struck in the turnout that spawned the first labor conspiracy trial, in Philadelphia in 1806, employed from twenty to twenty-four men—hardly the close relationship between master and journeyman or apprentice that had once been the rule. Many journeymen were by this time becoming confident that they needed to unite in order to exclude unqualified cheap labor and to preserve both their well-being and their idea of what the workplace ought to look like.[13]

They not only combined, therefore, but they used a variety of tactics to try to improve their position, some of which might result in criminal prosecution. They utilized some noncoercive methods, such as appeals to employers and to the public, and even formed journeyman-operated shops. And in many cases they struck, leaving the employment of uncooperative employers in some cases, and calling for general turnouts in others. But masters held the advantage: a surplus of labor meant they could simply ignore rebellious workers and their associations as quantity production and large-scale industry grew more common. So if journeymen were to succeed, it was apparent, they needed not only to work together but also to prevent others from working against them. It has been estimated that less than 3 percent of nonagricultural free laborers were members of labor unions during the 1830s, and though some trades were more unionized than others there was, nonetheless, a great pressure on union members to remain united and steadfast against employers who usually had a large pool of potential workers from which to draw. And thus it was that the nature of early American labor activism was not simply based on voluntary affiliation but was, out of necessity, also somewhat coercive in form. And most Americans certainly were not comfortable with the idea of involuntary association.[14]

Serious trouble began in 1805, when eight Philadelphia cordwainers were arrested after a failed strike. A demand for higher wages had ended in failure, with the cordwainers forced to return to work at the old rate. But in an attempt to bring the pressure of the law on the journeymen to prevent such a turnout from happening again, the masters sought criminal charges against the shoemakers. The defendants were charged with a criminal conspiracy, that is, they were charged with trying to exact "great sums of money" from their employers by refusing to work at the "usual prices and rates" but rather forming themselves into a club, refusing to work for anything below a given rate and pressuring other workmen to join their cause by means of "threats, menaces, and other unlawful means." Jared Ingersoll and Joseph Hopkinson argued the case for the prosecution, contending for the first time to an American judge that, although there was no statutory proscription making combining to set wages a crime, it fell under the common law prohibition on combinations, or "conspiracies," for private benefit that either injured the public welfare or violated the private rights of another citizen. That is, everyone agreed that it was both legal and ethical for one man to decide to work only for a certain wage and for nothing less. The crime was in the combination.[15]

Lacking any kind of statute on the matter, when labor associations sought to achieve better wages their actions were prosecuted under the common law's prohibition on what was called "criminal conspiracy." And the defense in virtually all of the conspiracy cases, from *Commonwealth v. Pullis* in 1806 Philadelphia through the explosion of conspiracy charges in the urban centers of 1830s America, challenged the idea that a common law crime of conspiracy could even exist in republican America. If the people or their representatives had never made it a crime, who could possibly justify prosecuting workingmen for agreeing to work only for a certain wage? Christopher Tomlins has shown that common law prosecutions for conspiracy were far more controversial in the United States than they ever were in England, despite the fact that there was great similarity in both labor unions and conspiracy cases between the Old World and the New. There were two distinct ways to conceive of the locus of legal authority in the United States: the ideally timeless principles of the common law, which existed outside of the constitutional structures of the post-Revolutionary polity; and the constitutionally ordained governing authority of the people, as embodied in their state and federal governments. Throughout the early nineteenth century, that issue was fiercely contested. Even if it had been conceded by the defense in *Pullis* that what the cordwainers had done was a crime under English common law (and it undoubtedly was not conceded), there was real debate about whether a common law crime of conspiracy was at all relevant in a nation committed to the principle of popular sovereignty. A crime was what the people said it was.[16]

The discussions about rival sources of authority in the first half century of American labor conspiracy trials, however, also occurred in another register.

Prosecutors, defendants, and judges were also forced to confront questions both about private, unsanctioned associational authority over a group's own members and about the use of compulsion to force the unwilling to join. There were twenty-three trials of labor associations on charges of criminal conspiracy in six of the United States between 1806 and 1850. The first (and there were no colonial cases of this kind) came in Pennsylvania in 1806 and ended with the conviction of eight shoemakers. The very formation of a society of this sort among mutually agreeing men was deemed by the judge in the case, Recorder Moses Levy, to be criminal, though the prosecution spent a great deal of time arguing that the means subsequently used by the organized cordwainers to improve their position were also arbitrary, coercive, and illegal. In 1842, the journeymen's right to organize finally found legal protection, when Chief Justice Lemuel Shaw in Massachusetts declared that the simple creation of an association to attempt to solicit higher wages was not in itself a criminal act. Unlawful purposes or unlawful means must be specifically shown. The key cases in the first half of the nineteenth century had a great deal to say about what membership ought to look like—and where the tradesmen's societies were thought to have gone wrong. In fact, seen in this way, conspiracy trials against journeymen become a remarkably useful means by which to trace the changing conceptions of what voluntary affiliation should and what it absolutely should *not* look like in the early American republic. Those notions initially worked in favor of restrictions on alliances among the workers of a trade, but, ultimately and over the course of about three decades, they developed in a way that came to include organized labor in America.[17]

The central questions to be answered by courts as early as the first labor conspiracy trial in 1806 had to do with associational authority. As the prosecutor Joseph Hopkinson asked the jury that year in Philadelphia, "Shall these, or any other body of men, associate for the purpose of making new laws, laws not made under constitutional authority, and compel their fellow citizens to obey them, under the penalty of their existence?" He went on: "If private associations and clubs, can make constitutions or laws for us . . . if they can associate and make bye-laws paramount, or inconsistent with state laws; What, I ask, becomes of the liberty of the people, about which so much is prated; about which the opening counsel made such a flourish!" Such questions were not merely rhetorical arguments. Although the conviction of the cordwainers for conspiracy did not necessarily hinge on whether the prosecution could show an illegitimate exercise of authority over individual shoemakers (it was enough, Recorder Levy said, to show that their joining together damaged the public good in some way, perhaps by raising the prices of goods), Hopkinson was explicit that the jury should "see the present cause in this double point of view," considering both "the general policy, as it relates to the good of our community," and this question of compulsion and associational authority. He said simply, "shall a secret body exercise a power over our fellow-citizens, which the legislature is not invested with? The fact is, they do exercise a sort of authority the legislature dare not assume." The jury was asked to decide whether the laws and constitution of the state ought to permit such claims of private governing power.[18]

Hopkinson had prefaced his case against the cordwainers by announcing to the jury that "we will shew you the nature of the pains and penalties they affix to disobedience; we shall also shew the mode by which they compel men to join their society, and the fetters with which they afterwards bind them." It was not as if they could even claim to be "an incorporated society," operating under the imprimatur of the state, he said. Rather, they were "merely a society for compelling by the most arbitrary and malignant means, the whole body of journeymen to submit to their rules and regulations; it is not confined even to the members of the society, it reaches every individual of the trade, whether journeyman or master." The "private confederacies" of laboring men, as Hopkinson called them, appeared to him to be a great threat to the consistent application of consent-based law and "the enjoyment of common and equal rights" thereby secured.[19]

The journeymen's society, however, claimed to be a fully legitimate, utterly democratic governing power over the journeymen of their trade. Their claim was a reasonable one, and it held true across a number of different occupations. Printers' organizations that formed at about the same time and in the same cities as the journeymen cordwainers' societies were obsessively democratic and participatory in their modes of operation. The Franklin Typographical Society formed in 1790s Philadelphia drew up an 1802 constitution that gave the bulk of its power to twelve directors, who were divided into four classes of three men, and elections were held quarterly. Theirs was a system that was, as historian Ronald Schultz has written, "designed to blur the distinction between leader and led." It was an intensely democratic arrangement. The Journeymen Cordwainers of the City of New York, who faced conspiracy prosecutions of their own between 1809 and 1811 and whose constitution survives, also elected officers annually and committee members twice annually. All evidence shows that, in New York and Philadelphia both, the journeymen made decisions to strike based entirely on direct democratic action.[20]

The historian Andrew Shankman has examined *Pullis* from that perspective, putting these claims of democratic action into the broader context of early national Philadelphia politics. The accused journeymen had formed an association that "put many of the Philadelphia Democrats' theories into practice." Thus, Shankman observes, "much of the testimony of the trial concentrated on the cordwainers' efforts to force individual journeymen to strike against their wishes." And yet prosecutor Joseph Hopkinson challenged the notion that the democratic form of the association—the fact that "the last turn-out was carried by a small majority . . . 60 against 50, or thereabout"—did anything to change the fact that the association claimed an unjust and, as it were, illegal authority over its members when it told the minority that they too could not work for anything less than the demanded rate. "Let the 60 put what price they please on their own work," he said, "but the others are free agents also: leave them free, or talk no more of equal rights, of independence, or of liberty." The defendants' attorney Caesar Rodney had argued the point directly, that "when you become a member of any institution, you engage to obey its rules." But Hopkinson would have none of it: the rules themselves must not abridge rights of the members that were and ought to be inviolable, in this case, the right to work for whatever wage one asked.[21]

And that was the key point. Hopkinson contended that the common law proscription on combinations for private benefit was vital to prevent that sort of tyranny, however democratically arrived at, and Recorder Levy would embrace that argument in his charge to the jury. But Hopkinson paired this with the argument that the association was also formed illegitimately, that it compelled participation rather than allowing people to join or refrain from joining as they wished. Even if you posit "that when men enter into a society, they are bound to conform to its rules," that "the majority ought to govern the minority," argued Hopkinson, "they ought to leave a man free to join, or not to join the society. If I go into a country I am bound to submit to its laws, but surely I may judge, whether or not I will go there. The society has no right to force you into its body, and then say you shall obey its rules under severe penalties." Both arguments were grounded in an emerging set of beliefs regarding the legitimate exercise of associational authority in the group life of the early American republic. There can be no doubt that the arguments also furthered the development of an increasingly capital-friendly economy in that it left individual workingmen relatively powerless. But the arguments themselves also accorded well with the attitudes and practices of American jurists regarding what voluntary affiliation and private governing power ought to look like in a wide array of other kinds of associations, granting the legal constraints on organized labor a cultural potency they would otherwise have lacked. And the echoes strengthened one another. The labor disputes of the era, then, helped to further a growing commitment to the idea that people ought always to have access to legal remedies against illegitimate claims of private, associational authority.[22]

Recorder Levy made different claims at different times about what authority was really being usurped by the journeymen cordwainers and where the injury lay: they claimed authority over nonmembers and coerced unwilling men into joining; they exercised an excessive amount of authority over their own members, even those there willingly; and they sought a price-fixing power (to set their own wages) that was dangerous to the public at large. As for the nonmembers, Levy believed that the journeymen's society left "no individual at liberty to join the society or reject it" but rather "compel[s] him to become a member." Levy asked the jury, "Is there any reason to suppose that the laws are not competent to redress an evil of this magnitude?" On the matter of associational authority over those who had already joined, Levy agreed with Hopkinson that majority rule in this instance was a patent violation of the rights of each individual member, who were being told by his society that he must remain steadfast to a cause he may not personally support any longer: "In the turn-out of last fall, if each member of the body had stood alone, fettered by no promises to the rest, many of them might have changed their opinion as to the price of wages and gone to work; but it has been given to you in evidence, that they were bound by their agreement, and pledged by mutual engagements, to persist in it, however contrary to their own judgment." As long as the society held fast to its rule that it would not work with any man who accepted a lesser wage, thereby compelling the master cordwainers to either abide by the union's demands or go unstaffed, they were in essence saying that "no one should work unless they all got the wages demanded by the majority; is this freedom?" The journeymen's society appeared to be claiming a power to make law and to dictate to both member and nonmember what the marketplace should look like. Besides our own legislature, Levy said, we seem now to have "a new legislature consisting of journeymen shoemakers." The jury agreed with Levy, and they fined George Pullis and the seven other cordwainers on trial eight dollars each, plus costs.[23]

If *Commonwealth v. Pullis* stood alone, it might seem as if these arguments regarding associational authority were merely rhetorical flourishes on a decision that had no other purpose but to protect capital from the combined power of labor. But three years later, when a journeyman shoemaker named

Edward Whitess was expelled from the Journeymen Cordwainers' Society of the City of New York for not paying fines and for "raising a rumpus" at a meeting, the matter of how to define and delimit associational authority again played the central role. Again, both sides spent a great deal of their time arguing whether the common law prohibition on conspiracy was applicable in the legal regimes of the new United States, in this case, in the courts of New York. But the question of the role of the common law again focused on what part the common law ought to play in constraining private claims to authority. And, again, the language of the prosecution and, in the end, of the court was one that emphasized individual rights over and against the power of a workingmen's society.

Some time in 1809, members of the society told Edward Whitess's employer, Charles Aimes, that he must fire Whitess or face a walkout of all the society members who worked for him. Aimes complied initially. When he would not dismiss an apprentice that the society insisted was also working in breach of their rules, though, they walked out. It became a general, city-wide strike when the society learned that other master shoemakers were taking in Aimes's work. Nine separate counts, all alleging a criminal conspiracy, were filed against twenty-four journeymen shoemakers at the city hall in New York. The case was tried in late 1809 and was reargued in the summer of 1810. In that trial, according to the defense attorney (and reporter of the case) William Sampson, the prosecution summed up its position in much the same way that Joseph Hopkinson had three years earlier in Philadelphia. They stressed that the journeymen violated the individual rights both of members and nonmembers, and they by those means formed an illegal combination strong enough to injure the common weal. The prosecutor, noted Sampson, made "strong remarks upon the imperious and tyrannical edicts of the constitution and by-laws of the society, and asked whether it was possible for any workman to enjoy without molestation, the indisputable rights of peace, neutrality, and self-government, in his own private and particular concerns." Second, just as had been the case in the Philadelphia trial, the prosecution in the New York case emphasized that journeymen infringed on the rights of nonmembers to decide for themselves whether they wished to join. Workingmen were "neither free to refuse entering into the society, nor at liberty, having done so, to leave it, without incurring ruin or unmerited disgrace." By these means, the journeymen's society "had exercised an aristocratic and tyrannical control over third persons."[24]

The journeymen's attorneys, William Sampson and Cadwallader Colden, read the situation differently, of course. But they too focused upon the exact nature of associational authority being claimed by the journeymen's society.

Sampson made the point this way: "Whitess had become one of their society, and agreed to their regulations. They are charged with combining not to work with Whitess (for such is the substance of it) till he should pay the fine he had agreed to pay for breaking their rules and orders. What is there indictable in all that, supposing it ever so true?" The members of the society had made an agreement to work neither with him nor for those who would employ him because Whitess had violated "the rules and ordinances, to the observance of which he had bound himself." That is, Whitess had consented to be governed by certain rules, rules that were neither arbitrary nor tyrannical but rather were fair, were democratically conceived, and most importantly were voluntarily agreed to. And where the prosecution contended that individuals' rights were violated by the society—specifically, the rights of Whitess and those who would otherwise employ him—the defense insisted that individuals were obliged to join together, and they knew it: "How a solitary poor workman shall resist a wealthy and powerful combination of masters I know not," argued Sampson. Collective action was essential, and the rules agreed upon by the workmen were both republican and just.[25]

The prosecution in the 1810 rehearing, however, argued powerfully that the journeymen had joined together in a way that was, simply put, criminal. And though no statute provided a remedy, the common law was sufficient to provide one, either for Whitess or the master shoemakers, and to break up the journeymen's combination. Thomas Addis Emmet, an Irish exile and Democratic Republican who closed the case for the prosecution, contended that "the constitution of the society" had provisions that tended "to erect an *imperium in imperio*, and overbear the rights of the citizen, and the law of the land." And the court would agree with Emmet, reading a charge to the jury to the effect that "the society of journeymen, of which the defendants were members, had established a constitution, or certain rules for its government," rules that "were made to operate on all the members of the society, on others of their trade who were not members, and through them on the master workmen, and all were coerced to submit, or else the members of the society which comprehended the best workmen in the city, were to stop the work of their employers." The journeymen's society had used illegitimate methods of association in the pressure they put on nonmembers to either join or suffer. Tomlins has noted that the court never did decide whether it would be the case that an agreement simply to seek higher wages constituted a criminal conspiracy, and so these discussions of illegal, coercive means to that end were central to the successful prosecution of the case. The court, in the end, did not want to come down terribly hard on the journeymen, who appeared to have "erred from a mistake of the law, and from supposing that they had rights upon which to found their proceedings." Each defendant was fined one dollar.[26]

Not even one year after the conclusion of *People v. Melvin,* members of the same journeymen's society were forced to defend themselves in court yet again, according to court documents unknown to historians before the 1980s. And, again, the case centered on the suffering of one workingman who claimed to have been injured by the actions of the Journeymen Cordwainers' Society. William Dougherty had taken on some outwork to make a pair of boots when members of the society came to inform him that a strike against the city's master cordwainers had begun. He then finished only the work he had on hand, he said, taking on no new projects until the strike was ended successfully. Impressed by their effectiveness and "knowing there was a Difficulty in obtaining work without being a member of said Society," Dougherty chose to join the union. Upon paying his initiation fee, he was charged by some thirty or forty members with having worked during the recent strike. Although he had not been a member at the time, they still voted to fine him three dollars. He refused to pay, and he was refunded his initiation fee and told to go on his way. From that time forward, however, when Dougherty sought work, he was denied because, as one master said in a deposition, "those Journeymen who were there at work for him would quit working and also prevent others from working." Though some employers were deposed to support the charges of Dougherty, historian Sean Wilentz, who uncovered the court documents, notes that the records provide no evidence that this was "an elaborate ruse with a willing journeyman" on the part of the city's master cordwainers. Twice in a year, New York City's journeymen cordwainers were forced to defend themselves in court based on charges brought by a member who disputed their authority over him. This time the journeymen's association won, and the charges were dismissed.[27]

The associational methods being used by these joiners and organizers were crucial. Though there is limited evidence extant, journeymen's societies of the first two decades of the nineteenth century appear to have almost always taken steps to coerce the unwilling practitioners of their trade to join. The constitution of a society of cabinetmakers in Baltimore formed at about the same time as the New York journeymen cordwainers included a clause almost identical to one in the New Yorkers' constitution, one that required any journeyman cabinetmaker to join the society within six weeks of arriving in the city, or face monthly fines. And the Pittsburgh cordwainers, who faced the next recorded conspiracy prosecution, in 1815, appear to have adopted practices quite similar to those of the Philadelphia journeymen.

An initiation fee of 50 cents and monthly dues of 25 cents were required, and they took an oath not to "work for any employer who did not give the wages and beside any journeymen who did not get the wages" that they set as a minimum. Like the Philadelphia cordwainers, they did not establish a permanent strike fund, but appeared to provide money to distressed members, allowing them to "take three or four dollars out of the box." When they struck in 1814, they opted to compromise, end the strike, and pay the court costs. In 1815, they were again brought into court on charges of criminal conspiracy.[28]

In the case of *Commonwealth v. Morrow,* the definition of conspiracy itself was beginning to become more refined from what had appeared in earlier cases. It was defined as "an agreement of two or more to the prejudice of the rights of others or of society." The freedom of each journeyman to decide for himself at what wage he would work was deemed as both a private and a public right, according to the court's summation for the jury: "It is the interest of the public, and it is the right of every individual, that those who are skilled in any profession, art, or mystery, should be unrestrained in the exercise of it." Admittedly, it was clear from how the court presented the case that the actual use of violence or threats of violence to pressure a journeyman to join need not be shown: the crime was complete if it could be shown that the agreement necessarily tended to impoverish another. Nonetheless, the prosecution and the defense argued at great length over whether the Pittsburgh cordwainers, as an association, allowed men to act freely.

It was the policy of the journeymen's society, argued the prosecution, to compel any man of their trade either to become a certificate-bearing member or to suffer the consequences of unemployment. And surely "every man was a freeman in this country—without a certificate from the journeymen cordwainers of this place." The defendants' attorney, on the other hand, told the court that the journeyman's oath and his "payment of the initiation fee are merely voluntary acts, the result of free will, the result of contract." Where one side insisted that the journeymen did not leave outsiders free to decide whether to join, the other stated quite clearly that all those who had joined had chosen to do so, in an exercise of their own free will. In one sense, of course, both sides were right: the members had made a deliberate choice to become members, but the prosecutor emphasized that the choice they made was between membership and poverty. And the court embraced that view, noting that it was clearly indictable "to conspire to compel men to become members of a particular association" even though "the means used was not in physical force, but exclusion from employment." And if the city of Pittsburgh lacked the authority to compel men to become members of a given association, the judge declared, surely the journeymen lacked it, too. The jury agreed, and the Pittsburgh shoemakers were fined one dollar apiece, with costs.[29]

There then came a lull in conspiracy prosecutions against journeymen's societies for more than five years, and in 1821 a society of master ladies shoemakers actually found themselves in the position of defendant in a criminal conspiracy trial. The journeymen ladies shoemakers of Philadelphia charged them with conspiring to lower their wages. In a habeas corpus hearing, Justice John Bannister Gibson examined the precedents before him and determined that the motive of combination must play a role in determining its criminality. In a stunning turn in a case that would shape all subsequent conspiracy trials in Pennsylvania and probably beyond, Gibson announced that "the mere act of combining to change the price of labour is, perhaps, evidence of impropriety of intention, but not conclusive." Simply joining together and demanding a certain wage was not in itself a crime, for it was becoming clear to many jurists such as Gibson that *both* sides in labor disputes were combining to attempt to check the other. And if it could be shown that one side had combined simply to return the going wage rate to what it would be "if it were left without artificial excitement by either masters or journeymen," for example, if the masters on trial could show that they had merely combined to "foil their antagonists" (their employed journeymen) from combining and raising their wage to "a value which it would not otherwise have, they will make out a good defence." It was a powerful statement that associations of employers or employees—even associations that had the stated aim of setting wages—were not guilty of criminal conspiracy per se. A specific injury, either to the public or to particular individuals, must be shown.[30]

Despite all of the arguments between defense attorneys and prosecutors in the earlier labor conspiracy trials about whether individual journeymen were harmed by the acts of the journeymen's society, there had always been a question about whether those individual injuries really mattered, whether their threats to prevent a poor journeyman from finding work were really crucial to determining guilt or innocence. In *Pullis* in 1806, as Gibson quoted Recorder Levy, the simple fact that the cordwainers had agreed among themselves to work only for a given wage was enough, regardless of whether their motive was "to *resist the supposed oppression of their masters,* or to insist upon extravagant wages," and—what is more important for this study—regardless of the means they used to achieve that end. Simply show that they had agreed to work only for a certain wage, and the crime was complete. Gibson disagreed. For him, under the common law an association of men that agreed among themselves to work only for a certain wage could be deemed a conspiracy only if one of two things was shown: that they raised the wage unnaturally high *or* that their actions necessarily tended to injure a specific person, e.g., a fellow journeyman who would not join a union. That this was Gibson's key point became clear when he noted that the cordwainers in 1806, in his reading, *still would have been guilty* of conspiracy because of the charge relating to "third persons," specifically, the charge that the cordwainers "would by threats and menaces and other injuries, prevent any other workmen or journeymen from working" for masters who paid a lesser wage. In the end, Gibson noted that he could not make a decision on the crucial question in the case before him, for it was a question of fact that only a jury could answer. The prosecution was probably dropped.[31]

Gibson displayed an awareness of the plural, diverse, and even competitive nature of the associational landscape in Philadelphia by 1821. Courts should not pretend that they were protecting the public weal by condemning any and all combinations. Because the relationship between employer and employee was, quite naturally, competitive (and could even descend into war[32]), there may well be times when an association of men may voluntarily and collectively agree to work only for a certain wage and no less (or, in the case of employers, to pay a certain wage and no more) and, in doing so, commit no crime. But if it could be shown that the combination was something other than a truly voluntary society, that there was some compulsion exerted on nonmembers to abide by the edicts of the society, the outcome was usually a guilty verdict. This was the case in the next two recorded labor conspiracy trials: a prosecution against New York hatters in 1823 and one against Buffalo tailors in 1824. In both, it was held that the crime was in the conspiracy to prevent a fellow journeyman from finding work and not in the agreement to work only for a certain wage. In the 1823 case, the defendants' refusal to work alongside a nonmember journeyman named Acker, thereby preventing his employment and impoverishing him, was the crime. In the 1824 Buffalo case, the crime was described this way: "A singular custom among the Jours. to coerce the refractory was proved to exist throughout the United States, by which the person who should refuse to come into the measures of the majority, or who subsequently to a turn out should, before an arrangement was had, labor at the same place for less than the wages demanded, was stigmatized by an appropriate name, and rendered too infamous to be allowed to labor in any shop where his conduct should be known." When the first jury could not reach a verdict in that case, a second was impaneled, which found the defendants guilty and fined them two dollars each. The decision was not well reported: its existence is known only by newspaper accounts. But it did suggest that the use of one of the most powerful tools at the disposal of workingmen—shame—might be indictable as a criminal conspiratorial act if it was intended to compel the unwilling to join their ranks.[33]

In sum, courts in the 1820s were beginning to develop a fairly articulate notion of the role of associated action in the labor market, and it was one that rested quite heavily on the idea that journeymen's societies can and should claim the allegiance only of those who had made a free and uncoerced decision to join. Among themselves, they could agree not to work for certain employers or below certain wages. Any moment that they attempted to prevent others from working, however, a charge of criminal conspiracy might succeed in court. In an 1827 conspiracy case, the defendant journeymen were explicit in their testimony about what "the rules among journeymen tailors" were, in a clear effort to persuade the court that theirs was a mere voluntary association that claimed authority over no one who had not chosen to join their ranks. As Thomas Carr testified, "The rule, as far as I know, is such, that, in case any journeyman in Robb and Winebrener's, or other shops should *strike* for higher wages, I should feel bound not to work for Robb and Winebrener, but not to prevent others working." The case, *Commonwealth v. Moore,* more popularly known as the *Case of the Twenty-Four Journeymen Tailors,* wound up hinging on one question: had coercion been used to prevent nonmember journeymen from working? In fact, every charge against them that did not involve threats against nonmember journeymen tailors was dropped, owing to the instructions to the jury by Recorder Joseph Reed, in which he deliberately invoked the authority of Justice Gibson (who by that time had become chief justice of the Pennsylvania Supreme Court) in *Commonwealth v. Carlisle*: simply combining was not in itself necessarily a crime, but rather the jury had to determine whether the association claimed and exercised any coercive authority over people that were not members.

Reed noted, for instance, that "the rules of the society of journeymen tailors . . . are, in some respects, illegal and oppressive, operating not only on the members, but on others." He explained that "these young men, have an undoubted right, by agreement among themselves, to regulate their own conduct, to ask as much as they please for their services, to continue, or to leave the service of any employer, as reason, inclination, or caprice should dictate." But, Reed went on, "the moment they interfere with the rights and privileges of others, equally valuable and sacred as those, which, in this prosecution, these defendants so jealously contend for, they are criminal." It was in their actions, by forming picket lines and preventing men who wanted to work from reaching their shops, that they committed a crime. It was on charges of threats against nonmember journeymen, and those grounds only, that the jury found the defendant tailors guilty. Criminal conspiracy charges in the courts of Pennsylvania would, more and more often after Gibson's influential 1821 opinion, include the matter of whether the defendants did anything to injure journeymen who would not join their association. When the journeymen shoemakers of Chambersburg, Pennsylvania, were indicted for conspiracy in 1829, for example, the charges were two, according to the lone newspaper account: they were charged with "conspiracy to raise their wages, and prejudice such as were not members of their association."[34]

The decade of the 1830s witnessed a great deal more labor organization, even on a national scale, and continued prosecutions against journeymen's societies for criminal conspiracy. Battles in the streets and in the courtrooms about the rights of workers to combine, even if that combination put pressure on all workers of a given trade to join their cause, would continue through the decade. But the tide had begun to turn. The conviction rate plummeted, and public support for the workingmen's combinations would grow.[35]

In 1831, in another case that is known to us only by scattered newspaper accounts, Pittsburgh carpenters were alleged to have combined with several hundred others in the streets of the city, massing in front of shops to discourage any carpenters from taking work until their dispute was ended. The jury took no time at all to deliver a verdict of not guilty. In Connecticut in 1834, a civil suit was brought against William Taylor and other carpet weavers for $15,000 based on the allegation that they did "wrongfully and injuriously by threats and falsehood induce a great number of Ingrain Carpet Weavers" to quit their work at the Thompsonville Carpet Manufacturing Company. Not only did Taylor win, but it was noted that "the result it is believed has met with public approbation," and he countersued for damages owing to his temporary imprisonment (though he withdrew the suit three years later). And of the eight conspiracy cases between 1836 and 1843, only three resulted in convictions, one of which was overturned. As Tomlins has observed, there had been nine convictions and five acquittals in all the previous recorded labor conspiracy trials. Workingmen in the decade of the 1830s united far more often than ever before, began their first efforts at transforming workplace organization into political activism, and even attempted to unite discrete trades into common organizations (hence the origins of the term "trades' union"). And even as perceptions of the American labor union were slow to change, the first national organization of journeymen cordwainers could announce that "combinations and associations among the mechanics and the laboring poor" were a legitimate means of regaining their "lost rights" and reasonably believe that more and more Americans agreed with them.[36]

And yet the plight of the lone suffering journeyman who might be injured by the union's efforts to enforce a closed shop continued to resonate. In 1835, for example, in the case of *People v. Fisher,* a conspiracy trial against journeymen shoemakers in Geneva, New York, Chief Justice John Savage of the Supreme Court of Judicature put great emphasis on the public injury that resulted from their combined efforts to drive up their own wages. Working with a statutory definition of conspiracy passed by the New York legislature in 1828 that criminalized any conspiracy "injurious . . . to trade or commerce," Savage focused on the public consequences of labor's organization. Nonetheless, he also decried the injustice of their insistence that the expelled journeyman, Thomas J. Pennock, work only for one dollar per pair. Savage wrote, "If the defendants cannot make coarse boots for less than $1 per pair, let them refuse to do so; but let them not directly or indirectly undertake to say that others shall not do the work for a less price. It may be that Pennock, from greater industry or greater skill, made more profit by making boots at 75 cents per pair than the defendants at $1. He had a right to work for what he pleased. His employer had a right to employ him for such price as they could agree upon." Savage's perspective was partially rooted in his notions of political economy—"competition is the life of trade," he declared, and this union sought to end it by insisting that Pennock work only at their level of efficiency—but his contention that what they had done was "wrong" rested not merely on Savage's ideas about free economic exchange but on the personal right that Pennock had to remain free from union regulations.[37]

Allegations of associational tyranny also took a new, xenophobic turn in the 1830s. Critics began to paint a picture of freeborn Americans under the thumb of unions that "are of foreign origin," as Judge Ogden Edwards said in a trial against twenty journeymen tailors in 1836. The *New York Commercial Advertiser* noted that the labor unions "are based on the same principles as the pernicious Trades Unions in England, and in almost every case, we are informed, they are managed and controlled by foreigners." Master carpenters in Philadelphia announced that "combinations of this description are indebted for their origin to the discontented and disorganizers in a monarchial government; they are not of American birth." In the 1830s, just as the labor movement was mounting its first organized political efforts, the image of the lone workingman, made "to march like some conscript militia through the streets, under the command of some foreigner," became a common motif.[38]

The workingmen remained committed to their rights of organization and collective self-rule. And yet both of the major political parties agreed that when journeymen made attempts to enforce their collective agreements on all the tradesmen of their industry they were unfairly stripping their fellow workingmen of the right to decide for themselves when, how, and for what wage they would work. Thus, the Whig *New York Journal of Commerce* could write unequivocally that "Trades Unionists" acted in a way that was "tyrannical, unfair, and a combination against the rights of other men." And the Democratic *Philadelphia Public Ledger,* in the midst of a lengthy editorial in support of the twenty tailors convicted of conspiracy in New York in the case of *People v. Faulkner* and fined the extraordinary sum of $1,150, would still draw a line between acceptable and improper associations based on perceived coercion of those unwilling to join the cause: "But while we contend that all men have a perfect right, by agreement, to settle the prices of their labor or merchandise, we contend that they have no right to coerce others into such agreement. Such coercion is a violation of the very principle upon which they claim the right of making such agreements." By the dawn of the 1840s, there had been almost four decades of public debate and legal dispute regarding concerted action among laboring men on their own behalf. Much of it centered on questions of how much authority such groups could claim over their own members and whether they acted coercively toward those who did not belong. In other words, the very definition of voluntary membership was at issue in one of the most important conversations in the early United States: the rights of workers to do something to improve their lot in a society that appeared to be remaking itself in ways that left them behind.[39]

Embracing Organized Labor in a Nation of Joiners

The most famous labor conspiracy trial in history was not a battle between masters and journeymen, or between factory owners and employees. It was a dispute between the Boston Society of Journeymen Bootmakers and one disgruntled member, Jeremiah Horne. Like so many of the conspiracy cases that came before, there were discussions of the rights of the people to a free market in goods and labor, and there were demands that the relevance of the common law of criminal conspiracy be rethought in a democratic republic such as the Commonwealth of Massachusetts. But the case of *Com-*

monwealth v. Hunt, which Hunt and the other union shoemakers lost in the Boston Municipal Court in 1840 and then won in a landmark decision by Lemuel Shaw in the Massachusetts Supreme Judicial Court in 1842, was at its core nothing more than a matter between member Horne and a journeymen's society he had joined. The most thorough study of the documents surrounding the case, written by Walter Nelles in 1932, noted that it was undeniably clear, "both from positive implications of the testimony and from the absence of any contrary suggestion in any of the reports, that there was no strike or threat or thought of a strike in 1840; no difference or friction whatever between masters and journeymen, or the Society; and that the prosecution was instigated single-handed by Jeremiah Horne." Horne's boss testified that he had never been injured by the society's actions, that "the wages fixed by the society were not unreasonably high," and that "society men were all good workmen." Other masters told the court that they had actually benefited from the society's policies. This was in every way a legal dispute about the authority of a journeymen's society over one of its own.[40]

As a member of the bootmakers' society, Horne had been fined for a violation of the society's rules. His employer, Isaac Wait, actually paid the fine for him. When more fines piled up, and the cantankerous Horne refused to pay, his employer even advised him to settle up with them and to try to remain on good terms. But Horne refused and lost his status as a member in good standing. Unwilling to run afoul of the society, Wait dismissed him. Horne then met with the local district attorney about pressing charges, and he sent his brother Dennis Horne, a member of the bootmakers' society, to attempt a reconciliation. When the journeymen's society said they would not settle, Dennis informed them that Jeremiah "wanted nothing but his rights" and would take the matter to court. And the district attorney, Samuel Parker, took the case with zeal to the Municipal Court of Boston, presided over by Peter Oxenbridge Thacher, a longstanding opponent of organized labor.[41]

The defense attorneys for John Hunt and the six other men charged with criminal conspiracy declared that there was nothing at all criminal about the means or goals of the Boston Society of Journeymen Bootmakers. After arguing halfheartedly that the common law of conspiracy was not in force in Massachusetts, John Kimball for the defense contended that no evidence had been shown that Wait had been compelled to dismiss Horne, or that any employers had been impoverished by the actions of the society (indeed, they had benefited), and that "similar societies have existed among the members of the legal and medical professions, and in almost every kind of business in which large numbers are engaged; and that it has been the custom of the people of this country to combine for any and every purpose not criminal or forbidden by law." Kimball even called members of the Suffolk Bar Association and the Boston Medical Association to make the point that they operated in a manner virtually indistinguishable from the bootmakers' union.[42]

Parker closed his two-hour speech for the prosecution this way. The journeymen's "society may have some good objects, and do some good," but it was "a coercive, rigid, persecuting society, to all who refuse to be members," such as the expelled Horne. He told the jury that they could have the rules of the bar association and the constitution of the journeymen's association before them to "compare them," and they will find that "they are wholly unlike." Thacher's charge to the jury was virtually a continuation of Parker's accusations: "The illegality of the agreement [among the journeymen] consists in the design and tendency, by a concentrated action, to injure and control others. If the defendants intended and expected, by means of this confederacy, to benefit themselves, at the expense of the rights of others, and by an unlawful invasion of those rights, it was an offence." He left to the jury only one question of fact—did John Hunt and the other members of the Boston Society of Journeymen Bootmakers intend to benefit themselves by their concerted actions?—and he implied the answer. More specifically, he asked the jury whether they believed that the defendants had a rule that they would not work for an employer "who should employ any workman or journeyman . . . who was not a member of their said club, after notice given to him to discharge such workman from his employ." If they did, "it is an unlawful means to effect an unjust and injurious purpose."[43]

Thacher also spent a great deal of time discussing the constitution, which he called "the soul of the club," and the apparent cohesiveness of the journeymen's society: "You may have perceived in this case, as in other secret associations," observed Thacher, "the strength of the spirit of the society." He told the jury that the members of the society had been "careful to conceal" their own roles and "were most unwilling to reveal any fact which might tend to impeach their associates." They were a tightly knit fraternity, a band of brothers that "[avowed] their intention to regulate their wages by a concentration of feeling and action with their brother craftsmen." To them, Horne was a "marked journeyman" or "*scab,* as he is called in this new vocabulary." In Thacher's telling, the members of the bootmakers' society had leagued together, and they claimed authority to fine Horne, to expel him when he refused to pay, and to cease working alongside him and thereby keep him from finding work in the city of Boston. Such authority, he said conclusively in a line that could have been lifted from the first American conspiracy trial in 1806, "was a new power in the state, unknown to its constitution and laws, and subversive of their equal spirit." The jury agreed, and John Hunt and the others were convicted of criminal conspiracy. The case was appealed.[44]

Robert Rantoul was the lead defense attorney who argued the case both before Thacher and at the Supreme Judicial Court, and his arguments at both the trial and the appellate court were nearly identical. When he argued the case before Chief Justice Lemuel Shaw, he centered on two things: the inapplicability of the common law in every case in the American republic, a crusade he would be on for his entire career; and the particular injustice of charging a society with conspiracy that did no more than was done every day by bar associations and medical societies, merely because it was made up of workingmen. Thus, the exception that Rantoul argued most closely for Shaw's court was that Thacher had not properly instructed the jury "that the indictment did not set forth any agreement to do a criminal act, or to do any lawful act by any specified criminal means, and that the agreements therein set forth did not constitute a conspiracy indictable by any law of this Commonwealth."[45]

Much to the surprise of many in Boston and around the nation, Shaw agreed. He "stripped" the indictment of "introductory recitals," "alleged injurious consequences," and "qualifying epithets," and he restated it this way: "the defendants and others formed themselves into a society, and agreed not to work for any person, who should employ any journeyman or other person, not a member of such society, after notice given him to discharge such workman." There was only one question: was that agreement unlawful, either in its aims or in the means it proposed to accomplish that purpose? Shaw answered those questions in a way conceivable only in a nation of joiners. His opinion in favor of the bootmakers can best be seen as a culmination of a slow drift among American jurists toward the idea that combination, by itself, was not a crime. Rather, as Gibson had been the first to suggest in Pennsylvania two decades earlier, to determine the lawfulness of any voluntary association, the actual deeds and goals of the group must be evaluated. And Shaw's opinion in *Commonwealth v. Hunt* shows the astonishing degree to which the law and experience of voluntary membership in all manner of associations had progressed to the point that many Americans, including Shaw himself, now had a well-developed vocabulary regarding voluntary affiliation, one that effectively framed their conceptions of organized labor.[46]

"The manifest intent of the association is, to induce all those engaged in the same occupation to become members of it," Shaw said. But this was not a condemnation. Similar attempts to "induce" people to join a cause, by signing a constitution and paying dues, had become commonplace in American society. And with the very next sentence he began to reshape American labor law in a way that brought it into line with all other kinds of associated action: "Such purpose is not unlawful." Nor, he said, was there any evidence that the association attempted to achieve its goal "by criminal means." Shaw was certain that a simple agreement not to work with or for a certain kind of person, in this case, someone who was not a member of their association, was nothing more than "an agreement, as to the manner in which they would exercise an acknowledged right to contract with others for their labor." Such an agreement was not a criminal act in the Commonwealth of Massachusetts.[47]

Though it would appear that Shaw had covered all of the charges made against Hunt and the other journeymen, there were two other matters that he addressed at length, ones that focused on what sorts of pressures a voluntary association ought to be permitted to bring to bear on nonmembers. First, he addressed the question of the society's demands that Wait must dismiss the disgruntled Horne. In the trial and at the appellate level, the constitution of the bootmakers was cited as evidence of their purposes and their means, and it included article 14, which stated the duty of members to quit the employ of a man who hired nonunion workers. And so Shaw stated directly that the accusation that they had attempted to "compel" Wait was "rendered harmless by the precise statement of the means, by which such compulsion was to be effected. It was the agreement not to work for him, by which they compelled Wait to decline employing Horne any longer." Clearly these men each possessed the individual right to work for whomever they pleased. And they were not culpable for having joined together to exercise that right more effectually.[48]

Even once Shaw had determined that the purpose of the journeymen's society was not unlawful, however, he had a tough argument to make regarding their means. And he opted to make his case by appealing to Americans' growing comfort with voluntary association. The long history of labor conspiracy trials had shown just how sticky the question of associational authority could be, even in cases in which it appeared that the association's purposes were not illicit and abusive to the public at large. Did it violate the rights of Horne, the man who began the prosecution, or of his employer, Isaac Wait, when Hunt and the other journeymen refused to work alongside Horne simply because he was not a member of their association, did not pay their fees and fines, and refused to work at their approved wage rate?

In a move that no one observing the arguments of counsel could have foreseen, Shaw answered that question by invoking the example of the temperance society. When he stated that "we cannot perceive, that it is criminal for men to agree together to exercise their own acknowledged rights, in such a manner as best to subserve their own interests," he immediately proposed "one way to test this." Imagine, he said, that they had joined together as a temperance society. "Suppose a class of workmen, impressed with the manifold evils of intemperance, should agree with each other not to work in a shop in which ardent spirit was furnished, or not to work in a shop with anyone who used it, or not to work for any employer, who should, after notice, employ a journeyman who habitually used it." The drinking workingman might suffer unemployment owing to their agreement, and an employer "might, at times, experience inconvenience in his work, in losing the services of a skilful but intemperate workman." But who could argue with the workingmen's right to agree among one another that they would work only in a dry shop? A decade earlier, Shaw had been a member of a committee of the Massachusetts Society for the Suppression of Intemperance that actually appealed in an open letter to "the Master and the Journeyman Mechanic" to form just that kind of association, a society in which the "principle" of temperance served as "the bond of union." He had been asked multiple times by the defense to draw a parallel between the bootmakers and the bar associations or the medical societies of the day, but he never did. Instead, Shaw deliberately compared the association of journeymen to a society that asked no dues of its members and asked only that members adhere to a shared belief and practice regarding the use of alcohol. There were many observers of this kind of associational commitment that did, indeed, have some concerns; in particular, some believed that the "pledge" taken by members of temperance societies created a new and dangerous burden on the freedom of the mind and of the soul. But Shaw was not one of them. He saw temperance societies as a powerful way for man to help his fellow man to act well. Again, who could argue with that?[49]

Defense attorney Rantoul had given the example of a temperance lecturer, "who induces men to forbear buying rum, to the impoverishing of sellers of rum," to contest the idea that every action seeking to impoverish another person was a crime or even morally objectionable. But Shaw did him one better. He adapted Rantoul's point into a discussion of a temperance *association*, something Shaw and many others of his social circle had long supported and thus could hardly be expected to condemn. In doing so he ignored an important component of the prosecution: that the bootmakers' society demanded dues and thereby claimed a power to tax upon penalty of unemployment. During the trial, Thacher had very clearly informed the jury that "the only authority which may rightfully impose a tax, in the shape of a fine or penalty, or in any other way, must be imparted by the legislature." But Shaw disregarded the contention, paying it no attention at all in his opinion. Even though it appeared that Shaw was attempting to deflect that question by his use of the temperance analogy, it was true that many groups did everything they could to "induce" people to become members and yet also required the payment of dues, for example, most every moral reform society. He apparently saw nothing objectionable in that practice. In his opinion, Shaw made a deliberate choice to situate the Boston Society of Journeymen Bootmakers within an associational world to which both he and so many of his contemporaries had become accustomed.

Additionally, Shaw knew that he had to address directly the accusation that the society had "a wicked and unlawful intent to impoverish one Jeremiah Horne, and hinder him from following his trade as a boot-maker." He proceeded by way of analogy to show that collective efforts to lessen someone else's profits, even to impoverish someone, were ordinary, lawful, and even "laudable." Here, too, he turned to the broader associational world of the early to mid-nineteenth century for analogy. He described a scene in which a baker was asked by a group of townspeople to lower his prices or they would join together, pool their funds, and "introduce another baker." The image he described was essentially that of a joint-stock company. As Shaw noted, "it might be said and proved, that the purpose of the associates was to diminish his profits and thus impoverish him," but "the same thing may be said of all competition in every branch of trade and industry." In short, "associations may be entered into, the object of which is to adopt measures that may have a tendency to impoverish another, that is, to diminish his gains and profits, and yet so far from being criminal or unlawful, the object may be highly meritorious and public spirited." From the temperance society to the joint-stock association, Shaw drew parallels that made the Boston Journeymen Bootmakers' Society look to be an acceptable, even agreeable part of American civil society.[50]

Shaw's decision has been interpreted a number of different ways over the years. For Walter Nelles, the decision was a way of weakening a radical workers' movement in politics, particularly their support for protective tariffs. For Mark DeWolfe Howe, it was a way of undercutting the legal codification movement by showing the flexibility of the common legal tradition. For legal scholars such as Wythe Holt and Raymond Hogler, the decision by Shaw was still decidedly procapitalist and founded on "deep economic interests," especially the way he "encouraged courts to persist in identifying the good of the community with *laissez-faire* ideology, or with the interests of entrepreneurs." For Alfred Konefsky, both *Hunt* (which specifically excluded the case of men who were under contract with their employers) and the fellow-servant ruling a week earlier in *Farwell v. Boston and Worcester Railroad,* a decision that seemed as anti-labor as *Hunt* seemed to be pro-labor, were really about the freedom of contract, the freedom of employees to choose. For Leonard Levy, Shaw was a realist who weighed competing rights and social consequences, a man more akin to Oliver Wendell Holmes, Jr., than to his conservative forebears on the Massachusetts bench. To Levy, *Hunt* signaled an acceptance by Shaw that the competition among organized forces in American society would benefit the public more than it would injure it. Christopher Tomlins, in a manner somewhat akin to both Konefsky and Levy, argued that Shaw was among the first judges to see a market-driven world, with "society as the sum of a congeries of diverse material interests that individuals pursued, self-consciously, by entering into voluntary transactions that bound them according to the terms they were able to negotiate with each other." Thus, Shaw could support the combined efforts of laboring men as being just one more component of, as Shaw stated, a "thousand other instances, where each strives to gain custom to himself, by ingenious improvements, by increased industry, and by all the means by which he may lessen the price of commodities, and thereby diminish the profits of others." That idea has been extended more specifically by Johann Neem to include Shaw's attitudes toward the pluralism of civil society, in which the sheer breadth and diversity of the voluntary associations of 1840s Massachusetts made any condemnation of the laborers' rights to join together "indefensible."[51]

What is most remarkable is that Shaw did not simply endorse the bootmakers' freedom of association. He spoke directly about the manner in which they had done so, and he approved heartily. It all accorded fully well with the law and practice of membership and association as it had taken shape over the preceding half century. Shaw would know. He himself was a joiner through and through. He was not only a member of a Massachusetts temperance society but was also a member of such associations as the Massachusetts Historical Society, the Society for Propagating the Gospel among the Indians, Phi Beta Kappa, the Friday Evening Club, and the Law Club. He even served as secretary and wrote out the constitution for the Washington Benevolent Society he had joined in 1812. He was, in sum, an active participant in the growing array of associational opportunities in the early nineteenth century. And he was willing, like no jurist before him, to contend that labor unions ought to be understood as part of that world. Thus, the laws and practices of voluntary membership that were being worked out in the culture at large became, for Shaw, the framework within which labor unions, too, operated. Seen that way, they were not criminal. They were common.[52]

As political theorists have long recognized, the associational world of civil society can have a positive and healthy relationship with a democratic political system. But individuals must be free to choose their affiliations, free to enter those groups that fit their beliefs and exit those that no longer do. Labor unions presented the most significant or, at least, most visible challenge to that idea in the early decades of the nineteenth century, for it was clear to the labor organizers that some level of coercion and near-compulsory membership were necessary for them to have any chance at all of succeeding in improving or at least preserving the position of those who worked for wages. And yet in the early nineteenth century, the journeymen's societies had come to act in ways virtually indistinguishable from the other sorts of associations that Americans were beginning to join in great numbers, except for the fact that they placed collective pressures on nonjoiners that were, for many, unsettling. But labor unions also drew up constitutions, distributed them to members, abided by mutually agreed-upon rules, and made decisions by direct democratic action or by the constitutionally circumscribed authority of elected officers.[53]

For years, advocates for organized labor had been attempting to state their case by insisting that the rich organized, too. "Who are they who complain of Trades Unions?" men such as Frederick Robinson could exclaim. "Are they not those whose combinations cover the land, and who have even contrived to invest some of their combinations with the sanctity of law? Are they not those, who are the owners of all kinds of monopolies, who pass their lives in perpetual caucuses, on 'change, in halls connected with banks, composing insurance companies, manufacturing companies, turnpike, bridge, canal, rail-road, and all other legalized combinations?" He could decry the conspiracy of the "Trades Union of lawyers" and announce that Judge Thacher was "a member of a combination of lawyers, better organized, and more strict and tyrannical in the enforcement of their rules, than even masonry itself." But only Shaw, more calmly, drew a parallel between the labor union and the temperance society, in which people joined together in support of a shared principle and did everything they could to induce their neighbors to join in. Only then did the labor union find its place in the American associational landscape.[54]

CONCLUSION

The Concept of Membership in the Age of Reform

Between the end of the American Revolution and the time that Alexis de Tocqueville and Gustave de Beaumont arrived on the shores of the American continent to explore the thriving democratic social order of the United States, the young republic had become filled with associations, clubs, societies, and corporations of all shapes and sizes. When seeking to accomplish much of anything, large or small, the American people appeared to be uniting together, finding in their own combined strength means to improve their own lives and to renovate their society. And some things about the United States witnessed by Tocqueville and Beaumont have remained true. Men, women, and children today would describe their experiences in the associations they create, organize, and join in ways that mirror the daily goings-on in the clubs and societies of the early American republic: a habit of using constitutions and rules to bring people together and, especially, a nearly universal and devoted attention to turn to those agreed-upon procedures if any conflict should ever arise. What is decidedly uncommon is the involvement of courts of law. When Frank Haas was expelled from his membership in the Ancient Free and Accepted Masons of West Virginia in 2008, for instance, the court turned away his request for redress despite the judge's declaration that, in her opinion, his ouster had been unfair and for fully illegitimate reasons. His expulsion began as a private matter, the jury believed, and it ought to remain so.[1]

How did we get there? How did Americans who had once seen the active hand of the law as an essential actor in the thriving of a republican civil society come to think that it ought to be at least an arm's length away? To be sure, there remained times and circumstances that might lead to judicial intervention in the internal affairs of private associations, but judges in the early American republic often displayed an eagerness and a deeply felt interest in their decisions to right some wrong done to an aggrieved member of a voluntary association: remember William Tilghman's point in restoring John Binns to membership, which the Pennsylvania chief justice chose to express in the first person: "I consider it as a point of very great importance, in which thousands of persons are, or very soon will be interested." That attitude would be replaced in the middle third of the century, as we saw in chapter 6, with a much more reticent and hesitant approach to judicial superintendence of private associations. In the astonishingly more diverse and pluralist civil society found in much of the nation during the Age of Jackson, Americans had come to the conclusion that this was a world that could function pretty well without the involvement of courts. By the time Tocqueville's observations on the American propensity for association were hitting the shelves in the United States, jurists who dealt with matters that arose out of the private associational life of nineteenth-century civil society had begun to declare that they would "not inquire into the merits" of decisions made "in a regular course of proceedings" regarding someone's membership in a private society. The only way to understand this jurisprudential shift is by setting it in the context of a post-Revolutionary nation full of individuals encountering the opportunities, the challenges, and the everyday experiences of voluntary association in an age full of promise and of discomfiting change.[2]

The earlier period of more active judicial involvement that had helped to create that world, however, was an important step in facilitating the creation of a pluralistic social landscape. By the end of the 1830s, William Novak's description of the diverse legal terrain confronting individuals held true, in which a person's rights and duties were determined "through the elaboration of a great hierarchy of very specific and highly differentiated legal statuses, his bundle of rights and duties the product of a very complicated and varied tally of the rules, regulations, and bylaws of the host of differentiated associations to which he belonged," including families, churches, unions, and mutual benefit clubs all the way up to cities, counties, and states. But it took a great deal of struggle and uncertainty to get there, to arrive at the conclusion that people ought, by and large, to be left alone to create their own clubs and to enforce their own rules without substantive review. Novak's description of the nineteenth-century legal landscape as it concerned associations and other privately formed organizations, while accurate in describing the antebellum era, was an unanticipated outcome of post-Revolutionary efforts to understand what membership ought to look like.[3]

How and why has this earlier epoch in American civil society has remained hidden from view? We know now that post-Revolutionary Americans had sincere and serious doubts about a diverse and fractured civil society, in which different interests and segments of society used formal association as a means of inscribing lines and divisions that many people thought ought to be downplayed in favor of a singular voice of "the people." By the second quarter of the nineteenth century, according to recent scholarship, these more conservative Americans, who had been critical of a secured and pluralistic public sphere, came to embrace it. By the early 1840s, even organized labor found acceptance as a legitimate actor on the stage of American public life.

The 1830s, however, also witnessed the rise of a new and, for some, particularly threatening way of joining together, a conception of membership that set a spark to new debates about the legitimacy and desirability of private associations that threatened the harmony of the nation. Many Americans—many who were coming to embrace and accept a pluralist and divided civil society unlike any in the Western world—would nonetheless speak out in horror at what they saw as a new kind of association. Over the same brief span of years that courts were beginning to opt out of an active role in the internal affairs of associations, and in which courts were finally coming to accept the legitimacy of labor organization, there was a growing debate in American society about the dangers of a particular, essentially new form of association: groups that sought to transform the nation by transforming and binding the individual, something accomplished by means of a particular kind of membership commitment that they called a pledge.

Many would come to believe that American temperance and antislavery societies of the 1830s had completely recast what individuals' voluntary membership ought to look like, from something centering on constitutional and procedural rules to something organized around a full-blown personal confession of faith, support, and allegiance in and for the shared cause—a pledge. And this was a transformation that, when added to the apparent political and social power of those mass movements by mid-decade, evoked new critiques of what the Reverend Baron Stow called, in capital letters, "the Voluntary Association" as something that potentially "crippled" any man's "personal independence." In certain moral reform associations there was a real danger, he wrote in 1837, that "the inward man is subjected to a species of control not far removed from despotism." Another minister, Dura Pratt, worried aloud in 1841 that joiners of voluntary associations, in some cases, "rush forward—sign the constitution—bind their consciences and all their future life to sentiments and efforts, the full nature and consequences of which, they, in many instances, comprehend but very little." In such cases, Pratt noted, associations "have a powerful tendency to interfere with the simple and invaluable rights, nay the very independence of individuals." But while evangelical ministers often took the lead in denouncing the formation of powerful voluntary societies that did damage to the individual conscience and appeared to be a new incarnation of a long-dismissed establishment's churchly control over society, they were not alone. Transcendentalist thinkers like Ralph Waldo Emerson as well as ordinary men and women who were being repeatedly asked to pledge their united commitment in ways they found troubling also began, in the 1830s, to speak out against these new and imposing bonds of membership.[4]

In April 1838, a week before his twenty-sixth birthday, a young seminary student in East Windsor, Connecticut, named Augustus Thompson spoke before the local temperance society about what he called the "Social Character of Ardent Spirits." Throughout, his address worked on two registers simultaneously. Drawing on a line in the third chapter of Amos, he asked, "Can two walk together except they be agreed?" Without harmony of interest, aim, or feeling, two cannot remain together. From there, he spoke about the destructive effects of alcohol for human beings, asking, "Can rum and health walk together? Can rum and thrift walk together?" and, most notably, "Can rum and self[-]rule walk together?" In discussing harmonious and discordant relationships, he wanted to show just how divergent and incompatible were strong drink and a strong individual. It would be his first published work in a lifetime of religious and motivational writings that spanned most of the nineteenth century.[5]

Thompson's analogy also spoke to the questions of how people could be and should be joined together, what means they should and should not use. The temperance association itself was a metaphorical comment on what he called "harmony of action." And all forms of collective action provided useful models. "If two individuals wish to pursue any of the walks of life in company, it is indispensable that they enter into some agreement, formal or implied, which shall operate as a common bond of union," he would note. "Is trade their object? They must form a co-partnership. Does an association for manufacture, insurance, or banking appear desirable? An act of incorporation is necessary." Indeed, for "all our relations, domestic, ecclesiastical, municipal, and international," some kind of agreement, formal or implied, was required. "It is the foundation of human society. It is a law of our being." Thompson, then, wanted to draw his listeners' attention—all of them, remember, members of a Connecticut temperance society—to the issues of cooperation, balance, and harmony. Both in the physical world and in human relationships, he would note, "affinity of nature and a proper adjustment of parts and bearings, is everywhere necessary to union and harmonious action." And he was clear: finding that "proper adjustment" might involve different forms and different kinds of agreements depending on what exactly the object was. What he did not say, but what his audience knew, was that the temperance society was a great exemplar of a new form entirely.[6]

The Law of Membership in the Age of Reform

The rise of American temperance and antislavery efforts took place in an associational world still shaped by the law and experience of membership in the early United States. Before American courts in the later 1830s began to remove themselves from associational disputes by insisting that they were private matters, we now know, there was a body of case law in which aggrieved members, believing their rights as members to have been improperly stripped or abridged, asked courts to intervene and found men there who were eager listeners. A common law of membership emerged, based largely on the writ of mandamus but drawing more broadly both on post-Revolutionary political culture and its abhorrence of arbitrary authority of all kinds and on the actual and everyday practices found in the group life of American civil society. Indeed, a certain level of judicial superintendence remained long after and even to the present day—a lasting consequence of a post-Revolutionary generation's embrace of common law methods of holding the private associations of civic life accountable for their actions. Patterns set as long ago as the dispute between John Binns and William Duane continued to shape legal and lay attitudes toward both the concept and the practices of voluntary association.

It was a development that allowed some jurists, in particular, to conclude that theirs was now a society in which the potential abuse of private authority had found its check. In 1835, for instance, New York Supreme Court justice Samuel Nelson drafted an opinion in a case that addressed the power of the Allegany County Medical Society to expel one of its own members. Henry Fawcett, it seemed, had joined the society under false pretenses, probably lacking in the qualifications to practice medicine and to join his county's medical society, which held a charter of incorporation from the state of New York. Fawcett found himself expelled from the medical society, and publications to that effect were circulated in the local papers. He sued for libel, claiming that the association had not followed the proper procedures and thus his reported expulsion was an illegal act. Announcing such a fraudulent expulsion to the world, he declared, was a libelous assault on his reputation. And the highest court in New York would agree.

The details of the particular conflict between Fawcett and the society are not important, because they were simply one set of variations on a remarkably frequent occurrence in the early American republic. The very next year, for instance, a Dr. John Bartlett was expelled from the Massachusetts Medical Society for consulting with a physician whom the society members believed to be a fraud and a "quack." His expulsion hearing before the medical society made national news, and Bartlett reacted to his ouster by declaring, "The public too shall hear of this matter; I will appeal to, and discuss this subject before another tribunal." True to his word, he made the case as public as he could, denouncing the society's improprieties over the next three years. Democrats in the Massachusetts assembly appointed a committee in 1839 to decide whether the medical society had acted unjustly and illegally: the members of the Massachusetts Medical Society were called to testify and "to show cause why their charter should not be declared void" for their alleged mistreatment of Bartlett, and the hearings lasted weeks. Only Bartlett's untimely death the next year prevented another round of inquiries planned for the next session.[7]

Joining together created new opportunities to exclude and expel, perhaps for good reason and perhaps not, and members had come to learn that they had a right to expect legal protections and judicial interventions when things went wrong. Indeed, in Fawcett's case, Justice Nelson took a moment to underscore the significance of that judicial superintendence, noting that Fawcett's expulsion, wrongful as it was, should not raise any concerns about the potential of a rampant abuse of power. Nelson was pleased to note that the power of a private society to expel its members is one "deemed essential to the fulfillment of the object of the institution, and the orderly and faithful administration of its affairs." But that same power of expulsion "cannot be considered very dangerous to the rights of the corporators, when so cautiously guarded, and subject also to review by the writ of *certiorari* or *mandamus*." Nelson appeared confident that something he treasured, the "individual rights" of each member or corporator, were not in any real danger. The superintending power of the law, he and many others had come to believe, was the best guarantor of the rights and freedoms of those Americans who chose to join ranks with one another.[8]

Nelson was writing at about the time that the influential Pennsylvania courts began to withdraw from a direct superintendence of these private organizations by limiting themselves to the less interventionist role of deciding whether the proper *procedures* had been followed. But a foundation had been laid, a conceptual and legal substructure that would have consequences for the development of American associational practices, particularly in states like Pennsylvania and New York but with a strong influence nationally, owing to the influence of its detailed treatment by treatise writers such as James Kent. Such jurisprudence reflected broader trends in American voluntary associations, even where there was no corporate charter to turn to. In those cases involving unincorporated societies, courts were less likely to involve themselves directly, though not entirely so—and there were cases, drawing on British precedents from the early nineteenth century (where very few voluntary associations held charters at all), in which American chancery courts would hold unincorporated societies to the terms of their bylaws. An 1839 decision in Vermont made clear that for such associations—in this case, a voluntary group called the Evangelical Society, founded in 1804, that held no official charter—it "become[s] necessary to examine their constitution or by-laws or articles of association" to determine how to adjudicate a particular dispute.[9]

Courts, then, continued to have a role to play in policing the boundaries of acceptable action in the private associational world of nineteenth-century America, at least when called upon by an aggrieved individual. The case of the expulsion of Edward V. Price from the American Institute of the City of New York in 1840, for instance, shows some of the ways that the common law of membership as set forth in the early nineteenth century remained useful and relevant long after. In this dramatic internal dispute regarding the alleged misappropriation of funds in an organization founded to champion agricultural and scientific innovation, Price came to serve as a stand-in for a much larger internal power struggle. After a group of members met at Howard House in Manhattan in April 1840, secretly, to discuss the possibility of actual misconduct on the part of the American Institute's officers, Price published a signed piece, addressed to New York senator Guilian C. Verplanck, in the *Morning Courier and New-York Enquirer* on April 23, 1840, to lay out their concerns that "the affairs of the institute . . . have been much neglected and mismanaged for the last two years" and that the officers had attempted "to prevent a candid investigation of its finances and management." The officers proceeded to launch an investigation, not into the potential misuse of funds, but into who had attended the Howard House meeting. Now following the letter of the bylaws, Price was notified that he would be brought up for expulsion at the next stated meeting for his "improper conduct."[10]

The controversy within the American Institute over the Howard House report and Price's open letter to Verplanck denouncing the officers was serious, heated, and procedurally complicated. Both sides organized formal meetings to debate and discuss the issues at hand. Both sides published broadsides or newspaper pieces to announce to the public what was going on and why one side or the other was guilty of scandal, deception, or libel. Philip Schuyler, appointed by the officers of the American Institute to chair a committee to investigate, could not learn the names of the nine members who had met at Howard House, and so he went after Price. In a thirty-five-page report Schuyler charged Price with making false accusations of official misconduct (there had been no misappropriation, Schuyler wrote, the books being "in the most perfect and mercantile order"), and he defended the right of "the majority," who "at all times posses powers equal to any emergencies of the internal government of the Institute," to expel anyone who "would recklessly jeopardy its interests." In the hearings, Price admitted that he had written the letter, which he defended as neither false nor malicious. He soon stopped cooperating, however, when he came to the conclusion that the inquiries had "taken on a most decided aspect of persecution towards me personally." In early 1841, Price was duly expelled by a vote of 77 to 24. And he petitioned for a writ of mandamus to restore him to membership.[11]

It was a typical instance of how courts of law could serve as new venues in ongoing associational disputes. The same cast would play the same roles but on a different stage. Instead of arguing their positions to one another or to the full membership of the organization, they now made their case before the New York Supreme Court. An attorney named Livingston Livingston, who had actually attended the Howard House meeting, served as Price's attorney. George Sullivan, who had taken a lead role in accusing Price of improper conduct in the internal hearings, represented the officers of the American Institute. In the end, the Supreme Court, in an opinion by Chief Justice Nelson, decided that there were flaws in the return filed by the American Institute to the alternative mandamus, and the court declined to allow them to file an amended return. The American Institute had "unjustly expelled" Price and "removed him from the exercise of the right of membership of said Institute, to the grievous damage of the said Edward V. Price." After a peremptory mandamus was issued ordering his readmission, a resolution was passed by the American Institute to restore him. More than two decades later, his name still appeared on the roster of members. Nelson's decisions in both the Fawcett and the Price cases reveal some of the ways that legal institutions continued to play a role in monitoring the boundaries of acceptable and unacceptable conduct in the internal affairs of certain associations.[12]

The period commonly known as the Age of Jackson or, more insightfully, the Age of Reform also witnessed the culmination of the post-Revolutionary generations' attempts to define the concepts of voluntary membership and voluntary association. And as American joiners, organizers, lawyers, and judges came, with increasing precision and forthrightness, to declare what the rights and obligations of membership were and what they ought to be, they also came to see many of the relationships that had once provided useful conceptual parallels—most importantly, stockholding—as sufficiently and substantially different. By the 1830s, courts became less willing to side with shareholding members against their corporation in instances in which the corporation attempted to change its policies in some way that the individual stockholder did not approve. In these conflicts between majority and minority, courts that a decade earlier had consistently sided with the individual member would reverse course, because Americans had begun to reimagine the relationship between stockholder and corporation in ways that minimized all but the pecuniary aspects of the connection. Member had become investor. Across the wide spectrum of associational forms and practices, both legal and lay understandings of the experience of membership in different kinds of organizations had become more fully developed by the fourth decade of the nineteenth century, and people were less apt to look for answers in parallel kinds of groups.[13]

Even as American civil society grew more diverse, an emphasis on procedural fairness and attentiveness to rules, bylaws, and constitutions remained ubiquitous, extending even beyond the shorelines of the young nation. As Matthew Raffety has recently shown, law and law-minded ways of acting together penetrated even into shipboard life on American seagoing vessels in the antebellum era. "Things that happened at sea," he notes, "whether they ended up in court or not, were shaped dramatically by the changing legal understandings of the age." The fact that, in some cases, appeal could be made to higher, land-based legal authorities over a ship's officers, typically in federal court, helped to nourish this attentiveness to fair procedures and law-bound conduct aboard ship. But he finds that the embrace both of rules and of the rule of law was not merely imposed from the top down but was becoming deeply ingrained in the everyday practices and ordinary goings-on of maritime life.[14]

The foundations of the world that Tocqueville and Beaumont witnessed in 1831 lay here, in the "background of general civil laws" (to use Michael Walzer's phrase) and in the shared, law-minded approach to association found among the first generations of American citizens. The widespread belief that people should, at the very least, be able to invoke minimal standards of fair treatment to hold their organizations accountable was immensely important. And this would last in certain ways even after courts had begun to withdraw from an active superintending role. Edward Price won his petition for compulsory readmittance, it would seem, because the justices of the New York Supreme Court believed that the leadership of the American Institute should not be allowed simply to excise any member that questioned its goals and methods. Even as courts were becoming less apt to intervene actively in internal disputes, Price's case revealed that the common law of membership still had an important role to play to prevent the worst kinds of practices such as expelling a man for attempting to notify outsiders of malfeasance—practices, that is, that may have seemed as malicious for society at large as for the lone, ill-treated man.

Law, then, continued to provide a language and a repertoire that could allow people to bind themselves together while limiting the potential for arbitrary abuses of private power. As the nineteenth century moved forward, however, many would call forth a language that emphasized the insufficiency of the law to create ties capable of knitting together a group of people as small as a voluntary association or as large as a nation. The dawn of a new and romantic age of nationalism, of emotional connections between individual and society, led some to ask whether more than law and procedure was needed. In 1839, a young idealistic Whig, Charles Janeway Stillé, would tell his fellow members of the Society of Brothers in Unity that "the social spirit" called for more than "paper laws and regulations." Though many supposed that these were enough "to bind society together and to answer its ends," he believed they created a mere "rope of sand," one that was insufficient to hold people "together as members of the social compact" and would instead "cast us adrift from every high and holy association." Without something sturdier than law—without, that is, the truer and stronger ties of human affection—"are we not by this means thrown upon the wide arena of the world," Stillé asked, "without sympathies, without attachment, uncared for and alone?"[15]

The post-Revolutionary preoccupation with legal superintendence and procedural regularity had laid the foundation for the tremendous expansion and diversification of antebellum civil society. But as that civil society fragmented, it came to comprise associations of all sorts, across a spectrum that included groups that called for little more than a dues-based, contractual membership as well as associations that asked for much more—for an internalized, emotional, but public commitment of the sort that some Americans would have difficulty believing was anything but a danger and a threat.

Remaking Membership in America

The creation of hundreds of societies to promote temperance, according to one writer for the American Education Society in 1829, was "a striking instance of the power of *combined action* when applied to moral subjects." They were that and more. Such associations, in some ways, were the fulfillment of the American embrace of voluntary affiliation; they were what historian Mary Ryan called "the apotheosis of association." No less a respected authority on American voluntarism than Alexis de Tocqueville said much the same thing. American temperance organizations, Tocqueville wrote in one of the alphabetic notebooks he carried on his journey, were essentially "the last word in the way of an association." For the French traveler, temperance societies were without doubt "one of the most notable things in this country." To understand democracy in America, one had to understand the temperance society.[16]

In other ways, however, the temperance movement represented a new direction for American civil society, one that has helped to obscure the law-minded and law-bound world of associations that came before. With the rise of the organized struggle to eliminate the harmful influence of alcohol in American life, joined quite soon by a comparably structured and similarly impassioned mass movement to destroy the institution of slavery, the concept of membership in America would be transformed. The work of sociologist Michael Young is particularly useful for historians on this point, for he has started to describe the ways that temperance and antislavery marked a "new form of collective action" that "deeply implicated the self in the campaign for change." There was something new here. These were associations that centered not on a shared willingness to abide by certain rules or constitutional principles, but rather on a personal transformation and a public confession of faith in the doctrine and the goals of the association. The temperance pledge and its parallels in other antebellum reform societies became a kind of personal and corporate covenant, one that was essentially novel to the world of post-Revolutionary American voluntarism.[17]

"At the outset," Young has noted, the pledge taken by members of temperance societies "did not pretend to any spiritual significance; it was simply a public display of membership and commitment to temperance principles." This kind of affiliation was voluntary, and it rested entirely on an individual's interest to join together with others to accomplish something beneficial to him- or herself and to society at large. On the face of it, such a pledge-oriented approach to voluntary membership would not have appeared to be something different in kind. At most, the pledge "inched toward a commitment of behavior and belief that the individual was duty bound to acknowledge in public." Within a very few years, however, the pledge took on a new significance for how people viewed the associational bonds of American civil society. When in 1829 William Ellery Channing fired the first salvo in a new assault on the American embrace of association as something potentially dangerous to the republic, a literature that took its fullest shape in the 1830s, he called certain voluntary associations "perilous instruments" that "ought to be suspected." Channing's essay has become a famous piece in historical appraisals of the Jacksonian era for his advocacy of individual energy, talent, and judgment and for his argument that some of the voluntary associations of his age appeared to threaten that self-sufficiency. And Channing noted, particularly, that it was "pledged Societies"—that is, voluntary groups that rested on the idea of a sworn commitment that was simultaneously public and personally transformative—that posed the greatest danger. It was the pledged society, Channing contended, that was "a dangerous engine at work among us." Francis Wayland, too, saw the act of members' "pledging themselves to each other and to the public" in temperance and antislavery societies as a deed that produced something new and dangerous, for it stripped men of "their feeling of moral responsibility" and instead turned them into an inflexible "solid column" that would see its will done.[18]

The belief that good Christians should combat the evils that accompanied drunkenness and insobriety were, of course, older than the antebellum era. The organized, orthodox religious struggle against drunkenness in the early national United States dated to the earliest associations formed to combat "vice" in the communities in and around New England. Moral societies, such as those organized by Lyman Beecher in the early nineteenth century, drafted rules and constitutions to help to structure their collective efforts to deal with growing immorality and a decline in the influence of the clergy. When Lebbeus Armstrong wrote a history of the temperance movement in the 1850s, he described the early years (which he dated from his own temperance society, which he founded in 1808, to the formation of the American Temperance Society in 1826) as being the "first epoch," and he "readily admitted that the pledge of the first organized temperance society was imperfect." The constitution of the Moreau and Northumberland Temperance Society that Armstrong had helped to establish specified that "no member shall drink . . . any distilled spirits" under pain of a 25-cent fine for every violation. This was a far cry from a personal and public profession of sworn commitment to the principle of abstinence and unceasing sobriety.[19]

It was, however, a step in that direction. Those early moral societies were innovators in the idea of organizing groups comprising those who adhered to a shared, socially conscious commitment and promised to act accordingly, requiring no dues and, in some cases, no votes of admission. Groups like the Concord Society for Discountenancing Vice and Immorality and the Greene and Delaware Moral Society emphasized, more than anything else, the value of uniting all those "of fair moral character" for the purposes of providing "example, affectionate persuasions, admonition, and in the extreme, legal coercion" of all those who persisted in profanity, drinking to excess, and "other prevailing immoralities." Even into the 1820s, these kinds of associational commitments were not atypical or even particularly obnoxious. These associations reduced social problems to moral ones, and they intended to fill their membership rosters with likeminded individuals who would join the fight.[20]

By the mid- to late 1820s, things began to shift toward a more profound, pledged commitment of associational loyalty that did not smack of patrician control of the unruly and intemperate poor. Rather, the pledge now stood to represent personal and social transformation. With the establishment of the American Temperance Society in 1826, from which Armstrong dated the second epoch of the temperance movement, there came into existence a new kind of voluntary commitment that focused on demanding abstinence even from the temperate (that is, not excessive) drinker. And in a short time, by the late 1820s and early 1830s, the pledge had become a defining element in the lives of hundreds of thousands of American men and women. The national organization added nearly eight hundred auxiliary societies in 1829, nearly a thousand more in 1830, throughout the Northern states, especially, but in large numbers in the South and the West—and it would continue to grow through much of the decade. In places like New York City, the movement swept up people in massive numbers, of diverse walks of life and of a wide range of ethnic and racial backgrounds.[21]

These local temperance societies organized themselves around the pledge. Their primary emphasis would be the call for individuals to swear to adhere to a shared course of action in combatting drinking and the liquor trade. This new movement appealed directly to the people and quite unlike the earlier moral societies was, according to historian Ian Tyrrell, "implicitly subversive of ministerial authority and of church dominance in social and moral matters." Linking it all together, alongside the print culture and the traveling agents of the American Temperance Society, was the pledge. So powerful was this new emphasis that the next great social reform movement to appear, a struggle to protect the sanctity of the first day of the week that was headlined by the creation of the General Union for the Promotion of the Christian Sabbath in 1828, also chose to emphasize a pledge, one "to honor the Sabbath and, in particular, to boycott all transportation companies that operated stagecoaches, steamboats, or canal packets seven days a week," according to Richard John. A vow to that effect, in fact, was the sole criterion of membership. While widely circulated petitions and massive amounts of printed promotional materials were the public face of the GUPCS, the life of the association came from an associational pledge that was meant to be personally binding and to be socially transformative.[22]

Within these pledged societies, many of the expected and usual practices and associational procedures—the sort of everyday constitutionalism found far and wide in American civil society of the nineteenth century—continued, giving a familiar shape the daily goings-on. Armstrong's first temperance society of 1808 had bylaws that called for annual and quarterly meetings, a library, a detailed fine and assessment structure, and provisions for expulsion and withdrawal. And even after the pledge became the defining characteristic of the group life of the movement, temperance societies maintained an emphasis on constitutional practices: the Hampden Youths Temperance Society recorded in their book of minutes that they opened each of their meetings by prayer and by "reading our Constitution and presenting it for signers as usual." All of these societies held regular meetings, elected officers, and acted in ways bound by their constitutions and bylaws. Organizers in a community utilized constitutions to promote and to establish these kinds of associations. In 1830, a minister in Andover, New Hampshire, wrote to a friend to tell him that, in his community, "a constitution for a Temperance Society has been circulated and received above forty names. The Society will probably soon be organized." Constitutions, then, continued to provide the framework of each and every temperance association.[23]

But the pledge was its heart. From the moment a pledge was taken, it was not so much constitutions and rules that held temperate men and women together but a shared, personal commitment to principle. The first article of the Kennebunk Temperance Society, founded in Maine in 1829, required every member to pledge "to wholly abstain from the internal use of ardent spirits and that we will not furnish them for our families or laborers or guests." The fifth article permitted the expulsion of those—and only those—who violated the first article. Raising funds, even just to offset the costs of association, was in most cases irrelevant and, in some cases, such as the Providence Association for the Promotion of Temperance in Rhode Island in 1830, was even constitutionally forbidden. No money could ever be called

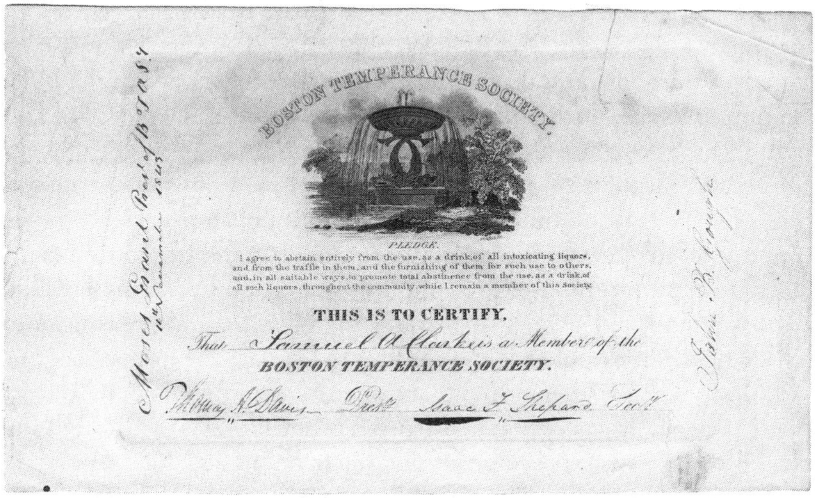
BOSTON TEMPERANCE SOCIETY.

PLEDGE.

I agree to abstain entirely from the use, as a drink, of all intoxicating liquors, and from the traffic in them, and the furnishing of them for such use to others, and, in all suitable ways, to promote total abstinence from the use, as a drink, of all such liquors, throughout the community, while I remain a member of this Society.

THIS IS TO CERTIFY,

That ______ is a Member of the

BOSTON TEMPERANCE SOCIETY.

6. Boston Temperance Society, membership certificate of Samuel A. Clarke, Nov. 11, 1843, Certificate File, PR 014, New-York Historical Society.

for, according to the constitution. The association was to be entirely about shared belief and shared commitment to the pledge.[24]

The details of the pledge varied from place to place, but the significance did not. The pledge was what defined membership. It appeared prominently on membership certificates, some of which, such as those produced by the Boston Temperance Society, included very little else.

The temperance pledge that was most commonly taken underwent a significant change in the mid-1830s, from one that permitted some alcohol to the "teetotal" pledge of complete abstinence. A tipping point was reached by 1835 and 1836, when teetotalers believed that they held majorities in state and local temperance organizations, and the teetotal pledge became a standard requirement of temperance membership. In the early 1840s, a new kind of temperance society, formed by and for "Reformed Drunkards," took shape under the name of the Washingtonians, and they, too, organized around a pledge of total abstinence.[25]

There was a profound emotional, even spiritual significance to this pledge in the lives of many Americans. One editor of a temperance magazine compared the temperance pledge to "the Sabbath, circumcision, baptism, the Lord's supper"—for all were "pledges or covenants." These pledged societies were, of course, fully voluntary and entirely oriented around shared commitment to a cause—characteristics of a great many associations of early American civil society. The temperance society, wrote Professor John Yates of Union College in 1834, "is republican in its character; free in its influence, demands no force, but appeals to reason." Indeed, it reminded him of nothing so much as the American Revolutionaries' "pledge of total abstinence from the use and traffic of tea," which in time gave life to a new nation. But it was also a transformative commitment, one made not to a church or to the nation but to a voluntary association.[26]

And it created fear. Some Americans such as Channing worried that it was an associational bond that would "interfere with, or restrain individual action, personal independence, private judgment, free, self-originated effort." Where Yates would see the pledged society as "the best school" for teaching a man "perseverance in that course of conduct, which he is rationally persuaded is correct," others, such as Francis Wayland, worried that such pledged societies risked producing rigidity of thought and a potential abuse of private power. "No man should join any voluntary association, under any pledge either express or implied," Wayland wrote, "which shall render his motives for change of opinion specially liable to be called in question." What is more, joining together in a shared commitment to a shared goal left each member vulnerable if those goals should change over time. "Suppose that a majority of those who have associated themselves with me, under the same pledge, but whom very likely I have never even seen, resolve that this pledge shall be altered, and that it shall include something else; that is assume to themselves the right to *pledge me, without my consent,* and to a matter wholly without the contract," Wayland prompted. (These were, we have seen, ongoing concerns in the law and practice of membership, ones dealt with repeatedly in the context of minority corporate shareholders' rights.) "Suppose they go farther," he wrote, "and discuss the ethical reasons of my pledge, and give to the world a reason for my conduct, which I have never given." Such concerns might seem hyperbolic, but they arose out of a deeply felt concern that associations might just be the greatest immediate threat to Wayland's faith in the inner guide to right conduct, the human conscience. The pledged society, this new form of collective action, left room for an abuse of associational power that Wayland believed it his duty to warn against. Perhaps these new bonds of membership were simply too strong, too dangerous to let be.[27]

It was not, however, the war on alcohol that produced the great profusion of anxieties and public pronouncements about the danger of the pledged society in the late 1830s. It was the assault on slavery. Abolitionist societies, too, embraced the pledge as their central feature. There, too, social transformation and individual obligation would be paired together. The model of temperance had a firm hold on the minds of those who took the lead in the early years of the abolitionist movement in 1830s America. To combat the sin of slavery, as the Ladies Anti-Slavery Society of Dover, New Hampshire, would make especially clear in its formative documents, "can be done, as in the case of intemperance, only by a radical reform in individual, and by consequence, in *public* sentiment." Any person who believed in their cause "may become a member of this Society by signing this Constitution." Those who joined the more than one thousand auxiliary societies of the American Anti-Slavery Society that were established in the 1830s were asked to hold to a similar conception of membership: William Jay quoted from their constitution in a short promotional work he published in 1835, and he emphasized the "great moral principles frankly and unequivocally avowed." The entire organization was "founded on principle," "availing itself, only of certain professed motives," demanding utter commitment to those goals, and eschewing the kind of "co-operation of motives of all sorts, however contradictory," that typified such earlier organizations as the American Colonization Society.[28]

The abolitionist societies of the 1830s rejected the idea that different people might join ranks for different reasons. The act of joining was an act of the conscience, one made meaningless if not motivated by shared moral considerations. And it created a newly powerful force in antebellum civil society. Orestes Brownson, though "decidedly opposed to slavery in any and every possible shape," believed he saw the consequences of "many hundreds of thousands of men, women, and children, all solemnly pledged to effect the immediate emancipation of the slaves." And he believed them to be dangerous, for the slaveholder and for the republic. "They are not formed for deliberation, for discussion, but for action," and as such they offered "neither a rational nor a moral argument for the abolition of slavery." They were "pledged to the 'immediate emancipation of the slaves,'" thought Brownson, and nothing that they offered was any more persuasive than "an associated multitude pointing the finger of scorn." Members of antislavery societies, like the women in Dover, were asked "to obey the injunction 'Remember those in bonds as bound with them'"—and those bonds were, for good or ill, extremely strong. This was not a commitment to become lifelong friends or anything of the sort. Rather, it was an associational bond oriented around a binding pledge to oppose a certain evil. William Lloyd Garrison, for instance, sought to calm the worries of some white women in the Ladies Anti-Slavery Society that their admission of black members would taint them in some way: "Remember," he said, "that you are not called upon to decide, that you will make bosom friends of colored females, or invite them into your parlors," but only whether they can "combine their influence with yours." And yet the pledge they each took was clearly no fleeting commitment. For some people, even those fully committed to the struggles against slavery or drink, the abolitionists and the temperance crusaders were asking for associational bonds of a new order, ones that destroyed the prospects of a truly deliberative democracy.[29]

What Channing called the pledged society, this new approach to voluntary affiliation and concerted action, is introduced here to help to better define and understand what came before. From a certain vantage, the pledged society was no more than a continuation of the law-minded, constitutionally bounded type of voluntary association that predominated in post-Revolutionary American civil society. In 1834, John Harrison told the Louisville Young Men's Temperance Society in Kentucky that "your subscriptions to the constitution of this voluntary association is a positive act, involving responsibilities and duties, pointed out in literal outline, by the words of that instrument, by which you are obligated to refrain from drinking ardent spirits." But he was aware that "this is but the letter of your free assumption of responsibleness to the furtherance of this excellent object." The spirit was something different. And it was the spirit of this new form of collective action that put doubts in the minds even of people who approved of the cause. When a group of citizens in Russia, New York, gathered to discuss and promote the cause of temperance in 1830, they were thrilled that people were beginning to give up alcohol, but only because it had thus far arose "from the judicious reflection and the independent resolutions of individuals." Forming a society to that effect would further a dangerous pattern, in which pledged societies were "all centering to one powerful and dangerous point, that of producing moral and intellectual slavery." Let men act on their own volition, "uninfluenced by the coercion" of even a voluntary association. They voted down the idea of forming a pledged temperance society.[30]

There were countless instances in the 1830s and 1840s of people who supported the goals of certain pledged societies but held onto doubts about the methods, and those doubts came not merely from public figures such as Channing and Wayland but from the grassroots of the movements as well. Historian Robert Hampel's study of the temperance movement in Massachusetts reveals some profound anxieties from the ordinary men and women who supported the efforts in support of temperance. Some worried that it echoed the hated Masonic oaths. More than anything, there were concerns that taking a pledge meant replacing one's self-reliance and personal strength with artificial rules and external bonds. Hampel discovered the minutes of a society in East Sudbury, Massachusetts, that listed seven men and two women "favorable to the cause, though unwilling to pledge." These were concerns that had nothing to do with whether someone supported efforts to create a more sober nation. Abraham Lincoln, for example—a temperate man, but a man who never signed a temperance pledge or joined a temperance society—gave decidedly mixed messages when asked to address a Springfield temperance society in 1842. He extolled the immense value of freeing men from "the chains of moral death" forged by intemperance, and the benefits for the republic of eliminating the abuse of alcohol might rival even those won in the Revolution of 1776. Still, Lincoln fretted about the lock-step practices of the movement and the threats that they might pose to public deliberation and to the democratic process.[31]

Were these pledged societies, then, a danger to or even a rejection of individual autonomy, or were they its fullest expression? At bottom, this was a question that hung over nearly every form of collective action, nearly every debate about the meanings and consequences of voluntary association in the post-Revolutionary United States. Temperance advocate John Harrison thought "the act of union to a Temperance Society is in itself meritorious, and demonstrative of decision and independence of character." The Reverend John Yates believed the temperance pledge revealed "the importance of decision [i.e., decisiveness] as a national trait." Whether it was the Revolutionaries' pledge to give up tea or his contemporaries' pledge to abjure alcohol, it occurred only when "the individual, after mature reflection—after testing the principle of abstinence, and under a full conviction of its truth and necessity, joins the association." From that moment of taking the pledge, however, he or she "is admitted . . . to the cordial sympathy and friendship of the good and virtuous." They can stand strong, for they do not stand alone. Even Wayland, worried as he was about the freedom of the individual conscience, believed that a temperance pledge simply "binds me to a particular and specified course of conduct," and this can, in the right circumstances, be a good thing. "I delegate nothing to any one. I put myself in no one's power. I surrender neither my understanding, nor my conscience, nor my liberty, to any man, nor to any set of men. I am in all these things as I was before"—unless, that is, his fellow members were to alter the nature of the pledged society, or begin to speak on his behalf in a way he could and would not accept.[32]

Personal Responsibility and the Bonds of Membership in America

By the 1830s and 1840s, in the midst of these debates about the potential dangers of the pledged societies of the antebellum era, there were signs that, as Brownson put it, "the spirit of association, is fast giving place to the more powerful engine of progress, individuality." When Ralph Waldo Emerson observed in Boston's Amory Hall in 1844 that the failure of the "New England Reformers" rested on their blindness to the fact that a true "union must be inward, and not one of covenants, and is to be reached by a reverse of the methods they use," he was not denying that people may well need to join together to accomplish ends true and good. He himself was an advocate of abolition and his wife a member in good standing of an antislavery society (there is no evidence that he ever joined one). But he nonetheless saw one of the two major defects of all of these "New England Reformers," alongside what he saw as their wrongheaded tendency to focus on one single wrong at a time, to be "their reliance on association."[33]

Emerson saw true reform as coming from the truly free and truly self-governed individual. "Each man, if he attempts to join himself to others, is all sides cramped and diminished of his proportion," Emerson believed, "and the stricter the union, the smaller and the more pitiful he is." As he was speaking, he made clear that he had in mind both the grandest, utopian collective efforts of his day, such as the commune at Brook Farm, as well as the more typical reform societies such as New England's countless antislavery associations. In both cases, "the union must be ideal in actual individualism." And that outcome came about when both association and individual member recognized the importance of "the adoption of simpler methods, and an assertion of the sufficiency of the private man." He described a recent moment in which "a church censured and threatened to excommunicate one of its members, on account of the somewhat hostile part to the church, which his conscience led him to take in the anti-slavery business." In response (and Emerson could hardly contain his glee at the outcome), "the threatened individual immediately excommunicated the church" instead of waiting for it to expel him. For a man who believed that society was constantly and perpetually conspiring against the individual, voluntary associations of any kind—and particularly those that asked the most of their members—were deeply suspect.[34]

For the romantic in antebellum America, then, formal association even for the greatest of causes must be a consequence of personal reformation. It could never be its cause. The pledged societies of the 1830s were vast, powerful, and united. Brownson in 1838 described "many hundreds of thousands of men, women, and children, all solemnly pledged to effect the immediate emancipation of the slaves," who were "banded together in some fifteen hundred Societies." The Reverend Leonard Withington noted in the context of temperance two years later that these pledges may serve a purpose: "If a man finds that a private vow, or a social pledge, animates his virtue, or assists his resolution, he is undoubtedly at liberty to make them." But for many people "the object of a social pledge is, in the present day, very greatly mistaken," for that pledge has become, "like the traditions of the Pharisees, a bar in the way of our duty." In the place of pure motive to do good, they substitute personal obedience to a pledge made to an association of fellow creatures. The pledges themselves "are like the very stimulating drink they oppose; they quicken the mind for a time, and then leave it flagging and dead." They replace individual spirit of action instead of complementing it. Much the same anxiety underlay Emerson's unwillingness to join his fellow Transcendentalists at Brook Farm, for to join such a "noble and humane" association of men and women in the hopes of finding a better life would simply "put on your community the task of my emancipation which I ought to take on myself." As Philip Gura accurately describes Emerson's views—and, we can add, the views of many critics of the pledged reform society—the task of personal reformation "was best accomplished in the privacy of one's closet."[35]

In time, it began to appear that well-meaning and serious men might just disagree on whether associational bonds facilitated or hampered the freedom of the individual. Emerson and others of his day, such as abolitionist Gerritt Smith, came to see in the voluntary principle a way to join together that emphasized what historian John Stauffer rightly calls the ideal of "sacred self-sovereignty." People should come together based solely on voluntary, mutual service to and for one another, without creating hierarchies or restraints: solidarity should go hand in hand with freedom and self-determination. Any organized group of human beings, including those societies formed in behalf of the providentially favored movements to end the evils of alcohol and slavery, must promote individual freedom, not external constraint—for only then could people act together as a moral force. Moral regeneration would emanate outward, from individual, to community, to nation.[36]

For decades, beginning with the growing numbers of voluntary societies of all kinds in the immediate wake of the American Revolution, people in the new republic had been confronting tensions between autonomy and association, between the powerlessness of individual isolation and the potential excesses of organized, private power. In 1836, a newspaper man named Orville Luther Holley addressed the Ontario County Temperance Society in upstate New York. He described how the nation had been confronted by a profound evil of drink and drunkenness, and "all modes of persuasion having been found unavailing . . . the only remaining alternative disclosed itself": the "voluntary pledge." There were dangers, of course, to this kind of collective effort, though something needed done and "in no department of social life do improvements drop from the air, or sprout from the ground." People must act, and act together, for "canals have not yet, that I am aware of been known to dig themselves;—railroads have not yet been seen coming, ready made, and stretching their inviting facilities across the country." In fact, "none of the admirable and useful institutions of a civilized and advancing condition of society, have ever yet started spontaneously into being and proffered their blessings gratuitously." But all of these combined and united efforts to effect change or to construct a better society came with risks. Indeed, the temperance societies had often been known to do too much, "to control the course of an individual, by unworthy means."[37]

Holley suggested an answer to this problem, this perhaps unavoidable conflict between personal autonomy and effective, collective action: if anyone should feel an "unjust interference," or "any thing in the nature of persecution, or oppression, in any form—let him spurn them, proclaim the iniquity of the attempt upon him, and assert his rights." For Holley, a man of liberal politics and firmly Anti-Masonic beliefs, there was a clear answer to the potential risks of joining together. "The true and proper way to thwart the acquisition is, not by opposing and decrying voluntary associations for wholesome purposes," he told a temperance association in Canandaigua, where William Morgan had gone missing just ten years earlier, "but by the prompt and thorough vindication of personal rights." Let people join together to do good work, for if anything should go awry, there was a recourse that would not destroy the potential for good simply to eliminate the prospect of evil. "If *personal rights* are invaded," he said, "let them be vindicated in every lawful and appropriate mode." The reform societies of the 1830s appeared to be both a new hope for progress and a new kind of possible oppression over the ideally free and independent mind. But for Holley there was no need to think beyond the solutions that had always worked, the rule of law and a commitment to personal rights that extended far and wide, in societies large and small.[38]

Orville Holley had been born in 1791, a citizen of a free and republican nation. He had always lived in a world without courtly corruptions or aristocratic distinctions of birth. Therefore, "the evils we have to complain of," he said, "are of those kinds, which are most intimately connected with *personal responsibility*. . . . They are not such as grow out of relations, *forced* and *fastened* upon us, *against our wills*, by *despotic* and *irresponsible power*, but they spring from such relations as are *voluntarily* assumed." It was in that world that he had always lived. He had seen dangers arise, and he understood the limits of what the American people had yet accomplished. He abhorred slavery, and he decried the racism of the post-emancipation North. He believed he had been a part of a just crusade against the dark and ominous threats of a Freemasonry that claimed the fealty of citizens and threatened the freedom of the nation. But as he looked about him in upstate New York in 1836, he believed that the greatest perils that citizens in the American republic faced were the results of choices they had made—the choice to drink, for instance, or the choice to let themselves "be trampled upon by sect, or party," without asserting their rights. Fortunately, "these are precisely the evils most within the reach of *individual* and *voluntary* reform, and under the control of that *personal free-agency*, which is the great basis of accountability to *society*, and to *God*." In a post-Revolutionary age in which the opportunities to remake the world seemed nearly limitless, people found new reasons and new ways to join together. And in a society in which free citizens were fettered only by the obligations that they assumed themselves, the potential risks and the possible rewards of voluntary affiliation rested heavy on the minds of men like Holley. When consent and personal choice formed the foundation of the social order, as he told his listeners, the "moral responsibility of every successive generation becomes more and more momentous."[39]

NOTES

INTRODUCTION

1. Wakefield Musical Society, Wakefield, NH, records, 1815–1825, New Hampshire Historical Society, Concord, NH.
2. Alexis de Tocqueville, *Democracy in America*, trans. George Lawrence (New York: Harper and Row, 1966), 513; Arthur M. Schlesinger, "Biography of a Nation of Joiners," *American Historical Review* 50 (1944): 1–25.
3. Francis Wayland, *The Limitations of Human Responsibility* (Boston: Gould, Kendall, and Lincoln, 1838), 90–91; Timothy Walker, *Introduction to American Law: Designed as a First Book for Students* (Philadelphia: P. H. Nicklin and T. Johnson, 1837), 203; Baron Stow, *Voluntary Associations—Their Use and Abuse: Discourse Delivered in the Meeting House of the Second Baptist Society, in Baldwin Place, Thanksgiving-Day, November 30, 1837* (Boston: Gould, Kendall, and Lincoln, 1837), 4, 19–20.
4. *Constitution of the Anti-Bell-Ringing Society, Instituted Oct. 26, 1838* (Boston: Henry P. Lewis, 1839), 3, 7; letter of Feb. 27, 1839, in papers relating to the Anti-Bell-Ringing Society, Henry E. Huntington Library, San Marino, CA.
5. A generic, "model" constitution for such groups was printed in Connecticut in 1810 and copied widely. *The Constitution of Particular Cent Societies: For the Purpose of Aiding Pious, Indigent Youths in Attaining an Education for the Gospel Ministry* (Hartford, CT: Peter B. Gleason, 1810).
6. See Joseph Raz, "The Politics of the Rule of Law," in *Ethics in the Public Domain: Essays in the Morality of Law and Politics* (Oxford: Clarendon, 1994), 377–78.
7. William J. Novak, "The Legal Transformation of Citizenship in Nineteenth-Century America," in *The Democratic Experiment: New Directions in American Political History*, ed. Meg Jacobs, William J. Novak, and Julian E. Zelizer (Princeton, NJ: Princeton University Press, 2003), 101–2; William J. Novak, "The American Law of Association: The Legal-Political Construction of Civil Society," *Studies in American Political Development* 15 (2001): 163–88; Theda Skocpol, "The Tocqueville Problem: Civic Engagement in American Democracy," *Social Science History* 21 (1997): 455–79; Theda Skocpol, Marshall Ganz, and Ziad Munson, "A Nation of Organizers: The Institutional Origins of Civic Voluntarism in the United States," *American Political Science Review* 94 (2000): 527–46; Richard R. John, "Governmental Institutions as Agents of Change: Rethinking American Political Development in the Early Republic, 1787–1835," *Studies in American Political Development* 11 (1997): 347–80.

8. [Samuel Blodget], *Economica: A Statistical Manual for the United States of America* (1806;reprint, New York: Augustus M. Kelley, 1964), 12, 19, 199–200; Richard D. Brown, "The Emergence of Urban Society in Rural Massachusetts, 1760–1820," *Journal of American History* 61 (1974): 29–51; Johann N. Neem, *Creating a Nation of Joiners: Democracy and Civil Society in Early National Massachusetts* (Cambridge, MA: Harvard University Press, 2008); Pauline Maier, "The Revolutionary Origins of the American Corporation," *William and Mary Quarterly*, 3rd ser., 50 (1993): 51–84; Oscar Handlin and Mary Flug Handlin, *Commonwealth: A Study of the Role of Government in the American Economy: Massachusetts, 1774–1861*, rev. ed. (Cambridge, MA: Belknap Press of Harvard University Press, 1969); Louis Hartz, *Economic Policy and Democratic Thought: Pennsylvania, 1776–1860* (1948; reprint, Chicago: Quadrangle, 1968); Harry N. Scheiber, "Private Rights and Public Power: American Law, Capitalism, and the Republican Polity in Nineteenth-Century America," *Yale Law Review* 107 (1997): 823–61.
9. The central work, of course, is Jürgen Habermas, *The Structural Transformation of the Public Sphere: An Inquiry into a Category of Bourgeois Society*, trans. Thomas Burger and Frederick Lawrence (Cambridge, MA: MIT Press, 1989). For recent work influenced by Habermas, see John L. Brooke, *Columbia Rising: Civil Life on the Upper Hudson from the Revolution to the Age of Jackson* (Chapel Hill: University of North Carolina Press, 2010); Albrecht Koschnik, "The Democratic Societies of Philadelphia and the Limits of the American Public Sphere, circa 1793–1795," *William and Mary Quarterly*, 3rd ser., 58 (2001): 626–27; Albrecht Koschnik, *"Let a Common Interest Bind Us Together": Associations, Partisanship, and Culture in Philadelphia, 1775–1840* (Charlottesville: University of Virginia Press, 2007); Neem, *Creating a Nation of Joiners*; John L. Brooke, "Ancient Lodges and Self-Created Societies: Voluntary Association and the Public Sphere in the Early Republic," in *Launching the "Extended Republic": The Federalist Era*, ed. Ronald Hoffman and Peter J. Albert (Charlottesville: University of Virginia Press, 1996), 273–377; Joanna Brooks, "The Early American Public Sphere and the Emergence of a Black Print Counterpublic," *William and Mary Quarterly*, 3rd ser., 62 (2005): 67–92. For an incisive examination of the relevant historiography, see John L. Brooke, "Reason and Passion in the Public Sphere: Habermas and the Cultural Historians," *Journal of Interdisciplinary History* 29 (1998): 43–67; John L. Brooke, "Consent, Civil Society, and the Public Sphere in the Age of Revolution and the Early American Republic," in *Beyond the Founders: New Approaches to the Political History of the Early American Republic*, ed. Jeffrey L. Pasley, Andrew W. Robertson, and David Waldstreicher (Chapel Hill: University of North Carolina Press, 2004), 207–50.
10. L. T. Hobhouse, *Liberalism* (1911; reprint, New York: Oxford University Press, 1964), 24; Nancy L. Rosenblum, *Another Liberalism: Romanticism and the Reconstruction of Liberal Thought* (Cambridge, MA: Harvard University Press, 1987), 162.
11. Hendrik A. Hartog, "The Constitution of Aspiration and 'The Rights That Belong to Us All,'" *Journal of American History* 74 (1987): 1014.

CHAPTER ONE

1. Edgar Erskine Hume, comp., *Society of the Cincinnati: Rules of the State Societies for Admission to Membership* (Washington, DC: Society of the Cincinnati, 1934), 3; Bryce Metcalf, *Original Members and Other Officers Eligible to the Society of the Cincinnati, 1783–1938: With the Institutions, Rules of Admission, and Lists of the Officers of the General and State Societies* (1938; rpt., Beverly Hills, CA: Historic Trust Eastwood,

1995); Minor Myers, Jr., *Liberty without Anarchy: A History of the Society of the Cincinnati* (Charlottesville: University Press of Virginia, 1983), chap. 2 and appendix; Diary of Thomas Jefferson, Mar. 6, 1788, in *The Writings of Thomas Jefferson*, ed. Andrew A. Lipscomb and Albert Ellery Bergh, vol. 17 (Washington, DC: Thomas Jefferson Memorial Association, 1903), 249–50; Charles Royster, *A Revolutionary People at War; The Continental Army and American Character, 1775–1783* (Chapel Hill: University of North Carolina Press, 1979), 355–56; North Callahan, *Henry Knox: General Washington's General* (New York: Rinehart, 1958), 216.

2. John Adams to Arthur Lee, Apr. 6, 1784, in *The Papers of John Adams*, vol. 16, *February 1784–March 1785*, ed. C. James Taylor et al. (Cambridge, MA: Belknap Press of Harvard University Press, 2012), 108–9; Cassius [Aedanus Burke], *Considerations on the Society or Order of the Cincinnati; Lately Instituted by the Major-Generals, Brigadier-Generals, and Other Officers of the American Army . . .* (Philadelphia: Robert Bell, 1783), 7; Kerby A. Miller et al., eds., *Irish Immigrants in the Land of Canaan* (New York: Oxford University Press, 2003), 576–85; John C. Meleney, *The Public Life of Aedanus Burke: Revolutionary Republican in Post-Revolutionary South Carolina* (Columbia: University of South Carolina Press, 1989), chap. 4. On the Cincinnati as a knighthood, see Richard Beale Davis, ed., *Jeffersonian America: Notes on the United States of America Collected in the Years 1805–6–7 and 11–12 by Sir Augustus John Foster, Bart.* (San Marino, CA: Huntington Library, 1954), 69, where Foster refers to Charles C. Pinckney as "a Knight of Cincinnati." From her vantage in England, Abigail Adams made a similar judgment, referring to "knights of the order" in a letter to another critic of the Cincinnati, Mercy Otis Warren, May 10, 1785. Richard Alan Ryerson, ed., *Adams Family Correspondence*, vol. 6, *December 1784-December 1785* (Cambridge, MA: Belknap Press of Harvard University Press, 1993), 139.

3. Quotation from "The Committee of both Houses of the General Court, appointed to enquire into the Existence, Nature, Object, and probably Tendency or Effect of an Order or Society called the Cincinnati . . . ," *Independent Chronicle*, Mar. 25, 1784, quoted in Johann N. Neem, *Creating a Nation of Joiners: Democracy and Civil Society in Early National Massachusetts* (Cambridge, MA: Harvard University Press, 2008), 42; Myers, *Liberty without Anarchy*, 1–90; Markus Hünemörder, *The Society of the Cincinnati: Conspiracy and Distrust in Early America* (New York: Berghahn, 2006), 5–56; Marc L. Harris, "'Cement to the Union': The Society of the Cincinnati and the Limits of Fraternal Sociability," Massachusetts Historical Society, *Proceedings* 107 (1995): 115–40; Wallace Evan Davies, "The Society of the Cincinnati in New England 1783–1800," *William and Mary Quarterly*, 3rd ser., 5 (1948): 3–25; Edgar Erskine Hume, "Early Opposition to the Cincinnati," *Americana* 30 (1936): 597–638; Charles William Janson, *The Stranger in America: Containing Observations Made during a Long Residence in That Country . . .* (London: Albion, 1807), 284–96.

4. Thomas S. Harding, *College Literary Societies: Their Contribution to Higher Education in the United States, 1815–1876* (New York: Pageant, 1971); McLachlan, "*Choice of Hercules*"; J. Jefferson Looney, "Useful without Attracting Attention: The Cliosophic and American Whig Societies of the College of New Jersey, 1765–1896," *Princeton University Library Chronicle* 64 (2003): 389–423; J. Jefferson Looney, *Nurseries of Letters and Republicanism: A Brief History of the American Whig-Cliosophic Society, 1765–1941* (Princeton, NJ: American Whig-Cliosophic Society, 1996).

5. Caleb Crain, *American Sympathy: Men, Friendship, and Literature in the New Nation* (New Haven, CT: Yale University Press, 2001); Andrew Burstein, *Sentimental*

Democracy: The Evolution of America's Romantic Self-Image (New York: Hill and Wang, 1999); David S. Shields, *Civil Tongues and Polite Letters in British America* (Chapel Hill: University of North Carolina Press, 1997); G. J. Barker-Benfield, *The Culture of Sensibility: Sex and Society in Eighteenth-Century Britain* (Chicago: University of Chicago Press, 1992); Lawrence E. Klein, *Shaftesbury and the Culture of Politeness: Moral Discourse and Cultural Politics in Early Eighteenth-Century England* (Cambridge: Cambridge University Press, 1994); Richard Godbeer, *The Overflowing of Friendship: Love between Men and the Creation of the American Republic* (Baltimore: Johns Hopkins University Press, 2009); Charles Janeway Stillé, *The Social Spirit: A Valedictory Oration, Pronounced at the Departure of the Senior Class from the Society of Brothers in Unity, Yale College, June 28, 1839* (New Haven, CT: B. L. Hamlen, 1839), quotation on 6.

6. Anthony Ashley Cooper, third earl of Shaftesbury, "Sensus Communis," in *Characteristics of Men, Manners, Opinions, Times, Etc.*, ed. John M. Robertson, 2 vols. (London: Grant Richards, 1900), 1:54; Shields, *Civil Tongues and Polite Letters*, 97–98, 175–208 (198 for quotation from Homony Club, Dec. 22, 1770); David S. Shields, "Anglo-American Clubs: Their Wit, Their Heterodoxy, Their Sedition," *William and Mary Quarterly*, 3rd ser., 51 (1994): 293–304; Peter Clark, *British Clubs and Societies, 1580–1800: The Origins of an Associational World* (Oxford: Clarendon, 2000); Daniel Defoe, *An Essay upon Projects*, ed. Joyce D. Kennedy, Michael Seidel, and Maximillian E. Novak (New York: AMS, 1999). On the terminology of emotion in use in the eighteenth century, see Nicole Eustace, *Passion is the Gale: Emotion, Power, and the Coming of the American Revolution* (Chapel Hill: University of North Carolina Press, 2008), appendix.

7. Catherine O'Donnell Kaplan, *Men of Letters in the Early Republic: Cultivating Forums of Citizenship* (Chapel Hill: University of North Carolina Press, 2008).

8. Thomas Paine, *Common Sense* (Philadelphia: R. Bell, 1776), 1; "The Institution of the Society of the Cincinnati," in Myers, *Liberty without Anarchy*, appendix, 258–59. For the original proposal by Henry Knox, the original text of the Institution, and "The Institution of the Society of the Cincinnati as Altered and Amended at their First General Meeting," see Edgar Erskine Hume, *Sesquicentennial History and Roster of the Society of the Cincinnati in the State of Virginia, 1783–1933* (Richmond, VA: Published for the Society of the Cincinnati, 1934), 26–41.

9. A Member of the Society of the Cincinnati, *A Reply to a Pamphlet, Entitled,* Considerations on the Society or Order of Cincinnati *&c.* (Annapolis, MD: Frederick Green, [1783]), 28; Morgan Lewis, address appended to Robert R. Livingston [chancellor], *An Oration Delivered before the Society of the Cincinnati in the State of New-York: In Commemoration of the Fourth Day of July* (New York: Francis Childs, 1787), 19–21. For a similar depiction, see John Sullivan to George Washington, Feb. 5, 1785, in *Letters and Papers of Major-General John Sullivan, Continental Army*, ed. Otis G. Hammond, vol. 3, in *Collections of the New Hampshire Historical Society*, vol. 15 (Concord: New Hampshire Historical Society, 1939), 394–97.

10. Kaplan, *Men of the Letters in the Early Republic*, chap. 1; Judith Nisse Shklar, "Politics and Friendship," *Proceedings of the American Philosophical Society* 137 (1993): 207–12; Ivy Schweitzer, *Perfecting Friendship: Politics and Affiliation in Early American Literature* (Chapel Hill: University of North Carolina Press, 2006), 9–10, 110–11.

11. George Washington to Thomas Jefferson, April 8, 1784, in *The Papers of George Washington: Confederation Series*, ed. W. W. Abbot (Charlottesville: University of Virginia Press, 1992), 1:275–76.

12. Thomas Jefferson to George Washington, Apr. 16, 1784, in ibid., 1:287–92.

13. Jefferson to Washington, Apr. 16, 1784. In granting Washington and his fellow soldiers the benefit of the doubt as to the purity of their motives, Jefferson was almost certainly being honest. He would repeat that version of the story two years later when he corrected the French encyclopedist Jean Nicolas Démeunier, who had painted a much more nefarious picture of the Cincinnati. The criticisms of the Cincinnati came about, Jefferson informed him, when men around the country read the plans for the Society "in their closets, unwarmed by those sentiments of friendship which had produced them, inattentive to those pains which an approaching separation had excited in the minds of the institutors." "Jefferson's Observations on Démeunier's Manuscript," in *The Papers of Thomas Jefferson*, ed. Julian P. Boyd, vol. 10 (Princeton, NJ: Princeton University Press, 1954), 49–50; Thomas Jefferson to George Washington, Nov. 14, 1786, in *The Papers of George Washington: Confederation Series*, vol. 4, *April 1786–January 1787*, ed. W. W. Abbot and Dorothy Twohig (Charlottesville: University of Virginia Press, 1995), 363–66.
14. George Washington, "Observations on the Society of the Cincinnati," [May 4, 1784] in ibid., 330–32; Hünemörder, *Society of the Cincinnati*, 91–101; Nathanael Greene to George Washington in *The Papers of Nathanael Greene*, ed. Roger N. Parks, vol. 13 (Chapel Hill: University of North Carolina Press, 2005), 382–84; William Moultrie, "Proceedings of the General Societe of the Cincinaty," b.v. Moultrie, Manuscript Department, New-York Historical Society; Winthrop Sargent's Journal, May 4–18, 1784, reprinted in *Papers of George Washington: Confederation Series*, ed. Abbot, 1:332–54.
15. Thomas Jefferson to John Taylor, June 4, 1798, in *The Papers of Thomas Jefferson*, ed. Barbara B. Oberg, vol. 30 (Princeton, NJ: Princeton University Press, 2003), 389; Gilbert Chinard, ed., *The Commonplace Book of Thomas Jefferson: A Repertory of His Ideas on Government* (Baltimore, MD: Johns Hopkins Press, 1926), 16–19, 107–8; Thomas Jefferson to James Madison, Jan. 30, 1787, in Boyd et al., *Papers of Thomas Jefferson*, 11:92–93; Thomas Jefferson, *Notes on the State of Virginia*, ed. William Peden (Chapel Hill: University of North Carolina Press, 1954), 59–60; James Wilson, Lectures on Law, in *The Works of James Wilson*, ed. Robert Green McCloskey, 2 vols. (Cambridge, MA, 1967), 1:233, quoted in Jan Lewis, "'Those Scenes for Which Alone My Heart Was Made': Affection and Politics in the Age of Jefferson and Hamilton," in *An Emotional History of the United States*, ed. Peter N. Stearns and Jan Lewis (New York: New York University Press, 1998), 57; Sarah Knott, *Sensibility and the American Revolution* (Chapel Hill: University of North Carolina Press, 2009), 3, 19. My thinking on this subject has been influenced by the important but nearly forgotten Yehoshua Arieli, *Individualism and Nationalism in American Ideology* (Baltimore, MD: Peregrine, 1966), chaps. 6–7.
16. See *Papers of George Washington: Confederation Series* 1:351–52n16, where Jefferson describes his conversations with Washington in a comment he drafted in response to John Marshall, *The Life of George Washington, Commander in Chief of the American Forces, during the War which Established the Independence of His Country, and the First President of the United States*, 5 vols. (Philadelphia: C. P. Wayne, 1804–1807), vol. 5. See Thomas Jefferson to Martin Van Buren, June 29, 1824, in *Writings of Thomas Jefferson*, ed. Lipscomb and Bergh, 16:62–64; Hünemörder, *Society of the Cincinnati*, 89–90; Dumas Malone, *Jefferson the Virginian* (Boston: Little Brown, 1948), 414–15.
17. *Papers of George Washington: Confederation Series* 1:330–32; see ibid., 332–54, for Winthrop Sargent's Journal of the first General Meeting, May 4–18, 1784, quotation on 335. For the letter from the Society of the Cincinnati to "Senior Land and Naval Officers and others, Members of the Society of the Cincinnati in France," May 1784,

see Winthrop Sargent, "Journal of the General Meeting of the Cincinnati in 1784," *Memoirs of the Historical Society of Pennsylvania* 6 (1858): 111–12.

18. John Sullivan to George Washington, Feb. 3, 1785, in *Papers of George Washington: Confederation Series*, ed. Abbott, 2:320–23; circular letter of Gen Sullivan of Exeter, NH, Feb. 3, 1785; Thomas C. Amory, *The Military Services and Public Life of Major-General John Sullivan, of the American Revolutionary Army* (Boston: Wiggin and Lunt, 1868), 197–98, 254–55; E. Wayne Carp, *To Starve the Army at Pleasure: Continental Army Administration and American Political Culture, 1775–1783* (Chapel Hill: University of North Carolina Press, 1984), 203–4; Charles P. Whittemore, *A General of the Revolution: John Sullivan of New Hampshire* (New York: Columbia University Press, 1961), 190; John Sullivan to George Washington, Feb. 5, 1785, in *Letters and Papers of Major-General John Sullivan, Continental Army*, ed. Otis G. Hammond, vol. 3, in *Collections of the New Hampshire Historical Society*, vol. 15 (Concord: New Hampshire Historical Society, 1939), 394–97; Gerald D. Foss, *Three Centuries of Freemasonry in New Hampshire* (Concord, NH: Grand Lodge of New Hampshire, 1972), 180–83.
19. "Observation on the Columbia Plan," 1783, Elbridge Gerry Papers, Massachusetts Historical Society, quoted in Hünemörder, *Society of the Cincinnati*, 152–53; *New Hampshire Gazette*, June 19, 1784, quoted in Myers, *Liberty without Anarchy*, 52, 197; "Convention of Members Chosen by the Towns of Westerly, North Kingston, South Kingston, Charleston, Exeter, Richmond, and Hopkinton," Apr. 1, 1784, Rhode Island Historical Society Manuscripts, Box 14, Folder 369, Rhode Island Historical Society, Providence, RI; William Manning, *The Key of Libberty: Shewing the Causes Why a Free Government Has Always Failed, and a Remidy against It* (Billerica, MA: Manning Association, 1922), 35–37, 61–67; Michael Merrill and Sean Wilentz, *The Key of Liberty: The Life and Democratic Writings of William Manning, "A Laborer," 1747–1814* (Cambridge, MA: Harvard University Press, 1993), 61–62, quotation on 160.
20. Jean M. Yarbrough, *American Virtues: Thomas Jefferson on the Character of a Free People* (Lawrence: University Press of Kansas, 1998), 166; Andy Trees, "Private Correspondence for the Public Good: Thomas Jefferson to Elbridge Gerry, 26 January 1799," *Virginia Magazine of History and Biography* 108 (2000): 239–40, 259; Andy Trees, *The Founding Fathers and the Politics of Character* (Princeton, NJ: Princeton University Press, 2004), chap. 1; Thomas Jefferson to Thomas McAuley, June 14, 1819, quoted in *Papers of Thomas Jefferson*, ed. Boyd, 1:32n; "Constitution for Proposed Agricultural Society of Albemarle," ca. Feb. 1, 1811, in *The Papers of Thomas Jefferson: Retirement Series*, ed. J. Jefferson Looney, vol. 3, *12 August 1810 to 17 June 1811* (Princeton, NJ: Princeton University Press, 2006), 347–52.
21. Francis S. Drake, *Memorials of the Society of the Cincinnati of Massachusetts* (Boston: Printed for the Society, 1873), 50; Davies, "Society of the Cincinnati in New England," 21–22; Thomas Fleming, *Duel: Alexander Hamilton, Aaron Burr, and the Future of America* (New York: Basic Books, 1999), 309–10; Nathan Schachner, *Aaron Burr: A Biography* (New York: Frederick A. Stokes Company, 1937), 251.
22. Edward Countryman, *A People in Revolution: The American Revolution and Political Society in New York, 1760–1790* (Baltimore: Johns Hopkins University Press, 1981), 293–94; Mary P. Ryan, "Civil Society as Democratic Practice: North American Cities during the Nineteenth Century," *Journal of Interdisciplinary History* 29 (1999): 583; *Commonwealth v. St. Patrick Benevolent Society*, 2 Binn. 441, 450 (1810); Roger Finke and Rodney Stark, *The Churching of America, 1776–2005: Winners and Losers in Our Religious Economy* (New Brunswick, NJ: Rutgers University Press, 2005), 23, 55; James Kent, *Commentaries on American Law*, 2nd ed. (New York: O. Halsted, 1832), 2:271.

23. Alexis de Tocqueville, *Democracy in America*, trans. George Lawrence (New York: Harper and Row, 1966), 514–17, quotation on 516; review [by Orestes Brownson] of William Ellery Channing's *Slavery*, in the *Boston Quarterly Review* (1838): 258; Andrew Sabl, "Community Organizing as Tocquevillean Politics: The Art, Practices, and Ethos of Association," *American Journal of Political Science* 46 (2002): 1–19.
24. Schlesinger himself saw the nation of joiners as arising from "the loins of religious voluntarism" (Arthur M. Schlesinger, "Biography of a Nation of Joiners," *American Historical Review* 50 [1944]: 21); Perry Miller, *The Life of the Mind: From the Revolution to the Civil War*, bks. 1–3 (New York: Harcourt, Brace, and World, 1965), 32–47; Kathleen D. McCarthy, *American Creed: Philanthropy and the Rise of Civil Society* (Chicago: University of Chicago Press, 2003); Robert H. Abzug, *Cosmos Crumbling: American Reform and the Religious Imagination* (New York: Oxford University Press, 1994), 40–41; H. Richard Niebuhr, *The Social Sources of Denominationalism* (1929; rpt., Hamden, CT: Shoestring, 1954); Anne C. Rose, "The Social Sources of Denominationalism Reconsidered: Post-Revolutionary Boston as a Case Study," *American Quarterly* 38 (1986): 243–64; Daniel Walker Howe, "The Evangelical Movement and Political Culture in the North during the Second Party System," *Journal of American History* 77 (1991): 1216; Peter Dobkin Hall, "Religion and the Origin of Voluntary Associations in the United States," working paper 213 (New Haven, CT: Program on Non-Profit Organizations, 1994); Nathan O. Hatch, *The Democratization of American Christianity* (New Haven, CT: Yale University Press, 1989), 170; Donald G. Mathews, "The Second Great Awakening as an Organizing Process, 1780–1830: An Hypothesis," *American Quarterly* 21 (1969): 39–43; James E. Block, *A Nation of Agents: The American Path to a Modern Self and Society* (Cambridge, MA: Belknap Press of Harvard University Press, 2002), 371–80. A variation on this explanation finds the organizational roots of American associational activity in the *First* Great Awakening: John L. Brooke, *The Heart of the Commonwealth: Society and Political Culture in Worcester County, Massachusetts, 1713–1861* (1989; rpt., Amherst: University of Massachusetts Press, 2005), 241, 246, 270. On social control, see Charles I. Foster, *An Errand of Mercy: The Evangelical United Front, 1790–1837* (Chapel Hill: University of North Carolina Press, 1960); Clifford S. Griffin, *Their Brothers' Keepers: Moral Stewardship in the United States, 1800–1865* (New Brunswick, NJ: Rutgers University Press, 1960); Daniel Walker Howe, *The Political Culture of the American Whigs* (Chicago: University of Chicago Press, 1979), chap. 7; and especially Lois W. Banner, "Religious Benevolence as Social Control: A Critique of an Interpretation," *Journal of American History* 60 (1973): 23–41.
25. [William Ellery Channing], Article V in *Christian Examiner and General Review*, 7 (1829): 106; Ronald G. Walters, *American Reformers, 1815–1860* (New York: Hill and Wang, 1978), 3–19; Thomas Bender, ed., *The Antislavery Debate: Capitalism and Abolitionism as a Problem in Historical Interpretation* (Berkeley: University of California Press, 1992). Gerald Gamm and Robert D. Putnam are critical of a connection between modernization and voluntarism in "The Growth of Voluntary Associations in America, 1840–1940," *Journal of Interdisciplinary History* 29 (1999): 511–57.
26. See Charles Sellers, *The Market Revolution: Jacksonian America, 1815–1846* (New York: Oxford University Press, 1991), 202–36; Paul E. Johnson and Sean Wilentz, *The Kingdom of Matthias: A Story of Sex and Salvation in 19th-Century America* (New York: Oxford University Press, 1994), 3–11; Mary P. Ryan, *Cradle of the Middle Class: The Family in Oneida County, New York, 1790–1865* (New York: Cambridge University Press, 1981), 107; John Patrick Diggins, *The Lost Soul of American Politics: Virtue,*

Self-Interest, and the Foundations of Liberalism (New York: Basic Books, 1984), 150; Rowland Berthoff, *An Unsettled People: Social Order and Disorder in American History* (New York: Harper and Row, 1971), 254–74.

27. Richard D. Brown, "The Emergence of Urban Society in Rural Massachusetts, 1760–1820," *Journal of American History* 61 (1974): 29–51; and his "Emergence of Voluntary Associations in Massachusetts, 1760–1830," *Journal of Voluntary Action Research* 2 (1973): 64–73; Conrad Edick Wright, *The Transformation of Charity in Postrevolutionary New England* (Boston: Northeastern University Press, 1992); Joyce Appleby, *Inheriting the Revolution: The First Generation of Americans* (Cambridge, MA: Belknap Press of Harvard University Press, 2000), 236–41; Gordon S. Wood, *The Radicalism of the American Revolution* (New York: Alfred A. Knopf, 1992), 328–29; Tocqueville, *Democracy in America*, 189, 513.

28. Josiah Woodward, *An Account of the Rise and Progress of the Religious Societies in the City of London . . .* , 2nd ed. (London: J. D., 1698), 35–36; David Hackett Fischer, *Paul Revere's Ride* (New York: Oxford University Press, 1994), 12–13; John Locke's "Rules of a Society, Which met once a week, for their improvement in useful Knowledge, and for the promoting of Truth and Christian Charity," in *A Collection of Several Pieces of Mr. John Locke, Never Before Printed, or Not Extant in His Works* (London: J. Bettenham, 1720), 358–62; Albrecht Koschnik, "Benjamin Franklin, Associations, and Civil Society," in *A Companion to Benjamin Franklin*, ed. David Waldstreicher (Chichester: Wiley-Blackwell, 2011), 338–39; Robert Micklus, ed., *The History of the Ancient and Honorable Tuesday Club*, 3 vols. (Chapel Hill: University of North Carolina Press, 1990), 1:33, 125–27.

29. Jessica Choppin Roney, *Governed by a Spirit of Opposition: The Origins of American Political Practice in Colonial Philadelphia* (Baltimore: Johns Hopkins University Press, 2014); Jessica Choppin Roney, "'Effective Men' and Early Voluntary Associations in Philadelphia, 1725–1775," in *New Men: Manliness in Early America*, ed. Thomas A. Foster (New York: New York University Press, 2011), 155–71; Jacquetta Mae Haley, "Voluntary Organizations in Pre-Revolutionary New York City" (PhD diss., State University of New York—Binghamton, 1976); Carl Bridenbaugh and Jessica Bridenbaugh, *Rebels and Gentlemen: Philadelphia in the Age of Franklin* (New York: Oxford University Press, 1962); Andrew J. Dalgleish, "Voluntary Associations and the Middle Class in Edinburgh, 1780 1820" (PhD diss., University of Edinburgh, 1991), 5; Clark, *British Clubs and Societies*, 60, 95.

30. Neem, *Creating a Nation of Joiners*, chap. 4; Sidney Tarrow, *Power in Movement: Social Movements, Collective Action, and Politics* (New York: Cambridge University Press, 1994); Jason Mazzone, "Organizing the Republic: Civic Associations and American Constitutionalism, 1780–1830" (JD diss., Yale Law School, 2004), chaps. 2–3; Theda Skocpol, *Diminished Democracy: From Membership to Management in American Civic Life* (Norman: University of Oklahoma Press, 2003); Brooke, "Ancient Lodges and Self-Created Societies," 273–377; Albrecht Koschnik, *"Let a Common Interest Bind Us Together": Associations, Partisanship, and Culture in Philadelphia, 1775–1840* (Charlottesville: University of Virginia Press, 2007); Brian Phillips Murphy, "'A Very Convenient Instrument': The Manhattan Company, Aaron Burr, and the Election of 1800," *William and Mary Quarterly*, 3rd ser., 65 (2008): 233–66.

31. James H. Kettner, *The Development of American Citizenship, 1608–1870* (Chapel Hill: University of North Carolina Press, 1978); Douglas Bradburn, *The Citizenship Revolution: Politics and the Creation of the American Union, 1774–1804* (Charlottesville: University of Virginia Press, 2009).

32. Marc Harris, "Civil Society in Post-Revolutionary America," in *Empire and Nation: The American Revolution in the Atlantic World*, ed. Eliga H. Gould and Peter S. Onuf (Baltimore: Johns Hopkins University Press, 2005), 202–3; Mazzone, "Organizing the Republic," chaps. 5–7.
33. Bullock, *Revolutionary Brotherhood*, 31; Paul Goodman, *Towards a Christian Republic: Antimasonry and the Great Transition in New England, 1826–1836* (New York: Oxford University Press, 1998), 12–13; *St. John's Lodge, No. 1, F. and A. M., Portsmouth, New Hampshire, Constituted 1736: By-laws of 1739 and 1755 with Names of Subscribers Thereto . . .* (Portsmouth, NH: Randall, 1973).
34. DeWitt Clinton, *Address Delivered by the Most Worshipful the Hon. De Witt Clinton, Esq., to the Grand Lodge of the State of New-York . . . 19th of June, 1806* (New York: Brothers Southwick and Hardcastle, 1806), 8–9.
35. Mark A. Tabbert, *American Freemasons: Three Centuries of Building Communities* (New York: New York University Press, 2005), 45; Brooke, "Ancient Lodges and Self-Created Societies," 274; Bullock, *Revolutionary Brotherhood*, 188; Dorothy Ann Lipson, *Freemasonry in Federalist Connecticut* (Princeton, NJ: Princeton University Press, 1977), 90–91.
36. John Dove, ed., *Proceedings of the M. W. Grand Lodge of Ancient York Masons of the State of Virginia; From Its Organization, in 1778, to 1822 . . .*, vol. 1 (Richmond, VA: James E. Goode, 1874), 210, 540–41; Josiah Holt to the Brethren of Frederick Lodge No. 26, Mar. 16, 1795, Records of Frederick Lodge No. 26, Farmington, CT, Masonic Papers, Connecticut Historical Society, Hartford, CT; Christopher P. Bickford, *Farmington in Connecticut* (Canaan, NH: Phoenix, 1982), 281–82.
37. Bullock, *Revolutionary Brotherhood*, 273; Lipson, *Freemasonry in Federalist Connecticut*, 224–25.
38. Dove, ed., *Proceedings of the M. W. Grand Lodge of Ancient York Masons*, 1:210, 540–41; John Dove, *The Masonic Text Book . . .* (Richmond: Shepherd and Colin, 1847), 258; Louisiana Grand Lodge to Virginia Grand Lodge, Aug. 12, 1824, Freemasonry Collection, Grand Lodge of Virginia, Robert Alonzo Brock Collection, Huntington Library; Clark Brown, *The Utility of Moral and Religious Societies, and of the Masonick in Particular: A Sermon, Delivered in Putney, Vt. On the Anniversary of St. John the Baptist, June 24th, 1814. . . . Anno Lucis, 5814.* (Keene, NH: John Prentiss, 1814), 21.
39. Holly Brewer, *By Birth or Consent: Children, Law, and the Anglo-American Revolution in Authority* (Chapel Hill: University of North Carolina Press, 2005); Edmund S. Morgan, *Visible Saints: The History of a Puritan Idea* (New York: New York University Press, 1963); Robert G. Pope, *The Half-Way Covenant: Church Membership in Puritan New England* (Princeton, NJ: Princeton University Press, 1969).
40. *Jewett v. Thames Bank*, 16 Conn. 511, 516 (1844).
41. "Introduction," *United States Magazine and Democratic Review* 1 (October 1837): 7.
42. Robert Baird, *Religion in America: The Origin, Progress, Relation to the State, and Present Condition of the Evangelical Churches in the United States: With Notices of the Unevangelical Denominations* (New York: Harper and Brothers, 1844), bk. 4; J. S. Buckingham, *America, Historical, Statistic, and Descriptive*, 2 vols. (New York: Harper and Brothers, 1841), 2:364. See Robert T. Handy, "The Voluntary Principle in Religion and Religious Freedom in America," in *Voluntary Associations: A Study of Groups in Free Societies*, ed. D. B. Robertson (Richmond, VA: John Knox, 1966), 129–39.
43. Isaac Backus, *A Letter to a Gentleman in the Massachusetts Assembly* (Boston, 1771), 506; Elisha Williams, *The Essential Rights and Liberties of Protestants. A Seasonable Plea for the Liberty of Conscience, and the Right of Private Judgment, in Matters of Religion . . .*

(Philadelphia: S. Kneeland and T. Green, 1744), 1–9, 38–51, 60–65, in *Puritan Political Ideas, 1558–1794*, ed. Edmund S. Morgan (Indianapolis: Bobbs-Merrill, 1965), 280, 287–88; Michael P. Zuckert, *The Natural Rights Republic: Studies in the Foundation of the American Political Tradition* (Notre Dame, IN: University of Notre Dame Press, 1996), 159, 195; Jack N. Rakove, "Beyond Locke, beyond Belief: The Nexus of Free Exercise and Separation of Church and State," in Robert Fatton, Jr., and R. K. Ramazani, *Religion, State, and Society: Jefferson's Wall of Separation in Comparative Perspective* (New York: Palgrave Macmillan, 2009), 37–52; Nathan Hatch, *The Democratization of American Christianity* (New Haven, CT: Yale University Press, 1989), 11, 64; Henry Pattillo, *Sermons &c.* (Wilmington, NC: James Adams, 1788), 42; Richard Carwardine, "Unity, Pluralism, and the Spiritual Market-Place: Interdenominational Competition in the Early American Republic," in *Unity and Diversity in the Church*, ed. R. N. Swanson (Oxford: Blackwell, 1996), 297–335; Finke and Stark, *Churching of America*, 112–13. Still essential reading on these themes is H. Richard Niebuhr, *The Social Sources of Denominationalism* (1929; rpt., Hamden, CT: Shoestring, 1954).

44. William Warren Sweet, *The American Churches: An Interpretation* (New York: Abingdon-Cokesbury, 1947), 63; William G. McLoughlin, *New England Dissent,1630–1833: The Baptists and the Separation of Church and State*, 2 vols. (Cambridge, MA: Harvard University Press, 1971), 2:514–25, 808, 934–37; Michael W. McConnell, "The Origins and Historical Understanding of the Free Exercise Clause," *Harvard Law Review* 103 (1990): 1469–1470; [William Smith?], *Some Remarks on the "Toleration Act" of 1819: Addressed to the Hon. John Taylor Gilman by a Friend to the "Public Worship of the Deity"* (Exeter, NH: Samuel T. Moses, 1823), 31–32.

45. Sweet, *American Churches*, 48; Hatch, *Democratization of American Christianity*, 102–13, Allen quotation on 109; Niebuhr, *Social Sources of Denominationalism*, chap. 9; Stephen Hum, "'When We Were No People, Then We Were a People': Evangelical Language and the Free Blacks of Philadelphia in the Early Republic," in Susan Juster and Lisa MacFarlane, *A Mighty Baptism: Race, Gender, and the Creation of American Protestantism* (Ithaca, NY: Cornell University Press, 1996), 235–58. On the West, see Hatch, *Democratization of American Christianity*, 30; Alan Taylor, "Agrarian Independence: Northern Land Rioters after the Revolution," in *Beyond the American Revolution: Explorations in the History of American Radicalism*, ed. Alfred F. Young (DeKalb: Northern Illinois University Press, 1993), 232–33; Stephen Aron, *How the West Was Lost: The Transformation of Kentucky from Daniel Boone to Henry Clay* (Baltimore: Johns Hopkins University Press, 1996); Robert M. Calhoon, "Religion, Moderation, and Regime-Building in Post-Revolutionary America," in *Empire and Nation: The American Revolution in the Atlantic World*, ed. Eliga H. Gould and Peter S. Onuf (Baltimore: Johns Hopkins University Press, 2005), 217–36.

46. Hatch, *Democratization of American Christianity*, 59; Jon Butler, *Awash in a Sea of Faith: Christianizing the American People* (Cambridge, MA: Harvard University Press, 1990), 258–60; Gordon S. Wood, *The Creation of the American Republic, 1776–1787* (Chapel Hill: University of North Carolina Press, 1969), 427–28; Thomas E. Buckley, *Church and State in Revolutionary Virginia, 1776–1787* (Charlottesville: University Press of Virginia, 1977). Pennsylvania's article on religious liberty was largely echoed by Kentucky, Missouri, Indiana, Ohio, Tennessee, Arkansas, and Illinois.

47. Thomas Jefferson, *Notes on the State of Virginia*, ed. William Peden (Chapel Hill: University of North Carolina Press, 1954), 160–61. See also Peter Onuf, "Thomas Jefferson's Christian Nation," in Robert Fatton, Jr., and R. K. Ramazani, *Religion, State, and Society: Jefferson's Wall of Separation in Comparative Perspective* (New York: Palgrave

Macmillan, 2009), 17–36; Lyman Beecher, *Autobiography, Correspondence, Etc., of Lyman Beecher, D.D.*, ed. Charles Beecher, 2 vols. (New York: Harper and Brothers, 1865), 344; Butler, *Awash in a Sea of Faith*, 270; Winthrop S. Hudson, *Religion in America: An Historical Account of the Development of American Religious Life*, 3rd ed. (New York: Charles Scribner's Sons, 1981), 129–30; Finke and Stark, *Churching of America*, chap. 3; Elizabeth Fox-Genovese and Eugene D. Genovose, *The Mind of the Master Class: History and Faith in the Southern Slaveholders' Worldview* (New York: Cambridge University Press, 2005), 730–32.

48. John M'Farland, *A Series of Letters, on the Relation, Rights, Privileges, and Duties of Baptized Children* (Lexington, KY: Joseph G. Norwood, 1828), 21.

49. Miller, *Life of the Mind in America*, chap. 2; Baird, *Religion in America*, 409; Susan Juster, *Doomsayers: Anglo-American Prophecy in the Age of Revolution* (Philadelphia: University of Pennsylvania Press, 2003), 162; Hatch, *Democratization of American Christianity*, 14; Christine Heyrman, *Southern Cross: The Beginnings of the Bible Belt* (Chapel Hill: University of North Carolina Press, 1998); Sidney E. Mead, "The Rise of the Evangelical Conception of the Ministry in America (1607–1850)," in H. Richard Niebuhr and Daniel D. Williams, *The Ministry in Historical Perspective* (New York: Harper and Brothers, 1956); and his "Denominationalism: The Shape of Protestantism in America," *Church History* 23 (1954): 291–320.

50. Chris Beneke, *Beyond Toleration: The Religious Origins of American Pluralism* (New York: Oxford University Press, 2006), 106, 177–78; Appleby, *Inheriting the Revolution*, 196–99. Such documents, containing full descriptions not just of the duties of members but also of their rights, e.g., to a certain mode of proceeding in any case affecting their status as member, became increasingly common. See, for example, *The Constitution of the Presbyterian Church in the United States of America: Containing the Confession of Faith, the Catechisms, and the Directory for the Worship of God: Together with the Plan of Government and Discipline as Amended and Ratified by the General Assembly at Their Sessions in May, 1806* (Philadelphia: Jane Aitken, 1806); *Constitution of the Presbyterian Church in the United States of America . . . as Ratified by the General Assembly, at Their Sessions in May, 1821; and Amended in 1833* (Philadelphia: Presbyterian Board of Publication, 1839); *A Compendium of Church Discipline, Shewing the Qualifications and Duties of the Officers and Members of a Gospel Church: To Which Are Prefixed the Constitution & Principles of Union of the Russell's Creek Association* (Bardstown, KY: S. Railey, 1825).

51. Philip N. Mulder, *A Controversial Spirit: Evangelical Awakenings in the South* (New York: Oxford University Press, 2002), 55–56; Richard D. Birdsall, "The Second Great Awakening and the New England Social Order," *Church History* 39 (1970): 357; Gregory A. Wills, *Democratic Religion: Freedom, Authority, and Church Discipline in the Baptist South, 1785–1900* (New York: Oxford University Press, 1997), 20; Ruth Bloch and Naomi Lamoreaux, "Defining Public and Private in Early America: The General Problem and Evidence mainly from New England" (unpublished paper for the Columbia Seminar on Early American History, April 2004), 43; Barry Alan Shain, *The Myth of American Individualism: The Protestant Origins of American Political Thought* (Princeton, NJ: Princeton University Press, 1994), 200.

52. Paul Goodman, *Towards a Christian Republic: Antimasonry and the Great Transition in New England, 1826–1836* (New York: Oxford University Press, 1988), 71; Susan Juster, *Disorderly Women: Sexual Politics and Evangelicalism in Revolutionary New England* (Ithaca, NY: Cornell University Press, 1994), 132; Seth Sweetser, "Review of my ministry for 14 years," Seth Sweetser Papers, Dec. 19, 1852, American Antiquarian

Society, quoted in Carolyn J. Lawes, *Women and Reform in a New England Community, 1815–1860* (Lexington: University Press of Kentucky, 2000), 61. The church member's manual was becoming an increasingly common form of publication: see John Mitchell, *The Practical Church Member: Being a Guide to the Principles and Practice of the Congregational Churches of New England* (New York: Leavitt, Trow, 1835) and his brief discussion in his Preface (vii) of this burgeoning form of literature.

53. Baird, *Religion in America*, 183–84 (emphasis in original); Michael G. Kenny, *The Perfect Law of Liberty: Elias Smith and the Providential History of America* (Washington, DC: Smithsonian Institution Press, 1994), 81, 139–40; E. Brooks Holifield, *Theology in America: Christian Thought from the Age of the Puritans to the Civil War* (New Haven, CT: Yale University Press, 2003), 292–93.

54. T. Scott Miyakawa, *Protestants and Pioneers: Individualism and Conformity on the American Frontier* (Chicago: University of Chicago Press, 1964), 42; Monica Najar, *Evangelizing the South: A Social History of Church and State in Early America* (New York: Oxford University Press, 2008), 8–9, 98; Certificate of William Baker, Apr. 26, 1797, Letters of Dismission, New York City Papers—Churches, box 31, Manuscript Department, New-York Historical Society. See also First African Baptist Church, in Philadelphia, to their brethren in the Lord, composing the Baptist Church, in Fayette Street New York, Feb. 11, 1812, ibid. Some English churches followed the same protocol in the nineteenth century: see the letter from a church in Reading, Berks, England, to a church "in the City of New York, or any other part of the United States of America," signed by John Dyer et al., May 26, 1816, ibid.

55. M'Farland, *Series of Letters*, 14; Joshua Leonard, *An Address, Presented to the Presbytery of Onondaga, at Homer, December 30, 1812, by Appointment* (Homer, NY: John W. Osborn, 1813), 9; Najar, *Evangelizing the South*, 8, 110; Wills, *Democratic Religion*, 51; John H. Rice, *An Illustration of the Character & Conduct of the Presbyterian Church in Virginia* (Richmond, VA: Du-Val and Burke, 1816), 8–9; Liam Séamus O'Melinn, "The Sanctity of Association: The Corporation and Individualism in American Law," *San Diego Law Review* 101 (2000): 136–43. Many of the churches that excluded women from voting on government matters such as the election of officers allowed them to vote in disciplinary cases.

CHAPTER TWO

1. *Columbian Centinel*, Dec. 27, 1794.
2. Thomas D. Mitchell, *The Tripod of the American Revolution, viz: Voluntary Association, Pledge, and Self-Denial: Being an Address to the Chamberlain Philosophical and Literary Society of Centre College, Kentucky, Delivered by Appointment, on the 4th of July, 1838, in the Presbyterian Church in Danville* (Lexington, KY: Intelligencer Print, 1838), 15; *Gazette of the United States*, May 24, 1794, quoted in Albrecht Koschnik, *"Let a Common Interest Bind Us Together": Associations, Partisanship, and Culture in Philadelphia, 1775–1840* (Charlottesville: University of Virginia Press, 2007), 35; Albrecht Koschnik, "The Democratic Societies of Philadelphia and the Limits of the American Public Sphere, circa 1793–1795," *William and Mary Quarterly*, 3rd ser., 58 (2001): 626–27; Matthew Schoenbachler, "Republicanism in the Age of Democratic Revolution: The Democratic-Republican Societies of the 1790s," *Journal of the Early Republic*, 18 (1998): 253–54. On the associations of the Revolutionary era, see Edward Countryman, *A People in Revolution: The American Revolution and Political Society in New York, 1760–1790* (Baltimore: Johns Hopkins University Press, 1981); Pauline Maier, *From*

Resistance to Revolution: Colonial Radicals and the Development of Opposition to Britain, 1765–1775 (New York: Alfred A. Knopf, 1972).

3. Alfred F. Young, *The Democratic Republicans of New York: The Origins, 1763–1797* (Chapel Hill: University of North Carolina Press, 1967), 393; Peter Van Ness Denman, "From Deference to Democracy: The Van Ness Family and Their Times, 1759 to 1844" (PhD diss., University of Michigan, 1977), 1:102–3; *New York Daily Advertiser*, Nov. 26, 28, Dec. 1, 3, 1789; John F. Roche, "The Uranian Society: Gentlemen and Scholars in Federal New York," *New York History* 52 (1971): 121–32; James McLachlan, "The *Choice of Hercules*: American Student Societies in the Early 19th Century," in *The University in Society*, vol. 2, *Europe, Scotland, and the United States from the 16th to the 20th Century*, ed. Lawrence Stone (Princeton, NJ: Princeton University Press, 1974), 449–94; Thomas Bender, *New York Intellect: A History of Intellectual Life in New York City, from 1750 to the Beginnings of Our Own Time* (New York: Alfred A. Knopf, 1987), 28, 52; Thomas S. Harding, *College Literary Societies: Their Contribution to Higher Education in the United States, 1815–1876* (New York: Pageant, 1971).
4. *New York Daily Advertiser*, Dec. 3, 1789; Eleanor Bryce Scott, "Early Literary Clubs in New York City," *American Literature* 5 (1933): 6; Diedrich Knickerbocker [Ralph Taft Heymsfeld], "Literary Societies and Associations in New York City, 1790–1830," submitted 1926 for New-York Historical Society Scholarship, Misc. Mss. Prize essays, box 2, New-York Historical Society, p. 19.
5. Thomas E. V. Smith, *The City of New York, in the Year of Washington's Inauguration, 1789* (1889; rpt., Riverside, CT: Chatham, 1972), 113–16, 194, 200; Roche, "Uranian Society," 121–27; Uranian Society, minutes, Mar. 15, 1791–June 15, 1793, New York Public Library.
6. J. G. de Roulhac Hamilton, "A Society for the Preservation of Liberty, 1784," *American Historical Review* 32 (1927): 550–52; Thomas Speed, *The Political Club: Danville, Kentucky, 1786–1790* (Louisville, KY: John P. Morton and Company, 1894); Michael Meranze, *Laboratories of Virtue: Punishment, Revolution, and Authority in Philadelphia, 1760–1835* (Chapel Hill: University of North Carolina Press, 1996), 144–45; Michael Vinson, "The Society for Political Inquiries: The Limits of Republican Discourse in Philadelphia on the Eve of the Constitutional Convention," *Pennsylvania Magazine of History and Biography* 113 (1989): 185–205; Koschnik, *"Let a Common Interest Bind Us Together,"* 19–21.
7. James Roger Sharp, *American Politics in the Early Republic: The New Nation in Crisis* (New Haven, CT: Yale University Press, 1993), 69–70; Seth Cotlar, *Tom Paine's America: The Rise and Fall of Transatlantic Radicalism in the Early Republic* (Charlottesville: University of Virginia Press, 2011), 183–88; Schoenbachler, "Republicanism in the Age of Democratic Revolution," 243; Noble E. Cunningham, Jr., *The Jeffersonian Republicans: The Formation of Party Organization, 1789–1801* (Chapel Hill: University of North Carolina Press, 1957), 63–66; Douglas Bradburn, *The Citizenship Revolution: Politics and the Creation of the American Union, 1774–1804* (Charlottesville: University of Virginia Press, 2009), 108–9; Rachel Hope Cleves, *The Reign of Terror in America: Visions of Violence from Anti-Jacobinism to Antislavery* (New York: Cambridge University Press, 2009), 64–67, 88–89.
8. Eugene Perry Link, *Democratic-Republican Societies, 1790–1800* (New York: Columbia University Press, 1942); Philip S. Foner, ed., *The Democratic-Republican Societies, 1790–1800: A Documentary Sourcebook of Constitutions, Declarations, Addresses, Resolutions, and Toasts* (Westport, CT: Greenwood, 1976), quotation on 34, from *New*

York Journal, Jan. 17, 1795; Ronald P. Formisano, *For the People: American Populist Movements from the Revolution to the 1850s* (Chapel Hill: University of North Carolina Press, 2008), 53–57; Joyce Appleby, *Capitalism and a New Social Order: The Republican Vision of the 1790s* (New York: New York University Press, 1984), 54–56, 63–69; Todd Estes, *The Jay Treaty Debate, Public Opinion, and the Evolution of Early American Political Culture* (Amherst: University of Massachusetts Press, 2006), 53–68; Schoenbachler, "Republicanism in the Age of Democratic Revolution," 237–61; David Waldstreicher, *In the Midst of Perpetual Fetes: The Making of American Nationalism, 1776–1820* (Chapel Hill: University of North Carolina Press, 1997), 131–33; Brian W. Dotts, *The Political Education of Democratus: Negotiating Civic Virtue during the Early Republic* (Lanham, MD: Lexington, 2012), chap. 5.

9. Koschnik, *"Let a Common Interest Bind Us Together,"* quotation on 26; Koschnik, "Democratic Societies of Philadelphia," 626–27; George D. Luetscher, *Early Political Machinery in the United States* (1902; rpt., New York: Da Capo, 1971), 41; Massachusetts Constitutional Society, "Rules and Regulations and Declaration, Jan. 13, 1794," in *Democratic-Republican Societies*, ed. Foner, 256; Sean Wilentz, *The Rise of American Democracy: Jefferson to Lincoln* (New York: Norton, 2005), 56.
10. Young, *Democratic Republicans of New York*, 396; Link, *Democratic-Republican Societies*, 111; Benson J. Lossing, *The Pictorial Field-Book of the War of 1812; or, Illustrations by Pen and Pencil, of the History, Biography, Scenery, Relics, and Traditions of the Last War for American Independence* (New York: Harper & Brothers, 1868), 88–89n3.
11. Wood's *Newark Gazette*, Mar. 12, 1794; Webb, *Correspondence and Journals of Samuel B. Webb*, 197–98, both cited in Link, *Democratic-Republican Societies*, 115–16.
12. A Faithful Watchman, "Traitors! Traitors! Traitors," *New York Evening Post*, Jan. 23, 1795; "Address of to the People of the United States of America," ibid.; Link, *Democratic-Republican Societies*, 115–16, esp. 116nn62, 65.
13. An American [Noah Webster], *The Revolution in France, Considered in Respect to Its Progress and Effects* (New York: George Bunce, 1794), 47–50.
14. *Columbian Centinel*, Dec. 27, 1794; *New York Evening Post*, Jan. 30, Feb. 4, 1795. On William Willcocks, a Revolutionary War veteran, attorney (even participating in the famous *Rutgers v. Waddington*), and New York assemblyman, see Joshua L. Chamberlain, ed., *Universities and Their Sons: History, Influence, and Characteristics of American Universities with Biographical Sketches and Portraits of Alumni and Recipients of Honorary Degrees*, vol. 4 (Boston: R. Herndon Company, 1900), 108–9.
15. Johann N. Neem, "Freedom of Association in the Early Republic: The Republican Party, the Whiskey Rebellion, and the Philadelphia and New York Cordwainers' Cases," *Pennsylvania Magazine of History and Biography*, 128 (2003): 259–90; Thomas P. Slaughter, *The Whiskey Rebellion: Frontier Epilogue to the American Revolution* (New York: Oxford University Press, 1986).
16. John Robison, *Proofs of a Conspiracy against All the Religions and Governments of Europe Carried on in the Secret Meetings of the Freemasons, Illuminati, and Reading Societies* (Philadelphia: T. Dobson, 1798), 125; Peter Porcupine [William Cobbett], *Detection of a Conspiracy Formed by the United Irishmen, with the Evident Intention of Aiding the Tyrants of France in Subverting the Government of the United States of America* (Philadelphia: William Cobbett, 1798).
17. Alexander Addison, *Charge to the Grand Juries of the County Courts of the Fifth Circuit of the State of Pennsylvania, at December Session, 1800* (Philadelphia: William Young, 1801), 20; Brooke, "Ancient Lodges and Self-Created Societies," 318–22. See also

David A. Wilson, *United Irishmen, Unites States: Immigrant Radicals in the Early Republic* (Ithaca, NY: Cornell University Press, 1998), chaps. 1–2; Gordon S. Wood, "Conspiracy and the Paranoid Style: Causality and Deceit in the Eighteenth Century," *William and Mary Quarterly*, 3rd ser., 39 (1982): 431–32; Waterman, *Republic of Intellect*, 72–76; Michael Lienesch, "The Illusion of the Illuminati: The Counterconspiratorial Origins of Post-Revolutionary Conservatism," in *Revolutionary Histories: Transatlantic Cultural Nationalism, 1775–1815*, ed. W. M. Verhoeven (New York: Palgrave, 2002), 152–65.

18. Koschnik, *"Let a Common Interest Bind Us Together,"* 42.
19. *New York Statutes*, 30th sess., chap. 92 (1807); *New York Evening Post*, Apr. 14, 1807; *Morning Chronicle*, Apr. 9, 1807.
20. *New York Evening Post*, Apr. 29, 1807; Oliver E. Allen, *The Tiger: The Rise and Fall of Tammany Hall* (Reading, MA: Addison-Wesley, 1993); Jerome Mushkat, *Tammany: The Evolution of a Political Machine, 1789–1865* (Syracuse, NY: Syracuse University Press, 1971), chaps. 1–2; Noble E. Cunningham, Jr., *The Jeffersonian Republicans: The Formation of Party Organization, 1789–1801* (Chapel Hill: University of North Carolina Press, 1957), 181; William L. Utter, "Saint Tammany in Ohio: A Study in Frontier Politics," *Mississippi Valley Historical Review* 15 (1928): 321–40.
21. *Weekly Inspector*, May 2, 1807; *Balance and Columbian Repository*, May 19, 1807.
22. *Report of the Trials of the Causes of Elisha Jenkins vs. Solomon Van Renssalaer . . . before Arbitrators, at Albany, August 16th, 17th, and 18th, 1808* (n.p.: Crowell and Frary, 1808), 13–16. When a meeting of Republicans responded to the Federalists' resolutions, they made no attempt to defend the Hibernian Society's decision to make membership hinge upon how each man voted (16–18).
23. Harvey Strum, "Federalist Hibernophobes in New York, 1807," *Éire-Ireland: A Journal of Irish Studies* 16 (1981): 7–13; Jason K. Duncan, *Citizens or Papists: The Politics of Anti-Catholicism in New York, 1685–1821* (New York: Fordham University Press, 2005), 144–46.
24. *American Citizen*, May 10, 1809. For Dempsey's occupation, see *Longworth's American Almanac, New-York Register, and City Directory: For the Thirty-Fourth Year of American Independence* (New York: David Longworth, 1809), 156.
25. George Washington to Bushrod Washington, quoted in Brooke, "Ancient Lodges and Self-Created Societies," 323; *New York Evening Post*, Jan. 30, Feb. 4, 1795.
26. Alexander Hamilton to James A. Bayard, Apr. 16–21, 1802, in *The Papers of Alexander Hamilton*, ed. Harold C. Syrett, vol. 25 (New York: Columbia University Press, 1977), 605–10; Colleen A. Sheehan, "Madison versus Hamilton," in Douglas Ambrose and Robert W. T. Martin, eds., *The Many Faces of Alexander Hamilton: The Life and Legacy of America's Most Elusive Founding Father* (New York: New York University Press, 2006), 196–97; Allan McClane Hamilton, *The Intimate Life of Alexander Hamilton* (New York: Charles Scriber's Sons, 1911), 334–35.
27. Hamilton to Bayard, Apr. 16–21, 1802, in *Papers of Alexander Hamilton*, ed. Syrett, 25:607–9. Though it was conventional in structure and purpose, Hamilton's proposal has not been well received by his historians: on the idea as "retrograde," see Ron Chernow, *Alexander Hamilton* (New York: Penguin, 2004), 658–59; on the proposal as "questionable" and forced, see Gerald Stourzh, *Alexander Hamilton and the Idea of Republican Government* (Stanford, CA: Stanford University Press, 1970), 125; and for the society as a "repulsive pressure group," see Douglass Adair and Marvin Harvey, "Was Alexander Hamilton a Christian Statesman?" *William and Mary Quarterly*, 3rd ser., 12 (1955): 308–29.

28. *Serious Considerations Addressed to the Electors of New Jersey concerning the Choice of Members of the Legislature for the Ensuing Year* (n.p., 1803), 3; *A Declaration of the Principles and Views of the Democratic-Federalists in the County of Cumberland, and State of New Jersey, with Their Form of Association* (Philadelphia: Mathew Carey, 1801), 9–10.
29. "Resolutions of the Philadelphia Washington Association," *Poulson's*, Aug. 1, 1811, quoted in Koschnik, *"Let a Common Interest Bind Us Together,"* 74.
30. William Buckner McGroarty, "The Washington Society of Alexandria," *Tyler's Quarterly Historical and Genealogical Magazine* 9 (1928): 147–63; Dixon Ryan Fox, "The Washington Benevolent Society," *Columbia University Quarterly* 21 (1919): 27–37; Robert W. July, *The Essential New Yorker: Gulian Crommelin Verplanck* (Durham, NC Duke University Press, 1951), 17–25; Dixon Ryan Fox, *The Decline of Aristocracy in the Politics of New York, 1801–1840*, ed. Robert V. Remini (New York: Harper Torchbooks, 1965), 88–99; David Hackett Fischer, *The Revolution of American Conservatism: The Federalist Party in the Era of Jeffersonian Democracy* (New York: Harper and Row, 1965), chap. 6; Samuel Eliot Morison, *The Life and Letters of Harrison Gray Otis, Federalist, 1765–1848*, 2 vols. (Boston and New York: Houghton Mifflin, 1913), 1:300–306.
31. Fischer, *Revolution of American Conservatism*, 116, table 19; Letter proposing organization (July 9, 1810) and constitution, Washington Benevolent Society of Providence, RI, Rhode Island Historical Society, Providence, RI; Washington Benevolent Society, February 1812–January 1816, Connecticut Historical Society, Hartford, CT.
32. *Constitution of the Washington Benevolent Society of the Town of Florida, and County of Montgomery, Instituted 11th December, 1810* (Albany, NY: Balance, 1811), art. 10; Letter proposing organization (July 9, 1810) and constitution, Washington Benevolent Society of Providence, RI, Rhode Island Historical Society, Providence, RI. On personal approbation and homogeneity of political and religious opinions, see Andrew J. Dalgleish, "Voluntary Associations and the Middle Class in Edinburgh, 1780–1820" (PhD diss., University of Edinburgh, 1991), chap. 3.
33. *A Summary Statement of the Origin, Progress, and Present State of the Washington Benevolent Society of Pennsylvania: With an Account of the Opening and Dedication of the Washington Hall, on the First of October, 1816* (Philadelphia: Office of the United States' Gazette, 1816); *Washington's Farewell Address, to the People of the United States: Published for the Benefit of the Washington Benevolent Society*, 2nd ed. (New York: J. Seymour, 1809); *The Text-Book of the Washington Benevolent Society: Containing a Biography and Character of George Washington, His Farewell Address to the People of the United States, and the Federal Constitution with the Amendments*, 3rd ed. (Concord: George Hough, 1814); Fischer, *Revolution of American Conservatism*, 122; "An Oration, Pronounced before the Washington Association, at Their Second Anniversary, July 19, 1812," *United States Gazette*, Aug. 10, 1813, quoted in Koschnik, *"Let a Common Interest Bind Us Together,"* 74–75; Jeffrey J. Malanson, "'If I Had It in His Hand-writing I Would Burn It": Federalists and the Authorship Controversy over George Washington's Farewell Address, 1808–1859," *Journal of the Early Republic* 34 (2014): 219–42.
34. David Hitchcock, *The Bond of Friendship: Being an Address Delivered before the Great-Barrington Branch of the Washington Benevolent Society—April 21, 1812* (Stockbridge, Vt.: Published for the author, 1812), 15; *Summary Statement*, sec. 24. Similar protections can be found in some but not all Washington Benevolent Society constitutions: see Constitution of the Washington Benevolent Society of Providence, RI, art. 11, Rhode Island Historical Society, Providence, RI (three-fourths vote, with notice); *The Constitution of the Washington Benevolent Society at Cambridge: Instituted the 22d of*

May, 1812 (Cambridge, MA: Hilliard and Metcalf, 1812), art. 8 (majority vote, with notice); *The Constitution of the Berlin Branch of the Washington Benevolent Society of the County of Renssalear . . .* (Albany: Websters and Skinners, 1814) (no clause regarding expulsion).

35. *Green Mountain Farmer*, Feb. 25, 1812; *Vermont Republican*, Feb. 24, 1812; *New Hampshire Patriot*, Mar. 2, 1813, *Vermont Republican*, June 1, 1812, Mar. 9, 1812, all quoted in William Alexander Robinson, "The Washington Benevolent Society in New England: A Phase of Politics during the War of 1812," Massachusetts Historical Society, *Proceedings*, 49 (1915–1916): 276n2, 280nn5, 8, 281nn1, 2.
36. *Eastern Argus*, Apr. 23, 1812, letter dated "Castleton, [Vt.,] March 21, 1812."
37. Resolution of Mar. 2, 1813, Records of the Washington Benevolent Society of Northwood [NH], New Hampshire Historical Society, Concord, NH.
38. Constitution of the Washington Benevolent Society, Washington Benevolent Society of Providence, RI, Rhode Island Historical Society, Providence, RI; Daniel Webster, *An Address Delivered before the Washington Benevolent Society, at Portsmouth, July 4, 1812* (Portsmouth, NH: Oracle, 1812), 5–6.

CHAPTER THREE

1. Thomas Paine, *Common Sense* (Philadelphia: R. Bell, 1776), 57; Zephaniah Swift, *A System of Laws of the State of Connecticut: In Six Books* (Windham, CT: John Byrne, 1795), 5; Christopher L. Tomlins, *Law, Labor, and Ideology in the Early American Republic* (New York: Cambridge University Press, 1993), 21; Christopher Tomlins, *Freedom Bound: Law, Labor, and Civic Identity in Colonizing English America, 1580–1865* (New York: Cambridge University Press, 2010), 390.
2. John Phillip Reid, *Law for the Elephant: Property and Social Behavior on the Overland Trail* (San Marino, CA: Huntington Library Press, 1980); Laura F. Edwards, *The People and Their Peace: Legal Culture and the Transformation of Inequality in the Post-Revolutionary South* (Chapel Hill: University of North Carolina Press, 2009); William J. Novak, *The People's Welfare: Law and Regulation in Nineteenth-Century America* (Chapel Hill: University of North Carolina Press, 1996); Johann N. Neem, *Creating a Nation of Joiners: Democracy and Civil Society in Early National Massachusetts* (Cambridge, MA: Harvard University Press, 2008). On the varied meanings of law and "the law," see E. P. Thompson, *Whigs and Hunters: The Origins of the Black Act* (New York: Pantheon, 1975), chap. 10.
3. An Obscure Individual [Stephen Moylan], *Observations on a Late Pamphlet Entituled "Considerations on the Society or Order of Cincinnati," Clearly Evincing the Innocence and Propriety of That Honourable and Respectable Institution* (Hartford, CT: Hudson and Goodwin, 1784), 13; Johann N. Neem, "Civil Society and American Nationalism, 1776–1865," in *Politics and Partnerships: The Role of Voluntary Associations in America's Political Past and Present*, ed. Elisabeth S. Clemens and Doug Guthrie (Chicago: University of Chicago Press, 2010), 28–53.
4. Albert O. Hirschman, *Exit, Voice, and Loyalty: Responses to Decline in Firms, Organizations, and States* (Cambridge, MA: Harvard University Press, 1970), 106–7.
5. Francis Lieber, ed., *Encyclopaedia Americana: A Popular Dictionary of Arts, Sciences, Literature, History, Politics, and Biography . . . on the Basis of the Seventh Edition of the German Conversations-Lexicon* (Philadelphia: Carey and Lea, 1830), s.v. "Corporation."
6. George Heberton Evans, Jr., *Business Incorporations in the United States, 1800–1943* (New York: National Bureau of Economic Research, 1948), table 9; William C.

Kessler, "Incorporation in New England: A Statistical Study, 1800–1875," *Journal of Economic History* 8 (1948): 43–47; Edwin Merrick Dodd, *American Business Corporations until 1860: With Special Reference to Massachusetts* (Cambridge, MA: Harvard University Press, 1954), 11; Joseph K. Angell and Samuel Ames, *Treatise on the Law of Private Corporations, Aggregate* (Boston: Hilliard, Gray, Little, and Wilkins, 1832; rpt., New York: Arno, 1972), quotation on 35; John Majewski, "Toward a Social History of the Corporation: Shareholding in Pennsylvania, 1800–1840," in *The Economy of Early America: Historical Perspectives and New Directions*, ed. Cathy Matson (University Park: Pennsylvania State University Press, 2006), 294–316.

7. Mark Douglas McGarvie, *One Nation under Law: America's Early National Struggles to Separate Church and State* (DeKalb: Northern Illinois University Press, 2004), 178–81. The best historical background to *Dartmouth* remains Bruce Arthur Campbell, "Law and Experience in the Early Republic: The Evolution of the Dartmouth College Doctrine, 1780–1819" (PhD diss., Michigan State University, 1973). On the public-private dichotomy in law, see Gerald Frug, "The City as a Legal Concept," *Harvard Law Review* 93 (1980): 1057–1154; Hendrik Hartog, *Public Property and Private Power: The Corporation of the City of New York in American Law, 1730–1870* (Chapel Hill: University of North Carolina Press, 1983).
8. William J. Novak, "The American Law of Association: The Legal-Political Construction of Civil Society," *Studies in American Political Development* 15 (2001): 163–88. The Georgia list draws on Milton Sidney Heath, *Constructive Liberalism: The Role of the State in Economic Development in Georgia to 1860* (Cambridge, MA: Harvard University Press, 1954), 293–308.
9. William P. Van Ness and John Woodworth, *Laws of the State of New York . . .* (Albany: H. C. Southwick, 1813), chaps. XLIII, XXXVIII, and LXVII; Lawrence M. Friedman, *A History of American Law*, 2nd ed. (New York: Simon and Schuster, 1985), 198–201; David Millon, "Theories of the Corporation," *Duke Law Journal* (1990): 205–7; Hartog, *Public Property and Private Power*, 22–24; Henry N. Butler, "Nineteenth-Century Jurisdictional Competition in the Granting of Corporate Privileges," *Journal of Legal Studies* 14 (1985): 138–43. According to Evans, *Business Incorporations in the United States*, the special-charter era can be thought to have ended as late as the 1870s (2).
10. Angell and Ames, *Treatise on the Law of Private Corporations, Aggregate*, 7–8, 35; James Willard Hurst, *The Legitimacy of the Business Corporation in the Law of the United States, 1780–1970* (Charlottesville: University Press of Virginia, 1970), 8–9; John Joseph Wallis, "Market-Augmenting Government? States and Corporations in Nineteenth-Century America," in *Market-Augmenting Government: The Institutional Foundations of Prosperity*, ed. Omar Azfar and Charles A. Caldwell (Ann Arbor: University of Michigan Press, 2003), 239–40; J. Alton Burdine, "Governmental Regulation of Industry in Pennsylvania, 1776–1860" (PhD diss., Harvard University, 1939), 34–35, 35n68; Handlin and Handlin, *Commonwealth*, 139–61; Neem, *Creating a Nation of Joiners*, esp. chap. 3.
11. William J. Novak, *The People's Welfare: Law and Regulation in Nineteenth-Century America* (Chapel Hill: University of North Carolina Press, 1996), 105–11; Scott Gregory Lien, "Contested Solidarities: Philanthropy, Justice, and the Reconstitution of Public Authority in the United States, 1790–1860" (PhD diss., University of Chicago, 2006).
12. Oscar Handlin and Mary F. Handlin, "Origins of the American Business Corporation," *Journal of Economic History* 5 (1945): 1–23; Gordon S. Wood, *Empire of Liberty:*

History of the Early American Republic, 1789–1815 (New York: Oxford University Press, 2009), 460–61; Pauline Maier, "The Revolutionary Origins of the American Corporation," *William and Mary Quarterly*, 3rd ser., 50 (1993): 51–84; [Anonymous], "Corporations," *American Jurist and Law Magazine* (October 1830): 300; David Ciepley, "Beyond Public and Private: Toward a Political Theory of the Corporation," *American Political Science Review* 107 (2013): 139–58.

13. Thomas E. Buckley, "After Disestablishment: Thomas Jefferson's Wall of Separation in Antebellum Virginia," *Journal of Southern History* 61 (1995): 445–80; Paul G. Kauper and Stephen C. Ellis, "Religious Corporations and the Law," *Michigan Law Review* 71 (1973): 1500–1574 (New York Act of Apr. 6, 1784, quoted on 1510); *Annals of Congress*, 22: 351, 982–83, quoted and discussed in David P. Currie, *The Constitution in Congress: The Jeffersonians, 1801–1829* (Chicago: University of Chicago Press, 2000), 318–23; Philip Hamburger, *Separation of Church and State* (Cambridge, MA: Harvard University Press, 2002), 182n 66.
14. *Laws of the State of New York*, 2 vols. (Albany: Charles K. and George Webster, 1802), chap. LXXIX, 336–43.
15. *Commonwealth v. St. Patrick Benevolent Society*, 2 Binn. (Penn.) 441, 443–45 (1810); Kevin Butterfield, "A Common Law of Membership: Expulsion, Regulation, and Civil Society in the Early Republic," *Pennsylvania Magazine of History and Biography* 133 (2009): 255–75.
16. 5 U.S. (1 Cranch) 137 (1803); Robert Lowry Clinton, Marbury v. Madison *and Judicial Review* (Lawrence: University Press of Kansas, 1989); William J. Nelson, Marbury v. Madison: *The Origins and Legacy of Judicial Review* (Lawrence: University Press of Kansas, 2000); Charles F. Hobson, *The Great Chief Justice: John Marshall and the Rule of Law* (Lawrence: University Press of Kansas, 1996); Maeva Marcus, "Judicial Review in the Early Republic," in *Launching the "Extended Republic": The Federalist Era*, ed. Ronald Hoffman and Peter J. Albert (Charlottesville: University of Virginia Press, 1996), 25–53; Gordon S. Wood, "The Origins of Judicial Review," *Suffolk Law Review* 22 (1988): 1293–1307; Gordon S. Wood, *Empire of Liberty: History of the Early American Republic, 1789–1815* (New York: Oxford University Press, 2009), chap. 12.
17. William Blackstone, *Commentaries on the Laws of England*, 4 vols. (Philadelphia: Robert Bell, 1771–1772), 3:109–11.
18. *James Bagge's Case*, 11 Co. Rep. 93b (1615), quotations on 95a, 98a (77 E.R. 1271); Edith G. Henderson, *Foundations of English Administrative Law: Certiorari and Mandamus in the Seventeenth Century* (Cambridge, MA: Harvard University Press, 1963), quotation on 72; J. H. Baker, *An Introduction to English Legal History*, 4th ed. (London: Butterworths Lexis Nexis, 2002), 147–48; Angell and Ames, *Treatise on the Law of Private Corporations, Aggregate*, 238n3.
19. Henderson, *Foundations of English Administrative Law*, 61–65, quotation on 65; Paul D. Halliday, *Dismembering the Body Politic: Partisan Politics in England's Towns, 1650–1730* (Cambridge: Cambridge University Press, 1998), 67–73, 131–43.
20. Halliday, *Dismembering the Body Politic*, 72–73; A. J. Harding, *Public Duties and Private Law* (Oxford: Clarendon, 1989), 82–133.
21. Kevin Butterfield, "The Right to Be a Freemason: Secret Societies and the Power of the Law in the Early Republic," *Common-Place: The Interactive Journal of Early American Life* 12 (2011). See also Halsey H. Moses, *The Law of Mandamus and the Practice Connected with It, with an Appendix of Forms* (Albany, NY: William Gould and Son, 1878), 182–93.

22. *Rex v. Blooer*, 2 Burr. 1043, 1045 (1760); *Rex v. Barker*, 3 Burr. 1265, 1267 (1762) (quotation); Henderson, *Foundations of English Administrative Law*, 141–42; Angell and Ames, *Treatise on the Law of Private Corporations, Aggregate*, 438.
23. Leonard S. Goodman, "Mandamus in the Colonies: The Rise of the Superintending Power of American Courts," *American Journal of Legal History* 1 (1957): 308–35, 2 (1958): 1–34, 129–47; J. W. Willcock, *The Law of Municipal Corporations: Together with a Brief Sketch of Their History and a Treatise on Mandamus and Quo Warranto* (1825; rpt., Philadelphia: John S. Littell, 1836), part 2, chap. 2, "Mandamus"; Angell and Ames, *Treatise on the Law of Private Corporations, Aggregate*, chap. 19.
24. Blackstone, *Commentaries on the Laws of England*, 3:111; William Selwyn, *An Abridgment of the Law of Nisi Prius: With Notes and References to the Decisions of the Courts of this Country by Henry Wheaton, Counsellor at Law*, 4th Am. ed. from 7th London ed., ed. Thomas I. Wharton, vol. 2 (New Haven, CT: E. F. Backus, 1831), 276–81; Angell and Ames, *Treatise on the Law of Private Corporations, Aggregate*, 455–62.
25. Alexander M. Burrill, *A New Law Dictionary and Glossary: Containing Full Definitions of the Principal Terms of the Common and Civil Law . . .* , 2 vols. (New York: John S. Voorhies, 1850), vol. 2, s.v. "Mandamus"; Zechariah Chafee, Jr., "The Internal Affairs of Associations Not for Profit," *Harvard Law Review* 43 (1930): 993–1029, esp. 1001–1006; Roscoe Pound, *Equitable Relief Against Defamation and Injuries to Personality*, 2nd ed. by Zechariah Chafee, Jr. (Cambridge, MA: Z. Chafee, Jr., 1930), sec. 3. See also "Judicial Control of Actions of Private Associations," *Harvard Law Review* 76 (1963): 983–1100.
26. Sir Frederick Pollock and Frederic William Maitland, *The History of English Law before the Time of Edward I*, 2nd ed., 2 vols. (Boston: Little Brown, 1905), 1:661–62.
27. Daniel J. Hulsebosch, "The Ancient Constitution and the Expanding Empire: Sir Edward Coke's British Jurisprudence," *Law and History Review* 21 (2003): 52 (see also Daniel J. Hulsebosch, "Writs to Rights: 'Navigability' and the Transformation of the Common Law in the Nineteenth Century," *Cardozo Law Review* 23 [2002]: 1049–1106); Michael Walzer, "The Civil Society Argument," in *Dimensions of Radical Democracy: Pluralism, Citizenship, Community*, ed. Chantal Mouffe (London and New York: Verso, 1992), 105.
28. Andrew Shankman, *Crucible of American Democracy: The Struggle to Fuse Egalitarianism and Capitalism in Jeffersonian Pennsylvania* (Lawrence: University Press of Kansas, 2004), 92–94, 173–74; David A. Wilson, *United Irishmen, Unites States: Immigrant Radicals in the Early Republic* (Ithaca, NY: Cornell University Press, 1998), 63; Sanford W. Higginbotham, *The Keystone in the Democratic Arch: Pennsylvania Politics, 1800–1816* (Harrisburg, PA: Pennsylvania Historical and Museum Commission, 1952), 136–39; Kim Tousley Phillips, "William Duane, Revolutionary Editor" (PhD diss., University of California, Berkeley, 1968), 228–34; Kim T. Phillips, "William Duane, Philadelphia's Democratic Republicans, and the Origins of Modern Politics," *Pennsylvania Magazine of History and Biography* 101 (1977): 365–87; Richard J. Twomey, *Jacobins and Jeffersonians: Anglo-American Radicalism and the United States, 1790–1820* (New York: Garland, 1989), 24–29, 54–56, 68–69, 108–11; Jeffrey L. Pasley, *"The Tyranny of Printers": Newspaper Politics in the Early American Republic* (Charlottesville: University of Virginia Press, 2001), 314–19; Worthington C. Ford, ed., "Letters of William Duane," *Proceedings of the Massachusetts Historical Society*, 2nd ser., 20 (1907): 257–394; *The Constitution of the St. Patrick Benevolent Society* (Philadelphia, 1804), 1; James Mease, *The Picture of Philadelphia* (1811; rpt., New York: Arno, 1970), 287.

29. *Freeman's Journal*, Apr. 10, 1805, quoted in Francis von A. Cabeen, "The Society of the Sons of Saint Tammany of Philadelphia," *Pennsylvania Magazine of History and Biography* 27 (1903); 29–48.
30. *Aurora*, Oct. 20, 1807, quoted in Wilson, *United Irishmen, Unites States*, 73; *Democratic Press*, Aug. 26, Sept. 2, Sept. 4, Sept. 25, 1807.
31. *Democratic Press*, Sept. 25, 1807.
32. *Aurora*, Oct. 3, 1807; *Democratic Press*, Oct. 5, Oct. 9, 1807.
33. *Democratic Press*, Oct. 5, Oct. 8, 1807; Shankman, *Crucible of American Democracy*, 179–80.
34. *Aurora*, Oct. 3, 1807; Alexander J. Dallas to Caesar A. Rodney, Feb. 6, 1809, Caesar A. Rodney Papers, Library of Congress, quoted in Shankman, *Crucible of American Democracy*, 181.
35. Binns's vote may have been the solitary dissent, but no records exist to confirm this. John Binns, petition for mandamus, Dec. 24, 1807, and deposition, Dec. 29, 1807, Mandamus and Quo Warranto Proceedings, Supreme Court of Pennsylvania, Eastern District, RG-33, Pennsylvania State Archives.
36. William Duane, return to mandamus, undated, ibid. Binns would later recall that he was certain his expulsion "was in itself absolutely null and void as it was contrary to the Constitution and Laws of the State, and the article of incorporation." *Democratic Press*, Apr. 2, 1810.
37. Laws of Pennsylvania, Apr. 6, 1791; *Commonwealth v. St. Patrick Benevolent Society*, 2 Binn. (Penn.) 441, 443–45 (1810). For an interpretation of the act of 1791, see *Case of the Medical College of Philadelphia*, 3 Wharton 445 (1838). For incorporations in Pennsylvania, see "Communication of the Secretary of the Commonwealth to the Constitutional Convention, June 29, 1837, listing all acts of incorporation since 1776," in *Journal of the Convention*, 2 vols. (Harrisburg, 1837–1838), 1:339–496.
38. *Commonwealth v. St. Patrick Benevolent Society*, 2 Binn. (Penn.) 441, 445–47 (1810); *Rex v. Richardson*, 1 Burr. 525 (1756).
39. Judith N. Shklar, *Ordinary Vices* (Cambridge, MA: Belknap Press of Harvard University Press, 1984), 101, 136; John H. Campbell, *History of the Friendly Sons of St. Patrick and of the Hibernian Society for the Relief of Immigrants from Ireland, March 17, 1771–March 17, 1892* (Philadelphia: Hibernian Society, 1892), 177–78, 349–50; Higginbotham, *Keystone in the Democratic Arch*, 214–16; Margaret H. McAleer, "In Defense of Civil Society: Irish Radicals in Philadelphia during the 1790s," *Early American Studies* 1 (2003): 176–97.
40. Mary Sarah Bilder, "The Corporate Origins of Judicial Review," *Yale Law Journal* 116 (2006): 502–66, quotation on 504; Mary Sarah Bilder, *The Transatlantic Constitution: Colonial Legal Culture and the Empire* (Cambridge, MA: Harvard University Press, 2004); Philip Hamburger, "Law and Judicial Duty," *George Washington Law Review* 72 (2003–2004): 1–41; Philip Hamburger, *Law and Judicial Duty* (Cambridge, MA: Harvard University Press, 2008); Novak, "American Law of Association," 163–88.
41. Angell and Ames, *Treatise on the Law of Private Corporations, Aggregate*, 239–43.
42. *Aurora*, Mar. 20, 1810. On the betrayal of James O'Coigley, see Wilson, *United Irishmen, Unites States*, 73–74; E. P. Thompson, *The Making of the English Working Class* (New York: Vintage, 1966), 169–74; [John Binns], *Trial of Edward Lyon (of Northumberland) for Subornation of False Swearing . . .* (Philadelphia, 1816).
43. *Commonwealth v. St. Patrick Benevolent Society*, 2 Binn. (Penn.) 441, 445–47 (1810); *Case of the Corporation of St. Mary's Church*, 7 Serg. and Rawle (Pa.) 517, 544 (1822).

44. Nancy L. Rosenblum, *Another Liberalism: Romanticism and the Reconstruction of Liberal Thought* (Cambridge, MA: Harvard University Press, 1987), 162.
45. Edwards, *The People and Their Peace*, 282.

PART TWO

1. Arthur M. Schlesinger, "Biography of a Nation of Joiners," *American Historical Review* 50 (1944): 1–25; John L. Brooke, *Columbia Rising: Civil Life on the Upper Hudson from the Revolution to the Age of Jackson* (Chapel Hill: University of North Carolina Press, 2010), 6, 79.
2. Joseph K. Angell and Samuel Ames, *A Treatise on the Law of Private Corporations, Aggregate* (Boston: Hilliard, Gray, Little, and Wilkins, 1832), v, vii; *Bushel v. Commonwealth Insurance Co.*, 15 Serg. and Rawle 173, 176–77 (1827).
3. Alexis de Tocqueville, *Democracy in America*, ed. Eduardo Nolla and trans. James T. Schliefer, 4 vols. (Indianapolis: Liberty Fund, 2010), 3:904.

CHAPTER FOUR

1. Constitution, book of records, and first annual address, Jan. 28, 1801, Ladies Literary Society, Norwich, CT, Connecticut Historical Society, Hartford, CT; Barbara E. Lacey, "Women in the Era of the American Revolution: The Case of Norwich, Connecticut," *New England Quarterly* 53 (1980): 539–40; Rosemarie Zagarri, *Revolutionary Backlash: Women and Politics in the Early American Republic* (Philadelphia: University of Pennsylvania Press, 2007), 56–57; Christoper Grasso, *A Speaking Aristocracy: Transforming Public Discourse in Eighteenth-Century Connecticut* (Chapel Hill: University of North Carolina Press, 1998), 420n43.
2. Alexis de Tocqueville, *Democracy in America*, trans. George Lawrence (New York: Harper and Row, 1966), bk. 2, chap. 5, " Of the Use That Americans Make of Association in Civil Life," p. 516.
3. Constitution, Ladies' Literary Society, Norwich, CT, Connecticut Historical Society, Hartford, CT.
4. Second annual address, Jan. 28 [27], 1802, in ibid.; minutes for Feb. 3, 1802.
5. Conrad Edick Wright, *The Transformation of Charity in Postrevolutionary New England* (Boston: Northeastern University Press, 1992), 206, was the first scholar to argue for "an examination of institutional processes and their consequences" in American voluntarism (206), a point further developed in another New England study, in Johann N. Neem's *Creating a Nation of Joiners: Democracy and Civil Society in Early National Massachusetts* (Cambridge, MA: Harvard University Press, 2008), esp. chap. 4.
6. Lyman Beecher, *The Practicability of Suppressing Vice, by Means of Societies Instituted for That Purpose: A Sermon, Delivered before the Moral Society, in East-Hampton (Long Island), September 21, 1803* (New London, CT: Samuel Green, 1804), 7.
7. Ibid., 7; *A Reformation of Morals Practicable and Indispensable: A Sermon Delivered at New-Haven on the Evening of October 27, 1812* (New Haven, CT: Eli Hudson, 1813), 22–23; Charles I. Foster, *An Errand of Mercy: The Evangelical United Front, 1790–1837* (Chapel Hill: University of North Carolina Press, 1960), 133n25. See Johann Neem, "Creating Social Capital in the Early American Republic: The View from Connecticut," *Journal of Interdisciplinary History* 39 (2009): 471–95; Peter Dobkin Hall, "Religion and the Origin of Voluntary Associations in the United States," working paper 213 (New Haven, CT: Program on Non-Profit Organizations, 1994).
8. Beecher, *Practicability of Suppressing Vice*, appendix.

9. Ronald G. Walters, *American Reformers, 1815–1860* (New York: Hill and Wang, 1978), 123–29; Lebbeus Armstrong, *The Temperance Reformation: Its History, from the Organization of the First Temperance Society to the Adoption of the Liquor Law of Maine, 1851 . . .* (New York: Fowlers and Wells, 1853); Lyman Beecher, *Autobiography, Correspondence, Etc., of Lyman Beecher, D.D.*, ed., Charles Beecher, 2 vols. (New York: Harper and Brothers, 1865), vol. 1, chap. 37.
10. "Records of the Female Reading Class, Colchester, Feb. 14th A. 1816," Connecticut Historical Society, Hartford, CT; Boscawen Juvenile Fraternity, Boscawen, NH, constitution and minutes, 1814–1815, New-York Historical Society, New York, NY.
11. Timothy Walker, *Introduction to American Law: Designed as a First Book for Students* (Philadelphia: P. H. Nicklin and T. Johnson, 1837), 203.
12. Samuel Stillman, "A Discourse Delivered before the Members of the Boston Female Asylum" (Boston, 1801), quoted in Neem, *Creating a Nation of Joiners*, 104; Wright, *Transformation of Charity*, 150.
13. William Patten, *The Advantages of Association to Promote Useful Purposes, Illustrated in a Discourse Delivered in the 2d Congregational Church, Newport, August 1st, A.D. 1805, at the Request of the Female Benevolent Society* (Newport, RI: Newport Mercury, 1805), 16.
14. Nancy F. Cott, *The Bonds of Womanhood: "Woman's Sphere" in New England, 1780–1835* (New Haven, CT: Yale University Press, 1977),149–51; Maternal Association of the First Congregational Church, Concord [NH], records 1827–1852, New Hampshire Historical Society, Concord, NH. See also the encomia about maternal societies in "Maternal Associations," *Observer and Telegraph* [Hudson, Ohio], Aug. 25, 1831, reprinted from the *New York Evangelist*; Richard A. Meckel, "Educating a Ministry of Mothers: Evangelical Maternal Associations, 1815–1860," *Journal of the Early Republic* 2 (1982): 403–23; Bruce Dorsey, *Reforming Men and Women: Gender in the Antebellum City* (Ithaca, NY: Cornell University Press, 2002), 23; Anne Firor Scott, *Natural Allies: Women's Associations in American History* (Urbana: University of Illinois Press, 1991), 13.
15. Ladies Benevolent Society, Dudley Street Baptist Church, Roxbury, Constitution and Minutes, 1842–43, Andover-Newton, quoted in Debra Gold Hansen, *Strained Sisterhood: Gender and Class in the Boston Female Anti-Slavery Society* (Amherst: University of Massachusetts Press, 1993), 60; *Proceedings of the Female Moral Reform Convention, Held in New York, May 8th, 9th, and 10th: With an Address to American Women* (New York: Published by the Convention, 1839), article 5. For a similar prohibition in an African American women's society, see the constitution of the Colored Female Religious and Moral Society of Salem," art. 4, quoted in Dorothy Sterling, ed., *We Are Your Sisters: Black Women in the Nineteenth Century* (New York: Norton, 1984), 109.
16. Constitution and minutes of the Ladies Sewing Society of St. James Church Ledyard, drafted Jan. 10, 1838, Connecticut Historical Society, Hartford, CT; Records of the Female Cent Society, 1812–1816, New Hampshire Historical Society, Concord, NH.
17. Donald B. Marti, *To Improve the Soil and the Mind: Agricultural Societies in the Northeastern States, 1791–1865* (Ann Arbor, MI: University Microfilms International, 1979), 15–20; Rodney H. True, "The Early Development of Agricultural Societies in the United States," *Annual Report of the American Historical Association for the Year 1920* (1925): 299; [Elkanah Watson], *Mr. Watson's Address, Delivered to the Members of the Berkshire Agricultural Society, at the Town-house in Pittsfield, September 24, 1811* (Pittsfield, MA: P. Allen, 1811); Elkanah Watson, *History of the Rise, Progress, and Existing State of the Berkshire Agricultural Society, in Massachusetts, with Practical Directions for*

Societies Forming in North-Carolina, on the Berkshire Model (Albany: E. and E. Hosford, 1819).

18. Isaac Briggs to Thomas Jefferson, Jan. 24, 1801, and Thomas Jefferson to Isaac Briggs, Feb. 8, 1801, in *The Papers of Thomas Jefferson*, vol. 32, *1 June 1800 to 16 February 1801*, ed. Barbara D. Oberg (Princeton, NJ: Princeton University Press, 2005), 501–3, 560.
19. "Constitution of Proposed Agricultural Society of Albemarle," ca. Feb. 1, 1811, in *The Papers of Thomas Jefferson, Retirement Series*, ed. J. Jefferson Looney, vol. 3 (Princeton, NJ: Princeton University Press, 2006), 347–52.
20. Ibid., 349–50.
21. Rodney H. True, *Early Days of the Albemarle Agricultural Society* (Washington, DC: Government Printing Office, 1920); Rodney H. True, ed., *Minute Book of the Albemarle (Virginia) Agricultural Society* (Washington, DC: Government Printing Office, 1920); Lucretia Ramsey Bishko, "The Agricultural Society of Albemarle and John S. Skinner: An Enduring Friendship," *Magazine of Albemarle County History* 31 (1973): 82.
22. True, ed., *Minute Book of the Albemarle (Virginia) Agricultural Society*, 270, 274.
23. Kathleen D. McCarthy, "Parallel Power Structures: Women and the Voluntary Sphere," in *Lady Bountiful Revisited: Women, Philanthropy, and Power*, ed. McCarthy (New Brunswick: Rutgers, 1990), 1–31; Nancy F. Cott, *The Bonds of Womanhood: "Woman's Sphere" in New England, 1780–1835* (New Haven, CT: Yale University Press, 1977), 134n15; Scott Gregory Lien, "The Centripetal Force of Benevolence: Social Unity and Voluntary Associations in the Early Republic," unpublished paper presented at the Omohundro Institute of Early American History and Culture, Fourteenth Annual Conference, June 2008, pp. 7–8; *Genius of Universal Emancipation*, May 12, 1827; Beth A. Salerno, *Sister Societies: Women's Antislavery Organizations in Antebellum America* (DeKalb: Northern Illinois University Press, 2005), 15–23.
24. Mary Kelley, *Learning to Stand and Speak: Women, Education, and Public Life in America's Republic* (Chapel Hill: University of North Carolina Press, 2006), 125.
25. Peter Clark, *British Clubs and Societies, 1580–1800: The Origins of an Associational World* (Oxford: Clarendon, 2000), 401; Neem, *Creating a Nation of Joiners*, 91; Theda Skocpol, *Diminished Democracy: From Membership to Management in American Civic Life* (Norman: University of Oklahoma Press, 2003).
26. A Citizen of the State of New York [William Jay], *A Memoir on the Subject of a General Bible Society for the United States of America* (New-Jersey: n.p., 1816), 15; Peter J. Wosh, *Spreading the Word: The Bible Business in Nineteenth-Century America* (Ithaca, NY: Cornell University Press, 1994), 40; Charles I. Foster, *An Errand of Mercy: The Evangelical United Front, 1790–1837* (Chapel Hill: University of North Carolina Press, 1960), chap. 7; Stephen P. Budney, *William Jay: Abolitionist and Anticolonialist* (Westport, CT: Praeger, 2005), 15–18; *Constitution of the American Bible Society: Formed by a Convention of Delegates, Held in the City of New-York, May 1816* (New York: G. F. Hopkins, 1816).
27. Neem, *Creating a Nation of Joiners*, chap. 4; Sidney Tarrow, *Power in Movement: Social Movements, Collective Action, and Politics* (New York: Cambridge University Press, 1994); Skocpol, *Diminished Democracy*; Jason Mazzone, "Organizing the Republic: Civic Associations and American Constitutionalism, 1780–1830" (JD diss., Yale Law School, 2004), chaps. 2–3; Jason Mazzone, "Freedom's Associations," *Washington Law Review* 77 (2002): 642–768.
28. Watson, *History of the Rise, Progress, and Existing State of the Berkshire Agricultural Society*, 43–68.

29. Cott, *Bonds of Womanhood*, 142–45; Kathleen D. McCarthy, *American Creed: Philanthropy and the Rise of Civil Society* (Chicago: University of Chicago Press, 2003), 81–82; Jane H. Pease and William H. Pease, *Ladies, Women, and Wenches: Choice and Constraint in Antebellum Charleston and Boston* (Chapel Hill: University of North Carolina Press, 1990), 119; *The Constitution of the Female Bible Society of Philadelphia, Instituted the Sixteenth of March, 1814: With an Address by the Right Reverend William White, D.D., Delivered at a Meeting of the Members* (Philadelphia: Printed by Order of the Society, 1814), 6. On the Worcester Female Association, see Carolyn J. Lawes, *Women and Reform in a New England Community, 1815–1860* (Lexington: University Press of Kentucky, 2000), 36–57. Other examples of heterosocial organizations include the Constitution of the Canaan Moral and Religious Tract Society, 1819, New Hampshire Historical Society, Concord, NH; Bible Society of the State of Rhode Island and Providence Plantations, Sept. 3, 1813, Rhode Island Historical Society, Providence, RI; Christian Benevolent Society, constitution and book of minutes, New-York Historical Society.
30. Scott, *Natural Allies*, 19, 195n32; Kelley, *Learning to Stand and Speak*, 28–29; Keith Melder, "Ladies Bountiful: Organized Women's Benevolence in Early Nineteenth Century America," *New York History* 65 (1967): 240. On a growing divergence between regions after this period, see John L. Brooke, "Cultures of Nationalism, Movements of Reform, and the Composite-Federal Polity: From Revolutionary Settlement to Antebellum Crisis," *Journal of the Early Republic* 29 (2009): 1–33.
31. *Origination and Constitution of the Sansom Street Baptist Female Society for Promoting Foreign Evangelical Missions, formed June 27, 1814* (Philadelphia: R. P. and W. Anderson, 1814); *The Fifteenth Report of the Female Bible Society of Philadelphia: Read before the Society, 25th March, 1829. With an Appendix, and a List of New Subscribers and Benefactors* (Philadelphia: John W. Allen, 1829), 9.
32. Branch Bible Society of Lebanon, Record Book, 1829–1856, Connecticut Historical Society, Hartford, CT; *Constitution and By-Laws of the New Haven Mutual Aid Association: Adopted April, 1833; Revised December, 1833* (New Haven, CT: Jas. F. Babcock, 1834).
33. "Female Charitable Societies," *Concord Observer*, Jan. 4, 1819; "Agricultural Societies," *Genesee Farmer and Gardener's Journal*, Mar. 11, 1837.
34. [Jay], *Memoir on the Subject of a General Bible Society*, 13.
35. Wapping Female Missionary Society, records, 1839–1861, Connecticut Historical Society, Hartford, CT.
36. *New Hampshire Juvenile Fraternity*, broadside (Concord, NH: William Hoit, Jr., 1808), New Hampshire Historical Society, Concord, NH. On the importance of publicity as a means of allaying fears, see Albrecht Koschnik, "'The Deeds of the Order so Carefully Concealed *Will Not Bear the Light*': Secrecy and Publicity in the Early Republic," unpublished paper presented at Society for Historians of the Early American Republic annual conference, July 2013.
37. Philadelphia Humane Society, *Directions for Recovering Persons, Who Are Supposed to Be Dead . . . To Which Is Prefixed the Constitution of the Said Society* (Philadelphia: Joseph James, [1788]), 6–16; *The Constitution of the Pennsylvania Society, for Promoting the Abolition of Slavery, and the Relief of Free Negroes, Unlawfully Held in Bondage. Begun in the Year 1774, and Enlarged on the Twenty-Third of April, 1787* (Philadelphia: Joseph James, 1787); Mazzone, "Organizing the Republic," 306–7; Amanda Bowie Moniz, "Saving the Lives of Strangers: Humane Societies and the

Cosmopolitan Provision of Charitable Aid," *Journal of the Early Republic* 29 (2009): 607–40.

38. Constitution, Ladies' Literary Society, Norwich, CT, Connecticut Historical Society, Hartford, CT.
39. *Constitution of the Female Charitable Society of Concord* (Concord, NH: George Hough, 1824); *Constitution of the Concord Female Charitable Society, and Names of Members* (n.d., n.p.), incorporated on Jan. 5, 1853: see *Acts of Incorporation and Constitution of the Concord Female Charitable Society: Catalogue of Members with Address and Reports at the Centennial Anniversary, 1812–1912* (Concord, NH: Ira C. Evans, 1912); Henry McFarland, "Concord Female Charitable Society," essay on file at the New Hampshire Historical Society; Sarah Kimball, "Concord Female Charitable Society" [1856], in Kimball-Jenkins Papers, New Hampshire Historical Society, Concord, NH; Records of the Concord Female Charitable Society, 1812–1840, New Hampshire Historical Society, Concord, NH; Samuel Ayer Kimball, receipts from memberships, subscriptions, etc., in Kimball-Jenkins Papers, New Hampshire Historical Society, Concord, NH; Maternal Association of the First Congregational Church, Concord [NH], records 1827–1852, New Hampshire Historical Society, Concord, NH; Minutes, Mar. 4, 1789, Providence Association of Mechanics and Manufacturers, Series II, Box 5, Rhode Island Historical Society, Providence, RI.
40. Kelley, *Learning to Stand and Speak*, 14; Zagarri, *Revolutionary Backlash*, chap. 2; Carolyn Eastman, *A Nation of Speechifiers: Making an American Public after the Revolution* (Chicago: University of Chicago Press, 2009), chap. 2.
41. Jeanne Boydston, "Civilizing Selves: Public Structures and Private Lives in Mary Kelley's *Learning to Stand and Speak*," *Journal of the Early Republic* 28 (2008): 55–57; Rosemarie Zagarri, "Politics and Civil Society: A Discussion of Mary Kelley's *Learning to Stand and Speak*," in ibid., 65. See also Lori D. Ginzberg, *Untidy Origins: A Story of Women's Rights in Antebellum New York* (Chapel Hill: University of North Carolina Press, 2005), 103–4; Cott, *Bonds of Womanhood*, chap. 2; Hewitt, *Women's Activism and Social Change*, chap. 2; Mary P. Ryan, "Civil Society as Democratic Practice: North American Cities during the Nineteenth Century," *Journal of Interdisciplinary History* 29 (1999): 559–84.
42. Records of the Literary and Philosophical Society of New York, meetings of Jan. 20, June 9, 1814, New-York Historical Society, New York, NY.
43. *The Constitution of the Social Society, Instituted at Schenectady, June 28th, 1798* (Schenectady, NY: John L. Stevenson, 1800), art. 24.
44. Charles Walker to Secretary of Am. Institute, Aug. 22, 1842, Records of the American Institute of the City of New York, box 76, folder 11, New-York Historical Society.
45. Ibid., art. 23; Christian Benevolent Society, constitution and book of minutes, pp. 22, 27, New-York Historical Society, New York, NY; Young Men's Association for Mutual Improvement, Norwich, CT, Record book, 1830–1831, June 25, July 9, 1830, Connecticut Historical Society, Hartford, CT; *Commonwealth v. Hunt*, Thacher's Criminal Cases, 609, 647, 650, 653 (1840). On the details of the appeal, see *Law Reporter* 3 (1841): 304.
46. For a good example of women's awareness that they needed to be clear and specific in order that new members would keep the association in the proper path, see Records of the Maternal Association of Clergymen's Wives in Cheshire County, NH, 1835–1870, New Hampshire Historical Society, Concord, NH, address in folder 5, dated January 1834.

47. Alexis de Tocqueville, *Democracy in America*, trans. George Lawrence (New York: Harper and Row, 1966), bk. 2, chap. 5, " Of the Use That Americans Make of Association in Civil Life," p. 516.
48. "Philanthropy of the Present Age," *New England Magazine* 6 (January 1834): 55.

CHAPTER FIVE

1. James Willard Hurst, *The Legitimacy of the Business Corporation in the Law of the United States, 1780–1970* (Charlottesville: University Press of Virginia, 1970), 14.
2. Roberta Romano, *Foundations of Corporate Law* (New York: Oxford University Press, 1993), 63.
3. *Ellis v. Marshall*, 2 Mass. 269 (1807); William E. Nelson, *Americanization of the Common Law: The Impact of Legal Change on Massachusetts Society, 1760–1830* (1975; Athens: University of Georgia Press, 1994), 134; Dale A. Oesterle, "Formative Contributions to American Corporate Law by the Massachusetts Supreme Judicial Court from 1806 to 1810," in *The History of the Law in Massachusetts: The Supreme Judicial Court, 1692–1992*, ed. Russell K. Osgood (Boston: Supreme Judicial Court Historical Society, 1992), 137–39; Oscar Handlin and Mary Flug Handlin, *Commonwealth: A Study of the Role of Government in the American Economy: Massachusetts, 1774–1861*, rev. ed. (Cambridge, MA: Belknap Press of Harvard University Press, 1969), 21–22; Morton J. Horwitz, *The Transformation of American Law, 1780–1860* (Cambridge, MA: Harvard University Press, 1977), 110–13.
4. *Ellis v. Marshall*, 2 Mass. 269, 279 (1807); Edwin Merrick Dodd, *American Business Corporations until 1860: With Special Reference to Massachusetts* (Cambridge, MA: Harvard University Press, 1954), 18–27; *Gray v. Portland Bank*, 3 Mass. 364 (1807); *Terrett v. Taylor*, 13 U.S. 43 (1815); *Dartmouth College v. Woodward*, 4 Wheat. 518 (1819). The first English cases making this sort of public/private distinction came a few years later (Dodd, *American Business Corporations*, 18).
5. *Dartmouth College v. Woodward*, 4 Wheat. 518, 560, 668–69, 708 (1819); U.S. Constitution, article 1, sec. 10; R. Kent Newmyer, "Justice Joseph Story's Doctrine of 'Public and Private Corporations' and the Rise of the American Business Corporation, *DePaul Law Review* 25 (1975–1976): 836; Joseph K. Angell and Samuel Ames, *A Treatise on the Law of Private Corporations, Aggregate* (Boston: Hilliard, Gray, Little, and Wilkins, 1832), 8–9, 21, 47. The importance of *Ellis* to the development of the public/private distinction is noted in Bruce Arthur Campbell, "Law and Experience in the Early Republic: The Evolution of the Dartmouth College Doctrine, 1780–1819" (PhD diss., Michigan State University, 1973), 223. *Ellis* was cited by both Daniel Webster, counsel for the school, and by Justice Joseph Story in *Dartmouth*. It should be no surprise that Webster and Story cited the same cases, as Story was an important contributor to Webster's case preparations: see R. Kent Newmyer, "Daniel Webster as Tocqueville's Lawyer: The 'Dartmouth College' Case Again, *American Journal of Legal History* 11 (1967): 127.
6. 6 Geo. I, c. 18 (1720); Joseph Stancliffe Davis, *Essays in the Earlier History of American Corporations*, 2 vols. (Cambridge, MA: Harvard University Press, 1917), 1:105–6; Shaw Livermore, *Early American Land Companies: Their Influence on Corporate Development* (New York: Commonwealth Fund, 1939); Winifred B. Rothenberg, "The Emergence of a Capital Market in Rural Massachusetts, 1730–1838," in *The Economy of Early America: The Revolutionary Period, 1763–1790*, ed. Ronald Hoffman (Charlottesville: University Press of Virginia, 1988), 135–36; Stuart Banner, *Anglo-American Securities*

Regulation: Cultural and Political Roots, 1690–1860 (New York: Cambridge University Press, 1998), 127–28; Edwin J. Perkins, *American Public Finance and Financial Services, 1700–1815* (Columbus: Ohio State University Press, 1994), 56–75; Charles Royster, *The Fabulous History of the Dismal Swamp Company: A Story of George Washington's Times* (New York: Vintage, 1999), 82–83, 375.

7. Evans, *Business Incorporations in the United States*, table 9; William C. Kessler, "Incorporation in New England: A Statistical Study, 1800–1875," *Journal of Economic History* 8 (1948): 43–47; Dodd, *American Business Corporations*, 11; John Majewski, "Toward a Social History of the Corporation: Shareholding in Pennsylvania, 1800–1840," in *The Economy of Early America: Historical Perspectives and New Directions*, ed. Cathy Matson (University Park: Pennsylvania State University Press, 2006), 294–316; John Majewski, *A House Dividing: Economic Development in Pennsylvania and Virginia before the Civil War* (New York: Cambridge University Press, 2000), chaps. 1–2.

8. Ron Harris, "Political Economy, Interest Groups, Legal Institutions, and the Repeal of the Bubble Act in 1825," *Economic History Review* 50 (1997): 675–96; A. W. B. Simpson, "The Rise and Fall of the Legal Treatise: Legal Principles and the Forms of Legal Literature," *University of Chicago Law Review* 48 (1981): 669–71; Perry Miller, *The Life of the Mind in America: From the Revolution to the Civil War*, bks. 1–3 (New York: Harcourt, Brace, and World, 1965), 99–116; Stewart Kyd, *A Treatise on the Law of Corporations*, vol. 1 (London: J. Butterworth, 1793); Hendrik Hartog, *Public Property and Private Power: The Corporation of the City of New York in American Law, 1730–1870* (Chapel Hill: University of North Carolina Press, 1983), 185–86. A work devoted solely to municipal corporations, noted by Angell and Ames as "very faithful" and helpful in their research on mandamus, quo warranto, disfranchisement, and amotion, was published in 1827: J. W. Willcock, *The Law of Municipal Corporations: Together with a Brief Sketch of Their History, and a Treatise on Mandamus and Quo Warranto* (London: W. Benning, 1827).

9. *Case of the Philadelphia Savings Institution*, 1 Whart. 461, 464–67 (1836); "An Act to Incorporate the Philadelphia Savings Institution," passed Apr. 5, 1834, *Laws of the General Assembly of the State of Pennsylvania . . .* (Harrisburg, 1834), no. 106; *Chester Glass Company v. Dewey*, 16 Mass. 94, 101 (1819); Angell and Ames, *Treatise on the Law of Private Corporations, Aggregate*, 294, 316–18; Robert E. Wright, *The First Wall Street: Chestnut Street, Philadelphia, and the Birth of American Finance* (Chicago: University of Chicago Press, 2005), 76–77; Samuel Williston, "History of the Law of Business Corporations before 1800," *Harvard Law Review* 2 (1888): 109–10; Joseph Edward Hedges, *Commercial Banking and the Stock Market before 1863* (Baltimore: Johns Hopkins Press, 1938), 27–55; Richard Sylla, "U.S. Securities Markets and the Banking System, 1790–1840," *Federal Reserve Bank of St. Louis Review* 80 (May-June 1998): 83–98; Abbott Lawrence Lowell and Francis C. Lowell, *The Transfer of Stock in Private Corporations* (Boston: Little Brown, 1884), chap. 5; Francis T. Christy, *The Transfer of Stock* (New York: Baker, Voorhis, 1929), 20–29.

10. Dodd, *American Business Corporations*, 74; Charles R. T. O'Kelley & Robert B. Thompson, *Corporations and Other Business Associations: Cases and Materials*, 4th ed. (New York: Aspen, 2003), 488–89; Massachusetts Statutes, 1805, chap. 14.

11. Albany and Schenectady Turnpike Company, articles of agreement and ledger, New-York Historical Society; Act passed March 30, 1802, Laws of New York, 25th Session, ch. 69

12. Eric Pawson, *Transport and Economy: The Turnpike Roads of Eighteenth Century Britain* (London: Academic Press, 1977); Walter K. Wood, "The Alleghany Turnpike

and Internal Improvements, 1800–1850" (MA thesis, Virginia Polytechnic Institute, 1969); Carter Goodrich, "The Virginia System of Mixed Enterprise: A Study of State Planning of Internal Improvements," *Political Science Quarterly* 64 (1949): 355–87; Joseph Austin Durrenberger, *Turnpikes: A Study of the Toll Road Movement in the Middle-Atlantic States and Maryland* (Valdosta, GA, 1931); Daniel P. Jones, "Commercial Progress versus Local Rights: Turnpike Building in Northwestern Rhode Island in the 1790s," *Rhode Island History* 48 (1990): 21–32; Robert F. Hunter, "The Turnpike Movement in Virginia, 1816–1860," *Virginia Magazine of History and Biography* 69 (1961): 278–89; Daniel B. Klein and John Majewski, "Economy, Community, and Law: The Turnpike Movement in New York, 1797–1845," *Law and Society Review* 26 (1992): 469–512.

13. *Jenkins v. Union Turnpike Road*, 1 Caine's Case Reports (NY) 86 (1805); *Union Turnpike Road v. Jenkins*, 1 Caine's Reports (NY) 381 (1803); Angell and Ames, *Treatise on the Law of Private Corporations, Aggregate*, 293; Dodd, *American Business Corporations*, 74–76.
14. *Goshen and Minisink Turnpike Company v. Hurtin*, 9 Johns. 217 (1812); *Dutchess Manu-Factory Company v. Davis*, 14 Johns. 238 (1817); Angell and Ames, *Treatise on the Law of Private Corporations, Aggregate*, 293–94; Dodd, *American Business Corporations*, 74–75. See also *Highland Turnpike v. M'Kean*, 11 Johns. 98 (1814); *Worcester Turnpike Corporation v. Willard*, 5 Mass. 80 (1809); *Gilmore v. Pope*, 5 Mass. 491 (1809).
15. *Andover and Medford Turnpike Corporation v. Gould*, 6 Mass. 40 (1809); Angell and Ames, *Treatise on the Law of Private Corporations, Aggregate*, 302; [Joseph K. Angell], "Law of Corporations: Personal Liability of the Members of an Incorporated Company for Stock Subscribed and for Assessments," *United States Law Intelligencer and Review* 2 (1830): 109–18; Dodd, *American Business Corporations*, 76. The point became especially clear when the Massachusetts Supreme Court extended this principle to a manufacturing corporation several years later: even though a group of unincorporated merchants have a legal right to compel one of their own to pay his share, the same cannot be said of a corporation, which "must derive all their rights and remedies from the provisions of the statute," barring only those instances in which a member had explicitly bound himself to pay assessments. *Franklin Glass Company v. White*, 14 Mass. 286 (1817).
16. *New Bedford and Bridgewater Turnpike Corporation v. Adams*, 8 Mass. 138, 139–40 (1811). The case is explained as hinging on the lack of mutuality of a consideration in *Trustees of Phillips Limerick Academy v. Davis*, 11 Mass. 113, 117 (1814), but in the *Adams* opinion the court was clear that the issue rested on the lack of any express promise at all. No effort at all was made to evaluate the contract, none being found.
17. *Bend v. Susquehanna Bridge and Bank Co.*, 6 Harris and J. (Md.) 128 (1823); *Hartford and N.H.R.R. v. Kennedy*, 12 Conn. 499, 528 (1838); *Instone v. Frankfort Bridge Co.*, 5 KY 576, 577 (1812); *Grays v. Turnpike Co.*, 4 Rand. (Va.) 378 (1826) (see also *Herkimer Manufacturing Co. v. Small*, 21 Wend. [NY] 273 [1839]); *Revised Code of the Laws of Virginia*, vol. 2 (Richmond: Thomas Ritchie, 1819), 213, sec. 6; Conway Robinson, *The Practice in the Courts of Law and Equity in Virginia*, vol. 1, *Containing Practice in the Courts of Law in Civil Cases* (Richmond, VA: Samuel Shepherd, 1832), chap. 20; Benj. Vaughan Abbott and Austin Abbott, *A General Digest of the Laws of Corporations: Presenting the American Adjudications upon Public and Private Corporations . . .* (New York: Baker, Voorhis, and Co., 1869), 38–39; John B. Minor, *Institutes of Common and Statute Law*, vol. 1, *The Rights Which Relate to the Person*, 2nd ed. (Richmond: Printed

for the Author, 1876), 530–31; Angell and Ames, *Treatise on the Law of Private Corporations, Aggregate*, 306.

18. Wright, *First Wall Street*, 76–77; President, Managers, and Company of the Delaware and Schuylkill Canal Navigation v. William Samson, "Case Stated for the opinion of the Judges of the Supreme Court," Folder 47, Miscellaneous Papers 1704–1899, Records of the Supreme Court, Eastern District, RG33, Pennsylvania State Archives; *Delaware and Schuylkill Canal v. Sansom*, 1 Binn. (Pa.) 70 (1803); Andrew M. Schocket, *Founding Corporate Power in Early National Philadelphia* (DeKalb: Northern Illinois University Press, 2007), 188.
19. Frank H. Easterbrook and Daniel R. Fischel, *The Economic Structure of Corporate Law* (Cambridge, MA: Harvard University Press, 1996), chap. 2; Richard A. Posner, "The Rights of Creditors of Affiliate Corporations," *University of Chicago Law Review* 43 (1976); Kevin F. Forbes, "Limited Liability and the Development of the Business Corporation," *Journal of Law, Economics, and Organization* 2 (1986): 163–77; Herbert Hovenkamp, *Enterprise and American Law, 1836–1937* (Cambridge, MA: Harvard University Press, 1991), chap. 5; Susan E. Woodward, "Limited Liability in the Theory of the Firm," *Journal of Institutional and Theoretical Economics* 141 (1985): 601–11; Stephen B. Presser, "Thwarting the Killing of the Corporation: Limited Liability, Democracy, and Economics," *Northwestern University Law Review* 87 (1992): 148–79.
20. Angell and Ames, *Treatise on the Law of Corporations, Aggregate*, 23–24; *Spear v. Grant*, 16 Mass. 9, 14 (1819); "On the Liability of Corporators," *American Law Magazine* 1 (1843), art. 5 (reprinted from *Carolina Law Journal* 1 [1831]: 217); "Law of Corporations," *Law Intelligencer and Review* 2 (1830): 109–9–18, 210–12, 240–47, 270–76; "Manufacturing Corporations," *American Jurist and Law Magazine* 2 (1829): 96–119; Perkins, *American Public Finance and Financial Services*, appendix.
21. Francis Wayland, *The Limitations of Human Responsibility* (Boston: Gould, Kendall, and Lincoln, 1838), 110; *Livingston v. Lynch*, 4 Johns. (NY) 573, 582 (1820); Hurst, *Legitimacy of the Business Corporation*, 25. Of course, anything can be amended, including any corporate charter or any contract, provided every single person involved agrees to the change. This was the rule at common law for good reason: with unanimous consent, there is no one left with either cause or standing to protest. On the unamendability of partnership agreements without unanimous consent of partners, see *Natusch v. Irving* (1824), reported in Niel Gow, *A Practical Treatise on the Law of Partnership*, 2nd American ed. (Philadelphia: Robert H. Small, 1830), appendix 2, 576–95.
22. Samuel Greenhow to Thomas Jefferson, May 29, 1809, in *The Papers of Thomas Jefferson, Retirement Series*, ed. J. Jefferson Looney, vol. 1 (Princeton, NJ: Princeton University Press, 2004), 243; Charles F. Mercer to Samuel Greenhow, May 18, 1809, Papers of the Mutual Assurance Society of Virginia, Correspondence, 1795–1866, Robert Alonzo Brock Collection, Henry E. Huntington Library, San Marino, CA (unless otherwise noted, all correspondence related to the Mutual Assurance Society is from the Brock Collection at the Huntington Library.); Dalit Baranoff, "Shaped by Risk: The American Fire Insurance Industry, 1790–1920" (PhD diss., Johns Hopkins University, 2003), 34–36; George Hay to William F. Ast, July 10, 1799.
23. Philadelphia Contributionship, *The Deed of Settlement of the Society for the Insuring of Houses, in and near Philadelphia* (Philadelphia: n.p., 1787?); Nicholas B. Wainwright, *A Philadelphia Story: The Philadelphia Contributionship for the Insurance of Houses from Loss by Fire* (Philadelphia: Willam F. Fell, 1952); Baranoff, "Shaped by Risk," 34–35; Humbert O. Nelli, "Insurance and the Bicentennial," *Journal of Risk*

and Insurance 43 (1976): 197–99; J. A. Fowler, *History of Insurance in Philadelphia for Two Centuries (1863–1882)* (Philadelphia: Review Publishing and Printing, 1888), 298–300.

24. John Bainbridge, *Biography of an Idea: The Story of Mutual Fire and Casualty Insurance* (Garden City, NY: Doubleday and Company, 1952), 20–21, 50–54; speech of Horace Binney, in *Centennial Meeting of the Philadelphia Contributionship for the Insurance of Houses from Loss by Fire* (Philadelphia: C. Sherman, 1852), 9–31; *Deed of Settlement*, 1; Sharon Ann Murphy, *Investing in Life: Insurance in Antebellum America* (Baltimore, MD: Johns Hopkins University Press, 2010).
25. *Rules and Articles of the Massachusetts Mutual Fire Insurance Company* (Boston, 1798), arts. 1, 11; report of Andrew Cunningham, secretary, Massachusetts Mutual Fire Insurance Company, Jan. 20, 1799, quoted in Edward R. Hardy, *Reports of 1888–1900, with an Account of the Early Insurance Offices in Massachusetts, from 1724 to 1801*, Insurance Library Association (Boston: Frank Wood, 1901), 86; Osborne Howes, Jr., "The Rise and Progress of Insurance in Boston," in *Memorial History of Boston*, ed. Justin Winsor, vol. 4 (Boston: James R. Osgood, 1883), 183–84; *The Deed of Settlement of the Mutual Assurance Company, for Insuring Houses from Loss by Fire in New-York* (New York: William Morton, 1787) (original, with appended signatures, at New-York Historical Society); Baltimore Equitable Society, "Deed of Settlement of the Society for Insuring of Houses in and near Baltimore," art. 33, *Maryland Journal and Baltimore Advertiser*, Feb. 28, Mar. 5, 1794; J. A. Fowler, *History of Insurance in Philadelphia for Two Centuries (1863–1882)* (Philadelphia: Review Publishing and Printing, 1888), 298–300; *The Constitution of the Stamford Mutual Insurance Company* (New York: J. Harrisson, 1797); *The Constitution, or Deed of Settlement, of the Providence Mutual Insurance Company* . . . ([Providence, RI]: J. Carter, [1800?]); chap. 26, "An Act for Establishing a Mutual Assurance Society against Fire on Buildings in this State," Dec. 22, 1794, *Acts Passed at a General Assembly of the Commonwealth of Virginia* (Richmond, VA: Augustine Davis, 1795); Henry St. George Tucker, writing in *Mutual Assurance Society v. Stone*, 30 Va. 218, 230 (1831) (quotation).
26. *Journal of the House of Representatives of the United States, being the First Session of the Third Congress* . . . , vol. 2 (Washington, DC: Gales and Seaton, 1826), 49; Walter Lowrie and Walter S. Franklin, eds., *American State Papers: Documents, Legislative and Executive, of the Congress of the United States* . . . , vol. 1 (Washington, DC: Gales and Seaton, 1834), no. 45, "Insurance against Loss by Fire," 77; "Memorial of Wm. F: Ast and of sundry inhabitants of the City of Richmond," in *The Papers of John Marshall*, ed. Charles T. Cullen and Herbert A. Johnson, vol. 2 (Chapel Hill: University of North Carolina Press, 1977), 296–97. Samuel Mordecai, writing in the 1850s, remembered Ast as "a small, shrivelled, wizen-faced man, who looked as if he was a descendant of the mother of vinegar." *Richmond in By-gone Days: Being Reminiscences of an Old Citizen* (Richmond, VA: George M. West, 1856), 253; see obituary in *Richmond Enquirer*, Sept. 26, 1807.
27. Form letter from William F. Ast to Henry Beatty, Sept. 26, 1796, in Mutual Assurance Society papers, 1796–1821, Virginia Historical Society; *Statement of the Subscribers and Members: Agreeable to Their Declarations for Insurance which are Filed and Recorded in the General Office of the Said Society* (Richmond, VA: n.p., 1802); W. F. Ast to Samuel Moody, June 8, 1807, Moody Family Papers, Virginia Historical Society.
28. "Constitution, Laws, Regulations, and Rules of the Mutual Assurance Society . . . Copied from the Journals of General Meetings," 16, Robert Anderson Papers, John D. Rockefeller, Jr., Library, Colonial Williamsburg Foundation; chap. 41, "An

Act to explain an act, intituled 'An act for establishing a mutual assurance society against fire on buildings in this state,'" Dec. 23, 1795, in *Statutes at Large*, 1:405–6; Richard Love, *Founded upon Benevolence: A Bicentennial History of the Mutual Assurance Society of Virginia*, ed. Shepherd (Richmond, VA: Valentine, 1994), 5; John B. Danforth and Herbert A. Claiborne, *Historical Sketch of the Mutual Assurance Society of Virginia, Richmond, Va.: From Its Organization in 1794 to 1879* (Richmond, VA: Wm. Ellis Jones, 1879), 3–4. In 1800, a decision was made at the general meeting to allow the senator or delegate from members' districts to serve as the proxy unless another had been specially appointed. Chap. 15, "An Act to amend the several acts passed for the establishment of the mutual assurance society against fire on buildings in the state of Virginia," Jan. 23, 1800, in *The Statutes at Large of Virginia, from October Session 1792, to December Session 1806, Inclusive . . .* , ed. Samuel Shepherd, 3 vols. (1835; rpt., New York: AMS, 1970), 2:210.

29. "Constitution, Laws, Regulations, and Rules," 14–15, Anderson Papers; Love, *Founded upon Benevolence*, 7.
30. "Act for Establishing a Mutual Assurance Society," Dec. 22, 1794, chap. 26, art. 6; Chap. 30, "An Act to amend the act, for establishing a mutual assurance society against fire on buildings in this state," Jan. 12, 1799, in *Statutes at Large*, ed. Shepherd, 2:160–61; Henry St. George Tucker, *Commentaries on the Laws of Virginia: Comprising the Substance of a Course of Lectures Delivered to the Winchester Law School*, 2 vols. (Winchester, VA: Republican, 1837), 2:242; Jefferson to Ast, Sept. 17, 1799, in *Papers of Thomas Jefferson*, ed. Oberg, 31:186–88.
31. Jefferson to Ast, Sept. 17, 1799, in *Papers of Thomas Jefferson*, ed. Oberg, 31:187–88.
32. William Frederick Ast to Jefferson, May 10, 1800, in *Papers of Thomas Jefferson*, ed. Oberg, 31: 571–72.
33. William Leigh to William Frederick Ast, May 30, 1806.
34. For accounts of losses broken down by year, see Samuel Greenhow, "To the Editor of the Enquirer," *Richmond Enquirer*, Oct. 27, 1809.
35. H. W. Burton, *The History of Norfolk, Virginia: A Review of Important Events and Incidents which Occurred from 1736 to 1877 . . .* (Norfolk: Norfolk Virginian Job Print, 1877), 6; Danforth and Claiborne, *Historical Sketch of the Mutual Assurance Society*, 20–21; *Statement of the Subscribers and Members: Agreeable to Their Declarations for Insurance which are Filed and Recorded in the General Office of the Said Society* (Richmond, VA: n.p., 1802), s.v. Tazewell; "View of 'The Mutual Assurance Society against Fire, on Buildings of the State of Virginia,'" pt. 3, *Richmond Enquirer*, Sept. 8, 1804.
36. "View of 'The Mutual Assurance Society against Fire, on Buildings of the State of Virginia,'" pt. 1, *Richmond Enquirer*, Aug. 29, 1804. At this time, Ritchie's newly formed newspaper had a small but quickly growing readership, between five and six hundred: see *Richmond Enquirer*, July 29, 1805 ("a few more than 500") and Nov. 3, 1804 (600). See Jerry W. Knudson, "The Jefferson Years: Response by the Press, 1801–1809" (PhD diss., University of Virginia, 1962), 50–52; Charles Henry Ambler, *Thomas Ritchie: A Study in Virginia Politics* (Richmond, VA: Bell Book and Stationary, 1913), 18–27; "On Banks," *Richmond Enquirer*, July 28-Aug. 25, 1804; Bert Marsh Mutersbaugh, "Jeffersonian Journalist: Thomas Ritchie and the Richmond *Enquirer*, 1804–1820" (PhD diss., University of Missouri, 1973), 76–80, 176–77.
37. *Richmond Enquirer*, Sep. 8, 1804; Francis Corbin to William Ast, Sept. 26, 1804. Writers have differed as to whom the division was intended to benefit: Samuel Mordecai

writing in the 1850s thought those in the towns supported the change because country members were notoriously slow or resistant in paying into the company funds (*Richmond in By-gone Days*, 254–57). In current scholarship, Bruce A. Campbell's argument ("John Marshall, the Virginia Political Economy, and the Dartmouth College Decision," *American Journal of Legal History* 19 [1975]: 40–65; Campbell, "Law and Experience in the Early Republic") that the country members adopted the change against town opposition has been generally accepted, e.g., in *The Papers of John Marshall*, vol. 7 (Chapel Hill: University of North Carolina Press, 1993), 217–18. That position finds support in Corbin's report and in Ast's letter to the *Richmond Enquirer*, Feb. 1, 1805. But evidence of the continued optimism within the society about effecting a general insurance across Virginia in 1804 and 1805, coupled with the fact that, in the end, it was the "country" branch of the Mutual Assurance Society that failed, lends credence to the idea that the move was part of a genuine attempt to balance the burdens of the society's roughly two thousand members.

38. Report of Edmund Randolph, Jan. 11, 1805, in Constitution of the Mutual Assurance Society as corrected by Samuel Greenhow, Robert Anderson Papers, John D. Rockefeller, Jr., Library, Colonial Williamsburg Foundation; *Richmond Enquirer*, Feb. 1, 1805; "An Act for carrying into execution the constitution of the mutual assurance society . . . ," chap. 24, Jan. 29, 1805, *Shepherd's Statutes*, 3:145–49; *Journal of the House of Delegates of the Commonwealth of Virginia* (Richmond, VA: Samuel Pleasants, Jr., 1804), 109. On the broad extent of Randolph's legal work during these years following his retirement from politics, see John J. Reardon, *Edmund Randolph: A Biography* (New York: Macmillan, 1974), 348–58.
39. Alexander McRae to William Ast, Apr. 21, 1805, and Charles Marshall to William Marshall, Feb. 18, 1806; John Marshall to Samuel Greenhow, Oct. 17, 1809, in *Papers of John Marshall*, ed. Hobson, 7:217–18.
40. *Currie's Administrators v. Mutual Assurance Society*, 4 Hen. and M. (14 Va.) 315 (1809). Campbell, "John Marshall, the Virginia Political Economy, and the Dartmouth College Decision," 40–65; Morton J. Horwitz, *The Transformation of American Law, 1780–1860* (Cambridge, MA: Harvard University Press, 1977), 111–14; and Timothy S. Huebner, *The Southern Judicial Tradition: State Judges and Sectional Distinctiveness, 1790–1890* (Athens: University of Georgia Press, 1999), 27–29, provide useful contextual information.
41. "An Act concerning the Mutual Assurance Society of Virginia . . . ," chap. 28, Feb. 16, 1809, *Acts Passed at a General Assembly of the Commonwealth of Virginia* (Richmond, VA: Samuel Pleasants, 1809), 36–38. The decision was handed down on Dec. 2, 1809, and was printed in full in the *Richmond Enquirer* on December 9.
42. 4 Hen. and M. (14 Va.) 315, 350 (1809); *Dartmouth College v. Woodward*, 4 Wheat. 518 (1819). On the scholarship seeing *Currie's Administrators* as reflecting a pre-*Dartmouth* position of unrestrained legislative authority to amend corporate charters, see Campbell, "Law and Experience in the Early Republic," 265–67; Campbell, "John Marshall, the Virginia Political Economy, and the Dartmouth College Decision," 49–52; Huebner, *Southern Judicial Tradition*, 27–29; Horwitz, *Transformation of American Law*, 111–14; as well as such legal history casebooks as Stephen B. Presser and Jamil S. Zainaldin, *Law and Jurisprudence in American History: Cases and Materials*, 5th ed. (St. Paul, MN: Thomson West, 2003), 327–32.
43. On the contests within this court, especially between Roane and St. George Tucker, who absented himself from this case, see F. Thornton Miller, *Juries and Judges versus*

the Law: Virginia's Provincial Legal Culture, 1783–1828 (Charlottesville: University Press of Virginia, 1994); Timothy S. Huebner, "The Consolidation of State Judicial Power: Spencer Roane, Virginia Legal Culture, and the Southern Judicial Tradition," *Virginia Magazine of History and Biography* 102 (1994): 58–60; and Hamilton, *Making and Unmaking of a Revolutionary Family*, 136.

44. "Constitution, Laws, Regulations, and Rules of the Mutual Assurance Society . . . Copied from the Journals of General Meetings," art. 17, passed Jan. 4, 1800, Robert Anderson Papers, John D. Rockefeller, Jr., Library, Colonial Williamsburg Foundation; "An Act for Carrying into Execution the Constitution of the Mutual Assurance Society . . . ," passed January 29, 1805, in *Statutes at Large of Virginia*, 3:145; *Constitution, Rules, and Regulations of the Mutual Assurance Society* . . . , ed. Shepherd (Richmond, 1810), art. 10, sec. 11; 4 Hen. and M. (14 Va.) 315, 352 (1809); Jefferson to Ast, Sept. 17, 1799, in *Papers of Thomas Jefferson*, ed. Oberg, 31:186–88; Michael Walzer, "Corporate Authority and Civil Disobedience," *Dissent* 16 (1969): 401; Albert Hirschman, *Exit, Voice, and Loyalty: Responses to Decline in Firms, Organizations, and States* (Cambridge, MA: Harvard University Press, 1970).
45. *Ware v. Hylton*, 3 U.S. 199 (1796); Campbell, "John Marshall, the Virginia Political Economy, and the Dartmouth College Decision," 63.
46. Policy of John Schultz, Mutual Assurance Society, Aug. 30, 1796, no. 251, Mutual Assurance Society papers, Virginia Historical Society; policy of Thomas Rutherfoord, Phoenix Assurance Company of London, Oct. 1, 1802, no. 136102, in Samuel Myers papers, Earl Gregg Swem Library, College of William and Mary. I am indebted to Margaret Pritchard of the Colonial Williamsburg Foundation for her help on the symbols and techniques apparent in the two prints.
47. W. F. Ast to Samuel Moody, June 8, 1807, Moody Family Papers, Virginia Historical Society; Greenhow to Jefferson, May 29, 1809, in *Papers of Thomas Jefferson, Retirement Series*, ed. Looney, 1:241–45; Samuel Greenhow, "To the Editor of the Enquirer," *Richmond Enquirer*, Oct. 27, 1809.
48. Mercer to Greenhow, May 18, 1809. Mercer was elected to the Virginia House of Delegates the following year and would become a leading Federalist, National Republican, and Whig until his death in 1858. Though this early episode of leadership in his home county goes unnoted, see Robert Allen Carter, "Virginia Federalist in Dissent: A Life in Charles Fenton Mercer" (PhD diss., University of Virginia, 1988); Douglas R. Egerton, *Charles Fenton Mercer and the Trial of National Conservatism* (Jackson: University Press of Mississippi, 1989), chap. 4; Norman K. Risjord, "The Virginia Federalists," *Journal of Southern History* 33 (1967): 486–517.
49. Mercer to Greenhow, May 18, 1809; Greenhow to Jefferson, May 29, 1809, *Papers of Thomas Jefferson, Retirement Series*, ed. Looney, 1:241–45 (see also the notes accompanying this letter in *Papers of Thomas Jefferson, Retirement Series*, ed. Looney, 1:244–45n); Cynthia Miller Leonard, comp., *The General Assembly of Virginia, July 30, 1619–January 11, 1978: A Bicentennial Register of Members* (Richmond, VA: General Assembly of Virginia by the Virginia State Library, 1978), 228, 232, 236; *Journal of the House of Delegates of the Commonwealth of Virginia . . . One Thousand Eight Hundred and Eight* (Richmond, VA: Samuel Pleasants, Jr., [1809]), 119–21; Heath to Greenhow, May 18, 1810. Thomas Jefferson provides one example of the delay in collecting quotas. He was billed all at once for two years' quotas, interest, and a recently added lawyers' commission. Benjamin Brown to Thomas Jefferson, Jan. 12, 1811, in *Papers of Thomas Jefferson, Retirement Series*, ed. Looney, 3:294.

50. Heath to Greenhow, May 18, 1810, and William Dawson to Samuel Greenhow, Dec. 5, 1811. Heath's novel *Edge-Hill; or, The Family of the Fitzroyals* (Richmond, VA: T. W. White, 1828), 2 vols., is now largely forgotten, but he was "almost the only person of any literary distinction" in Richmond, according to Edgar Allan Poe in 1841: "A Chapter on Autography," *Graham's Magazine*, December 1841, in *The Complete Works of Edgar Allan Poe*, ed. James A. Harrison, vol. 15 (New York: Thomas Y. Crowell, 1902), 241.
51. Marshall to Samuel Greenhow, Oct. 17, 1809, in *The Papers of John Marshall*, ed. Charles F. Hobson, vol. 7 (Chapel Hill: University of North Carolina Press, 1993), 217–18; Albert J. Beveridge, *The Life of John Marshall*, 4 vols. (Boston: Houghton Mifflin, 1919), 2:174. Either Marshall's frustration with the society was not long-lived or he simply resigned himself that it was better than any available alternative. He joined again, declaring in 1815 for insurance for his home, office, laundry, and kitchen in Richmond: Hobson, ed., *The Papers of John Marshall*, vol. 8 (Chapel Hill: University of North Carolina Press, 1995), appendix 2, 399, renewing in 1822 and 1829.
52. *Korn and Wisemiller v. Mutual Assurance Society*, 6 Cranch 192, 200–201 (1810); *Atkinson v. Mutual Assurance Society*, 6 Cranch 202 (1810); *Mutual Assurance Society v. Korn and Wisemiller*, 7 Cranch 396, 399 (1813); "Change of Contract of Insurance by Amendment of By-Laws of a Fraternal Mutual Benefit Association," *Yale Law Journal* 19 (1910): 379–80; Donald G. Morgan, *Justice William Johnson, the First Dissenter: The Career and Constitutional Philosophy of a Jeffersonian Judge* (Columbia: University of South Carolina Press, 1954); Oliver Schroeder, Jr., "The Life and Judicial Work of Justice William Johnson, Jr.," *University of Pennsylvania Law Review* 95 (1946–1947): 164–201, 344–86.
53. *Korn and Wisemiller v. Mutual Assurance Society*, 6 Cranch 192, 200 (1810); Heath to Greenhow, May 18, 1810. One area where courts, state and federal, intervened was in a series of cases centered on the lien of the Mutual Assurance Society on the property of members, which was held enforceable in some cases, but not all, against purchasers of the insured property: see *Greenhow, Principal Agent of the Mutual Assurance Society v. Barton*, 15 Va. 590 (1810); *Barton v. Price, Cashier*, bill of exceptions from Spotsylvania District Court, Sept. 16, 1805, Fredericksburg Circuit Court, Historic Court Records, Sharron S. Mitchell, clerk; *Mutual Assurance Society v. Watt's Executor*, 14 U.S. 279 (1816); *Stratton v. Mutual Assurance Society*, 27 Va. 22, 24 (1827); *Mutual Assurance Society v. Stone*, 30 Va. 218, 236–37 (1831).
54. St. George Tucker, *Blackstone's Commentaries: With Notes of Reference to the Constitution and Laws of the Federal Government of the United States, and of the Commonwealth of Virginia . . .*, 5 vols. (Philadelphia: William Young Birch and Abraham Small, 1803), 2:472, cited by William Fleming, concurring, *Currie's Administrators v. Mutual Assurance Society*, 6 Hen. and M. 315, 356 (1809); *Head and Amory v. Providence Insurance Company*, 2 Cranch 127 (1804); *Bank of the United States v. Deveaux*, 5 Cranch 61 (1809); Gregory A. Mark, "The Court and the Corporation: Jurisprudence, Localism, and Federalism," *Supreme Court Review* (1997): 425–26; John Marshall to Bushrod Washington, Aug. 3, 1819, in *The Papers of John Marshall*, ed. Charles F. Hobson, vol. 8 (Chapel Hill: University of North Carolina Press, 1995), 373; report of Mutual Assurance Society committee, appointed Apr. 5, 1822, chair, John Brockenbrough, quoted in Danforth and Claiborne, *Historical Sketch of the Mutual Assurance Society*, 52–53; chap. 25, "An act to abolish the Country Branch of the Mutual Assurance

Society against fire on buildings in the state of Virginia," Mar. 4, 1822, *Acts Passed at a General Assembly of the Commonwealth of Virginia . . .* (Richmond: Thomas Ritchie, 1822), 25–26 (quotation on 25).

55. Jefferson to Ast, Sept. 17, 1799, in *Papers of Thomas Jefferson*, ed. Oberg, 31:188; Carol Weisbrod, "Insurance and the Utopian Ideal," *Connecticut Insurance Law Journal* 6 (1999–2000): 397–98.

56. "View of 'The Mutual Assurance Society against Fire, on Buildings of the State of Virginia,' " pt. 3, *Richmond Enquirer*, Sept. 8, 1804; Greenhow to Jefferson, May 29, 1809, in *Papers of Thomas Jefferson, Retirement Series*, ed. Looney, 1:243; Charles Clay to William Ast, Sept. 18, 1805.

57. Angell and Ames, *Treatise on the Law of Private Corporations, Aggregate*, 304; Nathan Dane, *A General Abridgment and Digest of American Law: With Occasional Notes and Comments*, 8 vols. (Boston: Cummings, Hilliard, and Co., 1823), chap. 22, sec. 52., in vol. 1, 473–74; Andrew Johnson, "The Influence of Nathan Dane on Legal Literature," *American Journal of Legal History* 7 (1963): 28–50; Kevin Butterfield, "Stockholders as Members: The Rights of Membership and the Early American Business Corporation," paper presented at New York University Legal History Colloquium, April 2011.

58. Margaret M. Blair, "Locking in Capital: What Corporate Law Achieved for Business Organizers in the Nineteenth Century," *UCLA Law Review* 51 (2003): 387–455; Henry Hansmaan and Reiner Kraakman, "The Essential Role of Organizational Law," *Yale Law Journal* 110 (2000): 387–440; Henry Hansmaan, Reinier Kraakman, and Richard Squire, "Law and the Rise of the Firm," *Harvard Law Review* 119 (2006): 1335–1403; Kenneth Lipartito, "The Utopian Corporation," in *Constructing Corporate America: History, Politics, Culture*, ed. Kenneth Lipartito and David B. Sicilia (New York: Oxford University Press, 2004), 101–2; David Ciepley, "Beyond Public and Private: Toward a Political Theory of the Corporation," *American Political Science Review* 107 (2013): 139–58.

59. Eric Hilt, "When Did Ownership Separate from Control? Corporate Governance in the Early Nineteenth Century," *Journal of Economic History* 68 (2008): 645–85; Colleen Dunlavy, "From Citizens to Plutocrats: Nineteenth-Century Shareholder Voting Rights and Theories of the Corporation," in *Constructing Corporate America: History, Politics, Culture*, ed. Kenneth Lipartito and David Sicilia (Oxford: Oxford University Press, 2004), 66–93.

60. *Middlesex Turnpike v. Locke*, 8 Mass. 268, 272 (1811).

61. *Middlesex Turnpike v. Swan*, 10 Mass. 284 (1813); Angell and Ames, *Treatise on the Law of Private Corporations, Aggregate*, 304.

62. *Union Locks and Canals v. Towne*, 1 NH 44 (1817); Dodd, *American Business Corporations*, 81–82.

63. E. Merrick Dodd, Jr., "Dissenting Stockholders and Amendments to Corporate Charters," *University of Pennsylvania Law Review* 75 (1927): 585–613, 723–52; Edward O. Curran, "Minority Stockholders and the Amendment of Corporate Charters," *Michigan Law Review* 32 (1933–1934): 743–79; Lynn L. Dallas, "The Control and Conflict of Interest Voting Systems," *North Carolina Law Review* 71 (1992): 8n17; W. Lloyd Kitchel, "The Power of Stockholders to Bind a Corporation," *Yale Law Journal* 5 (1895): 83–92; Peter Karsten, "Supervising the 'Spoiled Children of Legislation': Judicial Judgments Involving Quasi-Public Corporations in the Nineteenth Century U.S.," *American Journal of Legal History* 41 (1997): 361n177; Dodd, *American Business Corporations*, 81–83.

64. *Indiana and Ebensburg Turnpike Road Co. v. Phillips*, 2 Pen. and W. (Pa.) 184, 196 (1830); Dodd, *American Business Corporations*, 82–83. In addition to *Dartmouth College v. Woodward*, the key arguments for the defense regarding contract were drawn from *Fletcher v. Peck*, 6 Cranch 87, 136–37 (1810); U.S. Constitution, art. 1, sec. 10; Pennsylvania Constitution of 1790, art. 9, sec. 17.
65. *Indiana and Ebensburg Turnpike Road Co. v. Phillips*, 2 Pen. and W. (Pa.) 184, 196 (1830).
66. *Hibernia Turnpike Co. v. Henderson*, 8 Serg. and Rawle (Pa.) 219, 223 (1822); *Irvin v. Susquehanna and Phillipsburg Turnpike Company*, 2 Pen. and W. (Pa.) 466, 470 (1831); A Citizen [Elkanah Watson], *Observations on the Real, Relative, and Market Value, of the Turnpike Stock of the State of New-York* (New York: S. Gould, 1806), 20–21; Klein and Majewski, "Economy, Community, and Law," 475–76; Banner, *Anglo-American Securities Regulation*, 142.
67. *Irvin v. Susquehanna and Phillipsburg Turnpike Company*, 2 Pen. and W. (Pa.) 466, 471, 474 (1831) (emphasis added); Burdine, "Governmental Regulation of Industry in Pennsylvania," 216–34. Gibson insisted that the *Irvin* case was distinguishable from the *Middlesex Turnpike* cases on the basis of the nature of the promissory notes, but I take the view of the chancellor of Vermont in *Stevens v. Rutland and Burlington Railroad Company*, 29 Vt. 545, 557–58 (1851), that "in the one case the court did not consider the alteration in the charter as a fundamental change in the structure of the association, while in the other[s] it was so considered." On the increasing specificity of charters regarding personal obligations, see *Hartford and New Haven Railroad Company v. Kennedy*, 12 Conn. 499, 524–25 (1838).
68. *Gray v. Monongahela Navigation Company*, 2 Watts and Serg. (Pa.) 156, 161 (1841); *Hartford and New Haven Railroad v. Crosswell*, 5 Hill (NY) 383, 386, 388 (1843).
69. *Delacy v. Neuse River Navigation Company*, 8 N.C. 274, 278–81 (1821).

CHAPTER SIX

1. James Kent, *Commentaries on American Law*, vol. 2 (New York: O. Halsted, 1827), 239, note D; Stewart Kyd, *A Treatise on the Law of Corporations*, vol. 2 (London: J. Butterworth, 1794), 50–94.
2. Ramsay MacMullen, *Roman Social Relations, 50 B.C. to A.D. 284* (New Haven, CT: Yale University Press, 1974), 78–79.
3. Elizabeth Kowaleski-Wallace, "The Needs of Strangers: Friendly Societies and Insurance Societies in Late Eighteenth-Century England," *Eighteenth-Century Life* 24 (2000): 53–72; Conrad Edick Wright, *The Transformation of Charity in Postrevolutionary New England* (Boston: Northeastern University Press, 1992), 64–65.
4. David Neave, "Friendly Societies in Great Britain," in *Social Security Mutualism: The Comparative History of Mutual Benefit Societies*, ed. Marcel van Linden (Bern: Peter Lang, 1996), 41–64; Peter Clark, *British Clubs and Societies, 1580–1800: The Origins of an Associational World* (Oxford: Clarendon, 2000), 368–77; P. H. J. H. Gosden, The Friendly Societies in England, 1815–1875 (Manchester: Manchester University Press, 1961); E. P. Thompson, *The Making of the English Working Class* (New York: Vintage, 1966), 418–20, 457–61; Michael Scarth, *The Rules and Regulations of the Castle Eden Friendly Society: With Extracts from the Proceedings &c. To Which Are Added Explanatory Notes and Observations* (London: W. Clarke, 1798); Frank Warren Crow, "The Age of Promise: Societies for Social and Economic Improvement in the United States, 1783–1815" (PhD diss., University of Wisconsin, 1953), 278–80; Wright, *Transformation of Charity*, 66; Martin Gorsky, "The Growth and Distribution of English Friendly

Societies in the Early Nineteenth Century," *Economic History Review* 51 (1998): 489–511, esp. 507–8; Walter S. Nichols, "Fraternal Insurance in the United States: Its Origin, Development, Character, and Existing Status," *Annals of the American Academy of Political and Social Science* 70 (1917): 109–22.

5. Steven C. Bullock, *Revolutionary Brotherhood: Freemasonry and the Transformation of the American Social Order, 1730–1840* (Chapel Hill: University of North Carolina Press, 1996), 193–97; *The Constitution of the Friendly Society of St. Thomas's African Church of Philadelphia* (Philadelphia: W. W. Woodward, 1797); "Private Benevolence and Moral Cures for Poverty," in *Welfare Reform in the Early Republic: A Brief History with Documents*, ed. Seth Rockman (Boston: Bedford/St. Martin's, 2003), 67–97; Wright, *Transformation of Charity*, 53; Crow, "Age of Promise," 281; James Mease, *The Picture of Philadelphia: Giving an Account of Its Origin, Increase, and Improvements in Arts, Sciences, Manufactures, Commerce, and Revenue, with a Compendious View of Its Societies, Literary, Benevolent, Patriotic, and Religious . . .* (Philadelphia: B. and T. Kite, 1811), 278–80.
6. *Rules and Regulations of the American Beneficial Society: Incorporated, March, 1804* (Philadelphia: John Hoff, 1804); Mease, *Picture of Philadelphia*, 278; affidavit of Joseph H. Vanderslice, Commonwealth v. American Beneficial Society, Filed Dec. 20, 1810, Writs of Mandamus and Quo Warranto, Supreme Court, Eastern District, Record Group 33, Pennsylvania State Archives, Harrisburg, PA.
7. Return of the American Beneficial Society, Dec. 26, 1810, ibid.; report of committee of Wm Meguire, Henry Snyder, Charles Snyder to American Beneficial Society, ibid.
8. Return of the Independent Beneficial Society, Dec. 20, 1813, ibid.; Petition of Charles Hepburn, Dec. 14, 1813, ibid.; *Constitution of the Independent Beneficial Society, of the City and County of Philadelphia* (Philadelphia: Joseph Rakestraw, 1811).
9. Petition of Charles Hepburn, Dec. 14, 1813, Writs of Mandamus and Quo Warranto, Supreme Court, Eastern District, Record Group 33, Pennsylvania State Archives, Harrisburg, PA.
10. Return of the Independent Beneficial Society, Dec. 27, 1813, and deposition of Cornelius Campbell, ibid.
11. Petitions of William Peter Roerig and Jacob Wolf, Dec. 31, 1813, and affidavit of John Stief, Jan. 13, 1816, Writs of Mandamus and Quo Warranto, Supreme Court, Eastern District, RG-33, Pennsylvania State Archives, Harrisburg, PA.
12. *Commonwealth v. Philanthropic Society*, 5 Binn. (Pa.) 486 (1813); William Miner to Jacob Beck, Apr. 1, 1817, folder 7, Mandamus and Quo Warranto Proceedings, Supreme Court of Pennsylvania, Eastern District, RG-33, Pennsylvania State Archives.
13. Deposition of William M. Stewart, July 22, 1811, folder 7, Mandamus and Quo Warranto Proceedings, Supreme Court of Pennsylvania, Eastern District, RG-33, Pennsylvania State Archives; *Constitution of the Philanthropic Society, Established at Philadelphia, May 6th, 1793: Incorporated the Seventh Day of January, 1799* (Philadelphia: Reprinted by Thomas T. Stiles, 1808); Mease, *Picture of Philadelphia*, 277; *Commonwealth v. Philanthropic Society*, 5 Binn. (Pa.) 486 (1813).
14. Ibid.; deposition of John Dennis, president of the Philanthropic Society, Apr. 3, 1812, and Minutes, Philanthropic Society, Apr. 9–23, 1811, folder 7, Mandamus and Quo Warranto Proceedings, Supreme Court of Pennsylvania, Eastern District, RG-33, Pennsylvania State Archives; Kent, *Commentaries on American Law*, 2:239n; Joseph K. Angell and Samuel Ames, *A Treatise on the Law of Private Corporations, Aggregate* (Boston: Hilliard, Gray, Little, and Wilkins, 1832), 243–45, 347.

15. Woodward, writing at nisi prius, Mar. 11, 1864, quoted in *Evans v. Philadelphia Club*, 50 Pa. 107 (1865).
16. "Return of George Ireland, late president, William Freeman now president, John Seisinger vice president, and Thomas Cotes junior secretary of the Penn. Ben. Inst.," Mandamus and Quo Warranto Proceedings, Supreme Court of Pennsylvania, Eastern District, RG-33, Pennsylvania State Archives; *Commonwealth v. Pennsylvania Beneficial Institution*, 2 Serg. and Rawle 141, 141–42 (1815).
17. *Rex v. May*, 5 Burr. 2681, 2682 (1770); Angell and Ames, *Treatise on the Law of Private Corporations, Aggregate*, 244–46, 276–77; J. W. Willcock, *The Law of Municipal Corporations: Together with a Brief Sketch of Their History, and a Treatise on Mandamus and Quo Warranto* (London: William Benning, 1827), 46–47. Angell and Ames drew upon Willcock's treatise heavily in their expositions on the right of notice, quoting one particularly powerful passage at length: "To a neglect of this notice alone, can be attributed those unconstitutional innovations which have crept into corporations, by which the body at large has in most cases been stript of their incidental rights, and the power of election, amotion, and disposing of corporate property, vested in them by their incorporation, have been arrogated to themselves by the select classes, until at length the antiquity of the usurpation has given them a semblance of right" (Willcock, *Law of Municipal Corporations*, 46–47, quoted by Angell and Ames on 278n3).
18. *Delacy v. Neuse River Navigation Corporation*, 1 Hawks. (8 N.C.) 274 (1821); Angell and Ames, *Treatise on the Law of Private Corporations, Aggregate*, 244–46.
19. David Hoffman, *A Course of Legal Study: Respectfully Addressed to the Student of Law in the United States* (Baltimore: Coale and Maxwell, 1817), 181–82; David Hoffman, *A Course of Legal Study: Addressed to Students and the Profession Generally*, 2nd ed., rewritten and much enlarged, 2 vols. (Baltimore: J. Neal, 1836), 1:320–21; William Selwyn, *An Abridgement of the Law of Nisi Prius; With Notes and References to the Decisions of the Courts of this Country*, by Henry Wheaton, *Fourth American from the Seventh London Edition with Additional Notes and References*, by Thomas I. Wharton, 2 vols. (Philadelphia: P. H. Nicklin and T. Johnson, 1831), vol. 2, chap. 28; Angell and Ames, *Treatise on the Law of Private Corporations, Aggregate*, chap. 11; Kent, *Commentaries on American Law*, 239n; James Kent, *Commentaries on American Law*, 2nd ed. (New York: O. Halsted, 1832), 297–98; Matthew Bacon, *A New Abridgement of the Law*, American ed., with notes by John Bouvier, vol. 2 (Philadelphia: Thomas Davis, 1846), 457–58.
20. Ronald P. Formisano and Kathleen Smith Kutolowski, "Antimasonry and Masonry: The Genesis of a Protest, 1826–1827," *American Quarterly* 29 (1977): 139–65; William Preston Vaughn, *The Antimasonic Party in the United States, 1826–1834* (Lexington: University Press of Kentucky, 1983), chap. 1; Paul Goodman, *Towards a Christian Republic: Antimasonry and the Great Transition in New England, 1826–1836* (New York: Oxford University Press, 1988), 3–9; Ronald P. Formisano, *For the People: American Populist Movements from the Revolution to the 1850s* (Chapel Hill: University of North Carolinas Press, 2008), 95–115; John L. Brooke, *The Heart of the Commonwealth: Society and Political Culture in Worcester County, Massachusetts, 1713–1861* (1989; rpt., Amherst: University of Massachusetts Press, 2005), chap. 10.
21. Frederick Whittlesey, *An Oration Delivered at Venice, the 4th of July, 1831: It Being the Fifty-Fifth Anniversary of the Independence of the United States* (Auburn, NY: T. M. Skinner, 1831), quoted in Elizabeth Bruchholz Haigh, "New York Antimasons,

1826–1833" (PhD diss., University of Rochester, 1980), 101; *Proceedings of a Convention of Delegates Opposed to Freemasonry, Which Met at Le Roy, Genesee Co. N.Y. March 6, 1828* (Rochester, NY: Weed & Heron, 1828), 5; Michael F. Holt, "The Antimasonic and Know Nothing Parties," *History of U.S. Political Parties*, ed. Arthur M. Schlesinger, Jr. (New York: Chelsea House, 1973), 584.

22. [William Morgan], *Illustrations of Masonry, by One of the Fraternity, Who Has Devoted Thirty Years to the Subject*, 2nd ed., *With an Account of the Kidnapping of the Author* (New York: Printed for the author, 1826), iii (introduction by David Miller).
23. *Proceedings of a Convention of Delegates Opposed to Freemasonry, Which Met at Le Roy, Genesee Co. N.Y. March 6, 1828* (Rochester, NY: Weed & Heron, 1828), 13.
24. Charles Thompson McClenachan, *History of the Most Ancient and Honorable Fraternity of Free and Accepted Masons in New York . . .*, 4 vols. (New York: The Grand Lodge, 1888–1894), 2:342; Bullock, *Revolutionary Brotherhood*, 371n16; *Proceedings of a Convention of Delegates Opposed to Freemasonry*, 13; Haigh, "New York Antimasons," 324–26; Charles W. Moore [g. sec. of grand lodge of MA], *Address Delivereed on the Centennial Anniversary of St. John's Lodge, No. 1, at Portsmouth, N.H., June 24, 1836* (Boston: Tuttle, Weeks, and Dennett, 1836), 78n26; *Truth's Proofs that Masonic Oaths Do Not Impose Any Obligations* (Norwich, CT, 1830), 13, quoted in Dorothy Ann Lipson, *Freemasonry in Federalist Connecticut* (Princeton, NJ: Princeton University Press, 1977), 310; Wright, *Transformation of Charity*, 165.
25. Bullock, *Revolutionary Brotherhood*, 189–91; Wright, *Transformation of Charity*, 161.
26. Derby [Shelton], King Hiram Lodge No. 12, letter from Jesse Bradley, Newton, 1823, and letter from George Bradley, Mar. 18, 1824, quoted in Lipson, *Freemasonry in Federalist Connecticut*, 209–10.
27. *Anti-Masonic Review, and Magazine*, Jan. 1, 1828, 4, 15.
28. Grand Annual Communication, Dec. 15, 1803, John Dove, ed., *Proceedings of the M. W. Grand Lodge of Ancient York Masons of the State of Virginia; From Its Organization, in 1778, to 1822 . . .*, vol. 1 (Richmond, VA: James E. Goode, 1874), 311, 324; Daniel Bradford, Grand Lodge of Kentucky [Lexington] to the Grand Lodge of Virginia, Sept. 29, 5804 [1804], Freemasonry Collection, Grand Lodge of Virginia, Robert Alonzo Brock Collection, Henry E. Huntington Library, San Marino, CA.
29. Wright, *Transformation of Charity*, 140; Albert G. Mackey, ed., *Encyclopedia of Freemasonry*, vol. 1, rev. and enl. by Robert I. Clegg (Chicago: Masonic History Company, 1929), 478; "An Act to Incorporate the Grand Lodge of Ancient Free Masons of South Carolina . . . ," no. 2203, in *The Statutes at Large of South Carolina*, ed. David J. McCord, vol. 8, *Acts Relating to Corporations and the Militia* (Columbia, SC: A. S. Johnston, 1840), 301–3; John Abbott, *An Address Delivered before the Grand Lodge of Massachusetts, at the Annual Communication, December, 5826* (Cambridge, [MA]: Hilliard, Metcalf, and Co., 1826), 4–5; Johann Neem, *Creating a Nation of Joiners: Democracy and Civil Society in Early National Massachusetts* (Cambridge, MA: Harvard University Press, 2008), 111–12; *Antimasonic Pamphlets No. 1: Memorial against the Masonic Incorporations of Connecticut: Together with the Report and Some of the Debates, in the General Assembly, May Session, 1832* (found at Connecticut Historical Society, printed but not bound), quotations on 2–3.
30. "Mr. Rush's Letter," *The Independence*, Apr. 4, 1832; Brooke, *Heart of the Commonwealth*, 327.
31. *Proceedings of the Antimasonic State Convention, holden at Montpelier, June 15 and 16, 1831. With Reports, Addresses, &c.* (Montpelier: Gamaliel Small, 1831), 5–6.

32. Bullock, *Revolutionary Brotherhood*, 194–95, 197. See also John Fabian Witt, *The Accidental Republic: Crippled Workingmen, Destitute Widows, and the Remaking of American Law* (Cambridge, MA: Harvard University Press, 2004), chap. 3.
33. Lipson, *Freemasonry in Federalist Connecticut*, 226–27; Lebbeus Armstrong, *The Man of Sin Revealed; or, The Total Overthrow of the Institution of Freemasonry, Predicted by St. Paul . . . to Which is Prefixed, Correspondence, shewing the Manner of the Author's Exclusion from His Pulpit, and Expulsion from the Royal Arch Chapter . . .* (Waterford, NY: J. C. Johnson, 1829), 29; "Mr. Rush's Letter," *The Independence*, Apr. 4, 1832; *The Address of the United States Anti-Masonic Convention, Held at Philadelphia, September 11, 1830. To the People of the United States* (Philadelphia: John Clarke, 1830), 3.
34. *Proceedings of a Convention of Delegates Opposed to Freemasonry*, 9.
35. Michael Wallace, "Changing Concepts of Party in the United States, 1815–1828," *American Historical Review* 74 (1968): 453–91; *Testimony Taken by the Committee Appointed by the House of Representatives, to Investigate the Evils of Freemasonry, Mr. Stevens, Chairman: Read in the House of Representatives, June 13, 1836* (Harrisburg, PA: Theo. Finn, 1836), 46; Haigh, "New York Antimasons," 91.
36. *Constitution of the Young Men's Anti-Masonic Association for the Diffusion of Truth* (Boston: Pollok, 1832); Papers of the Antimasonic Party in Suffolk, MA, 1821–1834, Henry E. Huntington Library, San Marino, CA; Brooke, *Heart of the Commonwealth*, 327.
37. James L. Ridgely, *History of American Odd Fellowship: The First Decade* (Baltimore: James L. Ridgely, 1878), chap. 4 (on grand lodge) and chap. 11 (on secrecy and ritual).
38. Mark C. Carnes, *Secret Ritual and Manhood in Victorian America* (New Haven, CT: Yale University Press, 1989), 26; Aaron B. Grosh, *The Odd-Fellow's Manual: Illustrating the History, Principles, and Government of the Order, and the Instructions and Duties of Every Degree, Station, and Office in Odd-Fellowship . . .* (Philadelphia: H.C. Peck and Theo. Bliss, 1853), 22n.
39. *Report of the Committee Appointed to Investigate the Evils of Freemasonry*, appendix; John W. Carter, *The World's Wonder; or, Freemasonry Unmasked: To Which Is Added a Key to the Phi Beta Kappa[,] Orangeman and Odd Fellows Society, with Notes and Remarks* (Madisonville, TN: Johnston and Edwards, 1835).
40. Vaughn, *Antimasonic Party*, 187.
41. Moore, *Address Delivered on the Centennial Anniversary of St. John's Lodge*, 78n26; Ronald P. Formisano, *The Transformation of Political Culture: Massachusetts Parties, 1790s–1840s* (New York: Oxford University Press, 1983), 207.
42. *Black and White Smith's Society v. Van Dyke*, 2 Whart. (Pa.) 309 (1837).
43. Ibid., 312–13. Emphasis added.
44. *Commonwealth ex. rel. Bryan v. Pike Beneficial Society*, 8 Watts and Serg. (Pa.) 247, 247–49 (1844).
45. Ibid., 250.
46. Jonathan Levy, *Freaks of Fortune: The Emerging World of Capitalism and Risk in America* (Cambridge, MA: Harvard University Press, 2012), chap. 6; *Otto v. Journeyman Tailors' Protective and Benevolent Union*, Note, *American State Reports* 7 (1889): 160–70; *Baird v. Wells*, 44 Ch.D. 861 (1890); *McGuiness v. Court Elm City, No. 1*, Note, *American and English Annotated Cases*, 3 (1906): 211–17; *Del Ponte v. Societa Italiana*, Note, *American State Reports*, 114 (1907): 24–30; *Tarbell v. Gifford*, Note, *American and English Annotated Cases*, 17 (1910): 1145–146; *Boston Club v. Potter*, Note, *American Annotated Cases* (1913C): 398–401; "Expulsion of Member of Club," *Solicitors' Journal and Weekly*

Reporter 70 (July 24, 1926): 828–29; Roscoe Pound, *Equitable Relief against Defamation and Injuries to Personality*, 2nd ed. by Zechariah Chafee, Jr. (Cambridge, MA: Z. Chafee, Jr., 1930), sec. III; *Robinson v. Templar Lodge*, Note, 117 Cal. 377 (1897); Seymour D. Thompson, "Expulsion of Members of Corporations and Societies," *American Law Review* 24 (1890): 537–58.

47. Carol Weisbrod, *The Boundaries of Utopia* (New York: Pantheon, 1980), 128–33; *Anderson v. Brock*, 3 Me. 243, 248 (1825); *Waite v. Merrill*, 4 Me. 102, 120 (1826).
48. Rosabeth Moss Kanter, *Commitment and Community: Communes and Utopia in Sociological Perspective* (Cambridge, MA: Harvard University Press, 1972); William R. Hutchison, *Religious Pluralism in America: The Contentious History of a Founding Ideal* (New Haven, CT: Yale University Press, 2003), chap. 2; *A Brief Exposition of the Established Principles, and Regulations of the United Society of Believers Called Shakers* (Albany, NY, 1830), 8, quoted in Weisbrod, *Boundaries of Utopia*, 73; *An Improved Edition of the Church Covenant, or Constitution of the United Societies Called Shakers* (Dayton, Ohio, 1833), 49. See also the legal materials compiled in *Investigator; or, A Defence of the Order, Government, and Economy of the United Society Called Shakers, against Sundry Charges and Legislative Proceedings: Addressed to the Political World* (Lexington, KY: Smith and Palmer, 1828).
49. Weisbrod, *Boundaries of Utopia*, 207.
50. See, for example, *Rules and Orders, to Be Observed by the Heart-in-Hand Fire Company, Instituted at New-York, January, 1781* ([New York]: Geo. Forman, 1805); *The Rules and Regulations of the Attentive Fire Society . . .* (Boston: Gilbert and Dean, 1803), 8; *Breneman v. Franklin Beneficial Association*, 3 Watts and Serg. (Pa.) 218, 220 (1842); Weisbrod, *Boundaries of Utopia*, chap. 11.

PART THREE

1. James Otis, *The Rights of the British Colonies Asserted and Proved* (Boston: Edes and Gill, 1764), 48.

CHAPTER SEVEN

1. Direct examinations of Job Harrison and Anthony Bennet and closing statement of Ingersoll in *Commonwealth v. Pullis* (1806), in *A Documentary History of American Industrial Society*, vol. 3, *Labor Conspiracy Cases*, ed. John R. Commons et al. (Cleveland: Arthur H. Clark, 1910), 72, 88–89, 212.
2. Closing statement of Rodney in ibid., 183.
3. Michael Merrill and Sean Wilentz, eds., *The Key of Liberty: The Life and Democratic Writings of William Manning, "A Laborer," 1747–1814* (Cambridge, MA: Harvard University Press, 1993), 180; Michael Merrill and Sean Wilentz, "'The Key of Libberty': William Manning and Plebeian Democracy," in *Beyond the American Revolution: Explorations in the History of American Radicalism*, ed. Alfred F. Young (DeKalb: Northern Illinois University Press, 1989), 264–65.
4. Howard B. Rock, *Artisans of the New Republic: The Tradesmen of New York City in the Age of Jefferson* (New York: New York University Press, 1979), 131–32; Gary John Kornblith, "From Artisans to Businessmen: Master Mechanics in New England, 1789–1850" (PhD diss., Princeton University, 1983), 49–130; Letter to the Mechanics and Manufacturers of Boston, Providence, April 30, 1789, Minutes, 1789–1877, Providence Association of Mechanics and Manufacturers, Series II, Box 5, Rhode Island Historical Society, Providence, RI; John S. Gilkeson, Jr., *Middle-Class Providence, 1820–1940* (Princeton, NJ: Princeton University Press, 1986), 14–17, 95–96. This

discussion of general societies is not intended to include the broader Workingmen's Party movement of the 1830s or the General Trades Union, formed in 1833, which had much broader goals.

5. Charles G. Steffen, *The Mechanics of Baltimore: Workers and Politics in the Age of Revolution, 1763–1812* (Urbana: University of Illinois Press, 1984), chap. 5; Rock, *Artisans of the Republic*, 131–32; Howard B. Rock, "'All Her Sons Join as One Social Band': New York City's Artisanal Societies in the Early Republic," in *American Artisans: Crafting Social Identity, 1750–1850*, ed. Howard B. Rock, Paul A. Gilje, and Robert Asher (Baltimore: The Johns Hopkins University Press, 1995), 155–75. On ritual and solidarity, see John Fabian Witt, *The Accidental Republic: Crippled Workingmen, Destitute Widows, and the Remaking of American Law* (Cambridge, MA: Harvard University Press, 2004), chap. 3.
6. *Charter of Incorporation of the Albany Mechanic's Society, Granted by the Legislature of the State of New-York, 6th March, 1801* (Albany, NY: C. R. and G. Webster, 1803), 9; *Constitution of the Associated Mechanics and Manufacturers of the State of New Hampshire: Instituted November 4, 1802. Incorporated June 11, 1803* (Portsmouth, NH: Beck and Foster, 1820); *The Charter and By-Laws of the General Society of Mechanics and Tradesmen, of the City of New-York* (New York: J. Seymour, 1814), 10–11; bylaws 15, 16, Minutes, 1789–1877, Providence Association of Mechanics and Manufacturers, Series II, Box 5, Rhode Island Historical Society, Providence, RI (quotation); Steffen, *Mechanics of Baltimore*, 113; Tho. R. Mercien, *An Address Delivered on the Opening of the Apprentices' Library of the City of New-York . . .* (New York, 1820), 4–5 (quotation); *Charter and By-Laws of the General Society*, 11. See also the mutual aid programs set up by the Mechanics Society of Hartford, incorporated nine years after their initial formation: *Act of Incorporation and By-Laws of the Mechanics Society of Hartford, Revision of 1829* (Hartford, CT: P. B. Gleason, 1829).
7. Leonard Bernstein, "The Working People of Philadelphia from Colonial Times to the General Strike of 1835," *Pennsylvania Magazine of History and Biography* 74 (1950): 323; Carl Bridenbaugh and Jessica Bridenbaugh, *Rebels and Gentlemen: Philadelphia in the Age of Franklin* (New York: Oxford University Press, 1962), 198; *The Carpenters Company of the City and County of Philadelphia: Celebration of the 200th Anniversary of Company and 150th Anniversary of the Meeting of the First Continental Congress* (Philadelphia, 1925), 5–6; Rock, "'All Her Sons Join as One Social Band,'" 159–60; Steffen, *Mechanics of Baltimore*, chap. 5, esp. pp. 102–5; Steven J. Ross, *Workers on the Edge: Work, Leisure, and Politics in Industrializing Cincinnati, 1788–1890* (New York: Columbia University Press, 1985), chap. 1.
8. Johann Neem, *Creating a Nation of Joiners: Democracy and Civil Society in Early National Massachusetts* (Cambridge, MA: Harvard University Press, 2008), 42–43; Conrad Edick Wright, *The Transformation of Charity in Postrevolutionary New England* (Boston: Northeastern University Press, 1992), 146; Kornblith, "From Artisans to Businessmen," 110–11.
9. Bruce Arthur Campbell, "Law and Experience in the Early Republic: The Evolution of the Dartmouth College Doctrine, 1780–1819" (PhD diss., Michigan State University, 1973), 255; *Charter of Incorporation of the Albany Mechanic's Society*, 6; New York *Laws*, 1804–1805, p. 410, quoted in John R. Commons, et al., *History of Labour in the United States*, 4 vols. (New York: Macmillan Company, 1918–1946), 1:86–87; [Peter Oxenbridge Thacher], *Monthly Anthology and Boston Review* 3 (1806): 609–10, quoted and identified in Christopher L. Tomlins, *Law, Labor, and Ideology in the Early American Republic* (New York: Cambridge University Press, 1993), 102–3.

10. Seymour Martin Lipset, "The Law and Trade Union Democracy," *Virginia Law Review* 47 (1961): 11.
11. Rock, *Artisans of the New Republic*, 317, 319; Sean Wilentz, *The Rise of American Democracy: Jefferson to Lincoln* (New York: Norton, 2005), 210; Sean Wilentz, *Chants Democratic: New York City and the Rise of the American Working Class, 1788–1850* (New York: Oxford University Press, 1984), 107–42; Bruce Laurie, *Artisans into Workers: Labor in Nineteenth-Century America* (New York: Noonday, 1989), 35–46; Richard Stott, "Artisans and Capitalist Development," in *Wages of Independence: Capitalism in the Early American Republic*, ed. Paul A. Gilje (Madison, WI: Madison House, 1997), 101–16; Leon Fink, "Labor, Liberty, and the Law: Trade Unionism and the Problem of the American Constitutional Order," *Journal of American History* 74 (1987): 907–9.
12. Steffen, *Mechanics of Baltimore*, 108–9; Rock, *Artisans of the New Republic*, 68, 243; Bruce Laurie, "Nothing on Impulse: Life Styles of Philadelphia Artisans, 1820–1850," *Labor History* 15 (1974): 337–66; Ian M. G. Quimby, "The Cordwainers Protest: A Crisis in Labor Relations," *Winterthur Portfolio* 3 (1967): 88–89.
13. Laurie, *Artisans into Workers*, 51; Ronald Schultz, *The Republic of Labor: Philadelphia Artisans and the Politics of Class, 1720–1830* (New York: Oxford University Press, 1993), 121–22; Daniel Walker Howe, *What Hath God Wrought: The Transformation of America, 1815–1848* (New York: Oxford University Press, 2007), 547; Cynthia Shelton, "The Role of Labor in Early Industrialization: Philadelphia, 1787–1837," in *New Perspectives on the Early Republic: Essays from the* Journal of the Early Republic, *1981–1991*, ed. Ralph D. Gray and Michael Morrison (Urbana: University Press of Illinois, 1994), 214–43; Rock, *Artisans of the New Republic*, 272–73; Lisa Beth Lubow, "Artisans in Transition: Early Capitalist Development and the Carpenters of Boston, 1787–1837" (PhD diss., University of California-Los Angeles, 1987), 199, 209; testimony of John Bedford, in *Commonwealth v. Pullis* (1806), in *Documentary History of American Industrial Society*, ed. Commons et al., 3:99.
14. Rock, *Artisans of the New Republic*, 273, 279–80; Maurice Neufeld, "The Size of the Jacksonian Labor Movement," *Labor History* 23 (1982): 599–607; Howe, *What Hath God Wrought*, 547–48.
15. Quimby, "Cordwainers Protest," 91–92; Commons et al., eds., *Documentary History of American Industrial Society*, 3:62–67; Robert Samuel Wright, *The Law of Criminal Conspiracies and Agreements: To Which Is Added the Law of Criminal Conspiracies and Agreements as Found in the American Cases, by Hampton L. Carson* (Philadelphia: Blackstone, 1887); John V. Orth, "English Combination Acts of the Eighteenth Century," *Law and History Review*, 5 (1987): 175–211.
16. Tomlins, *Law, Labor, and Ideology*, 32–33, 38n9, 94n119, 114–27; Walter Nelles, "The First American Labor Case," *Yale Law Journal* 41 (1931): 174–75; Kunal M. Parker, *Common Law, History, and Democracy in America, 1790–1900: Legal Thought before Modernism* (New York: Cambridge University Press, 2011), 102.
17. A full listing of cases can be found in Tomlins, *Law, Labor, and Ideology*, 128n1; Walter Nelles, "*Commonwealth v. Hunt*," *Columbia Law Review* 32 (1932): appendix, 1166–169. Tomlins (*Law, Labor, and Ideology*, 131–37) and Johann Neem ("Freedom of Association in the Early Republic: The Republican Party, the Whiskey Rebellion, and the Philadelphia and New York Cordwainers' Cases," *Pennsylvania Magazine of History and Biography* 128 [2003]: 259–90; *Creation a Nation of Joiners*, 161–63) were the first to explore how these labor debates were situated within broader discussions about compulsion, consent, and legitimate and illegitimate forms of association.

18. Commons et al., eds., *Documentary History of American Industrial Society*, 3:135, 142.
19. Ibid., 70, 68, 142.
20. Schultz, *Republic of Labor*, 122; Ethelbert Stewart, *A Documentary History of the Early Organizations of Printers* (Indianapolis, IN: International Typographical Union, 1907); George E. Barnett, "The Printers: A Study in Trade Unionism," *American Economic Association Quarterly*, 3rd Ser., 10 (1909): 3–379; Theodore W. Glocker, *The Government of American Trade Unions*, Johns Hopkins University Studies in Historical and Political Science (Baltimore: Johns Hopkins Press, 1913); Commons et al., eds., *Documentary History of American Industrial Society*, 3:364–65.
21. Andrew Shankman, *Crucible of American Democracy: The Struggle to Fuse Egalitarianism and Capitalism in Jeffersonian Pennsylvania* (Lawrence: University Press of Kansas, 2004), 161; Commons et al., eds., *Documentary History of American Industrial Society*, 3:139, 178.
22. Commons et al., eds., *Documentary History of American Industrial Society*, 3:139–40.
23. Commons et al., eds., *Documentary History of American Industrial Society*, 3:231, 234–35; Wythe Holt, "Labour Conspiracy Cases in the United States, 1805–1842: Bias and Legitimation in Common Law Adjudication," *Osgoode Hall Law Journal* 22 (1984): 623–24; Tomlins, *Law, Labor, and Ideology*, 131–38; Robert J. Steinfeld, "The *Philadelphia Cordwainers' Case* of 1806: The Struggle over Alternative Legal Constructions of a Free Market in Labor," in *Labor Law in America: Historical and Critical Essays*, ed. Christopher L. Tomlins and Andrew J. King (Baltimore: Johns Hopkins University Press, 1992), 20–43; Karen Orren, "Labor Regulation and Constitutional Theory in the United States and England," *Political Theory* 22 (1994): 109–10.
24. Rock, *Artisans of the New Republic*, 275–77; Commons et al., eds., *Documentary History of American Industrial Society*, 3:378–79.
25. *People v. Melvin*, 1 Yates Sel. Cas. (NY), 112 (1809). Though they initially balked at allowing a printed copy of their constitution to be submitted as evidence, they ultimately "thought proper to admit it," and it became part of the record. See Commons et al., eds., *Documentary History of American Industrial Society*, 3:364.
26. Commons et al., eds., *Documentary History of American Industrial Society*, 3:382, 384–85; Tomlins, *Law, Labor, and Ideology*, 139. See Barnett, "The Printers," 358, for how the New York journeymen described the course of events to another labor union.
27. Sean Wilentz, "Conspiracy, Power, and the Early Labor Movement: The People v. James Melvin et al, 1811," *Labor History* 24 (1983): 572–79, quotation on 578
28. "Constitution and Bye-Laws of the United Society of Journeymen Cabinet and Chair-Makers of the city of Baltimore," in Charles F. Montgomery, *American Furniture: The Federal Period* (New York: Viking, 1966), 21–22; Commons, et al, eds., *Documentary History of American Industrial Society*, 4:26, 34–35, 55, 87.
29. Ibid., 4:72, 75, 81–83, 85.
30. "The Commonwealth ex relatione Joseph Chew et al. v. John Carlise," *Journal of Jurisprudence* 1 (1821): 225–30, quotations on 229.
31. Ibid., 229; Thomas Lloyd, *The Trial of the Boot and Shoemakers of Philadelphia, on an Indictment for a Combination and Conspiracy to Raise Their Wages* (Philadelphia: T. Lloyd and B. Graves, 1806), 6; Nelles, "*Commonwealth v. Hunt*," appendix, 1167.
32. In a fascinating passage, Gibson used a slightly paraphrased quotation from Thomas Jefferson's Annual Address to Congress of December 3, 1805, in which Jefferson described war as "the unprofitable contest of trying which party can do the other the

most harm." Gibson noted that journeymen may well be "compelled to enter, with their employers, into 'the unprofitable contest of who can do the other most harm' " ("Commonwealth ex relatione Joseph Chew et al. v. John Carlisle," 229).

33. *People v. Trequier* (New York Hatters' Case), 1 Wheeler's Criminal Cases 142 (1823), in Nelles, "*Commonwealth v. Hunt,*" appendix, 1167; Arthur James Selfridge, "American Law of Strikes and Boycotts as Crimes," *American Law Review* 22 (1888): 236; Buffalo Tailors' Case, reported in the *Buffalo Emporium*, Dec. 25, 1824, in *Documentary History of American Industrial Society*, ed. Commons et al., 4:94–95. On shame as a tool for early American labor unions, see the comment by the secretary of the New York Typographical Society in 1809 on why they should exchange the names of members expelled for rule violations with other journeymen's societies: "There is nothing which acts more powerfully on the human mind than shame. . . . it is to be hoped it will ever deter a journeyman printer from conducting himself unworthily toward his brother when innate principle is wanting" (Barnett, "Printers," 287n12).

34. Marcus T. C. Gould, *Trial of Twenty-Four Journeymen Tailors, Charged with a Conspiracy: Before the Mayor's Court of the City of Philadelphia, September Sessions, 1827* (Philadelphia: n.p., 1827), 28, 160, 162; Tomlins, *Law, Labor, and Ideology*, 145; *Philadelphia National Gazette*, Nov. 19, 1829, in *Documentary History of American Industrial Society*, ed. Commons et al., 4:273.

35. See David Grimsted, "Ante-bellum Labor: Violence, Strike, and Communal Arbitration," *Journal of Social History* 19 (1985): 5–28.

36. *Allegheny Democrat*, Aug. 9, 1831, quoted in William A. Sullivan, *The Industrial Worker in Pennsylvania, 1800–1840* (Harrisburg, PA: Pennsylvania Historical and Museum Commission, 1955), 132–33; *Thompsonville Carpet Manufacturing Company v. Taylor* and *William Taylor v. Thompsonville Carpet Manufacturing Company*, in *Documentary History of American Industrial Society*, ed. Commons et al. (suppl.) 4:17–23, 110–36; *Proceedings of the Convention of Cordwainerse, Holden in the City of New-York, Commencing on the First Monday in March, 1836*, p. 17, quoted in ibid., 159; Tomlins, *Law, Labor, and Ideology*, 151–52.

37. *Revised Statutes of the State of New-York: Passed during the Years One Thousand Eight Hundred and Twenty-Seven, and One Thousand Eight Hundred and Twenty-Eight . . .* (Albany, NY: Packard and Van Benthuysen, 1829), 2:691; *People v. Fisher*, 14 Wend. (NY) 9, 19 (1834). Owing to the controversies over the applicability of the common law of criminal conspiracy, the legislature of New York in 1828 passed a statute that sought to eliminate the crime of conspiracy for mere private injuries (Act of Dec. 10, 1828, *New York Revised Statutes*, 1829, 2:691). As Tomlins notes, however, "There is no evidence to suggest that a desire to modify the conspiracy doctrine's impact on journeymen's combinations had any particular bearing on the New York legislature's action" (*Law, Labor, and Ideology*, 149). See also Wilentz, *Chants Democratic*, 286–90; Stephen Mayer, "*People v. Fisher*: The Shoemakers' Strike of 1833," *New-York Historical Society Quarterly* 62 (1978): 6–21.

38. *New York Commercial Advertiser*, reprinted in *The Saturday Evening Post*, Mar. 12, 1836; *The Pennsylvanian*, Mar. 17, 1837; *Poulson's Daily American Advertiser*, Apr. 10, 1835, quoted in Sullivan, *Industrial Worker in Pennsylvania*, 88–89; Nelles, "*Commonwealth v. Hunt,*" appendix, 1168.

39. Laurie, *Artisans into Workers*, 54–56; Tomlins, *Law, Labor, and Ideology*, 168–71; "Societies *vs.* Individuals," *New York Journal of Commerce*, May 25, 1839; *Philadelphia Public Ledger*, June 13, 1836, quoted in Tomlins, *Law, Labor, and Ideology*, 168.

40. Nelles, "*Commonwealth v. Hunt*," 1133; testimony of Isaac Wait in *Commonwealth v. John Hunt et al.*, Thacher's Criminal Cases 609, 614–15 (1840).
41. Ibid., 1132–33; Leonard W. Levy, *The Law of the Commonwealth and Chief Justice Shaw* (Cambridge, MA: Harvard University Press, 1957), 185–90; Peter Oxenbridge Thacher, *A Charge to the Grand Jury of the County of Suffolk, for the Commonwealth of Massachusetts, at the Opening of the Municipal Court of the City of Boston, on the First Monday of December, A.D. 1832* (Boston: Stimpson and Clapp, 1832), 13.
42. *Commonwealth v. Hunt*, Thacher's Criminal Cases, 609, 619, 621–22 (1840).
43. Ibid., 635–36, 643. Thacher's charge to the jury also found a large audience by its publication in Peleg W. Chandler's *Law Reporter* 3 (1841): 290–304. On the bar and medical societies, see Nelles, "*Commonwealth v. Hunt*," 1134n21, 1138 (When the district attorney read and commented upon the cordwainers' constitution, clause by clause, he too kept asking the jury to compare the Boot-Makers' Society to his own bar association. After reading their rule that disputes between members ought to be adjudicated by the club, he declared: "Despotic, tyrannical, illegal, etc." and asked them, "Is there any such bar rule?"); Holt, "Labour Conspiracy Cases in the United States," 638n216; *Law Reporter* 3 (1841): 303.
44. *Commonwealth v. Hunt*, Thacher's Criminal Cases, 609, 647, 650, 653 (1840). On the details of the appeal, see *Law Reporter* 3 (1841): 304.
45. Parker, *Common Law, History, and Democracy*, 126–32; *Commonwealth v. Hunt*, 45 Mass. 111, 127 (1842).
46. *Commonwealth v. Hunt*, 45 Mass. 111, 127 (1842).
47. Ibid., 129–30, 132.
48. Ibid., 132–33; Nelles, "*Commonwealth v. Hunt*," 1134n21.
49. *Commonwealth v. Hunt*, 45 Mass. 111, 130 (1842); *A Letter to the Mechanics of Boston, Respecting the Formation of a City Temperance Society: From a Committee of the Massachusetts Society for the Suppression of Intemperance* (Boston: Massachusetts Society for the Suppression of Intemperance, 1831), quotation on p. 4.
50. *Commonwealth v. Hunt*, 45 Mass. 111, 133–34 (1842).
51. Nelles, "*Commonwealth v. Hunt*," 1151–162; Mark DeWolfe Howe, *Readings in American Legal History* (Cambridge, MA: Harvard University Press, 1949), chap. 5; Holt, "Labour Conspiracy Cases in the United States," 644, 645n267; Raymond Hogler, "Law, Ideology, and Industrial Discipline: The Conspiracy Doctrine and the Rise of the Factory System," *Dickinson Law Review* 91 (1987): 697–745; Anthony Woodiwiss, *Rights v. Conspiracy: A Sociological Essay on the History of Labour Law in the United States* (Munich: Berg, 1990), 55–56; Alfred S. Konefsky, "'As Best to Subserve Their Own Interests': Lemuel Shaw, Labor Conspiracy, and Fellow Servants," *Law and History Review* 7 (1989): 219–39; Levy, *Law of the Commonwealth*, 203–6; Tomlins, *Law, Labor, and Ideology*, 215; Neem, *Creating a Nation of Joiners*, 162.
52. Frederic Hathaway Chase, *Lemuel Shaw: Chief Justice of the Supreme Judicial Court of Massachusetts, 1830–1860* (Boston: Houghton Mifflin, 1918), 250–55.
53. Geert Munichs, "Rational Politics? An Exploration of the Fruitfulness of the Discursive Concept of Democracy," in *Discourse and Democracy: Essays on Habermas's* Between Facts and Norms, ed. René von Schomberg and Kenneth Baynes (Albany: State University of New York Press, 2002), 186–87. On constitutionalism and associational practices, see the discussion in chap. 4. For labor-specific examples, see "Librarians Report," Aug. 6, 1831, New York Typographical Society papers, Manuscripts and Archives Division, New York Public Library (charged members 12½ cents to

purchase copies of the society constitution); Society of Mechanics and Workingmen, minutes, 1830–1831, New-York Historical Society (operated by ballot and parliamentary procedure, and distributed printed copies of the rules to members); Rock, *Artisans of the New Republic*, 290n17.

54. Frederick Robinson, *An Oration Delivered before the Trades Union of Boston and Vicinity, on Fort Hill, Boston, on the Fifty-Eighth Anniversary of American Independence* (Boston: Charles Douglas, 1834), 14–15.

CONCLUSION

1. *Haas v. Montgomery*, Circuit Court, Kanawha County, WV, civil action no. 08-C-1035 (2010); "Jury Sides with Grand Lodge in Mason Expulsion Case," *Charleston Gazette*, Dec. 15, 2010; "From Would-Be Reformer, to Former Mason, to Plaintiff," *New York Times*, June 16, 2008; Kevin Butterfield, "The Right to Be a Freemason: Secret Societies and the Power of the Law in the Early Republic," *Common-Place: The Interactive Journal of Early American Life* 12 (2011).
2. *Commonwealth v. St. Patrick Benevolent Society*, 2 Binn. (Pa.) 441, 445–47 (1810); *Commonwealth ex. rel. Bryan v. Pike Beneficial Society*, 8 Watts and Serg. (Pa.) 247, 240 (1844).
3. William J. Novak, "The Legal Transformation of Citizenship in Nineteenth-Century America," in *The Democratic Experiment: New Directions in American Political History*, ed. Meg Jacobs, William J. Novak, and Julian E. Zelizer (Princeton, NJ: Princeton University Press, 2003), 95, 101.
4. Baron Stow, *Voluntary Associations—Their Use and Abuse: Discourse Delivered in the Meeting House of the Second Baptist Society, in Baldwin Place, Thanksgiving-Day, November 30, 1837* (Boston: Gould, Kendall, and Lincoln, 1837), 19–20; Dura D. Pratt, *Voluntary Associations: A Discourse delivered Oct. 10, 1841, in the First Baptist Meeting House, Nashua, N.H.* (Nashua, NH: C. P. Danforth, 1841), 15, 18.
5. [A. C. Thompson], *Social Character of Ardent Spirits: An Address Delivered before the East Windsor Temperance Society at Their Annual Meeting, April 23, 1838* (Hartford, CT: Elihu Geer, 1838), 9; *Biographical and Historical Record of the Class of 1835 in Yale College for the Fifty Years from the Admission of the Class to College* (New Haven, CT: Tuttle, Morehouse, and Taylor, 1881), 217–21.
6. [Thompson], *Social Character of Ardent Spirits*, 3.
7. "Medical Impeachment: Doings of the Massachusetts Medical Society in the case of John S. Bartlett, MD, of Boston, One of Its Fellows," *Boston Medical and Surgical Journal*, 14, no. 18 (June 8, 1836): 288 (quotation); *Report of the Evidence in the Case of John Stephen Bartlett, M.D., versus the Mass. Medical Society, as Given before a Committee of the Legislature, at the Session of 1839* (Boston: Dutton and Wentworth, 1839); "Remonstrance of Abel L. Peirson of Salem Doctor of Medicine and a member of the Massachusetts Medical Society against the Petition of Dr. John S. Bartlett" [1839], in Abel Lawrence Peirson papers, Francis A. Countway Library of Medicine, Harvard University. For coverage, see *Boston Pilot*, Mar. 12, 1836; *Boston Daily Advertiser*, Oct. 15, 1836; "Consultation with Quacks—Puffing of Quack Medicine," *Western Journal of the Medical and Physical Sciences* 10 (1837): 293–96; *Boston Morning Post*, Mar. 11, April 26, 1839; "Dr. J. S. Bartlett, *versus* the Monster," *Thomsonian Manual and Lady's Companion* 5, no. 11 (Apr. 15, 1839): 169–71; "Societies *vs.* Individuals," *New York Journal of Commerce*, May 25, 1839.
8. *Fawcett v. Charles*, 13 Wend. (NY) 473, 477 (1835).

9. *Penfield v. Skinner*, 11 Vermont 296 (1839) (decision in chancery). For other instances, see Scott Gregory Lien, "Contested Solidarities: Philanthropy, Justice, and the Reconstitution of Public Authority in the United States, 1790–1860" (PhD diss., University of Chicago, 2006); *Babb v. Reed*, 5 Rawle (Pa.) 151 (1835); *Duke v. Fuller*, 9 NH 536 (1838). An articulate early opinion on the incorporated/unincorporated distinction is *Hess v. Werts*, 4 Serg. and Rawle (Pa.) 356 (1818).
10. January–December 1841, *The People ex relat. Edward G. Price v. The American Institute of the City of New York*, Dec. 8, 1840, General and special term minute books, January–December 1841, Supreme Court of Judicature (Albany), New York State Archives, Albany; "Notice of motion to expel Mr. E. V. Price Charge & Specification. Read & ordered on file Dec. 10 1840," "[Torn] of Indictment vs. Edward V. Price on the complaint of Thads. B. Wakeman for the District Attorney and the grand jury. Evidence of publication. The Newspaper," "Letter to Guilian C. Verplanck," *Morning Courier and New-York Enquirer*, Apr. 23, 1840, American Institute of New York, series 1, subseries 2, Administrative, Box 77, New-York Historical Society, New York.
11. *Report of the Nominating Committee of the American Institute, Intended to Be Read at the Stated Meeting in April: Which Report, (Though the Committee was Elected at a Stated Meeting of the Institute in March, after the Resolution for Its Appointment, Presented at the Previous Stated Meeting, Had been Lying on the Table a Whole Month for Consideration,) Was Not Permitted to be Read, and the Committee Discourteously Discharged by the Institute, at a Meeting Packed for the Purpose (New York: Narine, 1840); To the Members of the American Institute* [1840, printed single sheet published by trustees of the American Institute]; "Report of the Investigating Committee appointed under resolution of Jan. 11 1840," pp. 30–31, 34; Edward v. Price to Philip Schuyler, June 25, 1840, American Institute of New York, series 1, subseries 2, Administrative, Box 77, New-York Historical Society, New York.
12. *The People ex. relat. Price v. The American Institute of the City of New York* (July 1842), *New-York Legal Observer* (July 15, 1843): 170–76; *Catalogue of the Life & Annual Members of the American Institute of the City of New York: Showing the Date of Their Election, and Occupation When Elected, New York, Jan. 2, 1868* (New York: New York Printing Company, 1868).
13. For debate on the emerging distinction between shareholding and membership, see the *Case of the Philadelphia Savings Institution*, 1 Whart. 461, 464–65 (1836); deposition of William G. Bridges, Case of the Philadelphia Savings Institution, Mandamus and Quo Warranto Proceedings, folder 9, Supreme Court of Pennsylvania, Eastern District, RG-33, Pennsylvania State Archives, Harrisburg, PA; "An Act to Incorporate the Philadelphia Savings Institution," passed Apr. 5, 1834, *Laws of the General Assembly of the State of Pennsylvania . . .* (Harrisburg, 1834), no. 106; return of Peter Fritz, president of the Philadelphia Savings Institution, to the petition for mandamus, Mandamus and Quo Warranto Proceedings, folder 9, Supreme Court of Pennsylvania, Eastern District, RG-33, Pennsylvania State Archives, Harrisburg, PA.
14. Matthew Taylor Raffety, *The Republic Afloat: Law, Honor, and Citizenship in Maritime America* (Chicago: University of Chicago Press, 2013), 42–43, 71–77, 115, 212.
15. Charles Janeway Stillé, *The Social Spirit: A Valedictory Oration, Pronounced at the Departure of the Senior Class from the Society of Brothers in Unity, Yale College, June 28, 1839* (New Haven, CT: B. L. Hamlen, 1839), 10–11, 20.
16. *Quarterly Register and Journal of the American Education Society* (August 1829): 43; Mary P. Ryan, *The Cradle of the Middle Class: The Family in Oneida County, New*

York, 1790–1865 (New York: Cambridge University Press, 1981), 132–36; Alexis de Tocqueville, *Journey to America*, ed. J. P. Mayer and trans. George Lawrence (New Haven, CT: Yale University Press, 1960), 212

17. Michael P. Young, *Bearing Witness against Sin: The Evangelical Birth of the American Social Movement* (Chicago: University of Chicago Press, 2006), 199.
18. Young, *Bearing Witness against Sin*, 120; [William E. Channing], Article V in *Christian Examiner and General Review*, 7 (1829): 123; Francis Wayland, *The Limitations of Human Responsibility* (Boston: Gould, Kendall, and Lincoln, 1838), 95–96; Matthew Hill, *Law, Morality, and Abolitionism: Francis Wayland and Antislavery in America* (Newcastle upon Tyne: Cambridge Scholars, 2011), chap. 3; Maartje Janse, "A Dangerous Type of Politics? Politics and Religion in Early Mass Organizations: The Anglo-American World, c. 1830," in *Political Religion beyond Totalitarianism: The Sacralization of Politics in the Age of Democracy*, ed. Joost Augusteijn, Patrick Dassen, and Maartje Janse (London: Palgrave Macmillan, 2013), 64–69. See also William E. Channing, *Remarks on Creeds, Intolerance, and Exclusion* (Boston: James Munroe and Co. for the American Unitarian Association, 1837), 12, 20.
19. Lebbeus Armstrong, *The Temperance Reformation: Its History, from the Organization of the First Temperance Society to the Adoption of the Liquor Law of Maine, 1851 . . .* (New York: Fowlers and Wells, 1853), 25; Charles W. Ferguson, *Fifty Million Brothers: A Panorama of American Lodges and Clubs* (New York: Farrar and Rinehart, 1937), 56; Frank Warren Crow, "The Age of Promise: Societies for Social and Economic Improvement in the United States, 1783–1815" (PhD diss., University of Wisconsin, 1953), 498–99.
20. *New-Hampshire United Society, for the More General Diffusion of Knowledge and for the Promotion of Good Morals*, broadside ([Concord, NH]: n.p., 1818); Articles of Agreement of the Plymouth Moral Society, Plymouth, NH, New Hampshire Historical Society, Concord, NH; *The Concord Society for Discountenancing Vice and Immorality* (n.p., 1817); [Nathanial Appleton Haven, Jr., and Nathan Parker], *Extracts from a Report, Made to the Board of Council of the Portsmouth Society for the Suppression of Vice, at Their Monthly Meeting in February 1817* (Portsmouth, NH: Charles Turell, 1817); "Greene and Delaware Moral Society," *Utica Christian Magazine* (April 1815): 315–17; Joel Bernard, "Between Religion and Reform: American Moral Societies, 1811–1821," Massachusetts Historical Society, *Proceedings* 105 (1994): 1–38; Yehoshua Arieli, *Individualism and Nationalism in American Ideology* (1964; rpt., Baltimore, MD: Penguin, 1966), 267.
21. "Abstract of the Eleventh Annual Report of the New York City Temperance Society," 1840, in "Minutes of the Proceedings of the Executive Committee of the New York City Temperance Society," Manuscripts and Archives Division, New York Public Library; Young, *Bearing Witness against Sin*, chap. 5.
22. Ian R. Tyrrell, *Sobering Up: From Temperance to Prohibition in Antebellum America, 1800–1860* (Westport, CT: Greenwood, 1979), 67; Young, *Bearing Witness against Sin*, 76; Richard R. John, "Taking Sabbatarianism Seriously: The Postal System, the Sabbath, and the Transformation of American Political Culture," *Journal of the Early Republic* 10 (1990): 538; Janse, "A Dangerous Type of Politics?," 65.
23. Armstrong, *Temperance Reformation*, 20–25; Hampden Youths Temperance Society, formed Mar. 9, 1832, constitution and minutes, Francis A. Countway Library of Medicine, Harvard University; Samuel Kingsbury to Abraham Burnham, Aug. 18, 1830, Records of the New Hampshire Home Missionary Society: Letters, ca. 1810–1840,

New Hampshire Historical Society, Concord, NH; See *Constitution of the Tiverton Society for Promoting Temperance*, n.p., n.d.; Woonsoket Falls Temperance Society, Constitution of the Centre Village Association for the Promotion of Temperance, 1832, and Constitution of the Coventry Union Temperance Society, October 1831, all in Rhode Island Historical Society, Providence, RI; First Annual Report of Avon Temperance Society, Aug. 17, 1830; Constitution of the Groton Temperance Society, [March 1830?], Connecticut Historical Society, Hartford, CT; *Proceedings of the Temperance Society of Columbia, S.C.: Together with Their Constitution, and Report of Their Committees on the Influence of Intemperance upon the Health, Morals, and Prosperity of the Country* (Columbia, SC: M'Morris and Wilson, 1829).

24. Kennebunk Temperance Society minutes, 1829–1838, entry for Aug. 19, 1829, Kennenbunk, Maine, New-York Historical Society, New York; *Constitution of the Providence Association for the Promotion of Temperance. Adopted March 29, 1830—Amended May 30, 1831*, in Papers of the Providence Association of Mechanics and Manufacturers, Rhode Island Historical Society, Providence, RI.
25. Tyrrell, *Sobering Up*, 140, 144, 159–60; Armstrong, *Temperance Reformation*, 35–36; Membership book, Rose Temperance Society, entry for Feb. 18, 1829; and "Minutes of the Proceedings of the Executive Committee of the New York City Temperance Society," entry for Apr. 18, 1832, both in Manuscripts and Archives Division, New York Public Library; Washington Temperance Society of Farmington, Records, Feb. 22, 1842–Feb. 22, 1854, Connecticut Historical Society, Hartford, CT; Ami Pflugrad-Jackisch, *Brothers of a Vow: Secret Fraternal Orders and the Transformation of White Male Culture in Antebellum Virginia* (Athens and London: University of Georgia Press, 2010), chap. 2.
26. *American Quarterly Temperance Magazine*, Feb. 1833, pp. 315–17, quoted in Young, *Bearing Witness against Sin*, 124–25; John A. Yates, *The Temperance Society, a National Institution for Decision of Character: An Address* (Schenectady, NY: S. S. Riggs, 1834), 6, 10–11.
27. Yates, *Temperance Society*, 11; Channing, Article V in *Christian Examiner and General Review*, 7 (1829): 124; Wayland, *Limitations of Human Responsibility*, 111–13; Francis Wayland, *The Elements of Moral Science*, ed. Joseph L. Blau (1835; rpt., Cambridge, MA: Belknap Press of Harvard Univerity Press, 1963), 42–75; Steven C. Bullock, *Revolutionary Brotherhood: Freemasonry and the Transformation of the American Social Order, 1730–1840* (Chapel Hill: University of North Carolina Press, 1996), 300–302. See also Henry Ware, Jr., *The Combination against Intemperance Explained and Justified: An Address Delivered before the Cambridge Temperance Society, March 27, 1832* (Cambridge: Hilliard and Brown, 1832).
28. Ladies Anti-Slavery Society, Dover, NH, entry for Feb. 9, 1835, New Hampshire Historical Society, Concord, NH; William Jay, *An Inquiry into the Character and Tendency of the American Colonization and American Anti-Slavery Societies*, 3rd ed. (New York: Leavitt, Lord, and Co., 1835), 12–13, 127–28; Stephen P. Budney, *William Jay: Abolitionist and Anticolonialist* (Westport, CT: Praeger, 2005); William Lloyd Garrison, *Thoughts on African Colonization; or, An Impartial Exhibition of the Doctrines, Principles, and Purposes of the American Colonization Society . . .* (Boston: Garrison and Knapp, 1832); Richard S. Newman, *The Transformation of American Abolitionism: Fighting Slavery in the Early Republic* (Chapel Hill: University of North Carolina Press, 2002), 107–20; Eric Burin, *Slavery and the Peculiar Solution: A History of the American Colonization Society* (Gainesville: University Press of Florida, 2005).

29. Ladies Anti-Slavery Society, Dover, NH, entry for Feb. 9, 1835, New Hampshire Historical Society, Concord, NH; [Orestes Brownson], review of Francis J. Grund, *The Americans in Their Moral, Social, and Political Relations* [1837], *Boston Quarterly Review* 1 (1838): 191–92; review of William E. Channing, *Slavery* [1836], in ibid., 252, 254; William Lloyd Garrison to the Ladies Anti-Slavery Society, Apr. 9, 1834, quoted in Beth A. Salerno, *Sister Societies: Women's Antislavery Organizations in Antebellum America* (DeKalb: Northern Illinois University Press, 2008), 32–33.
30. John P. Harrison, *On the Intellectual and Moral Benefits Resulting to Young Men, from Connexion with a Temperance Society: A Lecture* (Lousiville, KY: Settle and Johnston, 1834), 7; *Oneida Observer*, Feb. 23, 1830.
31. "Minutes of meetings of Temperance Society of East Sudbury," Wayland Public Library, quoted in Robert L. Hampel, *Temperance and Prohibition in Massachusetts, 1813–1852* (Ann Arbor, MI: UMI Research Press, 1982), 29; Abraham Lincoln, "Address to the Washington Temperance Society," Feb. 22, 1842, Roy P. Basler, ed., *The Collected Works of Abraham Lincoln*, 8 vols. (New Brunswick, NJ: Rutgers University Press, 1953–1955), 1:272–78; Stewart Winger, *Lincoln, Religion, and Romantic Cultural Politics* (DeKalb: Northern Illinois University Press, 2003), 185–91; Lucas E. Morel, "Lincoln among the Reformers: Tempering the Temperance Movement," *Journal of the Abraham Lincoln Association* 20 (1999): 1–34.
32. Ibid.; Yates, *Temperance Society*, 15, 20; Wayland, *Limitations of Human Responsibility*, 112.
33. "Thoughts on Unity, Progress, and Government," *Boston Quarterly Review* 1 (1838): 194; "New England Reformers," *Collected Works of Ralph Waldo Emerson*, vol. 3, *Essays: Second Series* (Cambridge, MA: Belknap Press of Harvard University Press, 1983), 155, 157; Linck C. Johnson, "Emerson, Thoreau's Arrest, and the Trials of American Manhood," in *The Emerson Dilemma: Essays on Emerson and Social Reform*, ed. T. Gregory Garvey (Athens: University of Georgia Press, 2001), 35–37; Len Gougeon, *Virtue's Hero: Emerson, Antislavery, and Reform* (Athens: University of Georgia Press, 1990), 23.
34. "New England Reformers," 150–51, 157; Michael Strysick, "Emerson, Slavery, and the Evolution of the Principle of Self-Reliance," in *Emerson Dilemma*, ed. Garvey, 165–66.
35. Brownson, Review of William E. Channing, *Slavery* [1836], in *Boston Quarterly Review* 1 (1838): 254; Leonard Withington, *A Review of the Late Temperance Movements in Massachusetts* (Boston: James Munroe and Company, 1840), 5; Ralph Waldo Emerson to George Ripley, Dec. 15, 1840, in *The Letters of Ralph Waldo Emerson*, ed. Ralph L. Rusk and Eleanor M. Tilton (New York: Columbia University Press, 1939–1995), 2:368–71; Philip F. Gura, *American Transcendentalism: A History* (New York: Hill and Wang, 2007), 154; Lawrence Buell, *Emerson* (Cambridge, MA Belknap Press of Harvard University Press, 2003), 249–51; Robert H. Abzug, *Cosmos Crumbling: American Reform and the Religious Imagination* (New York: Oxford University Press, 1994), 99–102.
36. John Stauffer, *The Black Hearts of Men: Radical Abolitionists and the Transformation of Race* (Cambridge, MA: Harvard University Press, 2002), 96; Lawrence J. Friedman, *Self and Community in American Abolitionism, 1830–1870* (New York: Cambridge University Press, 1982), chap. 4; Arieli, *Individualism and Nationalism*, 284; Neal Dolan, *Emerson's Liberalism* (Madison: University of Wisconsin Press, 2009); Christopher Newfield, *The Emerson Effect: Individualism and Submission in America* (Chicago: University of Chicago Press, 1996); Daniel Walker Howe, *Making the American Self: Jonathan Edwards to Abraham Lincoln* (Cambridge, MA: Harvard University Press, 1997),

chap. 4; Douglas M. Strong, *Perfectionist Politics: Abolitionism and the Religious Tensions of American Democracy* (Syracuse, NY: Syracuse University Press, 1999), 24–25.

37. O. L. Holley, *A Discourse on the Temperance Organization: As Delivered at a Meeting of the Ontario County Temperance Society, in Canandaigua, February 18th, 1836* (n.p.: Morse and Harvey, 1836), 5–6, 14.

38. Holley, *Discourse on the Temperance Organization*, 11–12; Frank Luther Mott, *A History of American Magazines, 1741–1850* (Cambridge, MA: Belknap Press of Harvard University Press, 1957), 297. In response to public criticisms, many temperance societies would emphasize a similar point in their own materials, such as the New York Temperance Society's profession that the organization "presumes not to tyrannize over conscience and usurp the rights of private judgement." Circular, 1838, "Minutes of the Proceedings of the Executive Committee of the New York City Temperance Society," Manuscripts and Archives Division, New York Public Library.

39. Holley, *Discourse on the Temperance Organization*, 36; O. L. Holley, *An Oration on the Permanency of Republican Institutions, Delivered at Troy, July 5, 1824* (Troy, NY: Tuttle and Richards, 1824), 13–15; *New-York Whig*, ed. Henry Dana Ward and Orville L. Holley, Dec. 31, 1831.

INDEX